A. S. Byatt's

PASSIONS OF THE MIND

"*Passions of the Mind* will demonstrate the aesthetic principles that have guided [Byatt's] fiction writing. Her arguments are...never overly academic, always well-informed. They are also highly opinionated and contentious, full of snap."
—*San Francisco Chronicle*

"Impressive."
—*Chicago Tribune*

"Provocative...Byatt writes a clear, supple prose, has a formidable intellect, [and] does not hesitate to come to grips with vast metaphysical and philosophic ideas. [*Passions of the Mind*] is appropriately titled, for these are passions—literary subjects of urgent and immediate concern—which demand closer reading than the popular press can generally provide...refreshing."
—*Boston Globe*

"Byatt is a novelist whose imagination is steeped in literature. Judged as a literary critic...[she] proves an illuminating guide to writers she admires."
—*Christian Science Monitor*

"[Byatt] shares with us the daily joys, hopes, disappointments [and] afterthoughts of an almost lifelong love affair with books."—*Houston Chronicle*

"If *Possession* was a reminder that a good novel can also be a consummated act of criticism, then these wise and sophisticated essays manage at many moments to take on the contours of art."   —*Sunday Tribune* (London)

"These essays evoke all the pleasures of lounging indefinitely in a well-stocked library at one end of which a large table groans with a delicious buffet supper."
—*New Statesman*

A. S. Byatt

PASSIONS OF THE MIND

A. S. Byatt is author of the dazzling bestseller and Booker Prize-winning *Possession*. She has taught English and American literature at University College, London, and is a distinguished critic and reviewer. Her critical work includes *Degrees of Freedom* (a study of Iris Murdoch) and *Unruly Times: Wordsworth and Coleridge in Their Time*. She has also written five novels—*Shadow of a Sun, The Game, The Virgin in the Garden, Still Life,* and *Sugar and Other Stories*.

INTERNATIONAL

PASSIONS OF THE MIND

A. S. Byatt

PASSIONS
OF THE MIND

Selected Writings

VINTAGE INTERNATIONAL
VINTAGE BOOKS
A DIVISION OF RANDOM HOUSE, INC.
NEW YORK

FIRST VINTAGE INTERNATIONAL EDITION,
APRIL 1993

Library of Congress Cataloging-in-Publication Data
Byatt, A. S. (Antonia Susan), 1936–
Passions of the mind: selected writings / A. S. Byatt.—1st
Vintage International ed.
p.   cm.
Includes index.
ISBN 0-679-73678-6 (pbk.)
I. Title.
[PR6052.Y2P3   1993]
824'.914—dc20   92-50586
CIP

For D. J. Enright

Acknowledgments

First, I would like to express my gratitude to the various people who have in one way or another, at different times, prompted these essays: Michael Worton, Jean-Louis Chevalier, Warwick Gould, Malcolm Bradbury, Alan Hollinghurst, Jacqueline Simms and Carmen Callil. Various literary editors have set me off in new directions and the three I am particularly indebted to are Frank Kermode, Michael Ratcliffe and the late Nicholas Tomalin.

I am very grateful to my friend and editor Jenny Uglow for her help with the choice and arrangement of these essays, and also for the considerable assistance given by Julian Loose, Francis Spufford and Jane Turner. I would also like to thank Michael Worton and Jenny Chapman for their translations.

Details and dates of first publication of the individual essays are given in the end-notes but I am grateful to the following for permission to reproduce particular pieces: The Society for French Studies for "Still Life/Nature morte"; Editions des Cendres for " 'Sugar'/"Le Sucre' "; Penguin Books for "George Eliot: A Celebration" and the introductions to *George Eliot: Selected Essays, Poems and Other Writings,* and to Elizabeth Bowen, *A House in Paris*; the *Times Literary Supplement* for reviews of Ford Madox Ford and Barbara Pym and "The *TLS* Poetry Competition"; Oxford University Press for the preface to Ford Madox Ford's *The Fifth Queen* and "A Sense of Religion: Enright's God," from *Life by Other Means: Essays on D. J. Enright,* ed. Jacqueline Simms; The Macmillan Press and St. Martin's Press for "The Omnipotence of Thought" from *Sir James Frazer and the Literary Imagination*, ed. Robert Fraser; Edward Arnold Ltd. for "People in Paper Houses," from *The Contemporary English Novel*, eds. Malcolm Bradbury and David Palmer; *The Literary Review* for "William Golding: *Darkness Visible*"; Virago Press for an afterword and introductions to Willa Cather's *O Pioneers!*, *The Professor's House* and *Death Comes for the Archbishop*; *The New Statesman* for reviews of Aurelia Schober Plath's *Letters Home*, Norman Fruman's *Coleridge*, *The Damaged Archangel* and Charles Rycroft's *The Innocence of Dreams*; *The Guardian* for a review of Toni Morrison's *Beloved*; and IPC Magazines for "An Honourable Escape: Georgette Heyer."

Finally, for extracts within the essays, I should like to thank Watson, Little Ltd for quotation from D. J. Enright's *Collected Poems*, *A Choice of Milton's Verse* and *Fields of Vision*; Thames and Hudson, from *The Complete Letters of Vincent Van Gogh*; Faber & Faber, from Wallace Stevens's *Collected Poems*; Les Editions de Minuit and George Borchardt, from Jacques Derrida's *Marges de la philosophie*; Farrar, Straus & Giroux, from Antonin Artaud's *Selected Writings*, ed. Susan Sontag; Editions Gallimard, from Georges Bataille's *Œuvres Complètes*; Jonathan Cape, from Rainer Maria Rilke's *Letters on Cézanne*, trs. Joel Agee.

Contents

THE FEMALE VOICE?

VISION AND REALITY

Introduction

Novelists sometimes claim that their fiction is a quite separate thing from their other written work. Iris Murdoch likes to separate her philosophy from her novels; David Lodge says that his critical and narrative selves are a schizoid pair. I have never felt such a separation, nor wanted to make such claims. From my early childhood, reading and writing seemed to me to be points on a circle. Greedy reading made me want to write, as if this were the only adequate response to the pleasure and power of books. Writing made me want to read—it is often argued with some justice that a university training in English Literature is inhibiting to the desire to write, but I thought this out at eighteen and decided that the only way to deal with it was to read so much and so variously that no particular writer or system could overpower me. I have also taught—A Level, Liberal Studies for painters and craftsmen, adult education, and eleven years in the English Department at University College, London. Most of my solid training in the form of the novel was done in my years as an extra-mural lecturer, when I came to grips with Tolstoy and Dostoevsky, George Eliot, Lawrence and Joyce, Proust, Kafka and Mann. I am still grateful to my adult students for refusing to be confined to the English, or the "contemporary" novel. My teaching always felt to me only a more complicated extension of the reading and writing circle—a seminar on *The Prelude* was a lesson in how to use language, and an encounter with other minds.

The essays in this book are of two kinds—the reviews of a working writer, written to length and for money, and longer pieces, written in response to invitations from conferences or anthologies. I have tried to be scholarly where that was appropriate, and I have used recent literary theory where that seemed useful, though my temperament is agnostic, and I am a non-believer and a non-belonger to schools of thought. I grew up in Dr. Leavis's Cambridge, in an atmosphere of moral seriousness which placed English Literature at the centre of university studies and also of social morality. I felt then that these claims were extravagant and absurdly exclusive—all sorts of other things are good and beautiful, paint, philosophy, mathematics, biology—there are many ways of coming at inevitably partial visions of truth. I was and am excited by T. S. Eliot's observation that our literature is a substitute for religion, and so is our religion. Just because I cared so much and so precisely for the written word I was worried by the believers and, indeed, my early novels are in one aspect a sort of questioning quarrel with Leavis's vision and values, which nevertheless I inherit and share.

What we did learn was Leavis's word-by-word, questioning method of close reading, and what I cannot forgo is the habit of extended quotation involved in a criticism which has this at its centre. In the 1960s I attended Frank Kermode's graduate seminars at UCL, where the French structuralists and other theoretical approaches were arriving, and listened to much argument about interpretation being a matter of selecting and privileging certain parts and patterns in a work. I thought that Leavis's long quotations were a protection against such distorting interpretative fervour, and as an editor of George Eliot's essays I did not do as many modern editors have done and cut the long exemplary passages that were part of her text and her argument. Writing is reading and reading is writing, and I hope the readers of these essays will both bear with, and read, the quotations.

More seductive than Leavis, in the world I grew up in, was T. S. Eliot, and most seductive in Eliot, to me, was his admiration for the metaphysical poets, for their mixture of intellect and passion, sense and sensuousness. My lost paradise was Eliot's elegant fiction of the undissociated sensibility, in which Donne felt his thought as immediately as the odour of a rose, unlike Tennyson and Browning (who of course, and in fact, do exactly the same, as an examination of the yew trees in *In Memoriam,* or of "Karshish," will demonstrate). Moved by this vision of a historical fulcrum between fallen and unfallen worlds, I embarked on a doctoral dissertation on religious allegory in the seventeenth century. This was partly because I wanted to study the sensuous metaphors of Herbert and Marvell, in which the unfallen world of the spirit was embodied in exquisite images of the fallen world of the body, and partly—the allegory bit of it—because I wanted to write novels, and was interested in narrative. Before I abandoned it, this project had narrowed itself to a discussion of temptations in gardens between *The Faerie Queene* and *Paradise Regained,* between the Bower of Blisse, the serpent's address to Eve, and Satan's temptation of the incarnate Christ, the Word in human form, in the wilderness. It is not too much to say that this unwritten work, with its neoplatonic myths, its interest in the incarnation, in fallen and unfallen (adequate and inadequate) language to describe reality, has haunted both my novels and my reading patterns ever since. I came to the conclusion that *Paradise Regained* was, by the skin of its incarnate teeth, the last *believed*—or believed without a large dose of riddling and qualifying and fictionalising scepticism—Christian narrative in the language.

My interest in the novel as a form came later than my interest in poetry, and was partly a purely practical interest in narrative method. Two statements about the nature of fiction that influenced me very early were Iris Murdoch's 1961 essay "Against Dryness" and a remark of Graham Greene's, in his essay on Mauriac, about the relationship between the religious sense and the experienced reality, or irreality, of fiction. "Against Dryness" is both a text about morality in a post-Christian world and a text about the appropriate fictive form with which to explore that world, in its complexity and depth. It rejects what Blake might have called the single vision both of the crystalline novel, or jewel-like artefact, and of the journalistic report, and defends, on moral grounds, the Tolstoyan "old-fashioned naturalistic idea of character." Graham Greene argues that "with the death of James the religious sense was lost to the English novel, and with the religious sense went the sense of the importance of the human act. It was as if the world of fiction had lost a dimension: the characters of such distinguished writers as Mrs. Virginia Woolf and Mr. E. M. Forster wandered like cardboard symbols through a world that was paper-thin."

The problems of the "real" in fiction, and the adequacy of words to describe it, have preoccupied me for the last twenty years. If I have defended realism, or what I call "self-conscious realism," it is not because I believe that it has any privileged relationship to truth, social or psychological, but because it leaves space for thinking minds as well as feeling bodies. It is closely related to ideals of accuracy, as exemplified by those very self-conscious artists, Ford Madox Ford and Willa Cather. It is, however, Ford who discusses the problem of solipsism in the impressionistic modern novel. I am afraid of solipsism, and find it frustrating as a reading experience.

It has been justly observed that in Virginia Woolf's world, the only sensibility the reader meets truly is the novelist's own. I think the same could be argued of those recent heroes of the aleatory, reader-written text, Sterne, late Joyce, and Beckett. I was recently at a conference where it was argued with some force and elegance that Sterne left space for the reader to be free and creative as George Eliot, an instructive narrator, did not. And yet if we think about it, which is really the more *coercive,* the more exclusive of mental activity in the reader, Eliot's measured exposition and solidly sensible embodiment, or Sterne's legerdemain playfulness? It is Sterne who manipulates, who teases the reader and demands total admiration and assent. Eliot lays out her evidence and conclusions, speaks sometimes as "I," sometimes to "you" and sometimes as "we." But despite her passionate morality, her reasonable proceedings leave room for dissent and qualification—indeed, she demonstrates and argues the case for independent thought, in reader as in characters and writer. Eliot, like Leavis, says "This is so, is it not?" and sometimes does not seem to envisage the possibility of *real* divergence from her vision. But in Sterne's world, and in Beckett's and Robbe-Grillet's, the reader's freedom is framed quite differently by the novelist's strategies. You—or I—may "play freely" or "create"—but with the freedom of the judo player, or the magic slate-pencils of my childhood, rather than that of the moral daydreamer who temporarily inhabits the world of *Middlemarch,* feeling out its spaces and limitations, knowing that daydreaming is indeed daydreaming and is also discovery.

My work on incarnation and truth in Browning's dramatic poems and in George Eliot's thought, although it had its roots in my very early reading, is a product of my university-teaching years, and in a sense fills in part of the intellectual space between my immediate, writer's interest in the fictive problems posed by Murdoch and Greene, and the earlier world of Spenser, Herbert, T. S. Eliot and Milton. I was put onto Emery Neff's *The Poetry of History* by a footnote in Thomas Pinney's edition of George Eliot's essays, and from there went on to think about Michelet and Browning, and George Eliot and Feuerbach, the mythological studies of the great nineteenth-century linguists, and the relations of the Sacred Book to all other books, and its triune Protagonist to all other protagonists in our culture.

I think these essays do have some sort of a coherence and continuity. The first two essays are concerned with my own writing, and also tie my seventeenth-century preoccupations into later versions of the same concerns, Milton's language-flower to Mallarmé's, Browning's fictive rose in the Garden to Foucault's ideas of innocent language. Victorian essays on language and incarnation are followed by modern essays on the language of truth and fiction, myth and religion. Enright's God is rather like my own, an omnipresent absentee whose linguistic essence is reduced to traces of moral and cultural nostalgia, touched with savagery. The same might be said for whatever God or little gods inhabit the papery worlds of the novelists who make a kind of nihilistic use of the world of *The Golden Bough*.

The section on women contains two admired women, both Americans, both working in that world where accuracy touches cultural metaphor and myth. Willa Cather's accurately described land is made of mimetic word patterns and Virgilian myth. Toni Morrison's "coloured" people are coloured in every sense, and add a savage new dimension to the old guilty American play with the absolute of black and white, in writers like Hawthorne, Poe and Melville. Monique Wittig's *Lesbian Body*, reviewed in 1974, was a precursor of much more curious correlation of text and body, a new version of my anxieties and interests in the relations between language and the world, and one I find baffling and reductive. Wittig like the Leavisites and literary theorists is a believer who, in ascribing too much power to language, reduces its range. One could add Plath and Pym to this knot of ideas too. Pym's novels are cosy and sad, full of inhibiting conventions and bodily limitations. So are Plath's letters, as opposed to the fiercely accurate metaphors of her poems.

The essay on Van Gogh, written for his centenary, pulls together many of the ideas in the other essays, both on writing and on reading, on metaphor, incarnation and the impossibility of pure representation without added human meaning. This essay takes up many of the thoughts of "Still Life/Nature morte," which was written when I was working out the aesthetic problems of *Still Life*. Van Gogh stands, for me, between Browning and Wallace Stevens, sharing some of the preoccupations of each. The Van Gogh essay follows the Browning essay, and was written when I had just finished *Possession*, in which I tried to find a narrative shape that would explore the continuities and discontinuities between the forms of nineteenth- and twentieth-century art and thought.

December 1990

AS A
WRITER

1

Still Life/ Nature morte

THREE OR FOUR YEARS AGO I decided to try and write a novel which should be as plain as possible—a novel eschewing myths and cultural resonances—a novel, I even thought, which would try to forgo metaphor. This essay is an account of the failure of that project, and of some things I learned about the language of fiction through that failure. I offer it—irrespective of the merits of the novel—as an example of the self-conscious novelist brooding about the choice of words.

The novel in question—its title is *Still Life*—is the second book in a projected tetralogy of which the first is *The Virgin in the Garden*. A little history of the first one is necessary to understand the second. The first novel, set in 1953 at the Coronation of Elizabeth II, contains a verse drama about Elizabeth I, and makes great play with the iconography of the first Elizabeth as Diana, Virgo-Astraea, the Virgin Mary, Idea, Cynthia and so on—it owes a lot to Frances Yates. Intellectually it is—among other things—a response to T. S. Eliot's ideas of the history of poetic language and the nature of the poetic image. In 1953 when I left school, we *believed* the myth of the "dissociation of sensibility," which had taken place sometime in the seventeenth century. Donne, T. S. Eliot said, felt his thought as immediately as the odour of a rose: this in practice we took to mean that he *thought* with, in, sensuous images, gold to a ayery thinnesse beat, the spider love which transubstantiates all. The play in my novel, and the novel itself, are nostalgia for a *paradis perdu* in which thought and language and things were naturally and indissolubly linked or, to use an Eliot metaphor, fused. In my experience I know what the form of a novel is when I find what I think of as the "ruling" metaphor. In the case of this novel this was a metaphor of metamorphosis—of flesh into stone, or of flesh into grass—and a concomitant metaphor of language itself as flowers. Human passion frozen into works of art—there is a chapter on the marble men and maids of the Grecian Urn. Also on the statue of Hermione in *A Winter's Tale*. I played with the clichés: "You can't get blood out of a stone." Or, "All flesh is grass." My second-rate verse-dramatist's language is described as "florid": in my mind, and subsequently in the text, this became linked to the very concrete image of the flowers spilling from the mouth of the nymph in Botticelli's *Primavera*—flowers which became the dress of Flora (language is the dress of thought) and are also part of the earth itself—which I thought of in Philip Sidney's phrase about enamelled flowers and "Whatever else may make the too much loved earth more lovely." Words are literally things.

Again in my visual imagination Botticelli's tumbling florets became Elizabeth's Tudor roses, red and white, in a circle round her image in the Phoenix Jewel. There is a poem in praise of Elizabeth which runs: "Under a tree I saw a Virgin sit/The red and white rose quartered in her face." And the metaphorical imagination caused me to see that heraldic quartering also as the quartering of butchery or execution—flowers back to flesh, back to death's immobility. Below the metaphoric patterning of the text there runs a colour-patterning—red for blood, white for stone, green for grass. I should say that this is made explicit and is also the patterning of the metaphoric structure of the verse-drama in the play. I should add that one of the critical essays I most admire and have most learned from is Michel Butor's *Les Œuvres d'art imaginaires chez Proust,* in which he shows how the works became metaphors for Proust's undertaking, the colour patterning of imaginary paintings, stages, music, spills over into and patterns the shape and texture of the *Recherche* itself. It is a classic description of coherent *thinking with* metaphors at a very complex level. And I found I was writing into my text echoes of parts of sentences from what I think of as Milton's language-flower, the flower of analogy with which the archangel Raphael describes the relations of sense and thought to Adam in Paradise.

> so from the root
> Springs lighter the green stalk, from thence the leaves
> More airy: last the bright consummate flower

> Spirits odorous breathes. Flowers and their fruit
> Man's nourishment, by gradual scale sublim'd
> To *vital* spirits aspire: and *animal:*
> To *intellectual* . . .[1]

Another undissociated sensibility. It is significant that Coleridge affixes this passage, in its entirety, to the opening of *Biographia Literaria,* chapter XIII, on the Imagination or Esemplastic Power.

The idea of the second novel of the series—*Still Life*—was that it should, by contrast, be very bare, very down-to-earth, attempt to give the "thing itself" without the infinitely extensible cross-referencing of *The Virgin.* I wanted to write about birth, about death, plainly and exactly. There were ideological reasons for this, as well as a vague sense that my novel must move from an undissociated paradise to our modern dissociated world. I wanted both to demythologise my novel and to describe the demythologising of the Church in the novel. I am afraid of, and fascinated by, theories of language as a self-referring system of signs, which doesn't touch the world. I am afraid of, and resistant to, artistic stances which say we explore only our own subjectivity. I was very struck by Gabriel Josipovici's use, in *The World and the Book,* of the term "demonic analogy" (derived from Mallarmé's "démon de l'analogie"). He says that our discovery of correspondences is not an indication "that we inhabit a meaningful universe"—on the contrary "we realise with a shock of recognition . . . that what we had taken to be infinitely open and out there," was in reality "a bounded world bearing only the shape of our own imagination."[2] I am also resistant to the idea that the world hits us as a series of random impressions (V. Woolf) and that memory operates in a random manner. I wanted at least to work on the assumption that order is more interesting than the idea of the random (even if our capacity to apprehend it is limited): that accuracy of description is possible and valuable. That words denote things.

When I began *Still Life* I was working—in an academic capacity—on Ford Madox Ford and Pound and William Carlos Williams, whose dictum "no ideas but in things" informs the novel. Ford was an "impressionist," he said, but this word did not carry for him primarily connotations of randomness. Ezra Pound put it like this: "Madox Ford's aim towards the just word was right in his personal circle of reference. He was dealing mainly with visual and oral perceptions, whereinto come only colours, concrete forms, tones of voices, modes of gesture. Out of these you build sane ideogram.

You build your congeries in validity."[3] I felt that something might be learned of what I wanted from Flaubert and the *mot juste* so admired by Ford and Pound. Hugh Kenner says of Flaubert:

> What Flaubert did was arrange not primarily words but things; or words as *mimesis* of things. Out of an odour, a waft of talk, a plume of smoke, the flare of gaslight, the disposition, relative to carpets and windows, of certain furniture in a certain room, the world of Frédéric Moreau emerges with palpable and autonomous immediacy. The significant action of the novel, in contradistinction to the diagrammable 'plot', obstructed by dull descriptions, that emerges from a poor translation, consists in the interactions of the tensions set up between these items. That is the meaning of *le mot juste*.[4]

"Words *as mimesis* of things" begs a lot of theoretical questions, but the phrase meant something to me about how to write my bare book, my still life. The idea of not only demythologising but dispensing with metaphor came from reading Proust's defence of Flaubert's style:

> I must admit I was astounded to see how a man with such little writing talent has, by the entirely novel and personal use which he makes of the past perfect, the past imperfect, the present participle, of certain pronouns and prepositions, revived our vision of things almost to the extent that Kant did with his *Categories,* with the theories of the Knowledge and the Reality of the exterior world. It is not that I adore Flaubert's writing nor even his style. For reasons that would be too long to explain here, I believe that only metaphor can lend some kind of timelessness to a writer's style, and there is perhaps not one single beautiful metaphor in the entire Flaubert repertoire.[5]

And Genette quotes, in "Métonymie chez Proust," a sentence in which he speaks of the beauty of the homogeneous style of Flaubert, a style in which "toutes les choses, perdant leur aspect premier des choses, sont venues se ranger les unes à côté des autres dans une espèce d'ordre, pénétrées de la même lumière, vues les unes dans les autres" ("all things, losing their initial thing-like aspect, came to line up beside each other in some sort of order, penetrated by the same light, each of them being seen in all the others").[6] As Genette says, this arrangement of things suggests both continuity—"les unes à côté des autres"—and analogy—"les unes *dans* les autres." I had the idea that I could emphasise contiguity rather than analogy. I found that this was in fact impossible for someone with the cast of mind I have.

A concrete example might help here: a thing, or a metaphor. Another flower. I was describing a woman whose mother-in-law has come to live with her falling over the potted cyclamen she has put as a welcoming gesture on the dressing-table. The mother-in-law has stood it in the corridor outside her bedroom door (fear of it breathing out carbon dioxide). The cyclamen *would not stay* at the level of exact description. I asked myself about the derivation of the word—what have cycles to do with this flower?—and answered myself wrongly, that it represented the fact that it came early in spring, cyclically, and connected it to all my metaphors in *The Virgin in the Garden,* of death, and rebirth, resurrection and renaissance. (In fact the cyclamen is so called, the *OED* says, because the corm is circular.) Worse than that—I *saw* in my mind's eye some archetypal metamorphosing procession of flowers, from the odour of a rose, through Milton's language-flower and Mallarmé's language-flower, "l'absente de tous bouquets." The mental colours shifted very beautifully from various rosy cyclamens to a distressing purple I associate with death and depression. The text came alive, but the cyclamen was interesting because it was bristling with threads of connection to the earlier text, to the purple-fleshed purple-dressed mother-in-law, to language-flowers in general.

I don't know how much is known about the difference between those who *think* with mental imagery and those who don't. I very much do—I see any projected piece of writing or work as a geometric structure: various colours and patterns. I *see* other people's metaphors—if there is an iconic content to a metaphor I will "see" a visual image on some inner mental screen, which can then be contemplated more precisely, described discursively (the sap rising inside Milton's "light" green stalk, like light). I take pleasure in the writing habits of Henry James, who reserves most of his sensuous vividness and exactness of description for his own metaphors and the mental imagery of his characters. Occasionally he will write a rapid, synaesthetic figure into the text—consider Sarah Pocock's dress, scarlet like the scream of someone falling through a skylight. Vernon Lee gives a marvellous example from James of a submarine description of fish in the dark, which are someone's thoughts.[7] In *The Golden Bowl* the visual images I remember are Maggie's metaphoric enamelled pagoda, closed and inscrutable and tinkling, or Adam Verver as a lamb led on a scarlet silken thread. Or James will rescue dead metaphors by expanding them into a page of description—Adam Verver decides to "burn his boats" and sees the whole sea from the Brighton promenade crimson and lurid with the flames of the flaring fleet; Mrs. Assingham, "in the same boat" as her husband, paddles across a kind of Charon's lake in her own drawing-room, with the splash of water and the bump of the shore.

I came to the conclusion that I was doing violence to something in my own mental constitution to try to write like Flaubert, or Proust's Flaubert, or Pound's Flaubert. But I didn't want to abandon my project of, in some sense, naming and describing a demythologised world. I read Ricœur's *La Métaphore vive* out of curiosity about the workings of metaphor; I read Foucault's *Les Mots et les choses* in search of post-Renaissance images of the relations between words and things. And I found what Eliot might have called an objective correlative for my anxiety about things and metaphors— Vincent Van Gogh's yellow chair, which seems initially to be very much a mimetic rendering of the thing itself, for its own sake, and later his floral still lifes, the sunflowers, the irises. The yellow chair rose up before my inner eye, as Coleridge said of the ideas of "Kubla Khan," like a *vivid spectrum*. It turned out to be a complex metaphor, psychological, cultural, religious, aesthetic. It was Day contrasted to the Night of Gauguin's chair. It was one of *twelve* Van Gogh had bought for an ideal community of artists (demythologised apostles). It bore a burned-out pipe in the workaday daylight, as opposed to the lit candle of Gauguin's chair, accompanied by a yellow French novel, painted in what Van Gogh called "the terrible reds and greens of human passion." Nevertheless it had an intention of accurate *rendering*, to use Ford's favourite word. Van Gogh began to assume the place in *Still Life* of the ambiguous Elizabeth-Virgin in the earlier book. The playwright wrote a play called *The Yellow Chair*—a colour word, a noun. I devised various strategies for indicating that the text was concerned with simple naming, with mimesis, whilst continuing, and changing, the metaphors of the first novel.

I found Ricœur's whole discussion of the iconic element, or moment, in metaphor invaluable. In his chapter on "Le Travail de la ressemblance" he argues that the "voir comme" of a metaphor is both an experience and an act, both the reception of mental image *and* a deliberate act of understanding. It is to perceive identity and difference simultaneously and dependent on each other. Ricœur uses Wittgenstein's ambiguous figure—the duck-rabbit—which can be *seen* as a duck or a rabbit, and is itself an ambiguous Gestalt between the two terms, partaking of both. In a metaphor, he says, the vehicle and tenor are given: it is the mind that forms the Gestalt, the figure in which the similarity coheres. "La métaphore, figure de discours, présente de manière *ouverte* par le moyen d'un conflit *entre* identité et différence, le procès qui, de manière *couverte*, engendre les aires sémantiques par fusion des différences *dans* l'identité." ("Metaphor, a figure of speech, presents in an *open* fashion, by means of a conflict *between* identity and difference, the process that, in a *covert* manner, generates semantic grids by fusion of differences *within* identity.")[8] He goes on to speak of the poetic image in Anglo-Saxon literary criticism as "un objet clos sur soi, à la différence du langage ordinaire de caractère foncièrement référentiel" ("an object closed in on itself, in contrast to ordinary language and its thoroughly referential character").[9] Language itself becomes stuff to be looked at, not looked through. Some such verbal icon might be my cyclamen, a named thing in a referential word.

Where Van Gogh becomes useful here is that his sunflowers, as Gestalts, as icons, are mimetic in a way no verbal icon can be, in that they are made of paint, the elements of their petals and seeds are brush-strokes and pigment, not evanescent mental imagery. Gauguin called them Sun upon Sun upon Sun: they, like the chair, *stand for* the painter, the earth, time. But they are *things,* and to write language about their thingness can be to comment on the doubleness of a metaphor that is both mimetic and an exploration of the relation between identity and difference. I found that my text was connecting Van Gogh's very solid irises, the heavy dying purple, with the brilliance of Mallarmé's imaginary flowers, in the *Prose pour des Esseintes,* and in "Toast funèbre." Ricœur speaks eloquently of the Aristotelian *voir—voir le semblable.*" I found myself connecting this with "une île que l'air charge / De vue et non de visions," where "Toute fleur s'étalait plus large / Sans que nous en devisions." Mallarmé in the "Toast funèbre" speaks of the "frisson final" in an Eden which "éveille / Pour la Rose et le Lys le mystère d'un nom." Mallarmé's flowers are both named and described by metaphors—"pourpre ivre et grand calice clair." Again—it depends on one's visual imagination—it seems to me that to speak of these imagined images as most of the theorists quoted by Ricœur do, as "decayed sense" to use Hobbes's term for imagination, or as vestigial representations of sensations, as "percepts fanés,"[10] is to mis-describe what happens. Mallarmé's flowers are as bright as Vincent Van Gogh's, "a joyous abstract sensuality" as Bersani says.[11] He also says "the mystery of a name" is that it "creates an interval between itself and the object (or thought) to which it presumably adheres in the act of naming."

Foucault, in *Les Mots et les choses,* describes the Renaissance idea of language and the world, words and things, thoughts and sensations, in a way that is analogous to the theories of the dissociation of sensibility current in my youth. In that time there was no "gap" between words and things: the mystery of names was not Mallarmé's mystery. "Dans son être brut et historique du XVI siècle, le langage n'est pas un système arbitraire; il est déposé dans le monde et il en fait partie, à la fois parce que les choses ellemèmes cachent et manifestent leur énigme comme un langage, et parce que les mots se proposent aux hommes comme des choses à déchiffrer." ("In its raw sixteenth-century historical state, language is not an arbitrary system; it is deposited in the world and is part of the world, both because things themselves hide and reveal their enigma like a language and because words offer themselves to men as things to be deciphered.")[12] My first novel grew out of a Ph.D. thesis I never finished, on the nature of religious metaphor—the relations between the world of sense and the world of spirit—in the English Renaissance. My second became—in a playful way—informed by Foucault's vision of post-Renaissance nomination. In the Renaissance Garden, "ces mots qu'Adam avait prononcés en les imposant aux animaux, ils sont demeurés, au moins en partie, emportant avec eux dans leur épaisseur, comme un fragment de savoir silencieux, les propriétés immobiles des êtres . . ." ("Those words which Adam had spoken when allotting them to the animals survived, at least partially, bringing with them in their substantiality, like a fragment of silent knowledge, the immobile properties of living beings . . .")[13] In Renaissance thought, Foucault says, there are three elements—signifier, signified and resemblance—Wittgenstein's or Ricœur's Gestalt. In Classical thinking thought is organised on a binary system of identity and difference. He writes of mathematical ordering, and of classifying: "Nommer, c'est, tout à la fois, donner la représentation verbale d'une représentation, et la placer dans un tableau général." ("To name is simultaneously to give the verbal representation of a representation and to place that representation in an overall picture.")[14] Language is "un immense bruissement de dénominations qui se couvrent, se resserrent, se cachent, se maintiennent cependant pour permettre d'analyser ou de composer les représentations les plus complexes" ("a vast rustling of denominations which cover each other, draw close and tight, mask each other and nonetheless sustain each other in order to permit us to analyse or compose the most complex representations").[15]

This statement about seventeenth- and eighteenth-century language follows an analysis of the origins of speech as primitive syllables that were named, behind which is the mimetic babble of the infant. I found myself writing into my text "taxonomies"—from one girl's study of all young men in Cambridge to a formicary and an essay in field grasses, from children's pictures representing alphabets to a long discursus on a child's pre-speech.

"Là où le langage demandait la similitude des impressions, la classification demande le principe da la plus petite différence possible entre les choses." ("Whereas langage demanded similarity of impressions, classification demands the principle of the smallest possible difference between things.") Proust, in "Noms de pays," distinguishes between metaphoric names—names invested by his imagination with metaphoric life—and *les mots:* "Les mots nous présentent des choses une petite image claire et usuelle comme celles que l'on suspend aux murs des écoles pour donner aux enfants l'exemple de ce qu'est un établi, un oiseau, une fourmilière, choses conçues comme pareilles à toutes celles de même sorte." ("Words present us with a small, bright, everyday image like those pictures hung on school walls to give children an example of what a workbench, a bird or an anthill is, that is to say as things thought of as similar to all others of the same type.")[16] I tried to put in my novel lists of such simply denominated things—even an image, as I said, of such children's object-pictures on a nursery wall.

I tried also to look at ways of relating things that were not metaphoric. A geometric description of the order of the branches of an elm tree: a physical description of the way the light hit it and the colour waves were absorbed and refracted. Proust detected in Flaubert's use of parts of speech another rhythm, another beauty, from the vision of metaphor. What interested me was the abused and despised adjective, that delimiter of plain nouns which, if properly used, makes every description more and more particular and precise. A Tree, of many One. A large tree. A large, rugged tree. A large, rugged, lopsided tree. In a novel with paintings and adjectives somewhere in the centre, colour adjectives became particularly important. They behave rather like nouns, are often interchangeable—"that dividing and indifferent blue." Vincent van Gogh, I observed, often does not agree his colour adjectives with his nouns—"une pelouse vert," he says—referring to either pigment or colour as though, one might imagine, it was a separate being, had a life of its own. Wittgenstein, in his *Remarks on Colour,* sees colour perception as something partaking of the *private imagery* of sense-experience and as something exact, like mathematics: "I don't know whether red (i.e.) pure red is lighter or darker than blue; to be able to see that I would have to see them. And yet, if I had seen them, I would know the answer once and for all, like the result of a mathematical calculation."[17]

He asks himself: "Is there such a thing as a natural history of colours, and to what extent is it analogous to natural history of plants? Isn't the latter temporal, the former non-temporal?"[18] Rookmaaker in his book *Synthetist Art Theories*[19] quotes Aurier (Van Gogh's only serious critic during his lifetime) as a believer in lines, colour, light and shade as pure elements of thought, or a kind of immutable visual alphabet. I wanted my thoughts, my descriptions, to move between simply *naming,* like Proust's clear and usual images, and the kind of mental icons which are Mallarmé's language-flowers or the Sunflowers—"L'idée même et suave, l'absente de tous bouquets." Colour was one of the most powerful movements, from the purely descriptive to Van Gogh's idea of the world as a battleground between, or achieved resting-place of, the complementary colours, which he said he painted as the marriage between lovers.

One of the powerful forces behind my interest in naming and describing was the moment in *La Nausée* when Roquentin cannot name the root of the tree.[20] My novel is haunted by trees, including that one: Milton's banyan tree; an elm, which is genetically one individual; Darwin's Tree of the descent of Man; Wordsworth's "There is a Tree, of many One"—that is, *not* "pareille à tous ceux de même sorte." The description of Sartre's tree is verbally very interesting. He begins by saying: "Les mots s'étaient évanouis et, avec eux, la signification des choses, leurs modes d'emploi, les faibles repères que les hommes ont tracés à leur surface." ("Words had vanished, and with them had disappeared the meaning of things, directions for their use, the faint markers that men have traced on their surface.") He then thinks of the verb "to be" and rejects classification—does the sea belong to the class of green objects or is green part of the qualities of the sea? His inability to comprehend is expressed in attempts at formal thought—he tries to *count* the trees and fails: he tries to see whether the adjective, or quality, "black" can be ascribed to the thing—"la racine n'était pas noire . . . ce n'était pas du noir qu'il y avait sur ce morceau de bois . . . le noir, comme le cercle, n'existait pas": ("the root was not black . . . it was not black that was there on that piece of wood . . . black, like the circle, did not exist"). But there is a moment in all this when we, the readers, imagine the tree vividly. "Je pensais sans mots, *sur* les choses, *avec* les choses. L'absurdité, ce n'était pas une idée dans ma tête, ni un souffle de voix, mais ce long serpent mort à mes pieds, ce serpent de bois. Serpent ou griffe ou racine ou serre de vautour." ("I thought, without words, *on* things, *with* things. Absurdity was not an idea in my head, nor a murmuring voice, but that long, dead snake at my feet, that snake of wood. A snake or a claw or a root or a vulture's talon.") The metaphors in this passage of deliquescence and flux have their fat, precise, informative life.

I am aware that there is something illegitimate in offering you metaphors out of a novel you haven't read, ghosts of ghosts of roses. I'd like to end by offering you a kind of happy discovery I made when I decided to include in the text a list of names of grasses (as opposed to the "flesh is grass" metaphor of *The Virgin*).

Alopecurus (foxtail)—from alopex, a fox, oura, a tail
Phalaris—canary grass—from phalos, shining
Gastridium—nit-grass—from gastridion, a little swelling
Aira—hair-grass—from aira, to destroy (darnel)
Arrhenatherum—oat like grass—arrhen, male, ather, an awn
Panicum—panick-grass—from panis, bread
Anthoxanthum—vernal grass—anthos, a flower, xanthos, yellow

These names are all small metaphors—human perceptions, the nit, the little swelling, seeing the likeness in the difference of foxtail or haretail and grass. They are also double metaphors, out of etymological confusion. I like panick particularly. I see the grass both quaking with fear and providing wheat-ears for bread. Or Aira, where the sound (and visual image) of *hair* is at odds with the metaphorical—*and actual*—destructiveness of darnel in a hayfield. These names—differentiations, a taxonomy, Adamic names, muddled metaphors, shining yellow like fields of light, Gestalts combining fox and vegetable like Wittgenstein's duck-rabbit—these names to me stand for the relation of words to things, inventive, imprecise, denotative, practical, imagined. They are in their business a counter-image to Sartre's experience of namelessness. They are so because of their local metaphoric nature.

(1986)

2

"Sugar" / "Le Sucre"

T HE IDEA for this story presented itself to me initially as a kind of temptation. I had been thinking about the problem of the relations between truth, lies and fiction all my life, first in the moral atmosphere of my childhood and later as a professional matter, both as a writer of fictions and as a university teacher concerned with the nature of narrative. The formal patterns of "Sugar" rose up before me, seductively elegant, some years after my father's death, when I had spent much time rearranging my thoughts about life, death, families and time. It seems important to say that it was the formal element that came first. I did not find an "appropriate form," to quote Coleridge, in which to apprehend my father's death. Rather, I found I had used his dying—and secretly, my mother's later death also—in order to think about the nature of truth and writing. And that was something I had been brought up to think was wrong.

I grew up in an intensely literary family in which literature, art were nevertheless always considered to be matters of secondary importance. This was partly, in later stages, because we had a Quaker upbringing, in which the essential religious experience is a shared silence in a bare room: the early Quakers rejected all art as illusion and distraction from moral virtue and the Inner Light. My mother, whose own pleasures were largely, if narrowly, literary, would nevertheless make sharp speeches, over the washing-up, about the uselessness and self-regard of such persons as artists and mountain-eers, whom, for some reason, she always associated with each other.

Yet I, as a child, it is not too much to say, was in some way kept alive by fictions. I was asthmatic and spent much time in bed: I read Scott, Dickens, Jane Austen; I lived in those worlds. I told myself long tales of other lives, in which I lived with other people in other worlds, from fairy-tales through epics to the seventeenth century. I also retold my own life to myself to make sense of it. I recounted to myself the imagined sequence of events when my father would come back from the War, and occasionally looked, briefly, at the other possible events, when he would not. The wholly imagined worlds seemed simply good, the kings and princes, the flying horses, the paradisal forests. But these *real* imaginings, so to speak, had a contaminated quality. Fiction met lies. Necessarily, of course—we all tell our lives to ourselves, we must, to make sense of them—but the moment we do, we exert a kind of power of fantasy over them, which we feel to be corrupt.

My early attempts at fiction were, formally, very concerned with its dangers. My second novel, *The Game,* turned on various metaphors of the writer, the narrator, the storyteller, as one who eats up reality. The novel had a central character who was a herpetologist and television nature-personality. Coleridge used the image of the serpent for the Imagination. I saw novelists as consumers. I quoted Dr. Johnson, who wrote of "the hunger of the imagination that preys incessantly upon life," and used the cliché "food for thought" to represent the fate of people attacked by the novelist-in-the-novel with the sharp teeth and gaping jaws of her fiction. I have known, personally, human beings whose lives have been wrecked or mutilated by being made the object of other people's fictive attentions.

And if fiction does not eat up life, reality, truth, it rearranges it so that it is forever unrecognisable except in terms of the fixed form, the set arrangement.

When I began to write fiction, then, I felt, to say the least, ambivalent about its relation to my own life. If, nevertheless, in the 1960s, I set out to write a series of what might be described as self-consciously realist novels about my own time and my own culture, it was because I discovered Proust at exactly the right moment, at the moment when I had decided to abandon my doctoral dissertation on seventeenth-century religious allegory and con-centrate on writing novels. And what Proust taught me, in the early 1960s, was that it was possible for a text to be supremely mimetic, "true to life" in the Balzacien sense, and at the same time to think about form, its own form, its own formation, about perceiving and inventing the world. Proust could narrate what was his own life, *beside* his life, more truthfully and more exactly than any autobiographer, biographer or historian, because what he wrote contained its own precise study of the nature of language, of perception, of memory, of what limits and constitutes our vision of things.

I was trained to think about fiction in the arduously moral climate of the Cambridge of F. R. Leavis, who saw literature and art in Arnold's terms as a "criticism of life," who privileged these ways of looking over the more apparently exact ones of biography and history. When I was young, I was excited by the idea that history, biography, autobiography, were fictions. As a student—and still—I was moved by the huge poetic enterprise of Robert Browning's *The Ring and the Book*. In that poem Browning took the factual account of an eighteenth-century Roman murder trial and told it and retold it in an interlocking, endlessly modified web of brilliant narrative monologues: the lawyers, the innocent victims, various representatives of public opinion (Half-Rome, the Other-Half-Rome, Tertium Quid), the murderer, the writer himself, the Pope who judges the final issue (on earth) of life or death. Browning's Pope, in the eighteenth century, as described in the nineteenth century, sees human beings as essentially untruthful.

> But when man walks the garden of this world
> For his own solace, and unchecked by law,
> Speaks or keeps silent as himself sees fit,
> Without the least incumbency to lie,
> —Why, can he tell you what a rose is like
> Or how the birds fly, and not slip to false
> Though truth serve better?

Browning himself believed it was possible, indeed imperative, to tell the truth, that there was such a thing as "truth" that could be sorted out from all the intricate meshes of thought and opinion and partiality that make up our account of things. This makes him profoundly unfashionable now, however fashionable his narrative method of telling, retelling, making and remaking may initially seem to be. "Art," he claims roundly, having told us that "our human speech is naught, our human testimony false"—"Art remains the one way possible / Of speaking truth, to mouths like mine at least."

However initially attractive, even apparently "true" the idea might be that all our narratives are partial fictions, the wholesale enthusiastic acceptance of that way of thought removes both interest and power, in the end, from both art and the moral life. If my desire to write fiction came from my childhood reading and storytelling and my adult encounter with Proust, a further decisive encounter was with Iris Murdoch's extraordinary essay, a kind of credo, "Against Dryness," published in 1961. In this "polemical sketch" Murdoch argues that current views of the nature of the human personality are "shallow and flimsy" and that the two main views of human nature she describes—the rational one of the logical positivists and the existentialism of Sartre—both assume that human beings are "solitary and totally free" and that the fundamental virtue is "sincerity." "Sincerity" might, I suppose, be translated as "self-consistency" or "truth to oneself." Iris Murdoch finds it inadequate. What we need, she says, in a sentence that electrified and electrifies me, is "the hard idea of truth" as opposed to "the facile idea of sincerity."

"The hard idea of truth." The phrase persuades with a metaphor—truth is like stone, sincerity is slippery like butter. When I think about these matters, I always set this concept of Murdoch's against those paragraphs in Gabriel Josipovici's *The World and the Book* (which I mention in the essay "Still Life / Nature morte") in which he discusses Mallarmé's idea of "le démon de l'analogie." During my time as a writer such solipsist ideas of our experience of the world have increased largely in power. So that, whilst it was once attractive *(séduisant?)* to think that whatever we say or see is our own construction, it now becomes necessary to reconsider the idea of truth, hard truth, and its possibility. We may be, as Browning said, born liars. But that idea itself is only wholly meaningful if we glimpse a possibility of truth and truthfulness for which we must strive, however, inevitably, partial our success must be. I do believe language has denotative as well as connotative powers.

When my father was dying I wrote *Still Life,* which I had intended should be a bare, precise novel, telling things (birth, marriage, death) exactly, recognisably, without metaphor or analogy. A leitmotif in that novel was Vincent Van Gogh's painting of the yellow chair, which I took at first as a work of art that was made for the pure pleasure of exact mimetic knowledge—the chairness of the chair, the colour, the form. Later, of course, one discovered cultural and personal connotations. Van Gogh's chair was yellow and blue (colours of day), in contra-distinction to Gauguin's, which was red and green (the "terrible human passions" of the night). He had bought twelve, for the disciples of the new religion of secular art. And so on. But nevertheless it shone in its exact simplicity of representation.

There is a certain amount of defiance in "Sugar." Defiance of the moral imperative (my own, my family's, my culture's) that one should not "eat up" life with the order of art. Defiance of the aesthetic imperative that all good fiction now is overtly fictive and about fictiveness. "Sugar" is that, but it does try to be truthful. It does, also, indicate that there are truths its author chooses to omit, not to tell, to ignore. It does, indeed, also claim authorship for its author.

Translation gives one a new vision of the nature of exactness, accuracy, of the fitting of words to things. When I first read Jean-Louis Chevalier's translation of "Sugar" I felt, in a splendid paradox, both that "Le Sucre" was a new thing, a different piece of writing, and indeed vision, and that it was an exact translation, an *exact re-vision* both of my world and my words, and of the rhythms, part French, part English, in which I had been thinking when I wrote it. "Le sucre" in French is not "sugar" in English. The fact that words name things differently in two languages is part of our knowledge that we make up, we invent, what we experience and see, that naming it delimits and arranges it differently. But the fact that Jean-Louis Chevalier can find such exact equivalents for my English feelings, knowledge, history, shows that the ideas of truthfulness and accuracy also have their validity.

(1989)

VICTORIANS: INCARNATION AND ART

3

Robert Browning:
Fact, Fiction, Lies,
Incarnation and Art

I ONLY MAKE men and women speak," Browning wrote to Elizabeth Barrett, in perhaps his most often quoted remark about his own poetry, "—give you truth broken into prismatic hues, and fear the pure white light, even if it is in me, but I am going to try."[1] His subsequent attempt to speak with his own voice, *Christmas-Eve and Easter-Day,* is one of his interesting failures, and may also be seen as "dramatic" since none of the poet's self-representations strikes the reader as having a great deal to do with the subtle watching and feeling mind which inhabits the invented speakers of the great monologues. "Browning" is bluff and chatty, urgently affectionate and hortatory. Browning the animator is altogether more complex, wise and fierce, calculating and inspired, passionate and intelligent, exactly and sharply judging and endlessly, charitably, imaginatively curious about all sorts of small and obscene, trivial and terrible human desires and self-deceptions.

He is one of the very greatest English poets, and his greatness has never been fully acknowledged or described, in part at least because his prolific writing and his huge and idiosyncratic erudition make him hard to come to terms with all at once, and in part because he is difficult to docket in terms of the usual literary discussions of Victorian poetry. He is, in my view, one of the three great English love poets (the other two are Donne and Robert Graves) because (like them) he shows a precise curiosity about the psychological dramas of love's shifts, visions and failures, and also because, again like them, he sees women as complex human beings, with their own minds and desires, and hopes for dialogue. ("I only make men *and women* [my italics] speak . . .") He also understands and describes sexual passion with a freedom avoided by both novelists and poets in his time.

But in the end his central greatness rests on the dramatising monologues, the varied voices he brought to life. It has frequently been pointed out that the Romantics and Victorians were unable to write successful plays partly because their interest had shifted from the public conflict to the internal struggle of consciousness. But such an observation doesn't get us very far with the ferocious life and energy of Browning's characters in the poems, as opposed to those of his plays. For they are not at all obsessed with internal consciousness; they all have clear ideas of the external world, which they bring abundantly to life.

What is remarkable about the monologues, as a body of work, is the range of human history and geography they represent, from primitive Caliban on his island to the suave Bishop Blougram at his dinner, from Renaissance prelates and artists to ancient Greeks and Arab physicians, from the biblical David to the modern medium, squirming in his exposure, David Sludge. Each is both an individual and a type, a creature limited by his physical and temporal spot of existence, considering both time and eternity from his own point of view. The characters have been called Victorians in disguise, which does less than justice to Browning's very real sense of the differences between perception and frames of thought of different cultures. They do, however, taken together, represent a sustained attempt to embody and contemplate the problems which centrally occupied the nineteenth-century European mind: the problems of the relation of time to history, of science to religion, of fact in science or history to fiction, or lies, in both, and of art to all these.

"Wonder Tales": Strauss, Renan, Froude and Tennyson

The nineteenth-century loss of Christian faith is intricately bound up with the status of the Bible as a historical document. Genesis conflicts with geological and Darwinian accounts of the origin of species and the descent of man. The New Testament is called in question as eyewitness account, and its miracles are scrutinised as contrary to the new positivist excitement about the vision of societies, like solid bodies, as subject to inexorable and unvarying laws. Browning's two biblical poems, "Karshish" and "A Death in the Desert," deal with two of the cruxes of religious questioning at the time, the raising of Lazarus, Christ's most substantial miracle, recorded only in the Fourth Gospel, and the whole problem of the authenticity of that Fourth Gospel. Both poems are in themselves fictive eyewitness accounts of events much speculated about—what happened to the raised Lazarus? Why did he leave no description of life after death to inform the faithful?

The identity of the author of the Fourth Gospel was much discussed. Was the Evangelist also the Beloved Disciple? If he was, was he also John of Patmos, author of the Apocalypse?[2] Did he indeed die? The last chapter of St. John, studied by Mr. Gigadibs after his flight from Bishop Blougram's doubting casuistry to Australian husbandry, considers the claim that he did not.

Charles Darwin, in his *Autobiography,* discusses the evidence for Christianity in terms very relevant to both poems. He argues, like many of his contemporaries, that

> the clearest evidence would be requisite to make any sane man believe in the miracles by which Christianity is supported—the more we know of the fixed laws of nature, the more incredible do miracles become. . . . I gradually came to disbelieve in Christianity as a divine revelation.
>
> The fact that many false religions have spread over large portions of the earth like wild-fire had some weight with me. Beautiful as is the morality of the New Testament it can hardly be denied that its perfection depends in part on the interpretation which we now put on metaphors and allegories. But I was very unwilling to give up my belief.—I feel sure of this for I can well remember often and often inventing daydreams of old letters between distinguished Romans and manuscripts being discovered at Pompeii or elsewhere which confirmed in the most striking manner all that was written in the Gospels. But I found it more and more difficult, with free scope given to my imagination, to invent evidence which would suffice to convince me. Thus disbelief crept over me at a very slow rate, but was at last complete.[3]

"Karshish" might seem at first glance to be the fictive representation of Darwin's fantasy manuscript, a somewhat dubious reinforcement for belief. It is helpful, in this context, to look at the ideas of Strauss on lies, fiction and history. George Eliot translated Strauss's *Life of Jesus* in 1846, and

Browning knew the work well—Strauss appears as a major presence in *Christmas-Eve and Easter-Day*. His book was one of the most powerful influences in the demolishing of fundamentalist belief. In Volume III he puts succinctly the dispute between critical theologians and the Church. It is argued, he says, that "The theologian who is at once critical and speculative, must in relation to the Church be a hypocrite." He continues:

> The real state of the case is this. The Church refers her Christology to an individual who existed historically at a certain period: the speculative theologian to an idea which only attains existence in the totality of individuals; by the Church the evangelical narratives are received as history: by the critical theologian, they are regarded for the most part as mere myths.[4]

There are, Strauss says, various ways open to the theologian. He may attempt to bring the popular mind to understand the truths of religion as he does, or he "may descend from the sphere of the ideal into the region of the popular conception." In this region his truth is a kind of lying, or might be seen so. It can certainly be argued that Strauss at this point twists and turns like one of Browning's casuists, in the interests of saving his kind of truth.

> This expedient is commonly judged and understood too narrowly. The difference between the theologian and the Church is regarded as a total one; it is thought, that in answer to the question, whether he believes in the history of Christ, he ought to say exactly, no; whereas he says, yes: and this is a falsehood. It is true, that if in the discourses and instructions of the spiritual teacher, the main interest were an historical one, this would be a correct representation of the case: but in fact the interest is a religious one,—it is essential religion which is here communicated under the form of a history; hence he who does not believe in the history as such, may yet appreciate the religious truths therein contained, equally with one who does also receive the history as such: the distinction is one of form merely, and does not affect the substance. Hence it is evidence of an uncultivated mind, to denounce as a hypocrite a theologian who preaches, for example, the resurrection of Christ, since, though he may not believe in the reality of that event as a single sensible fact, he may nevertheless hold to be true, the representation of the process of the spiritual life, which the resurrection of Christ affords.[5]

Strauss's great argument was that the New Testament history contains mythic truth, akin to the truths of other myths, or to the abstract truths of philosophy, in an incarnate form in human lives and stories. Browning is popularly seen as a muscular Christian, using his emotional force of imagination to shore up the leap of faith in the dark. What he had to say to Mrs. Orr suggests that his position is not far from that of Strauss, and even with a touch of extra scepticism.

> I know the difficulty of believing . . . I know all that may be said against it [the Christian scheme of salvation] on the ground of history, of reason, of even moral sense. I grant even that it may be a fiction. But I am none the less convinced that the life and death of Christ, as Christians apprehend it, supply something which their humanity requires; and that it is true for them.[6]

Humanity, he says, requires Christ.

> The evidence of Divine Power is everywhere about us; not so the evidence of Divine Love. That love could only reveal itself to the human heart by some supreme act of *human* tenderness and devotion; the fact, or fancy, of Christ's cross and passion could alone supply such a revelation.

This could be seen as an uneasy half-way house between a warm faith clung to, and the cold truth of an empty universe of law. It gave Browning a way to study what it means to be human and incarnate, with, and in some cases without, the idea that infinite love could, in fact or fancy, inhabit finite human hearts. It also, in its riddling movement between one sort of truth and another, gave him a need to think out the uses of both fact and fiction.

"A Death in the Desert" was written partly in response to another rewriting of biblical history, Ernest Renan's *Vie de Jésus,* which appeared in 1863—Browning read it in November of that year. Renan, trained for the priesthood, and an Oriental scholar, wrote the *Vie de Jésus* during a visit to the Middle East, where he was entranced by the landscape and flowers of Galilee, which become characters in his narrative, which opposes the good and innocent Romantic countryman, Jesus, to the labyrinthine religious and political society of Jerusalem. Renan sees the miracle of the resurrection of Lazarus (about which he changed ground in later versions of the *Life*) as a pious fraud by the family at Bethany, a product of the Oriental imagination, which worked with gossip and the fabulous. He added to the *Vie de Jésus* a long appendix on the use to be made of the Fourth Gospel, which, unlike most leading biblical critics of his time, he saw as possibly descended from a factual source that differed from the Synoptic Gospels, though it was also informed by gnostic theology and the desire to equate Christ with the Logos of neoplatonism.

Renan's conception of his own task as a historian and biographer is particularly interesting. He was writing a life of Jesus as a hero of the history of Humanity which should succeed Sacred History. In his preface to the thirteenth edition of the book, he made a spirited rejoinder to his theological critics who believed in the supernatural.

> If the miracle has any reality, this book is but a tissue of errors. If the Gospels are inspired books, and true, consequently, to the letter, from beginning to end, I have been guilty of a great wrong in not contenting myself with piecing together the broken fragments of the four texts . . . If on the contrary the miracle is an inadmissible thing, then I am right in regarding the books which contain miraculous recitals as histories mixed with fiction, as legends full of inaccuracies, errors, and systematic expedients. If the Gospels are like other books, I am right in treating them in the same manner as the Hellenist, the Arabian, the Hindoo treated the legendary documents which they studied.[7]

But his method of study admitted the poetic imagination. If he used the idea of science to reject the miracle, he used the idea of artistic fiction to supplement scientific truth. (It is often seen as a modern discovery that history is necessarily fictive; it was in fact a pervasive nineteenth-century perception.) Renan's description of his own work in his introduction to the *Vie de Jésus* uses a contemporary scientific *metaphor* to endorse his inventions.

> A great life is an organic whole which cannot be exhibited by the mere agglomeration of small facts. It requires a profound sentiment to embrace the whole and to make it a perfect unity. The artistic method in such a subject is a good guide; the exquisite tact of a Goethe would discover how to apply it. The essential condition of the creations of art is to form a living system of which all the parts are mutually dependent and connected. In histories of this kind, the great indication that we hold to the truth is to have succeeded in combining the texts in such a fashion that they shall constitute a logical and probable

narrative in which nothing shall be out of tune. The secret laws of life, of the progression of organic products, of the action of minute particles, ought to be consulted at each moment, for what is required to be produced is not the material circumstance which is impossible to verify; it is the soul itself of history; what must be sought after is not the petty certainty of minutiae, it is the correctness of the general sentiment, the truthfulness of the colouring. Each detail which departs from the rules of classical narration ought to warn us to be on our guard; for the fact which requires to be related has been confined to the necessities of things, natural and harmonious.[8]

This passage is a pure delight in its sleight-of-hand movement between quite different discourses: scientific rigour, Romantic organicism, both as to lives and as to works of literature, with its argument by analogy, French classicism, with its rules of generality and harmonious narrative. Its shortcomings as argument are obvious; its pervasiveness as a set of ideas in the nineteenth century is as important in terms of the nature of art produced then as it is in terms of fictive history. Even Strauss, in a footnote on the Lazarus story, quotes Heydenreich's belief that Matthew omitted the miracle "because it required to be represented and treated with a tenderness and liveliness of feeling of which he did not think himself capable. Hence, the modest man chose to avoid the history altogether rather than to deprive it by his manner of narration, of its proper pathos and sublimity."[9]

Browning's reactions to the *Vie de Jésus* were critical, stringent and scholarly. He wrote to Isabella Blagden:

I have just read Renan's book, and find it weaker and less honest than I was led to expect. I am glad it is written: if he thinks he can prove what he says, he has fewer doubts on the subject than I—but mine are none of his. . . . The want of candour is remarkable: you could no more deduce the character of his text from the substance of his notes, than rewrite a novel from simply reading the mottoes at the head of each chapter: they often mean quite another thing,—unless he cuts away the awkward part—as in the parable of the Rich Man & Lazarus. His admissions & criticisms on St. John are curious. I make no doubt he imagines *himself* stating a fact, with the inevitable licence—so must John have done.[10]

Here Browning is intelligently remarking on the shortcomings of imaginative history, and coupling the evangelist with the scientific historian in their imaginations of themselves. Browning the poet demonstrated his characters' imaginations of themselves, including his St. John, who, despite Browning's strictures, has much in common with Renan's.★

He tells of the resurrection miracle in these terms (Ibid., p. 358):

Weary of the cold reception which the kingdom of God found in the capital, it would seem that the friends of Jesus wished at times for a great miracle which should powerfully impress Hierosolymite scepticism. A resurrection from the dead necessarily appeared most likely to carry conviction. We may suppose that Mary and Martha opened their minds to Jesus on this matter. Fame already attributed two or three acts of the kind to him. "If some one rose from the dead," the pious sisters no doubt said, "perhaps the living would repent." "No," Jesus must have replied, "even were a man raised from the dead they would not believe." Then, recalling a story familiar to him, that of the good beggar covered with sores who died and was carried by the angels into Abraham's bosom, he may have added, "Lazarus might return and they would not have faith." Later, singular misconceptions arose on this subject. The hypothesis was transformed into an actual fact. People spoke of Lazarus as having been raised from the dead, and of the unpardonable obstinacy of those who could resist such testimony. The sores of Lazarus and the leprosy of Simon the Leper were confused with one another, and the idea that Mary and Martha had a brother called Lazarus, whom Jesus caused to come forth from the tomb, became part of the tradition. When one knows of what inexact rumours and cock-and-bull stories the gossip of an Eastern town consists, one does not even regard it as impossible that a report of this nature may have been current in Jerusalem in the lifetime of Jesus, and that it may have had fatal consequences for him.

Before going on to consider Browning's poetic practice in detail, it is perhaps interesting to stay with the tale of Lazarus, and the loss, with a uniquely inspired Book, of a uniquely believed narrative. J. A. Froude, in *The Nemesis of Faith,* makes a telling comparison between the state of mind of a child believing a fairy story, a myth, or a biblical tale, and that of a sceptical adult.

★As I said earlier, Renan changed his position on Lazarus from time to time. His organic harmonising of the evangelical witness leads him to amalgamate the Lazarus of the Fourth Gospel with "Simon le Lepreux" in St. Matthew, and with the beggar in Christ's parable of Dives and Lazarus in Luke (Renan, *Vie de Jésus,* Folio 1974, p. 346 and n. 23).

This age is an age of fact—it believes only in experience—it is jealous and inquiring. It has rejected all these preternatural stories, and now clings only to the Bible. It halts here, for it is afraid of its conclusions . . .

There is life in the Parish School; the child's nature is the same as that which gave the old stories birth; but cross from the Parish School to the Parish Church, and we cross from life to death. Wonder Tales may live in the child; they die in the man, because his temper is changed—he has outgrown them. His mind is not tuned to the supernatural—he cannot believe it. And the result is that utter divorce between practice and profession which has made the entire life of modern England a frightful lie.[11]

Froude's word "lie" has a ringing sound which is part of the proceeding battle. But his other phrase, "Wonder Tales," and his sense of a felt need for them (for the sort of truth which they purvey?) is also part of that battle. Tennyson, in *In Memoriam,* doubting and hoping alternately about life beyond the grave, tells his own version of the Lazarus story, and asks his own questions.

Stanzas XXXI to XXXVII of *In Memoriam* deal with the nature of belief, incarnation, actual or fictive, and resurrection, in their own lucid, riddling way. Stanza XXXI reads:

> When Lazarus left his charnel-cave,
>   And home to Mary's house return'd,
>   Was this demanded—if he yearn'd
> To hear her weeping by his grave?
>
> 'Where wert thou, brother, those four days?'
>   There lives no record of reply,
>   Which telling what it is to die
> Had surely added praise to praise.
>
> . . . .
>
> Behold a man raised up by Christ!
>   The rest remaineth unreveal'd;
>   He told it not; or something seal'd
> The lips of that Evangelist.

In Memoriam XXXIII contrasts the masculine intellect whose religious faith is no longer in the Incarnate God, but is a kind of idealism which "has centre everywhere," with the piety of his sister who can pray. (Shades of Arthur Henry Hallam adjuring his fiancée, Tennyson's sister, not to bother her pure female intuitive wisdom with strenuous masculine doubt—and this in turn leads to an image of the woman as neoplatonic Matter, the body waiting for the form to be given by the male Logos.)

> O thou that after toil and storm
>   Mayst seem to have reach'd a purer air,
>   Whose faith has centre everywhere,
> Nor cares to fix itself to form,
>
> Leave thou thy sister when she prays,
>   Her early Heaven, her happy views;
>   Nor thou with shadow'd hint confuse
> A life that leads melodious days.
>
> Her faith thro' form is pure as thine,
>   Her hands are quicker unto good:
>   Oh, sacred be the flesh and blood
> To which she links a truth divine!
>
> See thou, that countest reason ripe
>   In holding by the law within,
>   Thou fail not in a world of sin,
> And ev'n for want of such a type.

This reads so easily, and is, I think, very complex in its implications. The "thou" addressed holds by the nineteenth-century certainties of reason and law, and fixes his faith everywhere, by virtue of such laws, which operate indifferently everywhere. The sister, who has, as I have argued, connotations of neoplatonic matter as opposed to mind, is the guardian of incarnate truth—the Logos linked to flesh and blood, the *form*, and also the *type*, which make life "melodious" and practical virtue natural. And this modern "sister" is linked to those eyewitnesses of embodied Truth and the resurrection of the body, Martha and Mary of Bethany. The poem itself is both deeply sceptical and deeply desirous of apprehending a "truth" beyond reason in the form and the type of the Incarnate One.

In Memoriam XXXVI continues the meditation on incarnation, truth, tales and books.

> Tho' truths in manhood darkly join,
>   Deep-seated in our mystic frame,

> We yield all blessing to the name
> Of Him that made them current coin;
>
> For Wisdom dealt with mortal powers,
>> Where truth in closest words shall fail,
>> When truth embodied in a tale
> Shall enter in at lowly doors.
>
> And so the Word had breath, and wrought
>> With human hands the creed of creeds
>> In loveliness of perfect deeds,
> More strong than all poetic thought;
>
> Which he may read that binds the sheaf,
>> Or builds the house, or digs the grave,
>> And those wild eyes that watch the wave
> In roarings round the coral reef.

The beginning of this lyric gives a generalised and mysterious vision of a generalised and mysterious incarnation: "Tho' *truths* in manhood *darkly* join." The Incarnate is to be praised because he gave rise to a standardised image of these truths, a type or counter—"current coin." The next verse contrasts the incapacity, in those of merely "mortal powers," to mediate truth directly or accurately, even in "closest words" (approximate words? accurate words? words *next* to truth, not inside it?), with the possibility of apprehending "truth embodied in a tale," which like the Christmas story shall "enter in at lowly doors." "Lowly" is Mary's word, and the stable's and also that of the uneducated human hearers or readers. Note the gentle shift from theological ideas of incarnation to aesthetic, or narrative, ones. "Truth embodied in a tale." Sleight of hand again, but part of the poetic process here. Tennyson's language, so plain, so clear, here so apparently commonplace, itself *embodies* the doubts and conflicts it deals with. The next verse adds the neoplatonic, or Johannine, Logos, and immediately by metonymy incarnates it.

> And so the *Word* had *breath,* and wrought
> With *human hands* the creed of creeds. [My italics]

The creed of creeds is a manual artefact, it is bodily, it is the incarnate *life* of Christ, both beautiful and active ("in loveliness of perfect deeds") here contrasted with art and the mind ("More strong than all poetic thought").

And these deeds, this creed made with hands, are to be *read,* though they are not poetic thought, they are the Book, or is it the Wonder Tale?

Resurrection and Life: Michelet and Browning

Michelet, the historian, tied a further knot in the threads which link poetry, history, the Fourth Gospel and its account of the miracle of Lazarus with a secular questioning about what can be saved of the idea of incarnation. He identifies his own work, the bringing to life of the dead in the history of Humanity, with that of the sage or thaumaturge or prophet who raised Lazarus. In his preface to *Le Peuple* he writes of his own contribution to history, which he sees as dependent on his own popular roots. He grew up like a blade of grass, he tells us, between paving-stones in the Paris of the Revolution, but his grass has kept its sap, quite as much as that of the Alps. He brings, with this popular sap, a new life and rejuvenation (a natural resurrection, one could say). He is part of the great tradition of French history-writing, and his contribution is to have given it a new name, a new definition.

> That this may have been my contribution to the future: that I have if not arrived at, then at least pinpointed, the aim of History, that I have given it a name no one has yet given it. Thierry saw History as a 'Narrative' and M. Guizot called it 'Analysis'. I have called it 'Resurrection', and this name will stick.[12]

He named history resurrection, and, as a child of the Terror, he was much obsessed by death. He tells how his most powerful childhood impression was of the now destroyed Musée des Monuments Français. Here he had his first impression of History, here he communed with the dead. "Je remplissais ces tombeaux de mon imagination, je sentais ces morts à travers les marbres . . ." ("I filled these tombs with my imagination, I could feel those dead men through the marble").[13]

In life, as in art, Michelet was preoccupied with the dead—like many of his contemporaries who, as the certainty of Heaven and the afterlife was disturbed or vanished, resorted to strange cults of ancestral tombs, or to the assurances of Swedenborg and the spiritualists that there was indeed life beyond the tomb. Michelet's much-loved father was buried in the Père-

Lachaise cemetery, over one gate of which appears a quotation from St. John XI: 25: "Qui credit in me, etiam si mortuus fuerit, vivet." This comes from Jesus' saying to Martha, before the resurrection of Lazarus: "Jesus said unto her, I am the resurrection and the life: he that believeth in me, though he were dead, yet shall he live." After his father's burial in November 1846, Michelet attacked the exclusivity of the Christian Grace reserved for believers, using this text. He was a staunch unbeliever all his life, and yet kept many church festivals, including All Saints, and thought in language derived from, and wound about with, theology. In 1850, in July, his son by his young wife was born after a struggle. Michelet recorded his symbolic naming in his journal.

> Thank God—she lives and will live. She has witnessed this soft fruit of life emerge from her own body without dying in the process. *Yves* is her in her father; *Jean* is her in her Christian upbringing and all that represents aspiration and hopes for the future; *Lazare* is her in myself: History and Resurrection.[14]

The child has two of the names of biblical dispute, John and Lazarus. In Michelet's scheme the Evangelist stands for the Christian hope for the future, and Lazarus for the new life conferred by the historian and history. Unfortunately the child lived only a few weeks, and was buried beside Michelet's father; their grave became a kind of shrine. His short life, and Michelet's passion for his fragile wife, gave rise to some instructive rhapsodising about resurrection. For instance, in August, he looks at his sick son and reflects that his death would be a grief, not only for themselves but "for all those who hope in this name of Lazarus. Consecrated by this name of resurrection, he will, in living, encourage these sick hearts. His death would discourage them . . ." And he writes of his wife, the "young heart" who demands from him the treasure of life:

> I am not a God, my child, I am a man. The life that is in me is not my own but the thinking of centuries. Its source is not from me but is the communal source of the World and of History. It came from God and still does flow from Him. It is the source of the human species, of universal actions and passions, the great river of life, work and pain.[15]

This is at once overweening and strangely humble, depending on how one looks at the idea of human life. Both Strauss and Feuerbach (to whom we shall come) see the species, *le genre humain,* as the true immortal incarnation of eternal truth, of which individuals are only finite parts. Michelet himself both incarnates and observes this superhuman creature.

In September 1850 he complains that his spirit languishes, "deux fois captif et deux fois dans la chair, deux fois lié d'incarnation" ("doubly captive and doubly in the flesh, doubly bound to incarnation"). He is held in his body by two mistresses, the woman, his wife, and his mistress, History. He sees life as a climb towards God by steps of a ladder—love, art . . .

> We can only glimpse God, that sun on high, through these clouds of art and of love which, like real clouds, provide the sun with its splendour and its charm for the earth's inhabitants whilst, at the same time, preventing them from seeing it face to face. The need to materialise and incarnate the spirit is our fate here below. There is still no religion which does not have a formula or a legend which gives it bodily form. Without doubt they are necessary; and yet as soon as the spirit uses them, it fixes on them, cannot transcend them and forgets how to ascend to the Spirit.[17]

Michelet is further than Tennyson from the need for the original Christian Tale, though he speaks of his work, and of himself, in terms of incarnation. Michelet's Christ is either Michelet, the raiser of Lazarus, or Le Peuple, the suffering, dying, unrecorded common man, or men. His use of Lazarus and resurrection has often been compared with Browning's own imagery for his own activities.

If *Men and Women* is fictive dramatic monologues, *The Ring and the Book* is history, in a way exactly comparable to Renan's activities in piecing together his artistic Tale out of the fragments of evidence available in the Gospels and Josephus. Browning's immersion in contemporary debate about evidence, eyewitness accounts, history and imagination must be involved in his interest in the "square old yellow Book" he found in Florence in 1860.

Browning's Book is a compilation of contemporary accounts of a murder trial and *cause célèbre* in Rome in 1698. From these Latin legal wrangles and pamphlets he made a twelve-book poem, of which the central ten books are dramatic monologues by speakers involved in the drama—the lawyers on each side, public opinion in three biased and conflicting personae, the murderer (twice), the murdered, the priest who organised her flight and the aged Pope who finally judges whether Count Guido shall in fact suffer death. The outcome of events is never in doubt—Browning summarises the story for the reader in the first Book, which is written in the poet's own voice. A writer who adopted a technique which gives ten different accounts of the same events in the twentieth century would almost certainly be reflecting on the knowable nature of human life, the unreliability of narrators, the relativity of truth. Browning, on the other hand, appears to be insisting on the need to pursue and determine truth as far as possible, even with all our shortcomings and fallibility amply acknowledged and demonstrated. Judges must judge, must assess evidence, as must historians. What Browning's method does is to demonstrate the difficulty for us, both as speakers and as readers, in picking our way through interpreted "facts." What we, as readers, experience is a series of other closed human beings, with their rhetoric, their prejudices, their sexual and social biases. We experience also our own provisional judgments and assents and dissents from the drift of the characters and the poet. We think to ourselves that the murdered girl, Pompilia, could not possibly be so innocent as the poem makes her out to be. We are made to experience, in the poem at least, the vulgarity and prurience of that pre-judgment, casual and perfunctory. Browning lies in wait for us, with the shallowness of other proponents of that view, with the full horror of the sadistic persecution of the bought child-bride by her husband—saved until the seventh Book, after the "reasonable" self-defence of the murderer and the rhetoric of Caponsacchi, whose very chivalric love for Pompilia makes the reader suspect her innocence even in admiring him.

Browning's own metaphor for his work, as poet and historian, is in the relation of Ring to Book. The poem opens with the Ring. It is made in imitation of

> Etrurian circlets found, some happy morn,
> After a dropping April; found alive
> Spark-like 'mid unearthed slope-side figtree-roots
> That roof old tombs at Chiusi: soft, you see,
> Yet crisp as jewel-cutting.

He uses the image of the mixing of gold with its alloy, to make it workable, for the working of his own imagination on the "pure crude fact" he finds in the yellow Book. Before considering this powerful image of the imagination, it is worth considering the peculiar beauty of the description of the discovery of the original, Etruscan rings, copied "by Castellani's imitative craft."

The surprising word in that first description is "alive," a word not naturally associated with gold rings. The "life" of the gold has both a natural and a supernatural connotation. It is found alive, in April, that is, in spring, among fig-tree roots, and appears spark-like, suggesting some renascent seed of light, like neoplatonic images for the divine spark in the human soul. It is found among old tombs, and is in some sense resurrected—fig trees carry a faint suggestion of Paradise, as does possibly the phrase "happy morn." Browning's nineteenth-century ring is an imitation of a mysterious one resurrected from some ancient past. So with his poem, the conventional length for an epic, but related intricately to the method of the *Comédie Humaine* rather than the *Divina Commedia*.

The physical image of the imagination as alloy, removed from the finished circle by a spirit of acid, to leave a "self-sufficient . . . shape," "Prime nature with an added artistry," is complemented, when we come to the Book, with a supernatural image of the poet as mage, thaumaturge or prophet. The finding of the Book is as instructive in its details as the finding of the original Ring. If the gold is natural, prime nature, the Book is cultural, and appears at the end of one of Browning's marvellous lists of objects, things randomly piled together in the market, things old and broken and dubious and intensely *physical* (we shall come back to Browning's lists of objects):

> 'Mongst odds and ends of ravage, picture-frames
> White through the worn gilt, mirror-sconces chipped,
> Bronze angel-heads once knobs attached to chests . . .

Browning has Balzac's skill, Dickens's skill, with objects both fascinating and threatening in their superfluity and lost meaning, abandoned artefacts, dead but speaking. The culmination of the list is five books, a Spicilegium, a vulgarised Horace, Dumas's *La Dame aux Camélias* ("the fond tale/O' the Frail One of the Flower"), and two Saints' Lives.

> The Life, Death, Miracles of Saint Somebody,
> Saint Somebody Else, his Miracles, Death and Life,—

It could be argued that the Dumas and the Saints' Lives are narrative forms rejected by Browning, for Pompilia is both suffering woman and partly sanctified. What attracts the Poet in the yellow Book is *fact,* as he says several times in different ways.

> Small-quarto size, part print, part manuscript,
> A book in shape but, really, pure crude fact
> Secreted from man's life when hearts beat hard,
> And brains, high-blooded, ticked two centuries since.

And

> Now, as the ingot, ere the ring was forged,
> Lay gold, (beseech you, hold that figure fast!)
> So, in this book, lay absolutely truth,
> Fanciless fact, the documents indeed . . .

Browning's startling description of himself as miracle-worker follows an apparently conclusive elaboration of the gold-alloy-ring figure. He appeals in ringing rhetoric to his readers—after his work.

> Lovers of dead truth, did ye fare the worse?
> Lovers of live truth, found ye false my tale?

But he goes on to meditate yet again, and differently, on fact and fiction.

> Well, now; there's nothing in nor out o' the world
> Good except truth: yet this, the something else,
> What's this then, which proves good yet seems untrue?
>
> . . . .
>
> Are means to the end, themselves in part the end?
> Is fiction which makes fact alive, fact too?
> The somehow may be thishow.
>   I find first
> Writ down for very A B C of fact,
> 'In the beginning God made heaven and earth.'

We are back to the authenticity of the Bible, though Browning does not insist on this, but goes on to say that man, made in God's image, makes images of his own,

> Creates, no, but resuscitates, perhaps.

He meditates on the mage who raised a ghost by sending out half of himself, and broods that if he has that skill,

> '. . . then write my name with Faust's!'
> Oh, Faust, why Faust? Was not Elisha once?—
> Who bade them lay his staff on a corpse-face.
> There was no voice, no hearing: he went in
> Therefore, and shut the door upon them twain,
> And prayed unto the Lord: and he went up
> And lay upon the corpse, dead on the couch,
> And put his mouth upon its mouth, his eyes
> Upon its eyes, his hands upon its hands,
> And stretched him on the flesh; the flesh waxed warm:
> And he returned, walked to and fro the house,
> And went up, stretched him on the flesh again,
> And the eyes opened. 'Tis a credible feat
> With the right man and way.

Why is this passage so disturbing? It is a truism that the Romantic poet came to see his own inspiration and creation as divine; poetry, as spilt religion; his work, as Coleridge said, an echo in the finite mind of the infinite I A.M. Browning makes no such high claims—he calls his work

> —Mimic creation, galvanism for life,
> But still a glory portioned in the scale.

It is partly the association of the word "galvanism" with the miracle of Elisha that gives to this image its charnel-house vitality. It is partly the lack of personality, even of gender, of the corpse in question. The corpse is very fleshly, a very solid piece of inanimate carnality. The act of resuscitation (which follows the biblical account very exactly) is not an act of love; it is a passing of life and identity from one figure to the identical other, which then warms. (Indeed, Browning has suppressed the fact that the corpse was that of a child.)

If Browning and Michelet are interested in the related topics of incarnation and resurrection, which are both in some sense *animation,* they are interested in the material part of the equation, in matter, in the body. I think this is obscurely and deeply connected to the fear, made beautiful and wonderful by the geologists and the prehistorians, that perhaps the body was all there was, that the one life ended once in death, which came increasingly to possess the century. The problems of mind, soul and body were older than Christianity, but Christianity, a historical religion, had had a vision of a unique divine event in Time and Space where the infinite was embodied in the finite, thus ensuring the connection forever between suffering flesh and triumphant spirit. With the fading of the historical faith, everything changed. Morality depended less on the hereafter and God's Judgment, more on individual judgment here and now, in the flesh. The relations between body and mind needed rethinking.

The Ring and the Book, a death-haunted text, moving as it does between a murder and an execution, provides a conventional Christian frame for Guido's sin and redemption, or can be seen as doing so, since it is his fear of his impending execution in his cell which strips away his casuistry and his cultural pride, reducing him to raw animal, and then to pleading with the authorities, human and divine:

> Sirs, have I spoken one word all this while
> Out of the world of words I had to say?
> Not one word! All was folly—I laughed and mocked!
> Sirs, my first true word, all truth and no lie,
> Is—save me notwithstanding! Life is all! . . .
>
> Abate,—Cardinal,—Christ,—Maria,—God,—
> Pompilia, will you let them murder me?

Is this last-minute repentance? Or the animal recognising the value of life, and the murderer fearing judicial murder?

The Pope, in the tenth Book, which precedes Guido's last speech, meditates on the nature of truth in his own way. The Pope is a believer, and is aware of the essential deficiencies of language when it comes to truth-telling. He opens his meditations with an apparently rambling dissertation on the history of his predecessors, notably Pope Formosus, tried by another Pope, Stephen, as an exhumed corpse:

> Read,—how there was a ghastly Trial once
> Of a dead man by a live man, and both, Popes:
> Thus—in the antique penman's very phrase.

It could be argued that the whole of *The Ring and the Book* is a trial of a dead man by a live man, which casts a complicating light on the Elisha metaphor for its making. The Pope quotes Ecclesiastes sagely, *en passant,* "Since of making of many books there is no end," and goes on to question

> Which of the judgments was infallible?
> Which of my predecessors spoke for God?

This is all a prelude to his own judgment of Guido, which he makes recapitulating the evidence once again, as judges do, and then comparing his judgment to a diagnosis made of a sick man, on inadequate evidence, which proved to be wrong.

> Mankind is ignorant, a man am I . . .
> If some acuter wit, fresh probing, sound
> This multifarious mass of words and deeds
> Deeper, and reach through guilt to innocence,
> I shall face Guido's ghost nor blench a jot.

He then thinks out the nature of truth and lies; lies are implicit in language itself. "What we figure as God's judgment-bar" has nothing to do with words.

> Not so! Expect nor question nor reply
> At what we figure as God's judgment-bar!
> None of this vile way by the barren words
> Which, more than any deed characterize
> Man as made subject to a curse: no speech—
> That still bursts o'er some lie which lurks inside,
> As the split skin across the coppery snake,
> And most denotes man! since, in all beside,
> In hate or lust or guile or unbelief,
> Out of some core of truth the excrescence comes,
> And, in the last resort, the man may urge
> 'So was I made, a weak thing that gave way
> To truth, to impulse only strong since true,

> And hated, lusted, used guile, forwent faith.'
> But when man walks the garden of this world
> For his own solace, and, unchecked by law,
> Speaks or keeps silence as himself sees fit,
> Without the least incumbency to lie,
> —Why, can he tell you what a rose is like,
> Or how the birds fly, and not slip to false
> Though truth serve better? Man must tell his mate
> Of you, me, and himself, knowing he lies,
> Knowing his fellow knows the same,—will think
> 'He lies, it is the method of a man!'
> And yet will speak for answer 'It is truth'
> To him who shall rejoin 'Again a lie!'
> Therefore these filthy rags of speech, this coil
> Of statement, comment, query and response,
> Tatters all too contaminate for use,
> Have no renewing: He, the Truth, is, too,
> The Word.

It proved impossible to cut this passage for quotation. Seen at its simplest it presents language as the fruit of original sin, or even as the satanic inhabitant of the natural serpent—language is the "coil" of speech in the "garden of this world." Natural man, the body, has natural "impulses" which are a form of truth, but thinking man, describing man, is inadequate and must lie. The trust and mistrust resemble the puzzles in the verses already quoted from *In Memoriam*. The woman in that poem has hands that are quick to good, and poetic thought is suspect compared with perfect deeds. Tennyson invokes the Incarnate in whom "the Word had breath and wrought / With human hands the creed of creeds." The Pope's human words "have no renewing." Whereas He, the Truth, is, too, the Word. And Browning's galvanic mockery, in the Pope's terms, his mimic creation, is words, and therefore lies. Yet Browning, at the end of the last book, makes claims for Art as truth, after all, at least in part because Art is a kind of deed, an artefact is a kind of incarnation, rather than the language of judgment or "estimation."

The lesson, he says, which "whatever lives should teach" is

> that our human speech is naught,
> Our human testimony false, our fame
> And human estimation words and wind.

Why take the artistic way to prove so much?
Because, it is the glory and good of Art,
That Art remains the one way possible
Of speaking truth, to mouths like mine, at least.

. . . .

But Art,—wherein man nowise speaks to men,
Only to mankind,—Art may tell a truth
Obliquely, do the thing shall breed the thought,
Nor wrong the thought, missing the mediate word.
So may you paint your picture, twice show truth,
Beyond mere imagery on the wall,—

. . . .

So write a book, shall mean beyond the facts,
Suffice the eye and save the soul besides.

Is this casuistry too? Fiction, mere imagery, are deeds and things—not testimony—are apprehended by "the eye" as pictures might be, sensuously, without the mediation of the partial and lying word. Fiction that makes fact alive is a kind of truth, to set beside human untruth, and the undifferentiated Divine Word-Truth.

Incarnation: George Eliot and Feuerbach

Browning's ideas of fictive truth in *The Ring and the Book* cast light on the nature of his use of the dramatic monologue, the particular speech, at particular spots in time and space, of thoroughly incarnate, essentially limited beings, who are also made of fictive imagining. His beliefs might be compared with those of George Eliot, who wished to make her ideas "thoroughly incarnate" in particular individuals, and feared to lapse from the picture to the diagram, who wrote:

But my writing is simply a set of experiments in life—an endeavour to see what our thought and emotion may be capable of—what stores of motive, actual or hinted as possible, give promise of a better after which we may strive—what gains from past revelations and discipline we must strive to keep hold of as something more than shifting theory. I become more and more timid—with less daring to adopt any formula which does not get itself clothed for me in some human figure and individual experience, and perhaps that is a sign that if I help others to see at all, it must be through the medium of art.[18]

George Eliot was much influenced in her desire for truths of feeling rather than theory by the ideas of Feuerbach, whose *Essence of Christianity* she translated in 1854. Feuerbach interpreted religion as human self-worship projected into fictive beings, imagined as objects of reverence and love. He wrote powerfully and persuasively of the workings of the human imagination (sensuous image-making power) in religious thought.

> The psychological truth and necessity which lies at the foundation of all these theogonies and cosmogonies, is the truth and necessity of the imagination as a middle term between the abstract and the concrete. And the task of philosophy in investigating this subject is to comprehend the relation of the imagination to the reason,—the genesis of the image by means of which an object of thought becomes an object of sense, of feeling.[19]

George Eliot described Dorothea's arrival at moral understanding in *Middlemarch* in terms of just such sensuous apprehension of an object of thought—the separate existence of her husband as an incarnate being. What is fascinating is that the resolute demythologiser Feuerbach not only insisted on the importance of truths of sense and feeling, but identified the incarnate Christ with the imagination as an object of worship.

> Man, as an emotional and sensuous being, is governed and made happy only by images, by sensible representations. Mind presenting itself as at once type-creating, emotional and sensuous, is the imagination. The second Person in God, who is in truth the first person in religion, is the nature of the imagination made objective. The definitions of the second Person are principally images or symbols; and these images do not proceed from man's incapability of conceiving the object otherwise than symbolically . . . because the thing itself is a symbol or image . . . The Son is the satisfaction of the need for mental images, the nature of the imaginative activity in man made objective as an absolute, divine activity.[20]

It is interesting in the context of Lazarus to note also Feuerbach's description of miracle, which for him is

> a thing of the imagination; and on that very account is it so agreeable: for the imagination is the faculty which corresponds to personal feeling, because it sets aside all limits, all laws which are painful to the feelings, and thus makes objective to man the immediate absolute satisfaction of his subjective wishes . . . It is true that miracle produces also an awful agitating impression, so far as it expresses a power which nothing can resist—the power of the imagination . . .

And later:

> Who can fail to recognize in the narrative of the resurrection of Lazarus the tender, pleasing, legendary tone . . .[21]

Whether Browning had thought of it or not, it is the truth of feeling and the subjective desire of the imagination which call Karshish to ask Abib what if in the thunder dwelt a human voice

> Saying, 'Oh heart I made, a heart beats here!'

a classic Feuerbachian making of God.

Strauss, in the Conclusion to the *Life of Jesus,* discusses the relation between the infinite and the finite, in scientific and theological terms. If we think of the infinite as that which lies beyond the finite, he says, we make it finite in that act of thought. The two are necessarily interdependent.

> As man, considered as a finite spirit, limited to his finite nature, has not truth; so God, considered exclusively as an infinite spirit, shut up in his infinitude, has not reality . . . The true and real existence of spirit, therefore, is neither in God by himself, nor in man by himself, but in the God-man . . .[22]

One could turn to others besides Strauss for a description of these relations. Browning, in a letter to Ruskin, who was puzzled by his abstruse meanings, wrote as a finite man.

> I know that I don't make out my conception by my language; all poetry being a putting the infinite within the finite. You would have

me paint it all plain out, which can't be; but by various artifices I try
to make shift with touches and bits of outlines which *succeed* if they
bear the conception from me to you.[23]

If we recall Browning's concession in the letter to Mrs. Orr that Christianity may be a fiction, and his reiteration that it nevertheless represents a
human need—a need for feeling, for "*human* tenderness and devotion"—
we can perhaps place his incarnate individuals as a series of infinites, put
within finites—the proper activity of Art, or "all poetry." We can also
suggest that the idea of "Him, The Truth, who is too the Word" is as much
an image of Feuerbach's "sensible representation" of the Imagination as
mediator between mind and matter.

Putting the Infinite Within the Finite: The Dramatic Monologues

What seems to me most remarkable about "Karshish," after thirty years of
reading and rereading it, is the peculiar appropriateness of Karshish himself
as an observer of Browning's Lazarus. By this I do not mean simply that an
Arab physician with different beliefs and preoccupations, and an epistolary
style related to the biblical epistles, makes an interesting dramatic hearer for
the unexpected ideas of resurrection and incarnation. Nor do I mean that
Karshish, scientist and doctor, provides an interesting sceptical mind, akin
to those nineteenth-century questioners of the miracle, with his reasonable
medical explanation of the "death." What I remember always about Karshish, what is vivid about him, are the descriptions he offers of his world, and
the intelligent curiosity and pleasure in detail with which he notes its
phenomena. His attention is directed by his profession, but outruns it,
which is why he is open to the possibilities of Lazarus's account of his state.
He makes his own vivid versions of Browning's heterogeneous lists:

> I have shed sweat enough, left flesh and bone
> On many a flinty furlong of this land.
> Also the country-side is all on fire
> With rumours of a marching hitherward:
> Some say Vespasian cometh, some, his son.
> A black lynx snarled and pricked a tufted ear;
> Lust of my blood inflamed his yellow balls:
> I cried and threw my staff and he was gone.

Karshish is more interested in a particular spider, which

> Weaves no web, watches on the ledge of tombs,
> Sprinkled with mottles on an ash-grey back;

than in large military and political movements.

His description of Lazarus is of a man equally interested in all details of his restored life.

> The man is witless of the size, the sum,
> The value in proportion of all things,
> Or whether it be little or be much.
> Discourse to him of prodigious armaments
> Assembled to besiege his city now,
> And of the passing of a mule with gourds—
> 'Tis one! Then take it on the other side,
> Speak of some trifling fact,—he will gaze rapt
> With stupor at its very littleness,
> (Far as I see)—as if in that indeed
> He caught prodigious import, whole results . . .

Karshish is intelligent enough to understand that this indifferent interest in everything is to do with the disturbed relation in Lazarus between finite and infinite. He ascribes Lazarus's "witlessness" to his death.

> So here—we'll call the treasure knowledge, say,
> Increased beyond the fleshly faculty—
> Heaven opened to a soul while yet on earth,
> Earth forced on a soul's use while seeing Heaven . . .

And Karshish uses of Lazarus a geometric image, of a man forced to hold on to some thread of life

> Which runs across some vast distracting orb
> Of glory on either side that meagre thread,
> Which, conscious of, he must not enter yet . . .

Browning himself used geometric imagery, of points and lines in fields, to represent individual incarnations. The characters he most approves, most loves, have a mixture of Lazarus's interest in all earthly details with Karshish's intelligent curiosity about them, his desire to do one thing well. The last Duchess offends her husband, confined by his limited human pride to a kind of savagery, by just such undifferentiated pleasure.

> Sir, 'twas all one! My favour at her breast,
> The dropping of the daylight in the West,
> The bough of cherries some officious fool
> Broke in the orchard for her, the white mule
> She rode with round the terrace . . .

Karshish, having said that Lazarus claimed that his healer was God himself, goes on:

> Why write of trivial matters, things of price
> Calling at every moment for remark?
> I noticed on the margin of a pool
> Blue-flowering borage, the Aleppo sort,
> Aboundeth, very nitrous. It is strange . . .

These lines are those that stay in the mind, in my experience. They appear to be poetic irony—Karshish does not know how to distinguish between the truly trivial and the cosmically shattering. But the lists do not work, in the poem, to that effect. They are beautiful, precise, a man connected to the earth, observing it. They are akin to Lazarus's interest in "trifling facts," so that the reader does a kind of double-take. In the world of the poem, the lynx and the borage are as sharp and vivid as the claims about incarnation, love and resurrection. They are part of what it is to be human, walking the meagre thread across glory.

Browning's artists, his theologians, and his lovers are made of this mixture of observation of solid fact, the direction of human energy, and live curiosity. Those of his artists who succeed, succeed because they have balanced these things adequately. The poet, in "How it Strikes a Contemporary," is described as an observer, simply, who noted everything—the poem is largely a list of what he noted. The poem's speaker sees him as a spy writing letters to the King, but the poem's reader knows that the poetry is in the watching itself, unadorned. Fra Lippo Lippi's superiors in the Church try to suppress his precise observation of the world and the flesh in the interests of the soul.

> Your business is not to catch men with show,
> With homage to the perishable clay,
> But lift them over it, ignore it all,
> Make them forget there's such a thing as flesh.
> Your business is to paint the souls of men—

Lippi's instinct is to concentrate on flesh.

> Or say there's beauty with no soul at all—
> (I never saw it—put the case the same—)
> If you get simple beauty and naught else,
> You get about the best thing God invents:
> That's somewhat: and you'll find the soul you have
>   missed,
> Within yourself, when you return him thanks.

Lippi's cheerful sensuality is a passion of love for creation, a living engagement with it, and so wholly admirable. Andrea del Sarto, in his world
silvered by a common greyness, lacks this living energy, the "soul" brought
by Michelangelo to his imperfect line, and not brought by Lucretia, to her
marriage or her work.

It is their engagement with the detail of the world of the senses that gives
to Browning's theological monsters their engaging, and somehow redeemed, quality. The Bishop of St. Praxed's, Caliban, and Mr. Sludge, the
Medium, are all very busy imagining and apprehending the sensuous world
they live in, and trying to make sense of it within the limits of their very
imperfect understandings and their not entirely pleasant natures. To compare these three with the achieved and "civilised" blandness of the worldly
Bishop Blougram is instructive. Blougram is very considerably more intelligent than any of these, and his riddling arguments for accepting Christianity
on balance are not wholly distant from Browning's own position. What is
wrong with him is a fatal complacency, a fatal easy *acceptance* of the limitations of his mediocrity. Blougram is so intelligent that he is even aware of
this accusation too, and turns on his interlocutor at the end, telling him that
he knows there are

> those exceptional
> And privileged great natures that dwarf mine—
> A zealot with a mad ideal in reach,
>
> . . . .
>
> A statesman with a scheme to stop this war,
> An artist whose religion is his art—
> I should have nothing to object: such men
> Carry the fire, all things grow warm to them,
> Their drugget's worth my purple, they beat me.

But he accuses himself even in this acknowledging phrase—he sees life as a competition, and measures Shakespeare by his own materialist standards (at least for argument's sake—it is truly difficult to know how far Blougram believes himself, and this is one of the glories of Browning's dramatic art).

> Himself, who only can, gives judgment there.
> He leaves his towers and gorgeous palaces
> To build the trimmest house in Stratford town;
> Saves money, spends it, owns the worth of things . . .

This is not untrue; it just has little to do with what we—or even Blougram, who is moved by a chorus ending from Euripides—value about Shakespeare. But Blougram's measured pleasure in second-rate honours and comforts betrays his inadequacy.

> I am much, you are nothing; you would be all,
> I would be merely much—you beat me there.

And in his vocabulary, the repeated "beat" of the competitive schoolboy, the "merely much" of his lack of drivenness, he displays his nature.

Compare that other Bishop, ordering his tomb in the sensuous confusion of approaching death. He is neither intelligent nor well-informed. He confuses the sex of his patron saint and confuses the discoveries of the Classical Renaissance hopelessly with the icons of the religion he professes. His thought for the afterlife is confined to that most material and earthly of things, the stone of his tomb. He is addressing his "nephews," who are in fact his sons, like many sons of worldly and only nominally celibate Renaissance priests. He can quote Ecclesiastes as well as the Pope in *The Ring and the Book*, but only, one feels, for the aphoristic poetry—the meaning escapes him, which is Browning's complex irony, since he is by no means simply mocked or exposed.

> Swift as a weaver's shuttle fleet our years:
> Man goeth to the grave, and where is he?
> Did I say basalt for my slab, sons? Black—
> 'Twas ever antique-black I meant! How else
> Shall ye contrast my frieze to come beneath?
> The bas-relief in bronze ye promised me,
> Those Pans and Nymphs ye wot of, and perchance
> Some tripod, thyrsus, with a vase or so,
> The Saviour at his sermon on the mount,
> Saint Praxed in a glory, and one Pan
> Ready to twitch the Nymph's last garment off,
> And Moses with the tables . . .

This is another list, a comical and powerful confusion of the rediscovered Classical world with the figures of Christianity, all as equal as the trivia observed by Lazarus or the last Duchess, all as beautiful and vivid. Behind all this lies Browning's knowledge of the conflicting traditions of the Church, the celibacy and austerity of the early Church at odds with the colours and liveliness of the Renaissance, when the infinite was embodied in a multitude of finite solid forms. This Bishop is a sensualist. His most powerful emotions, facing death, are attachment to the material of his tomb, competition with Gandolf, and the memory of the beauty of his dead mistress. We feel with him his limbs arranging themselves into the eternity of his monument. His vision of eternity is irredeemably incarnate.

> And then how I shall lie through centuries,
> And hear the blessed mutter of the mass,
> And see God made and eaten all day long,
> And feel the steady candle-flame, and taste
> Good strong thick stupefying incense-smoke!

These lines are great because of their directness and the largeness of their implications. The Bishop's imagination is confined to the five senses, all of which play a part in the eternal bliss he foretells. The words suggest to us comic and not wholly pleasant feelings—"mutter," "strong thick stupefying," "made and eaten." But they are the words of the acts of a religion which is based on incarnation, and the description of the mystery of the mass is an exact description—God is indeed made and eaten. And if the Bishop takes an incarnate pleasure in the eating, that is somehow as it should be, in some sense. The Bishop has lived his fleshly incarnation to the full, and sees the stones themselves as harbouring a kind of incarnation, deadly and terrifying, strangely beautiful in their grotesque way.

> Peach-blossom marble all, the rare, the ripe
> As fresh-poured red wine of a mighty pulse.

Or the unforgettable

> Some lump, ah God, of *lapis lazuli,*
> Big as a Jew's head cut off at the nape,
> Blue as a vein o'er the Madonna's breast . . .

The Bishop does not notice the cruelty in the image of the beheading, though the reader shivers at it, nor does he notice the unfortunate juxtaposition of the simile from the Madonna's breast. And yet the incongruity makes something beautiful, anticipating Fra Lippo's idea of simple beauty and naught else, in the imagined blue, flesh and stone.

Some kind of power comes through the Bishop's defined limitations, as it does through Caliban's attempts to sort out his world, ascribing to his God, Setebos, the random cruelty which he himself can exercise, and which he certainly senses in the "acts of God," and in the acts of men, in his island. But he also intuits the existence of something eternal and inhuman, the Quiet.

> There may be something quiet o'er His head,
> Out of His reach, that feels nor joy nor grief,
> Since both derive from weakness in some way.

Caliban's Setebos is the opposite of the infinite incarnate, he is the finite anthropomorphised into the Deity, and the finite is cruel.

> 'Believeth with the life, the pain shall stop.
> His dam held different, that after death

> He both plagued enemies and feasted friends:
> Idly! He doth His worst in this our life,
> Giving just respite lest we die through pain,
> Saving last pain for worst—with which, an end.
> Meanwhile, the best way to escape His ire
> Is, not to seem too happy.

And Natural Theology cannot in itself come at the Christian truth, though Caliban puzzles away at the problem of suffering most diligently, and produces an almost Darwinian vision of the anthropomorphic demon "growing" (developing) into the Quiet. Which will then, one assumes, be connected to the suffering earth.in a way in which it is not at present, though whether it will be equally cruel or indifferent, Caliban does not say.

> 'Conceiveth all things will continue thus,
> And we shall have to live in fear of Him
> So long as He lives, keeps His strength: no change,
> If He have done His best, make no new world
> To please Him more, so leave off watching this,—
> If He surprise not even the Quiet's self
> Some strange day,—or, suppose, grow into it
> As grubs grow butterflies: else, here are we,
> And there is He, and nowhere help at all.

This poem, too, is more than it says. The reader can sense that the conduct of civilised man, Prospero, has reinforced the savage creature's sense of the cruelty of the powers of the earth. But what, along the poem, remains in the memory is the fullness and sensuous abundance of Caliban's world, of which he is a fearfully living part, a world as swarming with life and interest as Lippo's gallery of incarnate faces or the Bishop's paradoxically living stones. These ideas, these thoughts—which are powerful thoughts, and hard to controvert—come out of this one world, which embodies them. The monologues together mean more, in this way, than they do singly. They are not part of one Book, one set of related evidences, as the speeches in *The Ring and the Book* are, but they make up an interlinked world of spots of time and space, more complex than the sum of its parts. Caliban exists alongside Blougram, and Cleon's civilised and frozen despair of eternity exists alongside not only the liveliness of his contemporary Karshish, but the analogous inertia of Andrea and the snarling striving of Mr. Sludge.

. . .

Nineteenth-century spiritualism is intricately and deeply involved in the crisis of faith amongst churchmen and thinking people. The Resurrection and the story of Lazarus promised a survival of death. Loss of certainty about these produced a host of Doubting Thomases who needed on this earth to hear and see the surviving spirits of the ancestors and the loved. Elizabeth Barrett Browning was a fervent believer in the mystical visions (very solid and carnal, moreover) of Swedenborg. Commentary on "Mr. Sludge"[24] has seen her belief as unusual, and Browning's robust rejection of the miracles wrought by the medium D. D. Home as a normal reaction to a distasteful eccentricity. But the desire to taste and see discarnate spirits was not at all unusual at the time. It was part of a whole shift of religious feeling. Swedenborg, the mineralogist who saw a life in stones, and who conversed in the most matter-of-fact way both with the angelic world and with the damned, was the hope of a whole world of believers. Spiritualism was the religion of a materialist age, in a simple sense, and also in a more complicated one. Emily Jesse (once Emily Tennyson, the bride-to-be of Arthur Henry Hallam) became a member of the Swedenborgian Church and raised the spirit of Hallam at a séance. Two of her sisters and one of her brothers also belonged. Tennyson's intense desire, in *In Memoriam,* to touch and grasp his lost friend, is not the excessive sensuality of a homosexual memory, as is now often argued, but part of the climate of the time.

> I loved thee, Spirit, and love, nor can
> The soul of Shakespeare love thee more

could be used as evidence for both kinds of feeling.

Sludge is unmasked as a fraud and a liar and a self-deceiver. He is also a casuist, in his uneducated way, quite as powerful as Blougram, more urgent, if less urbane. He fakes evidence, he fakes miracles, he fakes visions of the infinite beyond the limits of the body he is closed into. To have its full force, Sludge's definition of lies needs to be set beside all the other definitions of lies I have cited—from Browning's admission that Christianity may be a fiction, to Froude's Wonder Tales. For Sludge too comes into that circle of artists who give life and form to fictive truths.

> Strictly, it's what good people style untruth;
> But yet, so far, not quite the full-grown thing:

It's fancying, fable-making, nonsense-work—
What never meant to be so very bad—
The knack of story-telling, brightening up
Each dull old bit of fact that drops its shine.
One does see somewhat when one shuts one's eyes,
If only spots and streaks; tables do tip
In the oddest way of themselves: and pens, good Lord,
Who knows if you drive them or they drive you?

The imagery is not so far from Browning's account of his own poetic activity in *The Ring and the Book*—"Is fiction that makes fact alive, fact too?" Sludge too has a feeling for truth.

There's something in real truth (explain who can!)
One casts a wistful eye at, like the horse
Who mopes beneath stuffed hay-racks and won't munch
Because he spies a corn-bag: hang that truth,
It spoils all dainties proffered in its place!

Sludge, coddled and cossetted by the credulous company whom he sees as having an endless appetite for lies, feels like a child cossetted by nurse, aunt and grandmother who longs (like Caliban) for mud and earth.

I've felt a child; only a fractious child
That, dandled soft by nurse, aunt, grandmother,
Who keep him from the kennel, sun and wind,
Good fun and wholesome mud—enjoined be sweet,
And comely and superior,—eyes askance
The ragged sons o' the gutter at their game,
Fain would be down with them i' the thick o' the filth,
Making dirt-pies, laughing free, speaking plain,
And calling granny the grey old cat she is.
I've felt a spite, I say, at you, at them,
Huggings and humbug . . .

For Sludge, as for Caliban, *mutatis mutandis,* truth goes with spite and mud—like Caliban's his origins are despised and oppressed. His very name suggests a primeval or residual matter, as opposed to spirit, and he uses it often in this sense, mocking himself and his users, who see his earthy nature as the "medium" through which the spirit world will shine and speak. One of his images for his mediation between spirit and sense is the window; he says of the spirits:

> You see, their world's much like a gaol broke loose,
> While this of ours remains shut, bolted, barred,
> With a single window to it. Sludge, our friend,
> Serves as this window, whether thin or thick,
> Or stained or stainless; he's the medium-pane,
> Through which, to see us and be seen, they peep . . .

But he uses the image of mud in a pre-Freudian way to symbolise the materialism of the money world and the natural human propensity to lie as the Pope described it.

> I'll go beyond: there's a real love of a lie,
> Liars find ready-made for lies they make,
> As hand for glove, or tongue for sugar-plum.
> At best, 'tis never pure and full belief;
> Those furthest in the quagmire,—don't suppose
> They strayed there with no warning, got no chance
> Of a filth-speck in their face . . .
> Be sure they had their doubts,
> And fears, and fairest challenges to try
> The floor o' the seeming solid sand! But no!
> Their faith was pledged . . .
> And Sludge called 'pet' . . .

These are the religious fools, but there are the other fools, including the "literary man" who half-believes

> All for the book's sake, and the public's stare,
> And the cash that's God's sole solid in this world!
> Look at him! Try to be too bold, too gross
> For the master! Not you! He's the man for muck;
> Shovel it forth, full-splash, he'll smooth your brow
> Into artistic richness, never fear!
> Find him the crude stuff; when you recognize
> Your lie again, you'll doff your hat to it,
> Dressed out for company!

Here Carlyle's cash-nexus, the sludge of material existence, and the half-faith of art and fiction become one scatological vision. Yet Sludge too has his vision of God. He speaks of the doubt about the

> Strict sympathy of the immeasurably great
> With the infinitely small, betokened here
> By a course of signs and omens, raps and sparks,—
> How does it suit the dread traditional text
> O' the 'Great and Terrible Name'? Shall the Heaven of Heavens
> Stoop to such child's-play?

(There is another essay to be written on Sludge's images of the small, helpless and innocent, compared to Caliban's world of small persecuted creatures.)

From this concatenation of infinitely small and immeasurably great, Sludge produces his real image of divinity. In biblical days, he says, thunder and lightning were great and men were small and creeping. Now infinity, through the medium of the microscope, not the telescope, appears behind the "infinitely small."

> We find great things are made of little things,
> And little things go lessening till at last
> Comes God behind them. Talk of mountains now?
> We talk of mould that heaps the mountains, mites
> That throng the mould, and God that makes the mites.
> The Name comes close behind a stomach-cyst,
> The simplest of creations, just a sac
> That's mouth, heart, legs and belly at once, yet lives
> And feels, and could do neither, we conclude,
> If simplified still further one degree:
> The small becomes the dreadful and immense!

This passage could be compared with Michelet's account in *L'Insecte* of the seventeenth-century Dutch scientist Swammerdamm, who discovered the microscope, and the infinitely small, and feared (according to Michelet) the loss of faith that came with this fearful removal of man's central position in the universe, for which a religion had been built that made God incarnate once, and in human form. Sludge's Name is incarnate in the stomach-cyst—man has no privileged place in his muddy and earthy universe, a truth available to the unpleasant and unprivileged "medium" who is such a precise analyst of the human desire for self-aggrandisement and deceit. Or lies.

So, like the Bishop with his stones and incense-fumes, like Caliban with his slime and his busy creatures, Sludge is a particular incarnation with a particular vision of the infinite through his smeared window. It is worth remarking on his name, David, which can be no accident. David, King and Psalmist, meant a great deal to Browning, who presented him in "Saul" as an ecstatic visionary who sees the infinity of God in the finite universe around him, undifferentiated, as though he were able, as the reincarnate Lazarus is not, to see Heaven and Earth together and one.

> I report, as a man may of God's work—all's love, yet all's
>   law!
> Now I lay down the judgeship He lent me. Each faculty
>   tasked
> To perceive Him, has gained an abyss, where a dewdrop
>   was asked.
> Have I knowledge? confounded it shrivels at Wisdom
>   laid bare.
> Have I forethought? how purblind, how blank, to the
>   Infinite Care!
> Do I task any faculty highest, to image success?
> I but open my eyes,—and perfection, no more and no
>   less,
> In the kind I imagined, full-fronts me, and God is seen
>   God
> In the star, in the stone, in the flesh, in the soul and the
>   clod.

This David, the Old Testament prophet, is able to foretell to Saul the coming of the Incarnate Infinite who shall offer the love desired by Saul as by Karshish.

> 'Tis the weakness in strength, that I cry for! my flesh, that
>   I seek
> In the Godhead! I seek and I find it. O Saul, it shall be
> A Face like my face that receives thee; a Man like to me,
> Thou shalt love and be loved by, for ever: a Hand like
>   this hand
> Shall throw open the gates of new life to thee! See the
>   Christ stand!

Mr. Sludge apprehends the infinite after years of history, doubt, and speculation have intervened since David's vision, or St. John's dubious eyewitness. A poem which deals directly with this increasing distance and complexity is the "Epilogue" to *Dramatis Personae,* in which Browning speaks for himself, in riddles, dramatisations and images. It is a poem about incarnations and the Incarnation, the relationship between Face and face. It has three speakers, the first two of whom are identified in the second edition of *Dramatis Personae* as David and Renan.

David's poem is a song, akin to Christopher Smart's "Song to David" (see the "Parleying with Smart"). It describes an act of worship in the Old Testament Temple in which all the worshippers become *one man*

> When the thousands, rear and van,
>   Swarming with one accord,
> Became as a single man,
>   (Look, gesture, thought and word)
> In praising and thanking the Lord.

This act of praise and thanks in turn fills the Temple with the cloud of the presence of the Lord, and the three verses of the song join men, temple, song and God into one presence.

In the second poem, the speaker (as Renan), describes the Face as a vanishing star, moving out into the opening infinite distance. The star, like the Bishop's peachy marble, is riddlingly blooded (incarnate).

> Could man indeed avail, mere praise of his,
>   To help by rapture God's own rapture too,
>   Thrill with a heart's red tinge that pure pale bliss?

The imagery of "Renan's" speech here is related to the images St. John uses for the relation of heaven to earth in "A Death in the Desert." He speaks there of his belated telling of the facts of Christ's life which had "grown" in the "light" of John's own life with these facts.

> Since much that at the first, in deed and word,
>   Lay simply and sufficiently exposed,
> Had grown (or else my soul was grown to match,
>   Fed through such years, familiar with such light,
>   Guarded and guided still to see and speak)

> Of new significance and fresh result;
> What first were guessed as points, I now knew stars,
> And named them in the Gospel I have writ.

John might have made up fictive "stars" in his late interpretation of the "points" of the facts of the Life of Jesus. He himself, almost dead, is "bare to the universal prick of light," but his followers must learn to see the truth of love in the world. He compares historic truth to the distinct small objects seen through an optic glass that distanced them.

> Become succint, distinct, so small, so clear!
> Just thus, ye needs must apprehend what truth
> I see, reduced to plain historic fact,
> Diminished into clearness, proved a point
> And far away: ye would withdraw your sense
> From out eternity, strain it upon time,
> Then stand before that fact, that Life and Death,
> Stay there at gaze, till it dispart, dispread,
> As though a star should open out, all sides,
> Grow the world on you, as it is my world.

This difficult image seems to suggest that the experience of the open star is the experience of a world at once limited and limitless, like the Temple of David's song, the Infinite within the finite. It is certainly the same star which is dwindling into the distance in Renan's speech, taking with it music and worship. Renan too, sees "points,"

>   lesser lights, a mist
> Of multitudinous points, yet suns, men say—
> And this leaps ruby, this lurks amethyst,
>   But where may hide what came and loved our clay?
> How shall the sage detect in yon expanse
>   The star which chose to stoop and stay for us?

The Renan poem describes a dividing line between finite acting or suffering and the "disk's serene," now akin to Caliban's indifferent Quiet. Our passion blooded, or "crimsoned" it, but this time is past.

The third speaker, presumably the poet himself, uses a different image of man's separateness and incarnation. Like the vanishing stars, or St. John's historical facts about the Life of Christ, this image is a "point," but the point here is a rock in a waste of water. The point of rock becomes the focus of the activity of the water, until it is uprooted and swept over, when some other peak is chosen.

> Then, like me, watch when nature by degrees
> Grows alive round him, as in Arctic seas
> (They said of old) the instinctive water flees
>
> Toward some elected point of central rock,
> As though, for its sake only, roamed the flock
> Of waves about the waste: awhile they mock
>
> With radiance caught for the occasion,—hues
> Of blackest hell now, now such reds and blues
> As only heaven could fitly interfuse,—
>
> The mimic monarch of the whirlpool, king
> O' the current for a minute: then they wring
> Up by the roots and oversweep the thing,
>
> And hasten off, to play again elsewhere
> The same part, choose another peak as bare,
> They find and flatter, feast and finish there.

This is an image of the illusory sense a man has of his own central importance in his world, one might say. We are submersible points in a waste of waters, random and undifferentiated. This is not, however, the point Browning is making, although it is present in the feel of the narrative. He introduces the image of rock and water with the injunction

> Take the least man of all mankind, as I;
> Look at his head and heart, find how and why
> He differs from his fellows utterly:

What is important is the separateness and uniqueness of even the "least man." The movements of the waters—radiant with colours, feasting, flattering and finishing the points of rock—are described subsequently as the "dance" of nature about each man of us, at first making a pageant to "enhance his worth" and then rolling away elsewhere. This leads Browning to a gnomic reflection on one man's experience in one world—and that experience is defined as *his dividedness from others,* which could also be called his separate incarnation, his particular combination of infinite and finite.

When you acknowledge that one world could do
All the diverse work, old yet ever new,
Divide us, each from other, me from you—

Why, where's the need of Temple, when the walls
O' the world are that? What use of swells and falls
From Levites' choir, Priests' cries, and trumpet-calls?

That one Face, far from vanish, rather grows,
Or decomposes but to recompose,
Become my universe that feels and knows!

Before considering the nature of that final Face, I should like to look
quickly at Browning's habitual use of colour images in conjunction with
"points" to indicate separate and partial existences, divided from the whole.
I began with Browning's description of his activity of making men and
women speak in terms of light broken into its prismatic hues. I have shown
how he characteristically uses red to suggest blood and incarnation. At the
end of the first Book of *The Ring and the Book* he uses an image of shifting
colour for "This man's act, changeable because alive."

Action now shrouds, now shows the informing thought;
Man, like a glass ball with a spark a-top,
Out of the magic fire that lurks inside,
Shows one tint at a time to take the eye:
Which, let a finger touch the silent sleep,
Shifted a hair's-breadth shoots you dark for bright,
Suffuses bright with dark, and baffles so
Your sentence absolute for light or shade.

He moves almost immediately into his invocation to his "lyric Love,"
whose heavenly aspect, both deathly and infinite, is white, but which sang
a kindred heart out to the sun—"Yet human at the red-ripe of the heart."
The lyric Love is both Elizabeth and the Incarnate Love, which received the
summons to earth that blanched their heavenly chambers of their blue—
"And bared them of their glory." Infinity is white, the light that blazes
round Lazarus's dark incarnate line, or pricks at St. John through his now
fragile flesh. The finite is points of coloured light, which leap ruby and lurk
amethyst. Browning worshipped Shelley, and Shelley's image is to the point
here, "the Life that like a dome, of many-coloured light / Stained the white
radiance of eternity." And I have wondered whether the imagery of the

"point" owes anything to Swedenborg, who gave a geometric account of the beginning of things (in *Outlines of the Infinite*) and likened the mathematical or natural point to a two-faced Janus, which looks on either side toward either universe, both into infinite and into finite immensity. The rocky "point" amidst the varied and mythically "instinctive" waters of nature, with their radiance caught from particular aspects of light, is a beautiful image of particular incarnation in time and space. But the final verse adds another, whose metaphysical wit equals Donne's and is surprising, powerful and entirely appropriate where it stands. The Face, or star, grows as St. John's star grows. But it also "decomposes but to recompose." This image is threefold. It is to do with death and finitude, which bring decomposition with them (and, in some sense, the mud and clods and sludge of "Sludge"). It is to do with music, in the sense that David's Temple is made of music—and the music of swells and falls, analogous to the waves of the dominant image of the third speaker's poem. It is to do with poetry, also something which is composed. The connection between finite and infinite for David was the song of praise which made all men one in the Temple. The connection between finite and infinite for Renan was the sense of the infinite distance between light and human smallness, of reciprocity between speaker and hearer, life and the unearthly. What the third speaker seems to say is that even the least of men, in his individuality, is one incarnation of the infinite, that the walls of the world, which confine him, are at the same time his temple—as David saw God in the star, in the stone, in the flesh, in the soul, in the clod, indifferently. The Face is not resurrected but "recomposed" out of its death and decomposition, made by the poet, or singer, or perceiver, who, in knowing his separateness, knows also the existence of everything else, with both mind and heart, with both spirit and flesh. Because he differs from his fellows utterly (as opposed to becoming one man with others in the Temple), he composes his world with an essential difference, "my universe that feels and knows." He is a witness of difference. He is a poet who writes men and women, all separately incarnate, all separately aware in their necessarily and splendidly limited ways, of infinite passion and the pain of finite hearts that yearn.

4

George Eliot: A Celebration

MY FIRST INTRODUCTION to George Eliot was unpropitious. At the age of eleven I underwent a class "reading" of *Silas Marner* at Sheffield High School and remember finding it very tedious: no drama, or what there might have been subdued, too many comic country people who bore little relation to anyone I, a city child, had met, no romance of the simple sort I was looking for. In bed I read Scott, Jane Austen, Dickens, endless historical romances and a lot of poems. I was quite incapable of appreciating the economy and sober order of *Silas*. I don't think, although it's a legendary Tale, it should be given to children. Then I read *The Mill on the Floss,* which I found unbearable for different reasons. I didn't like the beginning because of its inexorable damping-down of the fire and energy of a lonely, clever girl. I didn't like the end, because it didn't seem appropriate: drowning *with her brother* was not (and I must say, is not) a fate for Maggie Tulliver that leaves one with any feeling of having really come to the end—tragic, passionate, despondent—of the complexities of cross, clever, ferocious Maggie. The author drowned the heroine for dramatic reasons—and I, as a child reader, felt cheated. So I didn't persevere.

When I was at Cambridge, good undergraduates were learning about the Great Tradition of the English novel from F. R. Leavis. Jane Austen, George Eliot, D. H. Lawrence, Henry James, Conrad. *Not,* in those days, Dickens or Scott, my early loves, and only one Brontë—Emily. I played safe by avoiding the whole issue and worked with poetry almost exclusively. So I came to George Eliot late, in the days when I was teaching the modern English novel in evening classes and trying to find out how to write a good novel myself. Meeting any great author is like being made aware of freedoms and capabilities one had no idea were possible. Reading *Middlemarch* and *Daniel Deronda* I learned several primitive yet crucial lessons about writing novels—and these lessons were also moral lessons about life. It is possible, I learned, to invent a world peopled by *a large number* of inter-related people, almost all of whose processes of thought, developments of consciousness, biological anxieties, sense of their past and future can most scrupulously be made available to readers, can work with and against each other, can lead to failure, or partial failure, or triumphant growth.

I suppose I was in my late twenties when I began teaching *Middlemarch,* and I taught it with passion because I perceived it was about the growth, use and inevitable failure and frustration of all human energy—a lesson one is not interested in at eleven or eighteen, but at twenty-six, with two small children, it seems crucial. George Eliot's people were appallingly ambitious and greedy—not always for political or even, exclusively, sexual power, as in most of the other English novels I read. They were ambitious to use their minds to the full, to discover something, to live on a scale where their life felt valuable from moment to moment. In *Middlemarch* Dorothea, the untutored woman who wishes to contribute to science, even Casaubon, the failed scholar, had hopes which meant something to *me,* as Madame Bovary's cramped, Romantic, confused sexual lunges towards more life did not. In *Daniel Deronda* the hero has humane and intellectual ambitions: Gwendolen Harleth is a sympathetic portrait on the grand scale of a deficient being whose conceptions of the use of energy never extended beyond power (sexual and social) and money (not for its own sake, but for social pride). Perhaps the most vital discovery I made about George Eliot at that time was that her people *think:* they worry an idea, they are, within their limits, responsive to politics and art and philosophy and history.

The next discovery was that the author thought. One of the technical things I had discovered during the early teaching of *Middlemarch* was George Eliot's authorial interventions, which were then very unfashionable, thought to be pompous Victorian moralising and nasty lumps in the flow of "the story." I worked out that on the contrary, the authorial "voice" added all sorts of freedom a good writer could do with. Sometimes it could work with firm irony to undercut the sympathetic "inner" portrayal of a character. Consider this early description of Dorothea:

Her mind was theoretic, and yearned by its nature after some lofty conception of the world which might frankly include the parish of Tipton and her own rule of conduct there; she was enamoured of intensity and greatness, and rash in embracing whatever seemed to her to have those aspects; likely to seek martyrdom, to make retractions, and then to incur martyrdom after all in a quarter where she had not sought it. Certainly such elements in the character of a marriageable girl tended to interfere with her lot, and hinder it from being decided according to custom, by good looks, vanity, and merely canine affection.

There is so much in there, in the style. The magisterial authority of a Greek Chorus, or God, who knows Dorothea's fate before her drama has really begun. Sympathy, in the author, towards the character's ambitions, and a certain wry sense that, unfocused as they are, they are doomed. And then, in that last sentence, which is biting social comedy, the choice of the crucial adjective—"merely *canine* affection"—to disparage the kind of "love" thought adequate by most planners of marriages, not only in the nineteenth century.

From close study of the novels, I went on to the life and read George Eliot's essays, written for the large part for the liberal *Westminster Review* in the years immediately preceding her shocking elopement with the married G. H. Lewes. They are intellectual, yes, and learned—very learned. George Eliot read Latin, Greek, French, Spanish, Italian and German: she was *au fait* with current philosophy, physiology, psychology and sociology: she wrote with ferocious authority. I liked that—I admire the deployment of a clear mind and a lot of information as one might admire Rembrandt's mastery of colour, chiaroscuro, space. But what is also marvellous about the essays is that they are sharp, trenchant, satirical, in places wildly funny. She takes the prose style of an unctuous Evangelical preacher to pieces with meticulous mockery: in "Silly Novels by Lady Novelists" she writes hilarious parodies of the ridiculous plots employed by female pen-pushers and ends with a moving plea for a novel with new depths of insight. As an example of the former, here is George Eliot's description of the archetypal heroine of a species of novel she designates as *mind-and-millinery:*

Her eyes and her wit are both dazzling; her nose and her morals are alike free from any tendency to irregularity; she has a superb *contralto* and a superb intellect; she is perfectly well-dressed and perfectly religious; she dances like a sylph and reads the Bible in the original tongues . . . Rakish men either bite their lips in impotent confusion at her repartees, or are touched to penitence by her reproofs; indeed there is a general propensity in her to make speeches, and to rhapsodize at some length when she retires to her bedroom. In her recorded conversations she is amazingly eloquent, and in her unrecorded conversations, amazingly witty.

At the end of the essay George Eliot produced eloquence of another order.

No educational restrictions can shut women out from the materials of fiction, and there is no species of art which is so free from rigid requirements. Like crystalline masses, it may take any form, and yet be beautiful; we have only to pour in the right elements—genuine observation, humour and passion. But it is precisely this absence of rigid requirement which constitutes the fatal seduction of novel-writing to incompetent women.

George Eliot was, I suppose, the great English novelist of ideas. By "novelist of ideas" I do not here mean novelists like Peacock, Huxley or Orwell, whose novels are dramatic presentations of beliefs they wish to mock or uphold, whose characters *represent* ideas like allegorical figures. I mean, in George Eliot's case, that she took human thought, as well as human passion, as her proper subject—*ideas,* such as thoughts on "progress," on the nature of "culture," on the growth and decay of society and societies, are as much actors in her work as the men and women who contemplate the ideas, partially understand them or unknowingly exhibit them. Part of the recent reaction against her, I suspect, is because her "ideas" have been too generally summed up as a belief in inevitable human progress, a gradual bettering of the human race, a slow movement upwards and outwards. This, with the fact that the societies she depicted were (with the notable exception of Deronda's Jewish plans for a new National Home) static, constricting, rigid in form, has led people to believe she has less to offer modern novelists than may be true.

George Eliot did indeed coin the word "meliorism" to describe a belief in gradual progress—the word is attributed to her in the OED. But she had a strong—stronger—sense of black comedy, black tragedy than she is now generally credited with, and a saving savagery in her vision of man's normal and natural inhumanity to man. She had no real heir as "novelist of ideas" in England: Lawrence's "ideas" are comparatively simple and strident, Forster's timid, and less comprehensive and forceful than hers. Her heirs are abroad—Proust in France, Mann in Germany. Which brings me to another reason for loving her: she was European, not little-English, her roots were Dante, Shakespeare, Goethe, Balzac, not just, as Leavis's Great Tradition implies, Jane Austen. She opened gates which are still open.

And I, as a woman writer, am grateful that she stands there, hidden behind the revered Victorian sage, and the Great English Tradition—a writer who could make links between mathematical skill and sexual inadequacy, between Parliamentary Reform and a teenager's silly choice of husband, between Evangelical hypocrisy and medical advance, or its absence. When I was a girl I was impressed by John Davenport's claim, in a Sunday newspaper novel-column, that "nobody had ever really described what it felt like to be a woman." I now think that wasn't true then, and isn't true now. People are always describing that, sometimes *ad nauseam*. George Eliot did that better than most writers, too—because it was not all she did: she made a world, in which intellect and passion, day-to-day cares and movements of whole societies cohere and disintegrate. She offered us scope, not certainties. That is what I would wish to celebrate.

(1980)

5

George Eliot's Essays

I N 1885 William Hale White wrote a letter to the *Athenaeum* in response to John Walter Cross's recently published *Life* of his dead wife, George Eliot.[1] It is worth quoting in full.

> As I had the honour of living in the same house, 142, Strand, with George Eliot for about two years, between 1851 and 1854, I may perhaps be allowed to correct an impression which Mr. Cross's book may possibly produce on its readers. To put it very briefly, I think he has made her too 'respectable'. She was really one of the most sceptical, unusual creatures I ever knew, and it was this side of her character which was to me the most attractive. She told me that it was worthwhile to undertake all the labour of learning French if it resulted in nothing more than reading one book—Rousseau's *Confessions*. That saying was perfectly symbolical of her, and reveals more completely what she was, at any rate in 1851–4, than page after page of attempt on my part at critical analysis. I can see her now, with her hair over her shoulders, the easy chair half sideways to the fire, her feet over the arms, and a proof in her hands, in that dark room at the back of No. 142, and I confess I hardly recognize her in the pages of Mr. Cross's— on many accounts—most interesting volumes. I do hope that in some future edition, or in some future work, the salt and spice will be restored to the records of George Eliot's entirely unconventional life. As the matter now stands she has not had full justice done to her, and

she has been removed from the class—the great and noble church, if I may so call it—of the Insurgents, to one more genteel, but certainly not so interesting.

It is this George Eliot—sceptical, unconventional, addicted to the daring, risqué, nakedly self-revelatory and subversive *Confessions*—whose presence can be sensed in her essays and reviews. She went to live in No. 142 Strand in 1851, when she was thirty-two, to lodge in the household of John Chapman, publisher and new owner of the *Westminster Review*. Chapman had already published her translation of David Friedrich Strauss's *The Life of Jesus* in 1846, and made her acquaintance in Coventry. Chapman was passionately addicted to women, and his family included his mistress, Elisabeth Tilley, as well as his wife, Susanna. Both women became very jealous of Miss Evans, and it is clear that there was good cause for this; her first visit to No. 142 lasted from January to March 1851, when a series of angry scenes and disputes culminated in her tearful departure. Chapman recorded in his diary: "M. departed today. I accompanied her to the railway. She was very sad and hence made me feel so. She pressed me for some intimation of the state of my feelings. I told her that I felt great affection for her, but that I loved E. and S. also though each in a different way. At this avowal she burst into tears."[2]

Chapman's offer for the *Westminster Review* was accepted in May 1851, and the deed of sale was signed in October of that year. He decided that the powerfully intelligent Marian Evans would be an ideal assistant; Susanna and Elisabeth were resolutely set against her return to No. 142 or indeed to London at all. For some months the two corresponded and Chapman negotiated with the other women. In September it was agreed that Marian Evans might return as a lodger; she lived there, apparently amicably, for the next two years.

She became, in effect, the secret editor of the *Westminster Review*. Chapman was known as chief editor; the letter sent out with the prospectus referred to "the Editors," and Marian Evans told Chapman, "In regard to the secret of the Editorship, it will perhaps be the best plan for you to state, that for the present *you* are to be regarded as the responsible person, but that you employ an Editor in whose literary and general ability you confide."[3]

Thomas Carlyle, who called himself "clear for silence at present," wrote to Robert Browning, suggesting that Browning contribute, and said Chapman had "an able Editor (name can't be given) and such an array of 'talent' as was seldom gathered before."[4] She edited ten numbers of the periodical;

Gordon Haight tells us the *Westminster* reviewed about a hundred volumes in each of these ten.[5] The reviews were arranged at first under the heading of "Contemporary Literature" of England, America, Germany and France; later, at Herbert Spencer's suggestion, they were rearranged under subject headings. The long articles were compilations of reviews by various authors: Marian Evans was responsible for running these together, editing and cutting. But it is not thought she wrote much herself, and some earlier attributions have been disproved. She did advise on the choice of authors and subjects, and was responsible for proofs and printing. She seems to have been paid nothing for all this work, but it transfigured her life. Chapman gave regular literary parties and took her to more; she met thinkers, poets and writers whose work she reviewed, such as R. W. Mackay and W. R. Greg, as well as Giuseppe Mazzini and Karl Marx. Her letters at the time are lively, incisive and busy. For a young woman from a merely respectable provincial family, this was an immense increase of freedom and life. She mixed with others of her own kind—the Insurgents; like herself, they were not part of the established social and religious hierarchy but were liberal, questioning, free-thinking, interested in reform.

The *Westminster Review* had a distinguished history. It was founded in 1824 by James Mill, with financial support from Jeremy Bentham. John Stuart Mill edited it from 1837 to 1840, when it gained its highest reputation for intellectual excitement and radical thought. The prospectus Chapman and Evans wrote for their first issue (January 1852) declared itself committed to advocating "organic change" according to the Law of Progress, whilst respecting the "variety of forms" in which "the same fundamental truths are apprehended." It would not ignore "the widespread doubts in relation to established creeds and systems" and would "fearlessly examine" the elements of ecclesiastical authority and of dogma; it would discuss "without reservation, the results of the most advanced biblical criticism." It advocated progress towards universal suffrage and reform of the judiciary, and a national system of education. There was to be an "Independent Section" to provide freedom for the expression of views that opposed those of the editors, though this section was found to be impracticable and was abandoned after the second number. The *Westminster,* under its anonymous editor, printed J.H. Froude on Tudor England, J.S. Mill on William Whewell's philosophy, and Herbert Spencer's theory of evolution.

Herbert Spencer's *Principles of Psychology* included a footnote thanking George Eliot for the happy phrase "Things which have a constant relation to the same thing have a constant relation to each other."[6] When he first met the "translatress of Strauss," he described her as "the most admirable woman, mentally, I have ever met."[7] In 1852 they spent much time together, and were rumored to be engaged. Her letters to him, kept secret until 1985, reveal a woman passionately and self-abasingly attached, begging for crumbs of attention, if not love. Spencer, who remained a bachelor, declined her affections and let it be known that this was because she was ugly. It says much for her generosity of spirit that she remained on good terms with him, even confiding in him that she was the "George Eliot" who had written *Scenes of Clerical Life,* a confidence he unwisely betrayed to the garrulous Chapman.

By the turn of the year, however, she had shifted her affections to Spencer's friend G. H. Lewes, whom at first she suspected of being flippant and lightweight. In 1850 Lewes was co-founder, with Thornton Leigh Hunt, of the *Leader,* a weekly newspaper, which, with the *Westminster,* published the bulk of George Eliot's reviews. Thornton Leigh Hunt was the father of the fifth son of Lewes's wife, Agnes (and subsequently of three more). Lewes was devoted to his own sons, and acknowledged this fifth one, thus rendering himself unable to seek a divorce, since he had condoned the adultery. But his marriage was over, and he was free, emotionally, to love Marian Evans. In September 1853 she moved from No. 142 Strand to lodgings in Cambridge Street. Her translation of Ludwig Feuerbach's *The Essence of Christianity* was written in the next few months and finally appeared in July 1854. It was in the same month that Marian Evans left for Germany with Lewes and embarked on the "marriage" that was to last his lifetime and lead directly to the work of George Eliot. This step also led directly to the writing of the major essays between 1854 and 1857, published in the *Westminster Review.* They were written for money, but they were also written with a new intellectual authority, freedom and sense of excitement. It is usual for critics of George Eliot to look for the weighty, the sibylline and the scrupulously just. But these essays are also at times savagely ironic, often very funny, and have a speed and sharpness that is less frequently remarked on.

It is possible to find in them hints of her private preoccupations at that time, and also thoughts about human nature, art and societies that will later form essential parts of the fiction of George Eliot. I shall discuss some of these and relate them to the development of her thought in other non-fictional work—translations, the poems, the correspondence with Frederic Harrison and the "Notes on Form in Art" (unpublished before Thomas Pinney's 1963 collection).

It is perhaps worth remarking at this stage, however, how much of her writing at this time drew its life from a kind of ferocious, witty and energetic rejection. The great essays on John Cumming and Edward Young are rejections of her own earlier religious and literary enthusiasms. "Woman in France: Madame de Sablé" questions English conventional ideas about female virtues and the nature of marriage. "Silly Novels by Lady Novelists" offers a radical rejection of the aims and moral vision of the novels currently being written by women, and ends with a statement of what women novelists *could* do, powered by anger as well as by hope. She was free, she was clearing the ground.

This is perhaps also the best point at which to discuss, at least briefly, the complex question of Eliot's attitude to "the woman question." At the height of her fame she was cautious, even ambivalent, in her support of Girton College and women's suffrage; she wrote: "there is no subject on which I am more inclined to hold my peace and learn, than on the Woman Question. It seems to me to overhang abysses, of which even prostitution is not the worst . . . I have been made rather miserable lately by revelations about women, and have resolved to remain silent in my sense of helplessness."[8] These inexplicit "abysses" seem related in their anxiety to her earlier fear of becoming "earthly sensual and devilish" at her father's death, and the removal of "that purifying, restraining influence."[9] She wrote brilliantly and passionately about the pain of thwarted intelligence, or artistic power, in women, but also insisted, throughout her life, on the importance of recognising the differences between the sexes. The "feminine" virtues of tenderness, sympathy and patience were to her real virtues, to be desired and respected *as feminine*. But at the same time she saw very clearly that to live only for personal affections was dangerously narrow: she wrote to a woman friend in 1870:

We women are always in danger of living too exclusively in the affections; and though our affections are perhaps the best gift we have, we ought also to have our share of the more independent life—some joy in things for their own sake. It is piteous to see the helplessness of sweet women when their affections are disappointed—because all their teaching has been, that they can only delight in study of any kind for the sake of a personal love. They have never contemplated an independent delight in ideas as an experience which they could confess without being laughed at. Yet surely women need this sort of defence against passionate affliction even more than men.[10]

Some feminists have criticised Eliot for accepting stereotyped ideas of "feminine" characteristics. Others have criticised her for trying too hard to have what they think of as the "male" patriarchal qualities of rationality and intellect (thus falling into the stereotyping trap themselves). She was a complex woman, at once freely independent and timidly clinging, powerfully intelligent and full of a compelled artistic ambition that sprang both from "feeling" and from the mind.

In the essay on Madame de Sablé (1854) she argued strongly both for the specificity of female talents and sensibilities and for "unions formed in the maturity of thought and feeling, and grounded only on inherent fitness and mutual attraction," as opposed to the "quiescence and security of the conjugal relation." In 1855, reviewing Thomas Keightley's *Life of Milton,* she supported Milton's plea for divorce, and drew the analogy between Milton's plight and the campaign of Caroline Norton, which brought attention to the iniquities suffered by women because of the divorce law. Milton's personal experience, she said, could be traced in his descriptions of the "baleful muteness of a virgin" hiding "all the unliveliness and natural sloth which is really unfit for conversation."[11] Her own personal pleading can be traced in the essay on Madame de Sablé, which ends with the lines, "Let the whole field of reality be laid open to woman as well as to man, and then that which is peculiar in her mental modification, instead of being, as it is now, a source of discord and repulsion between the sexes, will be found to be a necessary complement to the truth and beauty of life."

Eliot's sense of the "discord and repulsion" caused by the deformations and distortions of the female self uneducated is as constant as her sense of the importance of the relations *between* the sexes. In an essay on Margaret Fuller and Mary Wollstonecraft she remarks that "while men have a horror of such faculty or culture in the other sex as tends to place it on a level with their own, they are really in a state of subjection to ignorant and feeble-minded women." She goes on to quote Margaret Fuller's description of the "petty power" of the "ignorance and childish vanity" of uneducated women. Here is the hint of the beginning of both Rosamund Vincy in her complacent and destructive prettiness and Gwendolen Harleth in the aimless power-mongering of her fatal coquetry. Eliot saw both Fuller and Wollstonecraft as mirrors for her sense of herself. She wrote in 1852: "It is a help to read such a life as Margaret Fuller's. How inexpressibly touching that passage from her journal—'I shall always reign through the intellect, but the life, the life! O my god! shall that never be sweet?' I am thankful, as for myself, that it was sweet at last."[12] And in 1871, writing to the Jewish scholar Emanuel Deutsch, who was ill and despairing, she used Mary Wollstonecraft as an example of hope, comparing her with her own painful, youthful, hopeless self. "Remember, it has happened to many to be glad they did not commit suicide, though they once ran for the final leap, or as Mary Wollstonecraft did, wetted their garments well in the rain, hoping to sink the better when they plunged."[13]

Out of this sympathetic feeling for the young Mary Wollstonecraft and the despairing Jew came the suicide attempt of Mirah, the woman artist in *Daniel Deronda* who lived to be happy, in contrast to the fiercely separate and ambitious Alchirisi, Daniel's mother, who sacrificed her affections to her art, and told her son, "You can never imagine what it is to have a man's force of genius in you, and yet to suffer the slavery of being a girl."[14] In *Daniel Deronda* the problems of Fuller, Wollstonecraft and the author of the essay on Madame de Sablé are studied with a novelist's fullness and sceptical passion in Gwendolen, Mirah, the Alchirisi and also Catherine Arrowpoint, an intelligent and gifted heiress who gives up rich English philistinism for German-Jewish genius and seriousness. In her poetic drama *Armgart,* Eliot studied (in an earlier version) the conflict between female genius and the domestic and affectionate virtues; the singer rejects her suitor's definition of married love as her highest fulfillment, only to lose her voice, and learn how much egoism there was in her devotion to her talent. But the young woman who wrote the essays of the 1850s was, for the first time, happy as a woman, and full of new ambition as a writer. "Silly Novels by Lady Novelists" was written immediately before her own first attempt at fiction, and its lightness of tone is partly a result of her desire not to "undertake an article that would give me too much trouble."[15] The story she was beginning was "The Sad Fortunes of the Rev. Amos Barton," and it is easy to see in it a revision (in the Jamesian sense of revision, new looking at) of the works she characterised as the "white neck-cloth" school of evangelical fiction. "Why can we not have pictures of religious life among the industrial classes in England, as interesting as Mrs. Stowe's pictures of religious life among the negroes?" she asked, and went on, in "Janet's Repentance" and *Silas Marner,* to provide just such pictures. Gwendolen Harleth and Dorothea Brooke, with their very real human limitations, can in one sense be seen as corrective revisions of the beautiful, proficient, high-minded mind-and-millinery her-

oine, who, despite being "the ideal woman in feelings, faculties and
flounces," as often as not "marries the wrong person to begin with and
suffers terribly from the plots and intrigues of the vicious baronet." Gwendolen, with hideous irony, indeed resembles the type heroine, not an
heiress, who "has the triumph of refusing many matches and securing the
best, and she wears some family jewels or other as a sort of crown of
righteousness at the end." Gwendolen's jewels are a torturing crown of
iniquity, and she learns the Eliot lesson that resignation and suffering do *not*
produce "compensation" and some divine reward for virtue. Eliot began
this essay out of a desire to review the novel *Compensation,* and "fire away
at the doctrine of Compensation, which I detest."[16]

The "realism" of Eliot's fiction is partly a moral realism, rejecting "compensation" and other consoling doctrines, and partly a related technical
realism, a desire for accuracy. At the end of "Silly Novels" Eliot observed:
"No educational restrictions can shut women out from the materials of
fiction and there is no species of art which is so free from rigid requirements.
Like crystalline masses it may take any form, and yet be beautiful; we have
only to pour in the right elements—genuine observation, humour and
passion."

It is time to look at her ideas about the forms of art.

Realism

Eliot's review of John Ruskin's *Modern Painters,* vol. III, was published in
April 1856; in the summer of that year, at Tenby, "The Sad Fortunes of the
Rev. Amos Barton" was begun. In the essay on Ruskin, Eliot wrote: "The
truth of infinite value that he teaches is *realism*—the doctrine that all truth
and beauty are to be attained by a humble and faithful study of nature, and
not by substituting vague forms, bred by imagination on the mists of feeling,
in place of definite, substantial reality."

In the journal she kept at Ilfracombe earlier the same summer, she writes
of her observation of the countryside in terms of both art and nature-study.
It is "a 'Hunt' picture" and inspires in her a very clear linguistic ambition.
"I never before longed so much to know the names of things as during this
visit to Ilfracombe. The desire is part of the tendency that is now constantly
growing in me to escape from all vagueness and inaccuracy into the daylight
of distinct, vivid ideas. The mere fact of naming an object tends to give

definiteness to our conception of it—we have then a sign that at once calls up in our minds the distinctive qualities which mark out for us that particular object from all others."[17]

In the essays, particularly those on Cumming and Young, she comments again and again on inaccurate language.[18] She says of Young that one of his most striking characteristics was

his *radical insincerity as a poetic artist* . . . The source of all grandiloquence is the want of taking for a criterion the true qualities of the object described, or the emotion expressed . . .

> His hand the good man fixes on the skies,
> And bids earth roll, nor feels her idle whirl,—

may, perhaps, pass for sublime with some readers. But pause a moment to realize the image, and the monstrous absurdity of a man's grasping the skies, and hanging habitually suspended there, while he contemptuously bids the earth roll, warns you that no genuine feeling could have suggested so unnatural a conception . . . Examples of such vicious imagery, resulting from insincerity, may be found, perhaps, in almost every page of the *Night Thoughts*. But simple assertions or aspirations, undisguised by imagery, are often equally false. No writer whose rhetoric was checked by the slightest truthful intentions, could have said,—

> An eye of awe and wonder let me roll,
> And roll for ever.

Abstracting the more poetical associations with the eye, this is hardly less absurd than if he had wished to stand for ever with his mouth open.

In the essay on Cumming, she is even more uncompromising about the connection between accurate language and morality.

A distinct appreciation of the value of evidence—in other words, the intellectual perception of truth—is more closely allied to truthfulness of statement, or the moral quality of veracity, than is generally admitted. There is not a more pernicious fallacy afloat in common parlance, than the wide distinction made between intellect and morality. Ami-

able impulses without intellect, man may have in common with dogs
and horses; but morality, which is specifically human, is dependent on
the regulation of feeling by intellect.

Cumming, she says, is imprisoned, as an intellect, by the doctrine of verbal
inspiration that deprives his mind of "its proper function—the free search
for truth." Cumming's religious statements, as she wittily and devastatingly
demonstrates, are a series of overblown untruths.

In Cumming's case it is the freedom of the intellect and philosophical
truth that is at stake. In Lord Brougham's, whose style she also attacks, it is
Art. (It is interesting in this context that she defines Dr. Johnson's Wit, in
the essay on Heinrich Heine, as "reasoning raised to a higher power." Wit,
she says, has an affinity with ratiocination, and the higher the species of wit,
the more it deals "less with words and superficialities than with the essential
qualities of things.") She wrote to Charles Bray, defending her attack.

> The article on Lord Brougham was written conscientiously, and you
> seem to have misunderstood its purpose, in taking it for mere word
> quibbling. I consider it criminal in a man to prostitute Literature for
> the purposes of his own vanity, and this is what Lord Brougham has
> done. A man who has something vitally important to mankind to say,
> may be excused for saying it in bad English. In such a case criticism
> of style is irrelevant. But Literature is fine art, and the man who writes
> mere literature with insolvent slovenliness is as inexcusable as a man
> who gets up in a full drawing-room to sing Rossini's music in a
> cracked voice and out of tune. Because Lord Brougham has done
> some services to the public it does not follow that he is to be treated
> with anything else than justice when he is doing injury to the public,
> and I consider his *Lives, bad* and *injurious*.[19]

She was not herself afraid of clear distinct statements. There is a splendid
letter from her to Chapman, criticising his style, again on grounds of illogic
and inaccuracy. "I have a logical objection to the phrases 'it *would* seem',
'it *would* appear', 'we *would* remark'. Would—under what condition? The
real meaning is—it *does* seem, it *does* appear, we *do* remark. These phrases
are rarely found in good writers, and *ought* never to be found."[20] As editor
and essayist, she kept her own rules.

Also as novelist. Her early letters to her publisher about her fiction defend
the precision of the detail in terms of accuracy. John Blackwood told her
he would have liked to see, in her account of the confirmation in "Janet's

Repentance," "some allusion to the solemn and affecting sight that a confirmation ought to be."[21] Eliot replied:

> My own impression on rereading very carefully the account of the confirmation is, that readers will perceive, what is the fact—that I am not in the least occupying myself with confirmation in general, or with Bishops in general, but with a particular confirmation and a particular Bishop.
>
> Art must be either real and concrete, or ideal and eclectic. Both are good and true in their way, but my stories are of the former kind. I undertake to exhibit some things as they have been or are, seen through such a medium as my own nature gives me.

This clear statement also raises the problem of the relations between "realist" art and the philosophical distinction between idealism and realism. This, in its turn, leads on to a consideration of the religious scientific ideas (the two are inextricably interlinked) in Eliot's writings.

Development, Positive Science and Incarnation

Eliot's first review for the *Westminster,* that of Mackay's *The Progress of the Intellect,* was published in 1851, before she became an editor. In it can be found clear statements of her own beliefs, which resonate throughout her work. The essay is also important as her first reference to the work of Auguste Comte. Comte's Positive Philosophy was uncompromisingly realist. He held that the age of scientific discovery had succeeded the earlier stages of human thought, the Theological and the Metaphysical, which explained the facts of the universe in terms of "direct volitions of beings, real or imaginary, possessed of life and intelligence" (Theological) and of "realized" abstractions, forces, or occult qualities such as "Nature, or Vital Principles" (Metaphysical).[22] The age of Positive Science had understood that the world was governed by undeviating law—"that invariability of sequence which is acknowledged to be the basis of physical science, but which is still perversely ignored in our social organization, our ethics and our religion." *Duty,* Eliot says here, is "comprised in the earnest study of this law and patient obedience to its teaching." In F. W. H. Myers's famous account of his conversation with the sibylline author in Trinity College garden, he quotes her discourse on God, immortality and duty, and her saying how "inconceivable was the *first,* how unbelievable the *second,* and yet how peremptory and absolute the *third.*"[23] At the time of the *Westminster Review* essays, Eliot was negotiating a book on the "Idea of a Future Life" with Chapman (as well as her translation of Feuerbach) that might have addressed itself both to the untenable idea of "Compensation" for suffering or virtuous self-denial, and to the requirement of obedience to duty for itself alone. Eliot shared the Comtean belief that scientific truth had superseded the truths of revelation or philosophical intuition, but she was sceptical of his later doctrinaire recipes for happiness. Comte saw the laws of evolution of human society as laws of the same nature, once established, as those of physics—which makes the Positivist precept of "obedience" to these unavoidable laws a somewhat slurred and irrational idea.

Eliot quotes with approval Mackay's statements on faith.

Religion and science are inseparable. No object in nature, no subject of contemplation, is destitute of a religious tendency and meaning . . . Faith is to a great extent involuntary; it is a law or faculty of our nature, operating silently and intuitively to supply the imperfections of our knowledge. The boundary between faith and knowledge is indeed hard to distinguish . . . Faith as an inference from knowledge, should be consistently inferred from the whole of knowledge . . . Faith naturally arises out of the regular and the undeviating.

Eliot's own description of "our civilization, and yet more our religion" in this essay is one of "an anomalous blending of lifeless barbarisms, which have descended to us like so many petrifications from distant ages, with living ideas, the offspring of a true process of development." She calls Mackay's book "perhaps the nearest approach in our language to a satisfactory natural history of religion."

The idea of *natural history* is central, both to the thought of Eliot's time and to her own work as a novelist. The phrase "the natural history of religion" combines the ideas of objective science, the human past, the development of ideas and the study of morality conceived as a developing sequence of observations and "living ideas." The natural history of the earth included Charles Lyell's geology and Darwin's study of the origin of species. The "natural history" of societies sought to supersede a history that concentrated on the isolated acts of great men, or decisions of rulers, to study the whole structure and interrelations of families and groups as though they were organisms. Nineteenth-century work on philology and mythology sought to study the thoughts and beliefs, and acts and agriculture, of men as they developed speech and tales to describe themselves to themselves. Eliot's essay on Wilhelm von Riehl ("The Natural History of German Life") makes clear her enthusiastic acceptance of these ideas. As with Mackay's "natural history" of religion, Eliot stresses Riehl's interest in the life of the German people as "*incarnate history*," and, as in the Mackay essay, she warns against any attempt to detach ahistorical precepts or descriptions from it.[24]

> [Riehl] sees in European society *incarnate history,* and any attempt to disengage it from its historical elements must, he believes, be simply destructive of social vitality. What has grown up historically can only die out historically, by the gradual operation of necessary laws. The external conditions which society has inherited from the past are but the manifestation of inherited internal conditions in the human beings who compose it; the internal conditions and the external are related to each other as the organism and its medium, and development can take place only by the gradual consentaneous development of both.

Here the "inherited internal conditions" of men are presumably both biological and mental. Eliot goes on to say specifically that "The historical conditions of society may be compared with those of language" and to discuss the "subtle shades of meaning and still subtler echoes of association" that "make language an instrument which scarcely anything short of genius can wield with definiteness and certainty." She contemplates a future universal language constructed on a rational basis, "patent, deodorized and nonresonant," perfect and rapid as algebraic signs, a kind of prevision of computer language, made of ticks and dots. She uses a characteristic physiological analogy to reinforce her sense that the organism and its history must be respected.

> The sensory and motor nerves that run in the same sheath, are scarcely bound together by a more necessary and delicate union than that which binds men's affection, imagination, wit and humour, with the subtle ramifications of historical language. Language must be left to grow in precision, completeness, and unity, as minds grow in clearness, comprehensiveness, and sympathy. And there is an analogous relation between the moral tendencies of men and the social conditions they have inherited.

This passage—and the succeeding paragraphs—are crucial to understanding Eliot's thought, and also the nature of her fictive world, which she sees as a developing organism, incarnate history, much as Riehl sees his world. She continues with an approving quote from Ruskin's *Modern Painters,* vol. IV, about the continuity between old ruins, the ancient world and more recent buildings: "all is continuous; and the words 'from generation to generation' understandable here."[25] And then she expresses a conservative scepticism about the generalisations of Social Science, using the Comtean terms of progression "from the general to the special, from the simple to the complex, analogous to that which is found in the series of the sciences, from Mathematics to Biology." Social Science must study particular organisms. "A wise social policy must be based, not simply on abstract social science, but on the Natural History of social bodies." She approves Riehl's "social-political-conservatism," as opposed to "communistic theories which he regards as 'the despair of the individual in his own manhood, reduced to a system.' " And in the Riehl essay, her arguments for the specificity of natural history are also used for artistic realism: there is a moral obligation to depict peasants as they are, not in a pastoral idealisation. "Art is the nearest thing to life; it is a mode of amplifying experience and extending our contact with our fellow-men beyond the bounds of our personal lot. All the more sacred is the task of the artist when he undertakes to paint the life of the People. Falsification here is far more pernicious than in the more artificial aspects of life."

Images of natural history are intrinsic to her own art. One that foreshadows the natural-historical metaphors for the community of St. Ogg's in *The Mill on the Floss* is to be found in the "Ilfracombe Journal," where she describes Lantern Hill.

In hilly districts, where houses and clusters of houses look so tiny against the huge limbs of Mother Earth one cannot help thinking of man as a parasitic animal—an epizoon making his abode on the skin of the planetary organism. In a flat country a house or a town looks imposing—there is nothing to rival it in height, and we may imagine the earth a mere pedestal for us. But when one sees a house stuck on the side of a great hill, and still more a number of houses looking like a few barnacles clustered on the side of a great rock, we begin to think of the strong family likeness between ourselves and all other building, burrowing house-appropriating and shell-secreting animals. The difference between a man with his house and a mollusc with its shell lies in the number of steps or phenomena interposed between the fact of individual existence and the completion of the building.

Some such analogy as this underlies her description, in her 1855 review, of Lewes's *Life of Goethe* as such a "*natural history* of his various productions as will show how they were the outgrowth of his mind at different stages of its culture." And the same set of analogies and beliefs is at work in her review of *Wilhelm Meister,* where she describes Goethe himself, who "quietly follows the stream of fact and of life; and waits patiently for the moral processes of nature as we all do for her material processes."

The use of the word "incarnation" in phrases such as "incarnate history" calls up, of course, the whole problem of Christian theology and its partial, progressive and dubious abandonment. Many religious men and theologians clung to various forms of the idea of Christ as perfect or exemplary Man, or Ideal Man, even when they had conceded that the Bible as historical document was open to question, that the eyewitness evidence of the Miracles and the Resurrection were contradictory and unsupported, and that these were in conflict with the somehow more energetic and compelling universal and invariable laws of mind and matter. The young George Eliot was an evangelical Anglican; the growing George Eliot, compelled by Charles Hennell's *Inquiry into the Origins of Christianity,* by Strauss and by Feuerbach, was resolutely anti-Christian; the mature George Eliot saw Christian belief and morality as forms of human experience that must be studied and valued as part of our natural history. Nietzsche, in his only reference to Eliot (*Twilight of the Idols,* 1888), counted her among the English, who clung to the half-life of Christianity.

> G. Eliot.—They have got rid of the Christian God, and now feel obliged to cling all the more firmly to Christian morality: that is *English* consistency, let us not blame it on little bluestockings à la Eliot. In England, in response to every little emancipation from theology, one has to reassert one's position in a fear-inspiring manner as a moral fanatic. That is the *penance* one pays there.—With us it is different. When one gives up Christian belief one thereby deprives oneself of the *right* to Christian morality.[26]

Nietzsche, according to his translator, R. J. Hollingdale, probably knew about Eliot only from hearsay. It is interesting to juxtapose the views he attributes to her with the letter she wrote to Chapman in 1852, in the days of her editorial work.

I feel that I am a wretched helpmate to you, almost out of the world, and incog. so far as I am in it. When you can afford to pay an Editor, if that time will ever come, you must get one. If you believe in Free Will, in the Theism that looks on manhood as a type of the godhead and on Jesus as the Ideal Man, get one belonging to the Martineau 'school of thought' and he will drill you a regiment of writers who will produce a Prospective on a larger scale, and so the Westminster may come to have 'dignity' in the eyes of Liverpool.

If not—if you believe as I do, that the thought which is to mould the Future has for its root a belief in necessity, that a nobler presentation of humanity has yet to be given in resignation to individual nothingness, than could ever be shown of a being who believes in the phantasmagoria of hope unsustained by reason—why then get a man of another calibre and let him write a fresh Prospectus, and if Liverpool theology and ethics are to be admitted, let them be put in the 'dangerous ward', *alias,* the Independent Section.

The only third course is the present one, that of Editorial compromise.[27]

Incarnation

The long nineteenth-century debate about the precise meaning, or lack of meaning, of the Christian concept of the Incarnation, the meeting-point of the divine and the human, the infinite and the finite, is inextricably connected, consciously and unconsciously, to the development of the form of the novel. As the biblical narrative ceased to be privileged as unique truth, and became associated with partial histories of other kinds, or what Froude in *The Nemesis of Faith* calls "Wonder Tales," so there arose, for certain kinds of speculative minds, an interest in the nature of the individuals and the values they represented, as portrayed in secular narrative. If Piers Plowman in a religious culture is a Type of Christ, what is Adam Bede, breaking bread and drinking wine before Hetty Sorrel's trial and condemnation, in the fiction of a writer who explicitly rejected, in the letter I have just quoted, "the Theism that looks on manhood as a type of the godhead, and on Jesus as the Ideal Man"? George Eliot's nature, like Dorothea Brooke's, was both ardent and theoretic, and, like Margaret Fuller's, intellectual and sensuous, both analytic and observant, both idealising (theorising) and realist.

She was also the translator of two of the most influential documents in the Higher Criticism and the demythologising of Christianity: Strauss's *The Life of Jesus* and Feuerbach's *The Essence of Christianity*. Feuerbach's and Strauss's ideas on the meaning of the incarnation and its narrative, often illuminate the way in which Eliot thought about human nature and human stories.[28]

Particularly interesting ideas arise in Strauss's introduction and conclusion of his work. Strauss explains the biblical narrative as a series of "mythi" analogous to those of other religions. He rejects the historical claims of the Bible on the ground that individual acts of divine intervention in human affairs are inconsistent with the modern conviction "that all things are linked together by a chain of causes and effects which suffers no interruption." He also tries to distinguish myths from lies and deceptions, by making an analogy with poetry and quoting the mythologist Otfried Müller. "How," says Müller, "shall we reconcile this combination of the true and the false, the real and the ideal, in mythi, with the fact of their being believed and received as truth? The ideal, it may be said, is nothing else than poetry and fiction clothed in the form of a narration." Strauss then argues that this fiction cannot have *one* originator, but must be, in some now unimaginable way, the product of a common consciousness.

At the end of his book, Strauss discusses various ways in which philosophers have tried to preserve the meaning and importance of the concept of Incarnation, while acknowledging the fictiveness of a particular historical divine intervention. He examines the ideas of Spinoza and Kant, who believed that the ideal Christ, the eternal "wisdom of god" or "idea of moral perfection," could be believed; Strauss himself comes to a complicated definition of the union of idea and reality (infinite and finite) not in one historical individual but in *the species*.

> This is indeed not the mode in which Idea realizes itself; it is not wont to lavish all its fullness on one exemplar, and be niggardly towards all others—to express itself perfectly in that one individual and imperfectly in all the rest: it rather loves to distribute its riches among a multiplicity of exemplars which reciprocally complete each other—in the alternate appearance and suppression of a series of individuals. And is this no true realization of the idea? is not the idea of the unity of the divine and human natures a real one in a far higher sense, when I regard the whole of mankind as its realization, than when I single out one man as such a realization?

The connection of this description of "the alternate appearance and suppression of a series of individuals"—with the word "suppression" universalising and naturalising the tragedy of the Passion—is a good description of the moral, even religious sense we have of Eliot's world. Lydgate and Dorothea, Maggie and Adam Bede, are invested, in their limited individuality, with the religious *value* that has been displaced from the incarnate Man to the succession of human beings. They are Types and individuals. Our sense of the way in which Eliot saw the relationship between their general humanity and their particular identity is made more subtle and precise by considering Feuerbach's idea of the Incarnation.

"With the principles of Feuerbach I everywhere agree," Marian Evans wrote to Sarah Hennell, though she went on to add: "but of course I should, of myself, alter his phraseology considerably."[29] Feuerbach's book is still exciting to read, and her translation reads easily and urgently. The essential argument of *The Essence of Christianity* is that men invented religion—including the Persons of God, the sacraments and the Church—in order to be able to contemplate and worship their own nature. The book unravels the human needs that give rise to the particular beliefs it analyses, and passionately pleads for a recognition that mankind itself is the proper object of veneration and adoration. "Not abstract beings—no! only sensuous living beings are merciful. Mercy is the *justice of sensuous life*,"[30] he argues, in her words, and with sentiments that are apparent throughout her works. It is also Feuerbach who proposes that we should celebrate real bread and real wine, not as symbols of flesh and blood, alienated from their true nature, but for themselves. "Water is the purest, clearest of liquids; in virtue of this its natural character it is the image of the spotless nature of the Divine Spirit. In short, water has a significance in itself, as water." "But as religion alienates our own nature from us, and represents it as not ours, so the water of baptism is regarded as quite other than common water." U. C. Knoepflmacher has argued that Adam Bede's meal is a Feuerbachian "natural" sacrament in this sense.[31]

Two significant passages in *The Essence of Christianity* are concerned with the reinterpretation of the Incarnation. In the first, the chapter "The Mystery of the Cosmogonical Principle in God," Feuerbach identifies the Son—"i.e., God thought by himself, the original reflection of God"—with the principle of the *imagination,* the "middle term" between the mind and the Other, the maker of images. God making the world is "the mystic paraphrase of a psychological process," that is, human self-consciousness, the imagination of the self as an other.

> The psychological truth and necessity which lies at the foundation of all these theogonies and cosmogonies, is the truth and necessity of the imagination as a middle term between the abstract and the concrete. And the task of philosophy, in investigating this subject, is to comprehend the relation of the imagination to the reason—the genesis of the image by means of which an object of thought becomes an object of sense, of feeling.

Thus if Christ is for Strauss the Idea present in the succession of particular individuals who make up the race, he is, at least as the Son of the Creator, for Feuerbach, related to the Romantic Imagination, the creative principle that "bodies forth the forms of things unknown,"[32] that makes concrete and particular images in order to know and understand itself. "Consciousness of the world is consciousness of my limitation," Feuerbach goes on to say, a sentiment that is echoed in much of his translator's later commentary on human life. "The consciousness of my limitation stands in contradiction with the impulse of my egoism towards unlimitedness." She was the great analyst of egoism.

The other passage, "The Mystery of Mysticism," echoes Strauss's belief that the Species is the true object of our moral and religious attention—but he adds to this the idea that the essence of the Species is contained in the relation between the sexes, in the recognition of the Other, and in the sensuous passion of the flesh. "Flesh and blood is nothing without the oxygen of sexual distinction. The distinction of sex is not superficial, or limited to certain parts of the body; it is an essential one: it penetrates bone and marrow." (Here, perhaps, among other interesting thoughts, is one possible reason for George Eliot's conviction that the "woman question" must not lose sight of the essential *difference* between the sexes.) "Man is different in intercourse from what he is when alone. Love especially works wonders, and the love of the sexes most of all. Men and women are the complement of each other, and thus united they first present the Species, the perfect man." "In love, the reality of the Species, which otherwise is only a thing of reason, an object of mere thought, becomes a matter of feeling, a truth of feeling." If the young George Eliot rejected Christ as ideal Man and believed in resignation to individual nothingness, she was at the same time involved in translating a work that substituted sexual love, the union of the sexes, as "the perfect man." And again, in love, *thought* becomes transmuted into *feeling*.

It is with these ideas in mind that we should look at the correspondence with Frederic Harrison that took place in 1866–8.[33] It contains one of Eliot's best-known artistic statements of intent. What Harrison requires of her is to create a narrative that will embody "the idealization of certain normal relations," which is "the task of all art." ("Normal" here must be read as closer to "normative" than to "usual" or "humdrum.") Harrison wants her to describe a society, and a political, religious and moral state of affairs, that will show the "Positivist relations" of its people. Eliot replied that he laid before her "a tremendously difficult problem" of which he saw the difficulties,

> though they can hardly press upon you as they do on me, who have gone through again and again the severe effort of trying to make certain ideas thoroughly incarnate, as if they had revealed themselves to me first in the flesh and not in the spirit. I think aesthetic teaching is the highest of all teaching because it deals with life in its highest complexity. But if it ceases to be purely aesthetic—if it lapses anywhere from the picture to the diagram—it becomes the most offensive of all teaching.

The language here, in terms of the Positivist beliefs, is clearly related (as the language of Positivism itself was) to the revalued Christian concepts discussed above. Eliot saw her work as making *incarnate certain ideas* that she apprehended in the flesh, i.e. sensuously, materially, through feeling. I want to come back to the way in which in *Middlemarch* she dealt with Harrison's proposals, but first I want to write briefly about a related set of ideas that arises in the correspondence and in "Notes on Form in Art," which was written about the same time.

The correspondence opens with Harrison praising *Felix Holt* for having "the subtle finish of a poem" and being "a romance constructed in the artistic spirit and aim of a poem." Eliot went on to write *The Spanish Gypsy*, which was published in 1868, before returning to fiction with *Middlemarch*. Harrison welcomes *The Spanish Gypsy* as the statement he had been looking for. "I need not say I am sure what pleasure it gives me to recognize the profound truths and sacred principles which [that which] we call the Faith of the Future is preparing, for the first time truly idealized." But his distress at the characters of Zarca and Fedalma, in their idealism, reads comically in its honesty.[34] They are *idealisations* of love of the Species, the Race, Humanity. Fedalma's sacrifice of her personal love in her devotion to her race is a precursor of Daniel Deronda's, and both have their roots in Eliot's sense of Duty, which we have discussed, as "obedience" to the "laws" of social organisms. Harrison's instincts are surely right. Zarca and Fedalma are strained, horrible and *unreal*. They, and the correspondence, tell us something about what happened to Eliot when she shifted too far from one pole of the debate between idealism and realism towards the other.

In 1862 and 1863 Edward Bulwer-Lytton wrote a series of articles in *Blackwood's* in which he opposed an aesthetic doctrine of idealism in art to the current realism. *"The artist never seeks to represent the positive truth, but the idealized image of a truth* [Bulwer's italics]."[35] As Hegel well observes: "That which exists in nature is a something purely individual and particular. Art, on the contrary, is essentially destined to manifest the general." Characters in novels, as Richard Stang points out, "as embodiments of ideals created by the human imagination from the new facts of experience, are not individuals but types or symbols."[36] Stang suggests that Bulwer-Lytton's "general truths" seem "dangerously near a kind of never-never-land to which he periodically escaped to forget all about unpleasant reality." Gordon Haight thinks that Bulwer-Lytton's *Leila; or the Siege of Granada* (1838) is an unacknowledged source for *The Spanish Gypsy*.

Eliot's "Notes on Form in Art," dated 1868, the year of *The Spanish Gypsy*, can be seen, in one light, as a continuation of her thought about the ideal and the real, the particular and the universal, and incarnation; indeed, she begins with a discussion of "the philosophic use of the word 'Form' in distinction from Matter." Her idea of Form is intricately bound up with a series of images of organisms: she distinguishes between the "accidental" form of a stone and the "outline defining the wholeness of a human body" that is "due to a consensus or constant interchange of effects among its parts." It is part of the process of incarnation. Her definition of poetry is Feuerbachian. *"Poetry* begins when passion weds thought by finding expression in an image; but *poetic form* begins with a choice of elements, however meagre, as the accordant expression of emotional states." Poetic form grows like "the beautiful expanding curves of a bivalve shell," to go back to the imagery of Ilfracombe and Lewes's *Seaside Studies*. And earlier she writes a precise, clear sentence about the *range of poetry* that varies widely in the way it combines "emotive force" with "sequences that are not arbitrary and individual but true and universal." Poetry combines the particular with the ideal, the "true and universal" in its rhythms, its images, its sequences. Poetry, she says, has been defined to mean fiction, but fiction itself is only the expression of *predominant feeling* in "an arrangement of events in feigned correspondences"—i.e. in constructed images, such as those by which Feuerbach's imagination recognised its limitations and the existence of the other. Form in its "derivative meaning of outline" is "the limit of that difference by which we discriminate one object from another."

It could be argued that Eliot took to writing poetry because her interest shifted from the exactness and definiteness of her earlier realism to the system of correspondences, and general truths, and similarities and connections that make up the general reality. If her poem is a failure, her thoughts about poetic form surely affect the nature of the last two novels, *Middlemarch* and *Daniel Deronda*. The poetic web of metaphors in *Middlemarch* is unlike the forms of language in her earlier work. In the penultimate paragraph of "Notes on Form in Art" she says: "The old phrases should not give way to scientific explanation, for speech is to a great extent like sculpture, expressing observed phenomena, and remaining true in spite of Harvey and Bichat."

The desire for the solid and *perceptually particular* language expressed here is reminiscent of her defence, in the essay on Riehl, of "the subtle ramification of historical language." In the Riehl essay she opposed this to a new universal scientific "deodorized" code of scientific language. William Harvey and Marie François Bichat, the discoverers of the circulation of the blood and the hypothetical "universal tissue" that made up all particular organs, can be seen as representing, in the incarnate organism, the kind of *informing* principle of life that takes on particular individual forms. (Something also like Noam Chomsky's "deep structure" of language?) Bichat was one of Comte's heroes, and also the ideal of Lydgate, the Comtean scientist in *Middlemarch*. Bichat's universal tissue forms part of the recurring web of metaphors in *Middlemarch* that links and combines the diverse parts of the social organism in the novel. And that self-conscious web of metaphor itself is a conscious poetic strategy of universalisation.

Which brings us back to what Eliot made of Harrison's prescription for an idealising work of art. It has been pointed out, in subtle detail, just how far the plot of *Middlemarch* corresponds with Harrison's sketched plot.[37] We have the decayed and failing aristocracy and Church (Mr. Brooke, Casaubon); we have the new "positive" forces of scientist and capitalist (Lydgate and Bulstrode) combining to improve things (the hospital); we have in Dorothea the female influence Comte thought indispensable (which, according to him, must have *no other role* than maternity, no inheritance and no power that might corrupt its purity). If we look at Harrison's enthusiastic piety and the very dubious and bleak moral triumphs of *Middlemarch,* it seems clear that the novelist was actuated by something akin to the spirit of irony and contradiction that brought realism out of the genres described in "Silly Novels" and truth out of the rejection of Cumming and Young. The moral and artistic triumphs of *Middlemarch* are ultimately more Feuerbachian than Comtean, and have to do with a moral sense of finite human limitations rather than with the March of Humanity. Dorothea has to learn the Feuerbachian lesson: the "genesis of the image by means of which an object of thought becomes an object of sense, of feeling." Eliot's intelligence combined thought and feeling in a new form of poetic but ironic realist fiction.

The voice of the narrator of *Middlemarch* is more measured than that of the brilliant essayist; it speaks with a universalising "we" for the organic community, whereas the essayist (*vide* "Madame de Sablé" or "Heinrich Heine") often poses as a witty male. But the continuity is strong, and the essays and translations tell us vital things about the tone of the art.

> We are all of us born in moral stupidity, taking the world as an udder to feed our supreme selves: Dorothea had early begun to emerge from that stupidity, but yet it had been easier to her to imagine how she would devote herself to Mr Casaubon, and become wise and strong in his strength and wisdom, than to conceive with that distinctness which is no longer reflection but feeling—an idea wrought back to the directness of sense, like the solidity of objects—that he had an equivalent centre of self, whence the lights and shadows must always fall with a certain difference.[38]

(1990)

MODERNS:
VARYING
STRANDS

6

Accurate Letters:
Ford Madox Ford

FORD IS, as Malcolm Bradbury has pointed out, the writer to whom we turn when dissatisfied with the solipsism or insistent sensibility of Virginia Woolf, as the great English modernist prose writer. His ideas about prose, about language, about accuracy, are helpful to a writer trying to think out the relations between "realism" and "form" in fiction, in a way her "luminous envelope" is not.

"Accurate Letters" was first published in the *TLS* as a celebration of the Bodley Head reissue of *The Good Soldier,* the Tietjens trilogy (without the fourth volume, which Graham Greene disliked and claimed Ford himself had rejected) and *The Fifth Queen*. I have incorporated into the essay part of the preface I wrote for the World's Classic reprint of *The Fifth Queen*.

Ford Madox Ford, like Henry Green and Willa Cather, is a writer much admired by writers, but comparatively neglected by scholars and the general public. In the case of the scholars this was perhaps, as Hugh Kenner has said, because Ford had "no philosophy"—his work resists "thematic" analysis, or grouping in traditions of modernism, social realism or other isms. In the case of the general public the neglect is perhaps because, unlike Lawrence, Hardy, Woolf, Joyce, he projects no strong literary personality to which, in the phrase of today's innocent student, one can "relate." This elusiveness is odd and paradoxical, since he wrote many volumes of autobiographical memoirs and impressions, and other major writers—Ernest Hemingway, Robert Lowell, William Carlos Williams—have made minor works of art out of poems or anecdotes about him. Furthermore, he himself claimed that Henry James had modelled Merton Densher in *The Wings of the Dove* on the young Ford, his fervent admirer. Perhaps there is a superfluity of over-definite, epigrammatic evidence.

The matter is further complicated by the fact that it is easy, and not unhelpful at one level, to see his novels in terms of his biography—his Catholicism, his divorce problems, his desire to find a woman to talk to, his post-war paranoia and self-aggrandisement. Kenner calls this "impertinent." I would certainly argue that biographical aperçus tend to obscure in the reader's mind the qualities that astonish when he or she meets *The Good Soldier* or *No More Parades* purely as novels. It is ironic that Arthur Mizener's biography is entitled *The Saddest Story:* the title, so apt, so profoundly ironic, so grim, that Ford's publisher would not allow him to use it for *The Good Soldier* in case it depressed his readership, or the nation, in 1915.

In fact Ford's literary "character" is not unlike that of Samuel Taylor Coleridge, also his own worst enemy. Both were men with a passion for exact thought and exact use of words who nevertheless had justified reputations as appalling liars. Both wrote major works of art, and a considerable body of writing by any standard (Ford wrote eighty-one books). Yet both were felt not to have fulfilled their promise: to have wasted their talents. Both boasted, and both devoted themselves, with tact, humility and, most important, appropriate and adequate intelligence, to the furthering of the work, and the understanding of the work of writers they felt were greater than themselves. Both were grandiose and incompetent, journalistic entrepreneurs, whose periodicals are nevertheless literary landmarks. Both re-wrote, to our benefit, literary history. Both were not insular—Ford knew French, German, Italian, Provençal literature, and *used* it, as Coleridge knew German, French and Italian. Perhaps this last is another reason why Ford found his best reception, and his sharpest critics, among the Americans. He wrote about, and claimed he was, the English gentleman: he was in fact a polyglot, half-German, brought up amongst the aesthetes and Bohemians who frequented the house of his grandfather, the Pre-Raphaelite artist Ford Madox Brown.

It is time another attempt was made to re-establish his reputation, not only as the author of three or four novels better than most English novels, but as a thinker about the nature of writing, and the craft of fiction, whose injunctions and priorities, far from having become outdated, have not yet been fully explored or understood. Not by critics, not by novelists. Hugh Kenner, writing in 1950, on the occasion of the American republication of

Parade's End (remaindered eight years later), said: "It would be worth most novelists' while to spend some years of study and emulation of the procedures and felicities of *Parade's End*." And he locates the felicities in Ford's exact language, his orchestration of "a sort of scrupulous lexicography working by the exact reproduction of the tones of numerous speaking voices."

Ford in his lifetime worked out—to a considerable extent during his discussions and collaboration with Conrad—a theory of good prose-writing, of fictive construction, which derived immediately from the ideas of Henry James about the "rendering" of an "affair" and the organisation of "impressions," in English, and from the ideas of Flaubert, de Maupassant and their literary sympathisers about *le mot juste*, "the minutiae of words and their economical employment; the *charpente*, the architecture of the novel; the handling of dialogue; the rendering of impressions; the impersonality of the Author" (Ford's essay "Techniques," 1935). It was from Ford's belief that the novel of Flaubert was "the immensely powerful engine of our civilisation" that Ezra Pound derived his view that "No man can now really write good verse unless he knows Stendhal and Flaubert." In "The Prose Tradition in Verse" (*Poetry* [Chicago], 1914), Pound praised Ford as the "one man with a vision of perfection," "in a country in love with amateurs, in a country where the incompetent have such beautiful manners and personalities so fragile and charming that one cannot bear to injure their feelings by the introduction of competent criticism." Pound said of Ford: "It is he who has insisted, in the face of a still Victorian press, upon the importance of good writing as opposed to the opalescent word, the rhetorical tradition. Stendhal had said, and Flaubert, de Maupassant and Turgenev had proved, that 'prose was the higher art'—at least their prose." Because of this English amateurism, Pound asserted, it had been left to "a prose-craftsman like Arnold Bennett to speak well of Mr. Hueffer's prose, and a verse-craftsman like myself to speak well of his verses."

The situation has not much changed—except that English amateurism now perhaps values the casual, underwrought style more than the precise attention to diction of a Ford, whereas the Edwardians were still in love with the Pre-Raphaelite raptures and dreams. Pound added crisply that Ford did not learn from Wordsworth, because "Wordsworth was so busied about the ordinary word that he never found time to think about *le mot juste*." Students nowadays are apt to say that writers who use words "everyone doesn't know" are elitist. Ford believed there were three English languages: "that of *The Edinburgh Review* which has no relation to life, that of the streets which is full of slang and daily neologisms and that third one which is fairly fluid and fairly expressive—the dialect of the drawing-room or the study, the really living language." He could use all three, to effect, in fact, but we now need to insist again—for prose writers, for novelists—that the language "of the study," *thought* about (I do not mean "made" academic language), is living, and must be kept available.

Hugh Kenner, who is Ford's most acute critic—although his sharp and tempered remarks about him tend to appear in scattered essays incidental to his deepening understanding of the importance and formidable power of Pound's *paideuma*—claimed in 1972 that Ford offers an alternative tradition to the "aesthetic" one (Keats, Coleridge, Tennyson, Swinburne) which absorbed symbolism partly and led to the work of Yeats and Eliot. Ford stood for a "documentary" tradition (besides prose, Browning, Words-worth, Crabbe, Jonson), a plainness which, as Pound pointed out, depends on diction, "the limpidity of natural speech, driven towards the just word, not slopping down as he aimed more specifically not to slop into the ordinary Wordsworthian word." Impressionism, not imagism, was his aim; *progression d'effet,* architecture, not immediacy or symbol his method. He uses figurative speech rarely, though vividly: his metaphors stand out by their rarity, and his novels are not, as Lawrence's or Woolf's might be, best described as "extended metaphors," since that implies some kind of sym-bolic intention they don't have. William Carlos Williams, a good novelist and a good poet whose poetry—"no ideas but in things"—has a prose exactness related to Pound's belief that "the natural object is *always* the adequate symbol," was also a disciple and a good critic of Ford. And in the sense in which the red wheelbarrow is plainly descriptive, and yet means more than itself, so do Ford's fictive people, things, places, speech. The horses at the end of *The Rainbow,* the snake eating the frog in *Between the Acts*—these are mythic symbols of a kind Ford eschewed. But the world of a Ford novel is a way of seeing the world, as the prose of a Ford novel is a way of "revising" (in James's sense) the English language.

Ford and Conrad believed in impressionism—in the important thing, as the preface to *The Nigger of the Narcissus* claims, being "to make you *see*." Ford claimed often that it did not matter *what* subject you rendered, as long as you rendered it adequately. There is an inherent paradox in a form which requires the author to exclude his views, his presence, his ideas, and yet to give the impressions of things and events on a consciousness, or conscious-nesses. James tried to solve it with his angling of "points of view" or "vessels" of consciousness. At the time of writing *The Good Soldier* Ford said: "The Impressionist author is sedulous to avoid letting his personality appear in the course of his book. On the other hand his whole book, his whole poem, is merely an expression of his personality." It is unfortunate in some ways, though illuminating, that he claimed that his *Memories and Impressions* and the memoir *It Was the Nightingale* were works of art carefully structured on the same principles as his fiction. "I have employed every wile known to me as novelist—the timeshift, the *progression d'effet*, the adaptation of rhythms to the pace of action," he says of *It Was the Nightingale*, which does indeed present an entertaining and idiosyncratic picture of post-war life and letters in Provence, Paris and New York in the 1920s by just these means. In *Memories and Impressions* he claims that he has "for facts a most profound contempt. I try to give you what I see to be the spirit of an age, of a town, of a movement. This cannot be done with facts." His method of reworking his encounters with Galsworthy, Wells, Conrad and others led on the simple level to accusations of falsehood and distortion, for which his aesthetic justifications seem partly disingenuous. There are those who claim that the memoirs may come to be seen as his best work, but I think the half-genuine, half-spurious connection between their method and that of his good novels obscures the enormous difference between the artist of *Parade's End* and the "charming," occasionally whimsical (however wise) raconteur of *It Was the Nightingale*. "Impressions" are better without the first person.

I have, parenthetically, come to the conclusion that Hemingway's wickedly funny account, in *A Moveable Feast,* of Ford ponderously "cutting" a man he said was Belloc, who turned out to be Aleister Crowley, is itself a polished parody of the Fordian, inaccurate anecdote, true in its *impression*. As Arthur Mizener has shown, Ford at that time knew, and had known, Belloc well for years. But when we look at the novels, the "personality" conveyed by the "whole book," and its impressions, bears little relation to the personality of the raconteur. It is altogether sharper, clearer, grimmer, more purposeful than the convivial Ford.

The Fifth Queen: Realism, Romanticism and Rendering

The Fifth Queen, Ford's Tudor trilogy about Katharine Howard, is one of the most interesting historical novels in our language. Ford had done a lot of research for a life of Henry VIII, and for a monograph on Holbein which he produced in 1905, the year before *The Fifth Queen*. It is, aesthetically, a curious mixture of his Pre-Raphaelite heritage and his Impressionist beliefs: part of its force is the almost hallucinatory glitter and precision of detail about dress, plants, architecture, food and drink, which has something in common with the Victorian historical paintings, carefully researched, which Roy Strong has suggested we reconsider as works of art. Ford's early books include a life of Ford Madox Brown, a study of Rossetti, and a book on the Pre-Raphaelites. Some of the great set-piece descriptions in *The Fifth Queen* are reminiscent of the composition—and lighting—of Brown's historical paintings of Chaucer at the court of Edward III, or Oliver Cromwell—talking to Milton and Marvell or brooding on a white horse amidst farmyard muddle. (Compare Thomas Cromwell on his barge, the carefully composed interior portrait of Anne of Cleves, the farmyard muddle surrounding Mary Hall or Lascelles.) Katharine Howard herself is often described stretching out or dropping her arms, in hope or despair, like a posed figure "caught" by the painter at a historical crisis. Ford preferred Brown's historical paintings to his "decorative" work. "As a Teuton, I like to think—and I feel certain—that whatever of Madox Brown's art was most individual was inspired by the Basle Holbeins." The virtue of Brown's best work derived from "the study of absolute realism and of almost absolute minuteness of rendering."

This word "rendering" is a central word in Ford's many and varied discussions of the art of the novel. During the period of his collaboration with Conrad, the two of them discussed the techniques of narrative, the importance of "accurate letters," and developed a set of ideas which Ford referred to, on the whole, as Impressionism. "We saw," he wrote in his memoir of Conrad, "that Life did not narrate, but made impressions on our brains. We in turn, if we wished to produce on you an effect of life, must not narrate but render . . . impressions." Their masters were Stendhal, Maupassant and above all Flaubert, with his insistence on *le mot juste*—a crafted, exact, descriptive language from which the author, both as rhetorical stylist and as moral commentator, should be absent. In English, both novelists turned to Henry James, who in his essay on "The Art of Fiction" (1884) spoke of "the air of reality (solidity of specification)" as "the supreme virtue of a novel" and used the word "render" and the analogy with painting to illustrate his meaning. "It is here that the novelist competes with his brother the painter in *his* attempt to render the look of things, the look that conveys their meanings, to catch the colour, the relief, the expression, the surface, the substance of the human spectacle." While he admired their desire for accurate recording of natural objects, Ford mistrusted the moral fervour and nostalgic medievalising of Ruskin and the Pre-Raphaelites. All this helped to shape his highly visual "historical Romance."

His book on Holbein, unlike his book on Rossetti or his life of Brown, is written with moral and aesthetic passion. He opposes Holbein to Dürer on its first page in a way that directly prefigures the opposition of the two forces that battle for the soul of Henry VIII (and England) in the *Fifth Queen* novels. The painters are "the boundary stones between the old world and the modern, between the old faith and the new learning, between empirical, charming conceptions of an irrational world and the modern theoretic way of looking at life." Dürer "could not refrain from commenting upon life, Holbein's comments were of little importance." It seems that Dürer is greater. "Dürer had imagination, where Holbein had only vision and invention—an invention of a rough-shod and everyday kind." But it is Holbein whose accuracy Ford is praising. Praising Samuel Richardson's "craftsmanlike" approach to the novel, Ford said he was "sound, quiet, without fuss, going about his work as a carpenter goes about making a chair and in the end turning out an article of supreme symmetry and consistence." He compared Richardson to "the two supreme artists of the world—Holbein and Bach." He had already compared Holbein with Bach in the Holbein book itself, after praising Holbein's depiction of Henry VIII as "an unconcerned rendering of an appallingly gross and miserable man." "Holbein was in fact a great Renderer. If I wanted to find a figure really akin to his I think I should go to music and speak of Bach."

Ford, it seems, was interested in Holbein's art and in Henry VIII's court and the politics of Thomas Cromwell because of their "realism"—and the word "realism" draws together here both moral attitudes and aesthetic priorities. In the *Fifth Queen* novels Katharine Howard is presented as a virtuous, highly intelligent woman who wishes to reverse the political and religious changes worked by Thomas Cromwell, Lord Privy Seal—to reintroduce the old faith, feudal values, monastic virtues. This figure bears little relation to what evidence we have about the real Katharine, although Ford teases the reader delicately and inconclusively about the truth of his Katharine's early relations with her alarming cousin, T. Culpepper. Ford himself was a Roman Catholic, of a kind (with more or less fervour at different times of his life), and liked to refer to himself as a "radical Tory."

It is very illuminating to look at the books, collected as *England and the*

English, that Ford was publishing during the same years as the Tudor trilogy. *The Spirit of the People: An Analysis of the English Mind* appeared in 1907, in the same year as *Privy Seal*, and a year before *The Fifth Queen Crowned*.

In this book, Ford claims that England's greatness "begins with the birth of the modern world. And the modern world was born with the discovery of the political theory of the Balance of the Powers in Europe." *The Fifth Queen* is concerned with sex, love, marriage, fear, lying, death and confusion—it is also concerned with the idea of the balance of power as a real force in men's lives. The Ford of *The Spirit of the People* leaves us in no doubt about his admiration for the Cromwell who was "the founder of modern England." He describes Henry VIII's minister as "Holbein's type," the "heavy, dark, bearded bull-necked animal, sagacious, smiling, but with devious and twinkling eyes." He goes on:

> And indeed a sort of peasant-cunning *did* . . . distinguish the international dealings of the whole world at that date. Roughly speaking, the ideals of the chivalric age were altruistic; roughly speaking, the ideals of the age that succeeded it were individual-opportunist. It was not, of course, England that was first in the field, since Italy produced Machiavelli. But Italy, which produced Machiavelli, failed utterly to profit by him . . . England *did* produce from its depths, from amidst its bewildering cross currents of mingled races, *the* great man of its age; and along with him it produced a number of men similar in type and strong enough to found a tradition. The man, of course, was Thomas Cromwell, who welded England into one formidable whole, and his followers in that tradition were the tenacious, pettifogging, cunning, utterly unscrupulous and very wonderful statesmen who supported the devious policy of Queen Elizabeth—the Cecils, the Woottons, the Bacons and all the others of England's golden age.

The Tudor age, Ford said, was "a projection of realism between two widely differing but romantic movements." That is, the feudal-Catholic times were romantic because of the altruism, heroism and chivalry of their ideals. In Ford's view, the post-Stuart times, the days after William III and the Glorious Revolution, were paradoxically "romantic" in a deeper sense than the "picturesque" romanticism of the Stuart case.

> For in essentials the Stuarts' cause was picturesque; the Cromwellian cause a matter of principle. Now a picturesque cause may make a very strong and poetic appeal but it is, after all, a principle that sweeps

people away. For poetry is the sublime of common-sense; principle is wrong-headedness wrought up to the sublime pitch—and that, in essentials, is romance.

Consider this opposition: "the sublime of common-sense"/"wrong-headedness wrought up to the sublime pitch." It has much in common with the opposition, in these novels, between Cromwell and Katharine—the realistic Machiavellian with his belief in England, the King, the health of the country, and the in many ways "wrong-headed" Katharine, unprepared to come to terms with the greed of the nobles who have acquired the lands of the dispossessed monasteries, the venal nature of servants or the distress of Margaret Poins, who cannot be married in Katharine's restored Roman Catholic dispensation. There is a further twist to this opposition. Later in *The Spirit of the People* Ford blames Protestantism for "that divorce of principle from life which, carried as far as it had been carried in England, has earned for the English the title of a nation of hypocrites." Katharine's Catholicism is like the "female" Catholicism which Ford says these islands have discarded; the female saints, the Mother of God, "an evolution almost entirely of the sentiments and of the weaknesses of humanity." Katharine calls on the saints and on the Virgin throughout this book. But she also calls on the great classical moralists for what Ford would have called "principles" and Throckmorton sums her up, in this context, shrewdly, as a Romantic puritan as well as a romantic Catholic woman: "in all save doctrine this Kat Howard and her learning are nearer Lutheran than of the old faith." (We remember that Ford, in his Holbein book, describes Holbein's portrait of Katharine's "bitter, soured and disappointed" uncle, Norfolk, as "rigid and unbending in a new world that seemed to him a sea of errors" and pointed out that it was Norfolk who said "It was merry in England before the new Learning came in.")

Katharine's appeal to Henry is essentially romantic: they speak of the Fortunate Isles and bringing back a golden age. And her morals have the absolute quality of Ford's "principle" against which the despairing cynicism of Cicely Elliott is set. Cicely Elliott says, "God hath withdrawn himself from this world," and to Katharine, "Why, thou art a very infectious fanatic . . . But you must shed much blood. You must widow many men's wives. Body of God! I believe thou wouldst." And Katharine does not demur. She will kill out of her righteous principle as Cromwell will out of his expediency. In *The Spirit of the People* Ford remarks in parenthesis, contrasting his versions of Catholicism and Puritanism: "I am far from wishing to adumbrate to which religion I give my preference: for I think it will remain to the end a matter for dispute whether a practicable or an ideal code be the more beneficial to humanity."

A novel, Ford wrote, was "a rendering of an Affair: of one embroilment, one set of embarrassments, one human coil, one psychological progression." That the world of this novel is seen through Katharine's eyes more than any other's has tended to make her appear to be a "heroine"; but this is partly the result of Ford's attempts at what he called authorial "Aloofness." I believe she is morally judged, but she is judged by juxtaposition (another favourite term of Ford's, who admired Stendhal and Jane Austen for their gifts of dramatic juxtaposition of incidents which changed the reader's view of what had gone before). The moral work is done by the reader. We do not see so much of Cromwell, or Throckmorton, as we do of Katharine, and the King, passionate, bewildered, cunning, desiring, virtue, dangerous, generous, cruel, is seen almost—not entirely—from the outside, a looming body at the end of dark corridors, behind doors. We guess at their motives, with Katharine, but not through her view of them. In his later masterpieces, *The Good Soldier* and *Parade's End,* Ford used bewildered innocent minds to depict the muddle, the horror, the endless unsatisfactory and painful partiality of knowledge of human motive, of what has "really" happened or why. This novel is not so subtle, but it is recognisably by the same man. Ford as a writer was always preoccupied with the effect of lies, and the nature of worry and anxiety—they are his great themes, public and private. *The Good Soldier* and *Parade's End* are inhabited by grand, terrible liars. In *The Fifth Queen,* Udal's little lies run into Throckmorton's politic and murderous ones, as the sexual lies of Tietjens's wife in 1914–18 run into the public lies behind the Great War. In *The Spirit of the People* Ford wrote that the English are "a nation of hypocrites" *because* Protestant virtue divorced principle from life. In *The Fifth Queen* he displays the workings of the divorce.

The Good Soldier

Graham Greene has called *The Good Soldier* one of England's few major novels about sex—our answer to Flaubert. Ford, writing it at forty-two, felt it to be his masterpiece, the book he had been preparing to write, and it is both a technical and a psychological triumph. The narrator, Dowell, a rich American with a *mariage blanc* to chirpy Florence (whom he is finally able to talk himself into describing as a "cold sensualist"), describes his relations with the Ashburnhams: Edward, the English gentleman, generous to a fault, unable to control his physical desire for women other than his wife; his wife, Leonora, who "manages" him too well, an Irish (puritanical) Catholic who "controls" his relations with other women for his own good; and the girl, Nancy Rufford, an innocent, again Catholic, who is driven to insanity by Edward's suppressed love for her and by Leonora's jealousy and manipulation. Dowell recounts his slow (he is a naturally "faint," peaceful man) discovery of the raging passions of the others, partly as he remembers them, partly as he creates in himself, by the telling, the power to face what he feels, or believes. Thus pages of quiet, bewildered social commentary are suddenly lit up by visions of hell or heaven, moments of metaphor that alarm reader and speaker. (I do not accept the view that Dowell is an "unreliable narrator" because he is mad or sexually distorted or lying to make his own point look better. I think the tracing of his memory, the *structuring* of his vision through it, is too carefully done for this extra explanation to be necessary.) Dowell's *tone* is his own—as is his final incapacity to judge or assess the events he undergoes.

> Some one has said that the death of a mouse from cancer is the whole sack of Rome by the Goths, and I swear to you that the breaking up of our little four-square coterie was such another unthinkable event. . . .
>
> Permanence? stability? I can't believe it's gone. I can't believe that the long tranquil life, which was just stepping a minuet, vanished in four crashing days at the end of nine years and six weeks . . . No, indeed it can't be gone. You can't kill a minuet de la cour. You may shut up the music-book, close the harpsichord; in the cupboard and presses the rats may destroy the white satin favours. The mob may sack Versailles; the Trianon may fall, but surely the minuet—the minuet itself is dancing itself away into the furthest stars . . .
>
> No, by God, it is false! It wasn't a minuet that we stepped; it was a prison—a prison full of screaming hysterics. . . .
>
> I know nothing—nothing in the world—of the hearts of men. I only know that I am alone—horribly alone.

This is the beginning of the novel—at the end, after witnessing two suicides and enduring total insanity, his tone is still bewildered by the contrary visions of order and huge, meaningless destructive muddle.

Well, I am a nurse-attendant. Edward wanted Nancy Rufford and I have got her. Only she is mad. It is a queer and fantastic world. Why can't people have what they want? The things were all there to content everybody; yet everybody has the wrong thing. Perhaps you can make head or tail of it; it is beyond me.

Is there then any terrestrial paradise where, amidst the whispering of the olive-leaves, people can be with whom they like and have what they like and take their ease in shadows and in coolness? Or are all men's lives like the lives of us good people—like the lives of the Ashburnhams, of the Dowells, of the Ruffords—broken, tumultuous, agonised, and unromantic lives, periods punctuated by screams, by imbecilities, by deaths, by agonies? Who the devil knows?

This combination of the precisely, evocatively lyrical, or vivid, with the flat tone of normality—"Perhaps you can make head or tail of it; it is beyond me"—is one of the glories of the book. The others are the manipulation of the time-shift, and the difference between revelation by dialogue and terrible act—Florence's suicide is related quite coolly, Leonora's revelation that it *was* suicide is related much later, not coolly at all.

It is interesting that that very cool American novelist John Hawkes took the passage about the terrestrial paradise I have just quoted for the epigraph to his chilly, sunlit, amoral *Blood Oranges,* which parodies *The Good Soldier* both by creating Ford's hypothetical "terrestrial paradise" and sexual freedom, and by letting the story end in violence and madness as Ford's does. (It also parodies Hawthorne's *Blithedale Romance,* another terrestrial paradise torn apart by exclusive passions for inaccessible people.)

In many ways Ford's method with the narrating consciousness of *The Good Soldier* is nearer to James's than to Conrad's—what he exploits is Dowell's American innocence/ignorance, rather than something like Marlow's distant pseudo-judging storytelling memory. A book Ford particularly admired was *What Maisie Knew,* of which he wrote:

this is the story of a child moving among elemental passions that are veiled. But of course elemental passions can never be veiled enough not to get through to the consciousness, if not to the intelligence, of the child in the house. So in an atmosphere of intrigues, divorces, prides, jealousies, litigations, conducted as these things are conducted in this country, by what it is convenient to call the 'best people', Maisie always 'knows'. She knows all about concealed relationships as she knows all about intrigues, processes, and the points of view of old family servants. It is of course a horrible book, but it is very triumphantly true.

Parade's End

The Good Soldier is triumphant and horrible in a similar way. It is interesting, however, that it was to the Tietjens books that Ford compared the atmosphere of *What Maisie Knew* and its characteristic veiled and bewildering atmosphere of consciousness. Although *The Good Soldier* is, with justification, the critical favourite of Ford's works, I am not sure that the Tietjens epic, for all its very occasional moments of self-indulgent romanticism, is not Ford's greatest achievement. It was its misfortune that it was written much sooner after the Great War (1924, 1925, 1926) than many war novels, and was, with its apparent "Edwardian" realism and Galsworthy-like "condition of England" panoramic quality, easier for critics to consider already "old-fashioned." It is not, I think, a novel that can ever be "old-fashioned" or "dated" although Ford himself feared it might. It has the timeless authority of formal imagination, what James called "felt life" and "solidity of specification," as well as that exactness of diction which, as Kenner has admirably demonstrated, enabled Ford at once to know, and to detach himself sufficiently to understand and *place,* the values of his time.

Ford has told us in *It Was the Nightingale* what he wanted to achieve in *Parade's End.* He refers to it as "my immense novel" which was to dramatise "the public events of a decade." "The 'subject' was the world as it culminated in the war. You—or at least I—cannot make the world your central character. Perhaps it ought to be done. Perhaps that may prove to be the culmination of the novel." He is thinking of *L'Education sentimentale* and casting himself, somewhat dubiously, as the successor to the recently dead Proust (whom he had not read). In any case, he said, he could not manage "without the attraction of sympathy for a picturesque or upright individual" and so he invented Tietjens, mammoth in size, perfect in memory, of ancient English squirearchical lineage, Yorkshire, taciturn, absurdly honest and honourable to the point of self-immolation and annihilation, whose mind and morals are confused, destroyed, reordered by the Great War in public and by the sexual laxity and pointless, vicious lies of his streamlined, lovely wife, the aristocratic bitch Sylvia.

Ezra Pound, in Canto LXXIV, remembering "Lordly men are to earth o'ergiven/these the companions," opens his catalogue with "Fordie that wrote of giants." Giants is right: there is so *much* of Tietjens, in a way that only a long novel can make much—so many incidents to his life, so much harassed dialogue, so many moral decisions, so much recorded strain of war. It is experienced by Tietjens as chaos. It is presented by Ford with the controlled order of art, not fear or horror but "just worry." Fear ends in callousness, but "worry feeds on itself" until it "so destroys the morale that less than a grasshopper becomes a burden." "And it seemed to me that if the world could be got to see war from that angle there would be no more wars." It is in terms of "worry" that Ford makes his connection between Tietjens's conscious agony, as his memory fails, and James's technique of rendering the horrors of consciousness in the war world of the Tietjens books. He writes of the soldier as *homo duplex,* "a poor fellow whose body is tied in one place but whose mind and personality brood over another distant locality . . . I don't know what was going on at home: political intrigues, no doubt; strikes possibly. But there seemed to prevail a tenuous, misty struggle of schemes—just the atmosphere of *Maisie.*"

There are several things one would like simply to praise in *Parade's End.* One is fictive *plenty*—so many extraordinary characters, so many finely orchestrated scenes with so many actors, so many finely conducted dialogues of total incomprehension—between Tietjens and his equally taciturn brother; between Tietjens and General Campion, who has believed Sylvia's wanton lies about his sexual, financial and political disreputability; between lucid Valentine Wannop and Edith Ethel, once Duchemin, now Masterman, on the school telephone on Armistice Day. Who but Ford could have *invented* the scene at the breakfast table of the elegant, scopophiliac, ageing clergyman, Breakfast Duchemin, his Pre-Raphaelite wife, Tietjens, a prize-fighting bodyguard, a rising politician about to fall in love with Mrs. Duchemin, Valentine Wannop the suffragette, and her uninvited mother "who, Tietjens' father said, had written the one novel worth reading since the eighteenth century"? Who but Ford would have invented and narrated the military-sexual-caste-ridden tragic farce of the events outside Sylvia's hotel room at the front which lead indirectly to Tietjens's being sent to the Front to save an honour he had never lost. Or the Armistice Day party of mutilated soldiers and Old Pals around the camp bed in the empty room, where Tietjens and Valentine are about to give up their ingrained belief that "some do not . . ." and become lovers. Not only Flaubert and James are here, but the raw energy of Dickens, who always puts more in a *scène à faire* than any reader dare expect. Then there is the language—the exact ear for value words, for the voice of a Welsh soldier in a dugout contemplating

"Whatever could possess a cow that took a hatred for its cawve? Up behind Caerphilly, on the mountains . . . Overlooked, the cow must be."

William Carlos Williams, writing in 1951, claimed that *Parade's End* treats lying, public and private, as the major enemy. "Sylvia is the lie, bold-faced, the big crude lie, the denial . . . that is now having its moment." He makes a dangerous analogy, but an interesting one, with "the Russian position, the negative position, the lying position" in modern life, and goes on to claim:

> To use the enormous weapon of the written word, to speak accurately, that is (in contradiction to the big crude lie) is what Ford is building here. For Ford's novels are written with a convinced idea of respect for the meaning of words . . . He speaks of this specifically in *No More Parades*—that no British officer can read and understand a simple statement unless it be stereotypes . . . disrespect for the word and that, succinctly put, spells disaster.

At his loneliest, in *A Man Could Stand Up,* Tietjens wants "someone to talk to," remembers the accurate certainties of George Herbert, and asks himself: "What chance had quiet fields, accuracy of thought, heavy-leaved timbered hedgerows, slowly creeping ploughlands moving up the slopes . . . ?" In some ways a comic figure, whose heroic gestures cause major and minor catastrophes, Tietjens is, if not heroic, central, in his desire for accuracy of thought and his sense of its difficulty.

Frank Kermode, discussing *Middlemarch* and *Women in Love* as novels of crisis, claimed that *Middlemarch* had, for modern readers, the fault of "too much plotting and characterisation"—what Beckett, praising Proust, called "the vulgarities of a plausible concatenation." Whereas Lawrence, though respecting—just—contingency and fact, had a modern, for him "futuristic," interest in the primitive, the mythic, the "typical." Ford's novel may look at first sight more like *Middlemarch* than like *Women in Love*. If it is, it nevertheless, I would maintain, opens a way to a fiction that deals with the particularity of things and yet "places" their significance in a wider scheme of things.

Iris Murdoch in "Against Dryness" complained that modern novels were either "crystalline" or "journalistic": they were symbolic objects or random documentary. Ford, through his intentness on accuracy and form, on *technique,* combined the two with less strain than Lawrence, less idiosyncrasy and bias of personality than Woolf. Wallace Stevens begins an abstruse essay on metaphor with the gnomic statement, "The accuracy of accurate letters is an accuracy with respect to the structure of reality." Sceptically, but firmly, Stevens believed that words and things were necessarily related. So did Ford, and after him Pound and Williams. In our time, when we too often see language as a system singing to itself, conducting us and closing us from the world it tells to us, it is more than pleasant, it is necessary, to have a Ford, with his hopes of accuracy, to teach us to write fiction, to distinguish what Iris Murdoch called "the hard idea of truth" from "the great lie." Description is a great art: mimesis goes on. He was a master of it.

(1981)

7

"The Omnipotence of Thought": Frazer, Freud and Post-Modernist Fiction

P ERHAPS no book has had so decisive an effect upon modern literature as Frazer's," wrote Lionel Trilling in 1961. *The Golden Bough* stands at the head of his list of essential texts for understanding modern literary culture, and the reasons he gives are to do with the modern understanding of myth.

> Anyone who thinks about modern literature in a systematic way takes for granted the great part played in it by myth, and especially by those examples of myth which tell about gods dying and being reborn—the imagination of death and rebirth, reiterated in the ancient world in innumerable variations that are yet always the same, captivated the literary mind at the very moment when, as all accounts of the modern age agree, the most massive and compelling of all the stories of resurrection had lost much of its hold upon the world.[1]

When Trilling, in this context, talks about myth, he is thinking of the net of associations that are called up, for those who studied literature in the 1950s and 1960s, by T. S. Eliot's remark about *Ulysses* and the use of "myth" as a way of ordering and controlling the chaos and futility of modern life.[2] Joyce was an ex-Catholic; Eliot had a predisposition to belief; Pound saw Aphrodite. The literary atmosphere in which the Notes to *The Waste Land* were written, and even more read, was one in which, to quote Trilling again, many readers will feel that Frazer makes all faith and ritual indigenous to humanity, virtually biological. . . . Scientific though his purpose was, Frazer had the effect of validating those old modes of experiencing the world which modern men, beginning with the Romantics, have sought to revive in order to escape from positivism and common sense.[3]

I shall discuss a group of texts, all novels, which could ambivalently be categorised as modernist or post-modernist, which have in common an ironic or sceptical use of the idea, or the material, of Frazer's work, as a means of patterning their narratives. All of them are comic, though all are also serious social and spiritual explorations of the state of our lives. Some are more directly derived from *The Golden Bough* itself than others—all, probably, are at least as much concerned with responding to the high-modernist response to Frazer as with Frazer himself. Trilling in the essay I have quoted juxtaposes *The Golden Bough* with *Death in Venice, Beyond Tragedy* and Freud. Some of my chosen novels, again, are drawing on all these associations, rather than precisely on Frazer.

The texts I shall discuss are: Iris Murdoch's *A Severed Head, The Unicorn* and *The Good Apprentice,* Anthony Powell's *The Kindly Ones, Temporary Kings* and *Hearing Secret Harmonies,* Saul Bellow's *Henderson the Rain King,* Muriel Spark's *The Takeover* and Norman Mailer's *The Armies of the Night.*[4]

Iris Murdoch's reading of Freud is central to her stringent moral vision. Freud's reading of Frazer informs the thought and content of *Totem and Taboo,* and it is this work of Freud which, I think, particularly contributes to both the thought and the form of the drawing-room comedy *A Severed Head* and the Gothic romance *The Unicorn.*

There are three aspects of Freud's use of Frazer's work which are of particular interest in their relation to these novels. These are Freud's citation of Frazer on the true nature of forbidden acts, his discussion of magic as "omnipotence of thought" and his relation of obsessional neurosis to the taboos governing primitive kings.

In his essay "The Return of Totemism in Childhood," Freud makes a long and crucial quotation from Frazer in his discussion of the horror of incest. Frazer's arguments are, he says, "in essential agreement with the arguments which I put forward in my essay on taboo." He goes on to quote from *Totemism and Exogamy:*

It is not easy to see why any deep human instinct should need to be reinforced by law. There is no law commanding men to eat and drink or forbidding them to put their hands in the fire. Men eat and drink and keep their hands out of the fire instinctively for fear of natural not legal penalties, which would be entailed by violence done to these instincts. The law only forbids men to do what their instincts incline them to do; what nature itself prohibits and punishes, it would be superfluous for the law to prohibit and punish. Accordingly we may always safely assume that crimes forbidden by law are crimes which many men have a natural propensity to commit. If there was no such propensity there would be no such crimes, and if no such crimes were committed what need to forbid them? Instead of assuming, therefore, from the legal prohibition of incest that there is a natural aversion to incest, we ought rather to assume that there is a natural instinct in favour of it, and that if the law represses it, as it represses other natural instincts, it does so because civilised men have come to the conclusion that the satisfaction of these natural instincts is detrimental to the general instincts of society.[5]

The tone of this passage sounds like that of Freud himself, reasonable, assuming a consensus, measured in argument. The point it makes about desire and law is central to Freud's formulation of his theory of the repression of instinctive desires and to his study of the Oedipus complex. Its opposition of civilised men and "deep human instincts" echoes Freud's concerns in his studies of civilisation and its discontents, and, in another tone, is part of the irony of the fiction studied in this essay.

In the earlier essay "Taboo and Emotional Ambivalence" Freud also drew on Frazer to illustrate the sources of the neuroses, specifically the obsessional neurosis, which characteristically presents itself in a series of "magical" rituals to avert harm to the self or others. His discussion ties together public and private behaviour. He has earlier described the protective rituals surrounding primitive kings, quoting extensively from Frazer; he goes on to relate these rituals to the ambivalent practices of the neurotic:

The taboo does not only pick out the king and exalt him above all common mortals, it also makes his existence a torment and an intolerable burden and reduces him to a bondage far worse than that of his subjects. Here, then, we have an exact counterpart of the obsessional act in the neurosis, in which the suppressed impulse and the impulse that suppresses it find simultaneous and common satisfaction. The obsessional act is *ostensibly* a protection against the prohibited act, but *actually*, in our view, it is a repetition of it. The 'ostensibly' applies to the *conscious* part of the mind, and the 'actually' to the *unconscious* part. In exactly the same way, the ceremonial taboo of kings is *ostensibly* the highest honour and protection for them, while *actually* it is a punishment for their exaltation, a revenge taken on them by their subjects.[6]

Freud relates these ideas to his own discoveries: the fact that rulers attract "such a powerful unconscious element of hostility" is illuminated by "the child's complex of emotions towards his father—the father-complex." He expresses an interest in "more information on the early history of the kingship" and adds that "Frazer himself has put forward impressive reasons, though, as he himself admits, not wholly conclusive ones, for supposing that the earliest kings were foreigners who, after a brief reign, were sacrificed with solemn festivities as representatives of the deity."

I shall come back to these ideas, particularly in the context of *The Unicorn* and *Henderson the Rain King*. The third place where Frazer's influence on Freud's thought is of great importance seems to me to be the treatment of the concept of omnipotence of thought. In "Animism, Magic, Omnipotence of Thoughts," Freud quotes with approval Tylor's description of magic: "mistaking an ideal connection for a real one." He sets this beside Frazer's distinction between "imitative" and "contagious" magic, and points out that "the true explanation of all the folly of magical observances is the domination of the association of ideas." And again he cites Frazer: "Men mistook the order of their ideas for the order of nature, and hence imagined that the control which they have, or seem to have, over their thoughts, permitted them to exercise a corresponding control over things."[7]

Here again is a voice to compare to Auden's "rational voice," lamented in his elegy for Freud. Both doctor and anthropologist had a notion of what Iris Murdoch thinks of as the "hard idea of truth," an awareness of the limitations of mind, of the dangers of fantasy. Freud says, two pages later: "A general overvaluation has thus come about of all mental processes—an attitude toward the world, that is, which in view of our knowledge of the relations between reality and thought, cannot but strike us as an overvaluation of the latter."[8]

The phrase "omnipotence of thought," Freud goes on to tell us, was a coinage of his patient the Rat Man:

He had coined the phrase as an explanation of all the strange and uncanny events by which he, like others afflicted with the same illness, seemed to be pursued. If he thought of someone, he would be sure to meet that very person immediately afterwards, as though by magic. If he suddenly asked after the health of an acquaintance whom he had not seen for a long time, he would hear that he had just died, so that it would look as though a telepathic message had arrived from him. If without any really serious intention he swore at some stranger, he might be sure that the man would die soon afterwards, so that he would feel responsible for his death. In the course of treatment he was himself able to tell me how the deceptive appearance arose in the midst of these cases, and by what contrivances he himself had helped to strengthen his own superstitious beliefs. All obsessional neurotics are superstitious in this way, usually against their better judgment.[9]

What struck me about this passage, when I reread it in the course of thinking about these novels, was how well the Rat Man's description of the coherent patterning of his experiences coincided with the uncanny, coincidental and magical quality of the plotting of both Murdoch and Powell (both of whom are also interested in magic itself). Traditional realism works with probabilities, correcting the melodramatic or fairy-tale expectations of romance. Later magical realists use the conventions of older genres to explore unconscious fantasy or psychic truth. Powell and Murdoch, and indeed Bellow, Spark and Mailer, have the realist's sense, akin to Freud's and Frazer's, that there is a hard reality, not ourselves, which is not amenable to our planning, plotting and power-strategies. But they are also *technically* interested, in ways made available by Freud and Frazer, in the uncanny patternings we pursue and perceive. A study of Freud's interest in primitive stories about the nature of things and its relation to the scientific study of neurosis is one way to understand the atmosphere of their narratives, at once magical and sceptical.

It is interesting, in this context, that Freud sees art as the only field in which the omnipotence of thought still pertains:

In only a single field of our civilisation has the omnipotence of thoughts been retained, and that is in the field of art. Only in art does it still happen that a man who is consumed by desires performs something resembling the accomplishment of those desires and that what he does in play produces emotional effects—thanks to artistic illusion—just as though it were something real. People speak with justice of 'the magic of art' and compare artists to magicians. But the comparison is perhaps more significant than it claims to be. There can be no doubt that art did not begin as art for art's sake. It worked originally in the service of impulses which are for the most part extinct today. And among them we may suspect the presence of many magical purposes.[10]

One more quotation from the end of the essay "Taboo and Emotional Ambivalence" will lead us straight into the world of Iris Murdoch's novels, and to the centre of many of her preoccupying ideas:

The neuroses exhibit on the one hand striking and far-reaching points of agreement with those great social institutions, art, religion and philosophy. But on the other hand they seem like distortions of them. It might be maintained that a case of hysteria is a caricature of a work of art, that an obsessional neurosis is a caricature of a religion, and that a paranoic delusion is a caricature of a philosophical system.[11]

Iris Murdoch, *A Severed Head* and *The Unicorn*

(In what follows I shall to a certain extent recapitulate the argument of parts of my book *Degrees of Freedom* [1965], although with different emphases.)

A Severed Head might be called an anthropological drawing-room comedy, and *The Unicorn* an anthropological Gothic romance. Both are ambiguously patterned in ways that resemble Freud's description of the Rat Man's omnipotent thoughts and also in the way in which, like Freud's description of art as "omnipotence of thought," they offer a fantasy world of realised desires. Warwick Gould has remarked, in the seminar at which this paper was first read, on the way in which all Murdoch's novels have an atmosphere of "diffused sexuality," and I think that this is true at two levels. The subject of the novels is the relation between the public and the private, between morality and desire, between truth and fantasy. The sexualised atmosphere is partly to do with the nature of the novelist's own imagination and sense of pleasure and unpleasure, partly to do with a Platonic interest in Eros and the human desire for the Good, but partly also to do with a stringent and carefully thought out acceptance of Freud's account of human nature. In "On 'God' and 'Good' " Murdoch describes Freud's discovery which might "almost be called a doctrine of original sin."

Freud takes a thoroughly pessimistic view of human nature. He sees the psyche as an egocentric system of quasi-mechanical energy, largely determined by its own individual history, whose natural attachments are sexual, ambiguous and hard for the subject to understand or control. Introspection reveals only the deep tissue of ambivalent motive, and fantasy is a stronger force than reason. Objectivity and unselfishness are not natural to human beings.[12]

The psychoanalyst in *A Severed Head,* the sinister and bland Palmer Anderson, has his own version of this mechanistic description:

'The psyche is a strange thing,' he said, 'and it has its own mysterious methods of restoring a balance. It automatically seeks its advantage, its consolation. It is almost entirely a matter of mechanics, and mechanical models are the best to understand it with.' (p. 39)

This definition is offered at the end of the chapter in which Anderson has talked the novel's hero, Martin Lynch-Gibbon, into accepting Anderson's affair with Martin's wife, Antonia. " 'We are civilised people,' said Palmer. 'We must try to be very lucid and very honest. We are civilised and intelligent people.' " (p. 35)

Martin's name, Lynch-Gibbon, has often been interpreted as a gesture towards human origins, which it seems to wish to root out or obscure. Martin tries the "civilised" response, even bringing glasses of wine to the lovers in their bed. But this denial of his primitive feelings and passions is questioned by Palmer's half-sister, the anthropologist Honor Klein. In the quotations I have made from Freud and Frazer, the emphasis has been on the truthfulness of modern civilised man as opposed to the fantasy of the primitive. Honor Klein seems to suggest that the civilised behaviour desiderated by Anderson leads to fantasy and untruth as much as magic might.

'Truth has been lost long ago in this situation,' she said. 'In such matters you cannot have both truth and what you call civilisation. You are a violent man, Mr Lynch-Gibbon. You cannot get away with this intimacy with your wife's seducer.' (p. 81)

The anthropological imagery that runs through the novel reinforces this message. The image of the severed head itself is complex. Iris Murdoch has said it came from an interest in the Bog People. Martin's brother, Alexander, a sculptor who makes clay heads, specifically of Antonia, refers to "Freud on Medusa. The head can represent the female genitals, feared, not desired" (p. 54). In her book on Sartre, Murdoch contrasted this Freudian interpretation with Sartre's use of the image to represent "our fear of being observed."[13] (Martin's illicit affair with Georgie depends for its magic on its secrecy.) The clay head Alexander is making, with its "damp grey feature-less face" in its early stages, reminds Martin suddenly of the features of his mother under the sheet of her death-bed. (The female, feared and desired, of the incest taboo? Also the dead ancestor, ambivalently demon and beneficent spirit?)

The head is something to be questioned, an image of death and desire, connected to Orpheus and Medusa. But it has one very specific origin in *Totem and Taboo,* where Freud quotes Frazer on the placation of the dead:

> Other people have found a means for changing their former enemies after their death into guardians, friends and benefactors. This method lies in treating their severed heads with affection, as some of the savage races of Borneo boast of doing. When the Sea Dyaks of Sarawak bring home a head from a successful head-hunting expedition, for months after its arrival it is treated with the greatest consideration and ad-dressed with all the names of endearment of which their language is capable. The most dainty morsels of food are thrust into its mouth, delicacies of all kinds and even cigars. The head is repeatedly implored to hate its former friends and to love its new hosts since it has now become one of them.[14]

There are obvious and comic parallels in this passage with the attempts by Palmer and Antonia to placate and domesticate Martin after they have betrayed him.

In this context it is significant that the first vision of the anthropologist, Honor Klein, is in a fog in a railway station, of which Martin says, "It was the Inferno," and that, as Martin drives her back to Palmer and Antonia, he observes "Honor Klein's body sagged and jolted beside me like a headless sack." She has a strong, not entirely pleasant, physical presence, heavy and oily, down to earth, or below the earth. In a later scene she brandishes a Samurai sword and "decapitates" a thrown napkin. This use of the sword she connects with "a spiritual exercise," "not a trick." She begins to represent both the severing of the magically placated head Martin is to the lovers, the executioner who represents the hardness of moral truth, and indeed, "the female genitals, feared" but also desired now. After Martin makes an instinctive violent attack on her in the cellar of the house where Palmer and Antonia lie in bed like golden angels, he sees her like some underworld deity, her face black, her teeth white, the hair on her lip gleaming.

In the way of Murdoch heroes he falls suddenly and unpredictably in love with her, as though enchanted: "Her face was heavy and surly, like a face in a Spanish religious painting, something looking out of darkness, barbarous yet highly conscious" (p. 137). These contrasts are of her essence: physically solid, "religious," "looking out of darkness," "barbarous yet highly conscious." In the world of Palmer and Antonia, Freud's vision of original sin has been domesticated, "civilised," trivialised. Honor, even in her name, introduces older forces, darker truths.

'Being a Christian, you connect spirit with love. These people [the Japanese] connect it with control, with power.'
　'What do you connect it with?'
　She shrugged her shoulders. 'I am a Jew.'
　'But you believe in the dark gods,' I said.
　'I believe in people,' said Honor Klein. It was a rather unexpected reply. (p. 120)

The atmosphere of *A Severed Head* plays with riddling reversals of our ideas of the civilised and the primitive. Palmer is a Freudian scientist (or magician, but his words echo his author's analysis of Freud); Antonia is a descendant of Bloomsbury, who holds comfortable moral beliefs about the communion of souls which Martin describes as "a metaphysic of the drawing-room." Their civilised "morals" produce a kind of magical fantasy, whilst Honor Klein's infernal vision produces a kind of truth-telling. Yet one does not feel that Murdoch is expressing any Romantic nostalgia for pre-rational wholeness of the self, or for the "spilt religion" T. E. Hulme found in romanticism.

Honor Klein, it is true, is invested with some of the magical attributes of kingship or priesthood. Throughout the novel Murdoch plays with the idea of taboo; various women at various times become "taboo" to Martin, and Honor Klein herself has the electric quality Freud attributes to taboo. This extends to her sword: "It was hideously sharp. My hand stopped. The blade felt as if it were charged with electricity and I had to let go" (p. 122). Compare Freud's quotation from Frazer's *Encyclopaedia Britannica* article on taboo:

> Persons or things which are regarded as taboo may be compared to objects charged with electricity; they are the seat of a tremendous power which is transmissible by contact, and may be liberated with destructive effect if the organisms which provoke its discharge are too weak to resist it; the result of a violation of a taboo depends partly on the strength of the magical influence inherent in the taboo object or person, partly on the strength of the opposing *mana* of the violator of the taboo. . . .[15]

The way in which Martin Lynch-Gibbons acquires the strength of magical influence to stand up to Honor Klein is by observing her in bed with her brother, and thus becoming involved in the violation of the incest taboo. Honor Klein refers him to the myth of Gyges and Candaules, in which the invited voyeur of the king's love-making is ordered by the queen to choose death, which will close his eyes that have seen the forbidden thing, or to kill the king and replace him. This story in its turn is related to Frazer's accounts of the killing of kings, as well as to his accounts of the taboos placed on them by their subjects for their "protection."

If part of Honor's power is her violation of the incest taboo, which Martin gains power over, how can that mixture of myth, magic and primitive fear and desire work in a novel of this kind? It does not work in the same way in which, say, the appearance of the Eumenides works (if it does work) in *The Family Reunion*. Eliot felt that the myths of dying gods hinted at truths deeper than modern positive rationality, and came to believe that the religious sense of the community, the power of the old myths, was related to truth, that the Christian myth was a truth. What Harry sees are the dark gods unacknowledged by drawing-room comfortable morals and rationality. What Honor Klein represents is those dark forces and those uncomfortable truths, but the novel, in its powerfully elegant comic self-consciousness, recognises certain tough psychic forces, gives them deliberated symbolic form and does not give in to the world of magic or to the absolutes of religious belief. As I said, it is *sceptical*. Like Honor Klein, it does not claim *belief* in the dark gods; it is interested in people. And, post-Freud and post-Eliot, it knows that people are made up of conflicting systems of drives and values and images, and makes one possible pattern of these.

The Unicorn makes another. If *A Severed Head* uses Frazer and Freud to analyse civilisation and desire, *The Unicorn* is concerned with religion, with the spiritual life and the fantasies which parody the spiritual life. (It is also concerned with many other things that are not the concern of this essay, including Platonism and the Gothic vampires of Sheridan Le Fanu and Ireland.)

In "On 'God' and 'Good,'" later than the discussion of the Freudian "machinery," Iris Murdoch writes about the necessity of clear and steady attention and remarks:

> A chief enemy to such clarity of vision, whether in art or morals, is the system to which the technical name of sado-masochism has been given. It is the peculiar subtlety of this system that, while constantly leading attention and energy back into the self, it can produce, almost all the way as it were to the summit, plausible imitations of what is good. Refined sado-masochism can ruin art which is too good to be ruined by the cruder vulgarities of self-indulgence. . . . Fascinating too is the alleged relation of master to slave, of the good self to the bad self. . . .[16]

The plot of *The Unicorn* is a kind of knowing fairy-tale which examines a kind of semi-religious community in terms both of this ambiguity between sado-masochism and virtuous renunciation, and of Frazer's account of the imprisonment and restrictive rituals surrounding primitive kings, as interpreted by Freud.

The central figure of the story is Hannah Crean-Smith. Her name, it has been pointed out, is an anagram of Christ-Name, and in that capacity she is both the dying god and the sacrificial victim. She has married a very close relation, committed adultery and attempted murder of her husband, who survives, off-stage, terribly mutilated, a vindictive enchanter-figure, who is to return after seven years have elapsed.

Hannah is confined to Gaze Castle by some mysterious internal or external compulsion. The name Gaze suggests religious contemplation, and there is the suggestion that she is a figure of expiatory suffering and renunciation who will somehow "redeem" the court of anxious servants and lovers who surround her with their attention and reinforce her immobility. The plot opens with the arrival of Marian, the governess whose job turns out to be simply to be a companion for Hannah—Marian is "Maid Marian," and the arrival of this virgin alludes to the legend of the trapping of the unicorn by a pure virgin, which has been seen as an allegory of Christ and the soul, but has more ambiguous sexual connotations. Marian initially sees Hannah as "something very slightly unkempt, the hair tousled, the finger-nails not quite clean, the lovely face a little tired, a little sallow and greasy, like that of a person long ill." Marian is first repelled and then judges that "this person was harmless" (p. 30), which turns out not to be the case.

Hannah has her worshippers: the philosopher Max, in his house Riders, and his son, her ex-lover; Effingham, a visiting civil servant, the courtly lover *par excellence;* Denis, the servant; the unpleasant Evercreeches; and Gerald Scottow, ex-lover of Peter, a violent wielder of power. Their worship, in which Marian becomes involved, is worked out in terms of the idea of kingship, which is central to the argument of *The Golden Bough*. Frazer writes, and Freud quotes him at length:

> The idea that early kingdoms are despotisms in which the people exist only for the sovereign, is wholly inapplicable to the monarchies we are considering. On the contrary, the sovereign in them exists only for his subjects; his life is only valuable so long as he discharges the duties of his position by ordering the course of nature for his people's benefit. So soon as he fails to do so, the care, the devotion, the religious homage which they had hitherto lavished on him cease and are changed into hatred and contempt; he is dismissed ignominiously, and may be thankful if he escapes with his life. Worshipped as a god one day he is killed as a criminal the next. But in this changed behaviour of the people there is nothing capricious or inconstant. On the contrary, their conduct is entirely of a piece. If their king is their god he should also be their preserver; and if he will not preserve them, he must make room for another who will. So long, however, as he answers their expectations, there is no limit to the care which they take of him, and which they compel him to take of himself. A king of this sort lives hedged in by a ceremonious etiquette, a network of prohibitions and observances, of which the intention is not to contribute to his dignity, much less to his comfort, but to restrain him from conduct which, by disturbing the harmony of nature, might involve himself, his people, and the universe in one common catastrophe. Far from adding to his comfort, these observations, by trammelling his every act, annihilate his freedom, and often render the very life, which it is their object to preserve, a burden and sorrow to him.[17]

There is a telling little scene early in the novel in which Denis Nolan, the servant who at the end of the tale seems to have taken the burden of the suffering upon himself, is seen clipping Hannah's hair, though Marian would have thought him ill enough fitted to the role of *valet de chambre*. He tidies away and burns the clippings in a way which reminds us irresistibly of Freud's quotations from Frazer about the sacredness of the parts of the body of holy rulers.[18] Immediately after the passage I have just quoted from Freud, he goes on to quote Frazer, who was quoting Kaempfer, on the sacred person of the Mikado:

> There is such a holiness ascribed to all parts of his body that he dares to cut off neither his hair nor his beard nor his nails. However, lest he should grow too dirty, they may clean him in the night when he is asleep; because, they say, that which is taken from his body at that time hath been stolen from him and that such a theft does not prejudice human dignity.

Denis's ministrations emphasise both Hannah's sacredness and her immobility and helplessness. Frazer, in his section on the tabooing of hair, all of which is illuminating, says:

> It is obvious that the cutting of the hair must have been a delicate and difficult operation. There is first the danger of disturbing the spirit of the head. . . . Secondly there is the difficulty of disposing of the shorn locks. For the savage believes that the sympathetic connexion which exists between himself and every part of his body continues to exist even after the physical connexion has been broken, and that therefore he will suffer from any harm that may befall the severed parts of his body, such as the clippings of his hair or the parings of his nails. Accordingly he takes great care that these severed portions of himself shall not be left in places where they might either be exposed to accidental injury or fall into the hands of malicious persons who might work magic on them to his detriment or death. Such dangers are common to all, but sacred persons have more to fear from them than ordinary people. . . .[19]

And elsewhere he records that the ministrant who cuts the hair is also tabooed;[20] Denis is the priest who will inherit the kingship.

In the same scene Hannah is brought a bat by Denis, a damaged bat that will probably die, and which is in some way her totem animal: "Without knowing why, [Marian] felt she could hardly bear Mrs Crean-Smith and the bat together, as if they were suddenly the same grotesque helpless thing"

(p. 48). The bat, of course, also goes with the Gothic image of Hannah as vampire, Le Fanu's Carmilla, and Murdoch makes it both intensely alive, with its "strange little doggy face and bright dark eyes," and sinister, by implication. The novel as a whole is haunted by totemic animals. One character submerges herself in a pool like a seal; another is always accompanied by gun dogs. Denis is associated with fish, thus connecting him too with Christ and suffering. He protects goldfish from herons, and explains to Marian the meaning of the leaping salmon, of which Hannah has already said, "Such fantastic bravery, to enter another element like that. Like souls approaching God." Denis shows Marian the salmon and says, "Suffering is no scandal. It is natural. Nature appoints it. All creation suffers. It suffers from having been created, if from nothing else. It suffers from being divided from God" (p. 235).

Here a primitive totemic world is associated with a highly developed religious explanation of suffering. *The Unicorn,* like most of Murdoch's novels, but more intensely than most of them, is about the possibility and nature of the spiritual life, in a post- or un-Christian world. In that sense its use of the discoveries of Frazer and Freud might be thought to connect Murdoch's work to Trilling's description, quoted earlier, of Frazer's making "all faith and all ritual indigenous to the world . . . indeed almost biological," and also his contribution to the "old modes of thinking which modern men, beginning with the Romantics, have sought to revive."

But, again, there is a powerful element of scepticism and irony built into this mythic vision of the Princess in the Tower, the contemplative in her cell, the primitive ties between the community and the natural and spiritual worlds. For the Freudian implications of Frazer's narratives are insisted on and made clear. Hannah's suffering may be simply a sado-masochistic parody of virtue. It may too be an obsessional neurosis, "a caricature of a religion," and the behaviour of the worshippers carries a powerful charge of the ambivalence that Freud detects in their protectiveness. This ambivalence is frequently explored in Murdoch, starting with the pity of the enchanter, Mischa Fox, for maimed and destroyed insect life. The desire to protect, Freud says, in obsessional neurotics

> appears wherever, in addition to a predominant feeling of affection, there is also a contrary, but unconscious, current of hostility. . . . The hostility is then shouted down, as it were, by an excessive intensification of the affection, which is expressed as solicitude and becomes compulsive, because it might otherwise be inadequate to perform its

task of keeping the unconscious contrary current of feeling under repression. . . .[21]

When Hannah is subdued and seduced by Gerald Scottow (i.e., when the taboo of inviolability is broken) her worshippers feel free to gratify their own desires—Marian for instance makes love to Denis. As Freud says, "If one person succeeds in satisfying the repressed desire, the same desire is bound to be kindled in all the other members of the community."[22] And, when Hannah kills Scottow, she herself becomes vulnerable, dies and is succeeded by Denis, who takes on himself the crime of killing the enchanter, or power-centre, Peter, on his return. He loses his innocence and goes away.

> Marian had an eerie sense of it all beginning again, the whole tangled business: the violence, the prison house, the guilt. It all still existed. Yet Denis was taking it away with him. He had wound it all inside himself and was taking it away. Perhaps he was bringing it, for her, for the others, to an end. (p. 311)

In Denis's departure, and the new beginning of violence and guilt, we may perhaps see an echo of Frazer's repeated tragedy as one priest takes over in the grove of Nemi from his murdered predecessor, as well as a Christian allegory of scapegoat and suffering.

This account of *The Unicorn* leaves out the Platonic vision of truth and religion, introduced by Max, and leaves out also the relation of the story to Simone Weil's ideas of necessary suffering. It is a complex work of art, juxtaposing and mixing various genres and theoretical accounts of human nature into a tragicomic vision which has some dignity.

A constantly reiterated idea of Murdoch's is that "the spiritual life has no story and is not tragic"—a saying of the Abbess in *The Bell*. This idea is related to the willingness to experience, to attend to life, without imposing patterns or stories upon it. In *The Unicorn* Effingham Cooper's "intelligent" girlfriend Elizabeth, who never appears, says, "Art and psychoanalysis give shape and meaning to life and that is why we adore them, but life as it is lived has no shape and meaning, and that is what I am experiencing just now" (p. 120). We are reminded of the idea of "omnipotence of thought"—and here psychoanalysis is ironically, by implication, assimilated to art and indeed magic in that category.

The problem of death, Freud tells us, in his discussion of the origins of

animism, "must have been . . . the chief starting-point of all this theoriz-
ing."[23] What readers have generally seen as the most startling and memorable scene in *The Unicorn* is the one where Effingham, *l'homme moyen sensuel*,
finds himself trapped in a bog, and on the point of death. He has a vision
of nothing, of annihilation.

> The dark bog seemed empty now, utterly empty, as if, because of the
> great mystery that was about to be enacted, the little wicked gods had
> withdrawn. Even the stars were veiled now and Effingham was at the
> centre of a black globe. . . .
>
> Perhaps he was dead already, the darkening image of the self forever
> removed. . . . What was left was everything else, all that was not
> himself, that object which he had never before seen and upon which
> he now gazed with the passion of a lover. And indeed he could always
> have known this for the fact of death stretches the length of life. Since
> he was mortal he was nothing and since he was nothing all that was
> not himself was filled to the brim with being and it was from this that
> the light streamed. This then was love, to look and look until one
> exists no more, *this* was the love which was the same as death. . . . (pp.
> 197ff)

This vision, with its combination of the words "gaze," "passion" and
"love," is the true vision of which Hannah's story is the (so to speak)
animistic theorising. At the moment of death the acceptance of annihilation
brings a sense of the reality of things, underformed (to use another Murdoch
word) by human fantasy. I cite it now because it provides the example of
the experience of death and reality as one, which occurs, in a remarkably
similar form, at the end of *Henderson the Rain King*. It is a spiritual denial of
human stories constructed to avoid or evade meaninglessness.

Anthony Powell, *A Dance to the Music of Time*

"It is quite possible," says Freud,

> that the whole concept of demons was derived from the important
> relation of the living to the dead. The ambivalence inherent in that
> relation was expressed in the subsequent course of human develop-
> ment by the fact that, from the same root, it gave rise to two com-

pletely opposed psychical structures: on the one hand fear of demons and ghosts and on the other veneration of ancestors. The fact that demons are always regarded as the spirits of those who have died *recently* shows better than anything the influence of mourning on the origin of the belief in demons. Mourning has a quite specific psychical task to perform; its function is to detach the survivors' memories and hopes from the dead. When this has been achieved the pain grows less and with it the remorse and self-reproaches and consequently the fear of the demon as well. And the same spirits who to begin with were feared as demons may now expect to meet with friendlier treatment; they are revered as ancestors and appeals are made to them for help.[24]

Anthony Powell's long novel is claimed, impeccably, as part of the English tradition of observed social comedy. It is even disliked on these grounds by readers hostile to jokiness and the upper classes and Brideshead sentimentality, which is a pity, because it seems to me, in the subtlety of its construction, the way in which its episodes are juxtaposed and set up echoes along the whole work, the way in which its characters are both smaller (simpler) and larger than life, to be also an English version of the self-aware modernist novel, working with cutting and patterning rather than with distortions of consciousness or dislocating shifts of point of view.

At various points in the novel Powell, or his characters, explain that "naturalism" is a technique, like any other, no more and no less artificial, requiring skill in selection and writing. There is an essay to be written in this context about the choice of *length* of the episodes in the various novels, and the relation of selected scenes and dialogues to the reflections on life, art and history made by the narrator and the persons of the narrative— generals, artists, musicians, spivs and prophetesses. This is not the place for that essay. What I have to say about Powell's use of *The Golden Bough* and related ideas is to do with the sense of deliberate patterning in the narrative. It is also to do with ancestors. As the novel progresses and the narrator, Nicholas Jenkins, grows older, both the past and the present become fuller of both demons and ancestors and, with the war, of numbers of the dead. In a later novel, *The Fisher King,* Powell wrote an almost hieratically allegorical tale of an impotent photographer who loses his beautiful princess of a companion to a "poor knight"; the whole is interpreted in terms of the Arthurian myth by a chorus consisting of a best-selling historical novelist and a man in advertising. The matter of that tale is out of *From Ritual to Romance* and *Parsifal* rather than Frazer, and the manner is schematic rather than "naturalistic" insofar as it is successful, which it is, I think, as a grimly mythic study of impotence and age. I mention it here because it reinforces the sense that Powell's work is naturally haunted by the atmosphere of *The Waste Land,* and by what Eliot claimed came from Frazer.

The title of *Temporary Kings,* the eleventh and penultimate volume of *A Dance to the Music of Time,* is taken from Frazer (it is the title of Chapter XXV in the abridged *Golden Bough*). In a long novel about the passage and repetitions of time, the word "temporary" has its resonance and irony. But before considering that book, I want to look briefly at an earlier one, *The Kindly Ones,* which also has echoes of Eliot and the matter of ancestors and demons. This novel, published in 1962, is the last in the second peacetime trilogy and ends with the outbreak of the Second World War. It is thus a kind of Janus herm in the text, looking back and forward. It opens, not chronologically, but in the narrator's childhood in a military household at the outbreak of the First World War.[25] The household contains a house-maid who sees the "ghosts," is disappointed in love and appears stark naked in the drawing-room, "instantly metamorphosed" by Nick's mother's de-scription of this as "the end of the world," into "one of those figures—risen from the tomb, given up by the sea, swept in from the ends of the earth—depicted in primitive paintings of the Day of Judgment" (p. 62). These portents are juxtaposed with a childish confusion of Nick's between the suffragettes (referred to as Virgin Marys by Albert, the cooking footman) and the Furies: "At lessons that morning—the subject classical mythology—Miss Orchard had spoken of the manner in which the Greeks, because they so greatly feared the Furies, had named them the Eumenides—the Kindly Ones—flattery intended to appease their terrible wrath" (p. 6).

The double nature of the Eumenides, the pursuing ghosts of the *Oresteia* and *The Family Reunion,* as demons and domesticated household gods is close to Freud's description of the primitive attitude to the dead. In terms of the First World War, it is worth remarking that Nick's father was involved in the making of the Treaty of Versailles, which led inexorably to the Second. In terms of the relation of the ideas of magic and ritual to the structure of the novel, it is worth remarking that this reminiscent passage in 1914 sees the first appearance of Dr. Trelawney, who

conducted a centre for his own peculiar religious, philosophical—some said magical—tenets, a cult of which he was high priest, if not actually messiah. This establishment was one of those fairly common strongholds of unsorted ideas that played such a part in the decade ended by the war. Simple-lifers, utopian socialists, spiritualists, occultists, theosophists, quietists, pacifists, futurists, cubists, zealots of all sorts in their approach to life and art . . . a collection of visionaries who hoped to build a New Heaven and a New Earth through the agency of their particular crackpot activities, sinister or comic, according to the way you looked at such things. (p. 32)

Dr. Trelawney and his disciples go out for spiritual runs, he "in a short white robe or tunic, his long silky beard and equally long hair caught by the breeze."

Sinister or comic, Dr. Trelawney reappears at various points in the narrative, like Mrs. Erdleigh, the fortune-teller who calls up associations both of Madame Sosostris and of Wagner's prophetic Erda, and who also manages to call up, in *The Acceptance World,* the spirit of Karl Marx on *planchette.* Both preside over the fate of Nick's wandering Uncle Giles, whose death in a hotel run by Albert precedes the Second World War, and whose presence continues as an ambivalent ghost, present and absent, as such relations can, in the narrative of a novel, or in the memory. Nick, seeing to his dead uncle's effects, has to help Trelawney, now decidedly sinister, with an asthma attack, assisted by Dupont, his supplanter in the affections of his first love, Jean. Trelawney is a fake priest, not without power. Nick says, "There was something decidedly unpleasant about him, sinister, at the same time absurd, that combination of the ludicrous and the alarming soon to be widely experienced by contact with those set in authority in wartime" (p. 192).

This quotation is illuminating about Powell's method; the "real world" is shown to be infected by the attributes of the magical or charlatan, which reason can diagnose but not control. Widmerpool is of course "set in authority" during the war, and is indeed both ludicrous and alarming, coldly causing the death of Charles Stringham, now a saintly mess waiter: at the beginning of the sequence it was Stringham the glamorous and witty Etonian who mocked the ungainly Widmerpool and said he would be "the death of me."

Widmerpool marries Pamela, Stringham's niece, who is not kindly and deals out death. *Temporary Kings* opens in Venice, with a parody of the scene in *Death in Venice* where a very old singer (in the Mann story a persona of the destroying Dionysos) sings of the funicular and the kingdoms of the earth, and the characters of the novel discourse of death and the fear of death. "I feel like the man in the ghost story, scrambling over the breakwaters with the Horrible Thing behind him getting closer and closer" (p. 3). The language is full of comic echoes of Eliot's echo of Marvell's "At my back I always hear / Time's winged chariot hurrying near."

Nick is at a literary conference. Mark Members has talked him into attending.

'You'll live like a king once you get there.'

'One of those temporary kings in *The Golden Bough,* everything at their disposal for a year or a month or a day—then execution? Death in Venice?'

'Only ritual execution in more enlightened times—the image of a declining virility. A Mann's man for a' that. . . .' (p. 7)

A further twist in this sinister imagery is given by the visit of the conference guests to a palazzo with a Tiepolo ceiling depicting the myth of Gyges and Candaules, already discussed in terms of the sexual supplanting (and killing) of the king in *A Severed Head*. A Dr. Brightman adds to the story of the supplanting of Candaules the legend that Gyges descended under the earth and found a man in a hollow bronze horse. "The Hollow Horse, you remember, is a widespread symbol of Death and Rebirth" (p. 87). The story has repercussions in Powell's narrative; it is darkly suggested that Widmerpool, the indefatigable seeker after power, is impotent and gets his pleasure from what Pamela Widmerpool, who appears in this scene, calls "watching—looking on, being looked at."

(It is later revealed that Pamela Widmerpool, who comes into the story fresh from that scandalous death of the French writer Ferrand-Sénéschal, in her arms, has in fact been making love to him partly for the conniving benefit of Widmerpool, who was looking on.)

It is in that scene too that Pamela Widmerpool meets Russell Gwinnett (named with one of the names of the morbidly witty Ambrose Bierce, death-obsessed), who wishes to write a life of X. Trapnel, the writer who died as a result of his affair with Pamela and whose death and "apotheosis" in the Hero of Acre, a Fitzrovia pub, are recounted by Malcolm Crowding just before the scene under the painting. Both the account of Trapnel's death and the scene in the palazzo resound with echoes of Frazer's dying gods and slaughtered kings.

It was Lazarus coming back from the Dead. Better than that, because Lazarus didn't buy everybody a drink. . . .

The charnel cave was put behind him. It was Trapnel Unbound. (p. 31)

At closing time

> X walked through the doors of the Hero like a king. There was real dignity in his stride. It was a royal progress. Courtiers followed in his wake. You can imagine—free drinks—there was quite a crowd by that time, some of them singing, as it might be, chants in a patron's praise. (p. 33)

Trapnel finds that he has lost his stick—a stick with a death's head, which we know to be a swordstick. This loss of power—Pamela has already destroyed his novel—kills him:

> 'No,' he said. 'Of course I haven't got a stick any longer, have I? I sacrificed it. Nor a bloody novel. I haven't got that either.'
> Then he heeled over into the gutter. Everyone thought he was drunk. (p. 34)

There are echoes here of Frazer's descriptions of the celebratory mourners in the rituals of Dionysos and Adonis. There are further echoes in the scene in the palazzo, where Gwinnett, who is seen partly in terms of a dead ancestor, a signer of the Declaration of Independence, meets the terrifying Pamela, and makes a "frontal attack" declaring his interest in Trapnel. Pamela responds, "Poor X," and sounds "deeply moved."

> Now, it had become Trapnel's turn to join the dynasty of Pamela's dead lovers. Emotional warmth in her was directed only towards the dead, men who had played some part in her life, but were no more there to do so. That was how it looked. The first time we had ever talked together, she had described herself as 'close' to her uncle, Charles Stringham, almost suggesting a sexual relationship. . . .
> It was Death she liked. Mrs Erdleigh had hinted as much on the night of the flying bombs. Would Gwinnett be able to offer her Death? (p. 102)

Here Pamela is almost the goddess of the sacred grove, demanding successive sacrifices, the huntress. It is interesting that Stringham, Widmerpool's deposed victim, appears here both as ancestor and (incestuous) lover in the dynasty of the deposed and sacrificed. Dr. Brightman links Pamela's remarks about the need to be looked at to this aspect of things:

> You mean one facet of the legend [of Gyges] links up with kingship in another guise? I agree. Sacrifice is almost implied. Public manifestation of himself as source of fertility might be required too, to forestall a successor from snatching the attribute of regality.

Pamela characterised Candaules as "the naked man with the stand." Trapnel lost his attribute of regality, the stick without which he was never seen.

Gwinnett is attempting to make contact with Trapnel. His profession gives him a professional concern with the life of the dead; his temperament, too. Later in Venice he begins to take on certain aspects of Aeneas.

> Gwinnett had certainly entered the true Trapnel world in a manner no aspiring biographer could discount. It was like a supernatural story, a myth. If he wanted to avoid becoming the victim of sorcery, being himself turned into a toad, or something of that kind—in moral terms his dissertation follow *Profiles in String* into the waters of the Styx— he would have to find the magic talisman and do that pretty quickly. (p. 174)

He pursues Pamela, by now a personification of Death in Venice, through the Venetian midnight.

Gwinnett at the realistic level has the idea of "reconstructing in himself Trapnel's life, getting into Trapnel's skin, "becoming Trapnel." This project, the biographer as conjurer of the dead, leads to him living in Trapnel's old rooms, where he is visited at midnight by a naked woman; she is comically and frighteningly observed by an old man, Bagshaw Senior, going out to relieve himself. It is Christmas. Bagshaw tells Nick, "My father enacted the whole extraordinary incident under a sprig of mistletoe. In the middle of it all, some of the holly came down, with that extraordinary scratchy noise holly makes" (p. 191). The symbol is naturalised and embedded in the comic and the mundane, but the mistletoe is Frazer's mistletoe, the Golden Bough, and the woman, who is Pamela, is inviting Gwinnett into the Underworld. Her final act is to take an overdose and offer herself to Gwinnett, thus allowing him to "become" Trapnel as Gyges became Candaules, and enabling Pamela to "make the sacrifice of herself. Her act could only be looked upon as a sacrifice—of herself, to herself."

It seems to me important that the account of Stringham's "good death" in the camps in Singapore is delayed until this book, and appears in the middle of Pamela's tormenting progress to the Underworld, with its humiliation of Widmerpool. Stringham is the displaced and avenged ancestor. It is also important that Mrs. Erdleigh prophesies her descent to her, in portentously bathetic terms that are also impressive. Pamela the sorceress is a joke and deadly serious.

The last book of the sequence, *Hearing Secret Harmonies,* published in 1975, deals with that time we think of as "the Sixties," though it extended well into the Seventies—the time of hippies and Hobbits, of astrology and cults and gurus, of drugs and more sinister and threatening phenomena. It brings to an end the long journey of Widmerpool, first glimpsed on his solitary runs at Eton, famous for his overcoat, which was obscurely wrong. He has become a figure of political power, and ends in a search for quite different power, in a cult run by the unpleasant Scorpio Murtlock, who has taken over Dr. Trelawney's running-rites and claims to be resurrecting and restoring that sage. Widmerpool and Professor Gwinnett, pursuing other researches with his usual thoroughness, take part in unpleasant rites and dances round the "Devil's Fingers." Nick, a cool observer of this new crop of primitivism, as he was of Trelawney's version, observes:

> It was not quite the scene portrayed by Poussin, even if elements of the Seasons' dance were suggested in a perverted form; not least by Widmerpool, perhaps naked, doing the recording. From what Gwinnett had said, a battle of wills seemed to be in progress. If, having decided material things were vain, Widmerpool had turned to the harnessing of quite other forces, it looked as if he were losing ground in rivalry with a younger man. (p. 173)

The images Powell draws on in the descriptions of this last stage of Widmerpool's progress are in fact those of Ariosto's *Orlando Furioso,* rather than *The Golden Bough*. The fertility magic is generalised, and, when Widmerpool dies, in an attempt to outrun Murtlock in a naked magical run, his death is part of the whole history of his bizarre and monstrous competitiveness. Yet he is trying to be King of the Woods, and he is attempting to make his thought omnipotent in a recalcitrant world. Bithel, the army buffoon, now the Fool who survives, tells the last tale.

'Somebody heard Lord Widmerpool shout, "I'm leading, I'm leading you." '

'How did it end?'

'It was rather a twisty way through the woods. Nobody could see him, especially in the mist. When they came round a corner, out of the trees, he was lying just in the road.' (p. 269)

Widmerpool dies in an attempt to make time run faster, having never understood the cyclical graceful dance of the Poussin painting that gives its name to the sequence. His fate is informed and illuminated by the atmosphere spread by Frazer's studies and images throughout the modern period. As with Iris Murdoch, the use of the myths and the magic is partly comic, partly sceptical, partly almost elegant imagery for darker truths that in, say, Conrad or Lawrence would have been urgent with blood and darkness. But at the same time such references do connect readers to ancestors and demons, whatever their ambiguous provenance. They do, still, provide a way for forming our stories of mystery and the fact of death.

Saul Bellow, *Henderson the Rain King*

Henderson the Rain King was first published in 1959, before the Sixties explosion of interest in the irrational and the primitive; its primitivism is related to the mythopoeic ambitions of high modernism, and it is also, it seems to me, a daring and successful attempt to challenge *Moby-Dick* as the great American myth of travel and spiritual exploration. That said, it must immediately be remarked that it is also a comic and ironic novel, asking not for belief in its narrative, which offers itself as "mental travel" (quite aware of the echoes of Blake this phrase calls up), and not asking for assent to its central myth, either. It is self-conscious, and self-consciously patterned, in a way quite different from Melville's giddy and compelled discovery of Emersonian correspondences and natural emblems of spiritual riddles.

Henderson is a great novel, and what makes it great, paradoxically after what I have said, is the brilliance and sensuous immediacy of its physical world, and the voice of its hero and narrator, pugnacious, grumbling, tormented, comic, explosive, humiliated, but always questing, always energetic. Saul Bellow was a student of anthropology, and his novel is an anthropologist's novel, though critics are more likely to talk about it in terms of his interest in Reichian psychology.

Henderson escapes a civilisation with which he is at odds and becomes a kind of tourist in search of spiritual comfort. He wishes to satisfy an inner voice which cries, "I want, I want." He goes into the interior of Africa in search of some ultimate truth and finds two tribes, the gentle Arnewi, with a hugely fleshy female ruler, and the Wariri, whose king, Dahfu, becomes his friend. The Arnewi make him welcome, offer him a bride-price to marry the queen's sister and are plagued by frogs in their water cistern. Henderson offers his personal version of American aid to the Arnewi, and explodes their tank and the frogs with a home-made bomb. Moving on to the Wariri, he finds a more prosperous and extremely unpleasant society, which believes in its own luck, with reason, and survives on a philosophy of delivering blows. There are street executions; Henderson finds a dead man in his hut; he is tricked into using his huge strength in a rain-making ceremony, where he moves the effigy of the goddess Mummah, and becomes the Sungo, the Rain King. He takes part in a frenzied dance, whipping the gods to make them produce rain, which they do.

The king, Dahfu, is a powerful and beautiful man, living at ease in his harem, but surrounded with the restrictions already discussed in connection with Hannah in *The Unicorn*. He will be strangled when he can no longer satisfy his wives, he tells Henderson. He dances with the skull of his father, which he must not let fall; his father's spirit has become a maggot and then a lion, which the king must kill in a hunting-ceremony which is a proof of strength. He keeps a lioness in his cellar, learning her ways, "becoming" a lion, which annoys the witch-doctors and helps them to plot his downfall. He is killed by a lion, setting out to trap his father, and reveals to Henderson that Henderson has been tricked into becoming the Rain King by being made to take on a show of strength which the wise men in the tribe avoid. For the Sungo is heir to the kingship if there is no direct heir. He will inherit the wives, the restrictions, the dangerous rites and the eventual death. Henderson escapes, using his strength, and takes with him the lion cub provided by the witch-doctor to hold the soul of his dead friend.

The relations between this crude account of Bellow's plot and the world of Frazer's research are obvious. The king who will be strangled when he fails to satisfy his wives, the stranger who may be substituted for the king as sacrificial victim, the rulers who make rain and are vulnerable to destruction by their people if they fail, the animistic explanation of what happens to the soul of the dead ancestor, the reluctance of the people to take on the kingship, are all to be found amply recorded in Frazer, though no doubt not only in Frazer. Poor Henderson is, like Gwinnett and Widmerpool, a Temporary King.

A quotation from *The Golden Bough* may illustrate the general affinity between the rain-making in *Henderson* and Frazer's observations:

> Sometimes, when a drought has lasted a long time, people drop the usual hocus-pocus of imitative magic altogether, and being far too angry to waste their breath in prayer, they seek by threats and curses or even downright physical force to extort the waters of heaven from the supernatural being who has, so to say, cut them off at the main. In a Japanese village, when the guardian divinity had long been deaf to the peasants' prayer for rain, they at last threw down his image and, with curses loud and long, hurled it head foremost into a stinking rice-field. 'There,' they said, 'you may stay yourself for a while, to see how *you* feel after a few days scorching in this broiling sun that is burning the life from our cracking fields.' In the like circumstances the Feloupes of Senegambia cast down their fetishes and drag them about the fields, cursing them till rain falls.[26]

> And now I wanted to fall on the ground to avoid any share in what seemed to me a terrible thing, for these women, the amazons, were rushing upon the figures of the gods with those short whips of theirs and striking them. 'Stop!' I yelled. 'Quit it! What's the matter? Are you crazy?' It would have been different perhaps, if this had been a token whipping and the gods were merely touched with the thick leather straps. But great violence was loosened on these figures, so that the smaller ones rocked as they were beaten while the bigger without any change of face bore it defenseless. Those children of darkness, the tribe, rose and screamed like gulls on stormy water. Naked, I threw myself down, roaring, 'no, no, no!' . . . My hand, which had the whip still in it, was lifted once or twice and brought down so that against my will I was made to perform the duty of the rain king. . . .

> And then after a great neighing, cold blast of wind, the clouds opened and the rain began to fall. Gouts of water like hand grenades burst all about and on me. The face of Mummah, which had been streaked by the whips, was now covered with silver bubbles and the ground began to foam. The amazons with their wet bodies began to embrace me. (*Henderson*, p. 201)

If Frazer's passage is mocking and detached, Bellow's is alive and complex. The magic works. The prose is about the effectiveness of violent blows (note the hand grenades).

To what use is Bellow putting all this material? He has many purposes in this novel, all of which are inextricably part of each other. One is, like Iris Murdoch in *A Severed Head,* but also like Melville in *Moby-Dick,* to reflect ironically on the concepts of civilisation and savagery. The *Pequod* is among other things a symbol of American savagery, going out into the world of nature to slaughter and destroy. Its most civilised and heroic passenger is the cannibal, Queequeg, Ishmael's friend, who has filed teeth and is tattooed with a theory of the universe. Henderson, capitalist and tourist, is a descendant of Ishmael, and like other American heroes finds his black counterpart, a man much better educated and more urbane than himself, sitting in his silk trousers and servicing his wives. What Dahfu teaches Henderson, above all, is the "connection between truth and blows."

'Last winter as I was chopping wood a piece flew up from the block and broke my nose. So the first thing I thought was *truth!*'

'Ah,' said the king, '. . . As things are such may appear to be related to the case. I do not believe actually it is so. But I feel there is a law of human nature in which force is concerned. Man is a creature who cannot stand still under blows. . . . All wish to rid themselves and free themselves and cast the blow upon the others. And this I conceive of as the earthly dominion. But as for the truth content of the force, that is a separate matter.'

The room was all shadow, but the heat with its odor of vegetable combustion pervaded the air.

'Wait a minute now, sire,' I said, having frowned and bitten on my lips. 'Let me see if I have got you straight. You say the soul will die if it can't make someone else suffer what it suffers?'

'For a while, I am sorry to say, then it feels peace and joy.'

I lifted up my brows and with difficulty, as the whiplashes all over the unprotected parts of my face were atrocious. I gave him one of my high looks, from one eye. 'You are sorry to say, Your Highness? Is this why me and the gods had to be beaten?'

'Well, Henderson, I should have notified you better when you wished to move Mummah. To that extent you are right.' (pp. 212–13)

I have quoted so much partly to give the sense of the comic contrast between the tone of the king and that of the tourist, though the content of the exchange is of great importance, and resembles Iris Murdoch's interest in Simone Weil's idea of *Ate,* the automatic passing-on of blows, and virtue as the receiving of blows without returning them. There is a great deal here, too, about the nature of masculinity, which I have not space to go into;

Henderson's blundering aggression and desire, his disastrous relations with his wives and daughter, are illuminated both by his failure with the peaceful Arnewi (renewal? connected with the female reproduction of the species?) and his relations with the king of the Wariri (war? male aggression?), who looks after his potency and his body in a charnel-house atmosphere, with a caged female lion from whom he is trying to learn, by a kind of animal reciprocity, pacing in the cellars.

Something riddling is also discovered in the course of the novel about the relation of the world to the mind, which gave rise to the Freudian problem of "omnipotence of thought" already discussed. Henderson has a perfectly modern way of telling his own stories to himself, fitting reality to his own desires. Before the rain-making ceremony he has an excited sense that he is finding truth:

> What a person to meet at this distance from home. Yes, travel is advisable. And, believe me, the world is a mind. Travel is mental travel. I had always suspected this. What we call reality is nothing but pedantry. I need not have had that quarrel with Lily. . . . I proclaimed that I was on better terms with the real than she. Yes, yes, yes. The world of facts is real, all right, and not to be altered. The physical is all there and it belongs to science. But then there is the noumenal department, and there we create and create and create. As we tread our overanxious ways, we think we know what is real. And I was telling the truth to Lily after a fashion. I knew it better, all right, but I knew it because it was mine—filled, flowing, and floating with my own resemblances; as hers was with *her* resemblances. Oh, what a revelation! Truth spoke to me. To *me,* Henderson. (p. 167)

I used to think that this was the central message of the novel, but that was too simple; it was the spiritual excitement of a hungry and naïve man before the blows of truth. Later, Henderson thinks that

> chaos doesn't run the whole show. This is not a sick and hasty ride, helpless, through a dream into oblivion. No, sir! It can be arrested by a thing or two. By art, for instance. The speed is checked, the time is redivided. Measure! . . . The voices of angels! Why the hell else did I play the fiddle? And why were my bones molten in those great cathedrals of France so that I couldn't stand it and had to booze up and swear at Lily? (pp. 175–6)

The measure he is observing is the king's dance, his artistry, with the beribboned skulls of his ancestors. We might call that a primitive form of culture, the dead assimilated into the form of art. But Dahfu is still urgently involved in the knowledge of the fact of death inherent in that patterning.

Dahfu too has an idea of the whole planet as a mental whole, sleeping, waking, breathing and creating through the imagination. Men may work with the All-intelligent, he tells Henderson, to make not the monsters they have made—"The agony. The appetite. The obstinate. The immune elephant. The shrewd pig. The fateful hysterical" and so on (p. 217)—but "what gay, brilliant types, what merriment types, what beauties and goodness, what sweet cheeks or noble demeanors" (p. 217). Thought has power for him too, but in some organic possible way. Men dreamed of flying, he says, and now they fly. He associates this with his own understanding of the animal, the lioness, and this causes Henderson to think how he has chosen the pig as his own animal, in a fit of opposition to a Jewish friend who was to breed mink in the Catskills.

Henderson's pig-keeping, in its bizarre energy and doomed violence, is brilliantly done, and is part of a larger vision of the relations between human imagination and the animal world, partly totemic, partly animistic, playing the primitive perceptions of wholeness against the modern desire to recover that sense of wholeness without the primitive closeness. There are the Arnewi cattle in their patience, and the frogs in their watery tomb. There is Henderson's vision of the octopus in the aquarium at Banyuls, at the beginning of the novel, which offers him a vision of a universe of death, and is surely associated with the giant squid who appears as the apotheosis of meaninglessness in *Moby-Dick*—"an unearthly, formless, chance-like apparition of life."[27] Dahfu quotes the scientist Kepler on the breathing life of the planet; Henderson sees the deathliness of the octopus in scientific terms:

> I looked in at an octopus, and the creature seemed also to look in at me and press its soft head to the glass, flat, the flesh becoming pale and granular—blanched, speckled. But even more speaking, even more cold, was the soft head with its speckles and the Brownian motion in those speckles, a cosmic coldness in which I felt I was dying. . . . I thought, 'This is my last day. Death is giving me notice.' (p. 18)

The penultimate lion, who kills Dahfu, is also experienced as death and reality, but hotly, not coldly. There are similarities between Henderson's situation in the lion trap and Effingham's in the bog—both are brought face to face with "the fact of death that stretches the length of life." Henderson says:

> it was no vision. The snarling of this animal was indeed the voice of death. And I thought how I had boasted to my dear Lily how I loved reality. 'I love it more than you do,' I had said. But oh, unreality! Unreality, unreality! That has been my scheme for a troubled but eternal life. But now I was blasted away from this practice by the voice of the lion. His voice was like a blow at the back of my head. (p. 307)

As in *The Unicorn,* civilised life, even art, even the imagination, are perhaps seen briefly here as strategies for conjuring with or avoiding the fact of death. In that light Henderson comes to see clearly and differently, to be able to return, accompanying a Persian child and the lion cub who is fraudulently and symbolically Dahfu. This vision of this fact succeeds and modifies the visions of the power of the imagination, without perhaps undoing them entirely.

Another aspect of Bellow's choice of the making of rain for the central narrative image of this novel is its relation to the central image of *The Waste Land.* As Eliot used the imagery of the dying god and the Fisher King to express the dryness and the spiritual thirst of his culture as he saw it, Bellow in his comedy uses primitive rain-making as an image for the same thing, and conveys how men, anthropomorphically, associate water with their own fertility and potency. There is a marvellous speech in the middle of *Henderson* where Henderson talks to Dahfu about the seeding of clouds with dry ice by scientists to make rain, and the origin of all life in the foam of the sea, which recalls though Henderson doesn't mention it, the birth of Aphrodite from the foam of the semen of castrated Cronos. Human beings, savages and civilised, make the world in their own image—note the metaphor in "seeding." It is in this context that Henderson's vision of the clouds from the aeroplane on his return journey is so moving. He is carried over "the calm swarm of the water, the lead-sealed but expanding water, the heart of the water." (Note again the metaphors, not magical, but human, adding human vision to the fact of water.)

> I couldn't get enough of the water, and of these upside-down sierras of the clouds. Like courts of eternal heaven. (Only they aren't eternal, that's the whole thing; they are seen once and will never be seen again,

being figures and not abiding realities; Dahfu will never be seen again, and presently I will never be seen again; but every one is given the components to see: the water, the sun, the air, the earth.) (p. 333)

Here is a peaceful, clear and demythologised vision that glories in metaphor but does not use it as magic or religion. Like Iris Murdoch, Bellow uses Frazer's stories and knowledge to show our involvement in myth and ritual and in some way both to show their necessity, indeed inevitability, and to release us from them.

Norman Mailer, *Armies of the Night,* and Muriel Spark, *The Takeover*

Bellow's great novel was written at a time when there was still a strong sense of the interconnection of myth and art, of the search for the spiritual in the forms of cultural inheritance illuminated by work such as Frazer's. When Mailer came to write *The Armies of the Night,* his "faction" account of the 1967 march on the Pentagon, the interest in the irrational, or the pre-rational, had spilt over into public life. Powell, Murdoch and even Bellow use fictive sorcery, invocations of demons and ancestors, totem and taboo systems to explore our civilised culture, its forms and its roots. The army of hippies and witches in Mailer's work attempted by real sorcery and magical rites to attack the "Pentagon of power" with the Pentagram of magic. Mailer refers to them as "a striking force of witches" and heads a chapter "The Armies of the Dead," referring partly to the poem by Lowell (also present on the march), "For the Union Dead," but also to the appearance of the marchers, parodically got up in ancient uniforms, Indian costumes and so on. The marchers represent, intellectuals and magicians alike, the belief in the potency, or omnipotence, of thought.

They attempt to raise the Pentagon three hundred feet with a ring of exorcism: "In the air the Pentagon would then, went the presumption, turn orange and vibrate until all evil emissions had fled this levitation. At that point the war in Vietnam would end." They invoke an eclectic collection of gods: "God, Ra, Jehovah, Anubis, Osiris, Tlaloc, Quetzalcoatl, Thoth, Ptah, Allah, Krishna, Chango, Chimeke, Chukwu, Olisa-Bulu-Uwa, Imales, Orisasu, Odudua, Kali, Shiva-Shakra, Great Spirit, Dionysus, Yahweh, Thor, Bacchus, Isis, Jesus Christ, Maitreya, Buddha, Rama . . ."—a list which must have grown out of the comparative labours of Frazer and others. Frazer would have no doubt been interested also to know that sexual magic took place: "For the first time in the history of the Pentagon there will be a grope-in within a hundred feet of this place, within two hundred feet. Seminal culmination in the spirit of peace and brotherhood, a real grope for peace" (pp. 132ff).

Mailer himself has a different point to make. He is afraid that the hippies, who are destroying their own genes with their drugs, are destroying their past, and with it death and the reality of death. The powers in the Pentagon can put out life and thus death with the bomb; the new drug culture, blowing the mind, is destroying with fantasy the sense of the real, the past, using demons indeed to annihilate ancestors:

> On which acidic journeys had the hippies met the witches and the devils and the cutting edge of all primitive awe, the savage's sense of explosion?—the fuse of blasphemy, the cap of taboo now struck, the answering roar of the Gods—for what was explosion but connections made at the rate of 10 to the 10th exponent of the average rate of a dialogue and its habitual answer?—had all the TNT and nuclear transcendencies of TNT exploded some devil's cauldron from the past?—was the past being consumed by the present? by nuclear blasts, and blasts into the collective living brain by way of all exploding acids, opiums, whiskeys, speeds and dopes?—the past was palpable to him, a tissue living in the tangible mansions of death, and death was disappearing, death was wasting of some incurable ill. When death disappeared there would be no life. (p. 135)

Here, reached from a quite different point, is the sense that it is the reality of death, which cannot be conjured away, that provides the central meaning of our life. Mailer appears to fear that the destruction of the past, of continuity, biological or cultural, will lead to some form of annihilation by demons. He speaks after all for reason and humaneness, in the middle of an orgy.

I have quoted this scene, which is only tangentially connected with *The Golden Bough,* because I want to suggest that after the Sixties the use of this work, and indeed the exploration of myth, became more difficult. Some continuities were broken. The appropriation of Dionysos by those dionysiacs made wise, sceptical, riddling reference to his continuous presence, such as that of *Death in Venice,* less accessible. What Mailer foresaw partly took place. The past, the ancestors, and Frazer with them, moved away rather quickly. We need instant myths, instant gratification, now.

In this context, however, Muriel Spark produced *The Takeover* (1985), a chilly modern comedy set in a house in Nemi overlooking "the scene of the tragedy"—a phrase Spark quotes from Frazer himself, and follows with a long citation of the description of the whole tale of the priesthood of Diana, the King of the Wood, and the fateful branch, the Golden Bough.

The house is leased to Hugo Mallindaine, who claims he is descended from the goddess Diana, and in a silly way sets up in his garden, aided by some modern "ecological priests," a silly modern cult of Artemis, which gets out of hand, but, despite Spark's usual cutting contempt for modern religious cults and fashions, is not funny or sinister enough. The plot concerns the machinations of the very rich, Italians and Americans, who "own" the land around the lake, though they turn out not to own the site of Hugo's house, which belongs to the stolid fiancée of the servant Lauro, a gilded youth (or golden bough?).

All this is interesting, in its sense of the superficiality of our perch on the plundered earth, but there is one sense in which Spark has made a new, very modern metaphor out of Frazer's grove, which is fascinating in its suggestiveness.

At dinner they spoke of Hubert and of to where they were all planning shortly to return. It was not in their minds at the time that this last quarter of the year they had entered, that of 1973, was in fact the beginning of something new in their world; a change in the meaning of property and money. They all understood these were changing in value, and they talked from time to time of recession and inflation, of losses on the stock market, failures in business, bargains in real estate: they habitually bandied the phrases of the newspaper economists and unquestioningly used the newspaper writers' figures of speech. They talked of hedges against inflation, as if mathematics could contain actual air and some row of hawthorn could stop an army of numbers from marching over it. They spoke of the mood of the stock market, the health of the economy as if these were living creatures with moods and blood. And thus they personalised and demonologised the abstractions of their lives, believing them to be fundamentally real, indeed changeless. But it did not occur to one of those spirited and in various ways intelligent people around Berto's table that a complete mutation of our means of nourishment had already come into being where the concepts of money and property were concerned, a complete mutation not merely to be defined as a collapse of the capitalist system, or a global recession, but such a sea-change in the nature of reality as could not have been envisaged by Karl Marx or Sigmund Freud. Such a mutation that what were assets were to be liabilities and no armed guard could be found and fed sufficient to guard those armed guards who failed to protect the properties they guarded, whether hoarded in banks, or built on confined territories, whether they were priceless works of art or merely hieroglyphics registered in the computers. Innocent of all this future they sat round the table and, since all were attached to Nemi, talked of Hubert. Maggie had him very much on her mind and the wormwood of her attention focussed on him as the battle in the Middle East hiccuped to a pause in the warm late October of 1973. (p. 107)

The "takeover" has become a matter of high finance, and the threatened temporary kings are the owners of property, vulnerable to the new supplanters and thieves.

This sense of doom is resolutely comic, and quite deliberately contrasted with Frazer's word for his takeover, the "scene of the *tragedy*." In this new world, tragedy, religion and true priesthood are alike flimsy and ridiculously parodic. Like other of Spark's novels this one must be read in the light of its author's Catholicism, which entails a belief that there is one eternal, though also indeed one temporal, Event, one historical Truth (and, indeed, one significant Death) in the light of which all other stories are approximate fictions—including, it would logically appear, Frazer's demythologising "tragedy" also.

Iris Murdoch, *The Good Apprentice*

I should like to conclude by looking at a recent novel by Iris Murdoch which returns to the matter of *The Golden Bough* and considers the seductions, uses and dangers of myth in a clear and moving way.

The Good Apprentice contrasts the fates of two young men, stepbrothers, Edward Baltram and Stuart Cuno. The title is riddling—partly derived from Hogarth's contrasted apprentices, one virtuous, one profligate, partly alluding to the Sorcerer's Apprentice. Both young men are in a sense apprentices to Good. Stuart is one of Murdoch's good men who decide to be good. He has no religious faith, so must be, as his author has said we must be in our day, "good for nothing." He practises celibacy, chastity and attention. Edward is a guilty man—he has given a drug to his best friend, who has fallen to his death. Edward is consumed by guilt. Stuart's life, like the life desiderated by the Abbess in *The Bell*, "has no story and is not tragic," though other characters attempt to drag him into theirs. Edward's, on the other hand, *is* tragic, and is crammed with storied coincidences like the Rat Man's omnipotent thoughts.

He receives a strange "message," from a medium whose name he finds on a piece of paper, that he should come to his father. The psychoanalyst of this story, a wise man who sees himself as the mage, Prospero, about to renounce his powers, sends Edward to his real father, comparing this specifically to sending him into the "underworld." Edward's father is a painter called Jesse Baltram—a Frazerian name, since Jesse is the name of the ancestor of David and Christ, whose name is at the foot of the Tree of Jesse in church windows, a Tree Spirit, and "Baltram" recalls the magic of Beltane fires. When Edward arrives at Seegard (compare the earlier Gaze Castle) he finds a family consisting of three women, "Mother May" (compare Frazer's passages on the May Queen) and her two daughters. At one level this household is a decayed version of the William Morrissey communes of the 1920s and has things in common with Dr. Trelawney's group in Powell. The women wear home-made garments, eat fruit and nuts and do handicrafts—which are comically useless and incompetent. The house is full of mythic jokes. The absent Jesse has named the leisure room the "Interfectory," whose sinister meaning Edward, a classicist, can understand, but the women seem not to. On the chimneypiece is "a long piece of carved wood on which, between interwoven leaves and fruits, was written, *I am here. Do not forget me*" (p. 111). (Et Ego in Arcadia? And, if in the Interfectory, is the "I" Death?) Edward takes pleasure in the fact that the three women are "three taboo women": *This* is part of it all, of the pattern or the destiny or the doom or whatever it is (p. 105).

The house is surrounded by "tree men," literally treecutters who threaten the avenue of poplars, but also wood spirits. Jesse, when found, is the captive king, half crazed, with immensely long and vital hair and fingernails, who still has powerful sexual appetites, lusts after his daughters and is seen as a satyr with furry haunches. There is a sacred "dromos" with a "lingam stone" where one of the girls dances magically without touching the ground. Jesse appears to Edmund under the water, the drowned god, but reappears somewhere else. When he does die, Mother May asserts wildly, "He has metamorphosed himself. He has taken on some other form to renew his strength. He is lying in the woods in a trance, he has become something brown and small like a chrysalis, imperceptibly stirring with the force of a new life" (p. 320). Just before this remark, Edward, looking for Jesse, "reached the path which was so like a stairway made of the roots of trees, stepping upon the crackling brown fruitage of oak and ash and beech which lay before his feet like tiny sacrificial images of gods."

The whole of this part of the text is, as it were, soaked in vegetation myths and the uses made of them by popularisers, by literatures and sub-literatures, since Frazer and his predecessors. It is beautiful at times. It is, more importantly, seedy, sinister, run-down and plain incompetent. If Jesse's art is cruel but powerful, the women's art is neither beautiful nor useful. There is one splendidly funny wooden object, shaped like an elongated bird:

'How do you keep that on?' . . .
　'Oh you put it on your wrist and tie it on with a scarf. Or hang it around your neck with a leather thong, you can tie it here, round the bird's foot.'
　'But then the bird will be upside down.'
　'Does that matter?' (p. 162)

It might be observed that the whole atmosphere of tree gods and fertility rites, and dying and resurrected father-kings is a little tired, a little *déjà vu*. But that is precisely the point of the way in which they are presented. The light is murky; the life has gone out of it all. The girls can only play one tune properly, Ilona tells Edward, who says,

'And you used to weave.'
　'Used to, yes. There was something, it's like remembering history, something long ago to do with salvation by work, and it was anti-religious and anti-God, that was a point, a sort of socialism, and like a kind of magic too, and being beyond good and evil and *natural* and *free*—that's what's so tragic, it was something beautiful, but the spirit's gone, it's gone bad, perhaps it was always sort of too deep a kind of knowledge, with something wrong about it, or rather we failed, *we* failed, he was too great for us—but that's what made Jesse so alive and full of power and *wonderful* as he used to be, as if he could live forever. And of course we had to be happy and we *were* happy, I can remember that, and now we have to pretend to be happy, like nuns who can never admit that they made a mistake and that it has all become just a prison.' (p. 200)

Edward works out his salvation amongst these dying myths—including Arts and Crafts socialism and Nietzschean morality, beyond good and evil. His story began with drugs and a crime, and is involved in art and magic.

Stuart's story is by contrast austere. He demythologises and strips the human spirit. Thomas, the magian psychoanalyst, suggests to him that he may envy Edward "his extreme situation."

'No, why should I?' said Stuart, surprised.
'It's one method of breaking up illusions of self-satisfaction.'

But Stuart is suspicious of stories and resists mystery.

'It's dark inside, Stuart.'
'You mean original sin. I'm not concerned with those guilt stories. Oh, of course, you mean the unconscious mind!'
'Don't tell me you don't believe in it.'
'Nothing so positive. I don't fancy the idea. It doesn't interest me.'
'Perhaps you interest it. Don't despise the concept. It's not just an abode of monsters, it's a reservoir of spiritual power.'
'Spirits. Magic. No, I don't like what you've just said. It's a misleading bad idea.' (p. 141)

And Thomas reflects that "The dark powers, as the ancients knew, were essentially ambiguous, and thus, as Stuart instinctively perceived, enemies of morality."

Critics of the novel perceived Stuart as somehow horrible, thus echoing Jesse, who, brought face to face with him, cries out, "There's a dead man, you've got a corpse there, it's sitting at the table. . . . That man's dead, take him away, I curse him. Take that white thing away, it's dead" (p. 292). Stuart, that is, represents among other things the bare recognition of the *simple* "fact of death that stretches the length of life." He is part of Iris Murdoch's recurring debate between the saint and the artist, and, if Edward's tragic story is redeemed by art, Stuart's is redeemed by attention to unadorned facts and rejection of magic. Stuart too has his journey to the underworld. He tries to meditate in a church, and can't stay. He descends into Oxford Circus Underground station, and feels "a new and dreadful feeling of shame, a shameful loneliness and sadness and grief, as if he were both banished from the human race and condemned for eternity to be a useless and detested witness of its sufferings" (p. 447). He looks into the dark, onto

> the black sunken concrete floor of the track. Then he saw that there right down at the bottom something was moving as if alive. He frowned and focussed his eyes. He stared. It was a mouse, a live mouse. The mouse ran a little way along beside the wall of the pit, then stopped and sat up. It was eating something. Then it came back again, casting about. It was in no hurry. It was not trapped. *It lived there*.

The energy of the novel, despite the power of Edward's guilt and grief, is on the side of the simplicity of Stuart's attempts to strip himself of the tangle of habits and beliefs and rituals that are in some sense represented by the Seegard house and the power of Jesse's art and male presence. (Though at the end of the book "Jesse lives" is found written on walls.) The mouse is in a sense the fact of life, which is in some way the same thing as the fact of death, seen simply, and as a kind of revelation of truth, or reality.

(1990)

8

People in Paper Houses: Attitudes to "Realism" and "Experiment" in English Post-war Fiction

I

Much of the debate about appropriate form in the English novel since the war has been concerned with the acceptance or rejection of appropriate or inappropriate models. Thus what has been called the "reaction against experiment" of the 1950s was much preoccupied with rejecting the model of James Joyce and Virginia Woolf. We had C. P. Snow's reductive description of the innovations of these two writers as "a method, the essence of which was to represent brute experience through moments of sensation";[1] we had the linked complaints of Kingsley Amis: "The idea about experiment being the life-blood of the English novel is one that dies hard. 'Experiment' in this context boils down pretty regularly to 'obtruded oddity,' whether in construction . . . or in style; it is not felt that adventurousness in subject matter or attitude or tone really counts."[2] The "avant-garde" of the 1960s and 1970s have now rejected this rejection, declaring that the "nineteenth-century novel," with which many novelists of the 1950s felt a continuity, is the convention now leading novelists into bad faith, and a perverse ignorance of the revolution that was effected once and for all by Joyce, the "Einstein of the novel." Thus we have the desperately hectoring voice of B. S. Johnson, berating writers who do not realise that "literary forms do become exhausted, clapped out . . . ," and that "the nineteenth-century novel" was finished by the outbreak of the First World War: "No matter how good the writers are who now attempt it, it cannot be made to work for our time, and the writing of it is anachronistic, invalid, irrelevant and perverse." Johnson's description of the nineteenth-century novel is, in fact, quite as inadequate as was Snow's account of the modernist experiment. For him, its wrongness is that it tells a story—and "telling stories is telling lies."[3]

These irritable territorial definitions have taken place against the background of a critical discussion of contemporary fiction which has been, in this country, decidedly thin; and against a critical lore which has been—and this is important—characteristically moral and prescriptive. We have the Great Tradition. We have John Bayley's *The Characters of Love* (1960), an immediately attractive and sympathetic book—particularly, I suspect, to writers—which distinguishes the literature of Nature from the literature of the Human Condition, and advocates a realism, characteristically English, which depends on love, in author and reader, for characters as separate individuals. Related to this is Iris Murdoch's essay of 1961, "Against Dryness"—a "polemical sketch" pleading for a return to the realistic depiction of "free, separate" characters as a way out of a philosophical solipsism and a simple welfare utilitarianism we have too easily embraced. Iris Murdoch gives clear and good historical reasons why it is not now possible simply to mimic the nineteenth-century realists, and certainly her novels do not themselves do so. Nonetheless, her prescription is roughly the same as John Bayley's. We must *learn from* tradition—from Shakespeare, and the nineteenth-century novelists, especially the Russians. Bernard Bergonzi's *The Situation of the Novel* (1970) is extremely sympathetic to Bayley's position; it does, though, share B. S. Johnson's anxious sense that modern English realism is "no longer novel," but depends on exhausted forms and concepts. The paradox is, according to Bergonzi, that the most vital contemporary literature is also totalitarian and dehumanising, and as for his examples of that vitality they are French and American, not English: Heller, Pynchon, Burroughs, Mailer, Robbe-Grillet, Genet. There are similar anxieties in David Lodge's *The Novelist at the Crossroads* (1971); Lodge's crossroads mark the paths pointing away from realism, but he nonetheless offers "a modest affirmation of faith in the future of realistic fiction"—a faith that can be reasonably borne out by a look at the kinds of novels many writers today are publishing.

Behind that Great Tradition, there is, of course, the spirit of "Tradition and the Individual Talent." "But we *know* so much more than they did," protests T. S. Eliot's hypothetical artist, asked to contemplate his forebears;

"Precisely," replies the voice of authority. "And they are that which we know." It was Eliot who complained that our literature was a substitute for religion, and so was our religion. Respect for the tradition of the realist novel is apparently a very rooted fact, and is inextricably involved in a very complex set of responses to the decline of religion and the substitution of a Religion of Humanity. The fictional texts of the Great Tradition are indeed the texts of the Religion of Humanity, and many novelists now seem to feel that they exist in some uneasy relation to the afterlife of these texts, as the texts themselves once coexisted with the afterlife of Genesis and the Gospels. They are the source of enlightenment, but not true. Or not true for us.

Thus it seems that much formal innovation in recent English fiction has concerned itself, morally and aesthetically, with its forebears, and in a way for which I know no exact parallel in other literatures. This has its dangers: as Nathalie Sarraute declared, in "Rebels in a World of Platitudes," the true enemy of good art is not mass society or technology, but "the only real, the deadly danger, the great works of the past,"[4] which must be absorbed and rejected simultaneously. This is, of course, the anxiety of influence, of which Harold Bloom is the prophet.[5] This anxiety, in the English novel now, seems to operate in odd ways—with and against the moral force of the Great Tradition, which still exerts its power, to produce forms sometimes limp, sometimes innovatory, sometimes paradoxical, occasionally achieved, and sometimes simply puzzling. The state is recognisable; but traditional critical methods for the study of influence and of plagiarism are often distracting here. When Dr. Leavis isolated the ways in which James's *The Portrait of a Lady* is a reworking of part of Eliot's *Daniel Deronda,* he was pointing to a kind of "reader's greed" in the writer which is, in fact, perfectly characteristic of George Eliot's own work. I take it that some need both to reread, and to better, certain stories that caught her imagination was behind her own reworking of an episode from Gottfried Keller in the climax of *The Mill on the Floss;* of the description of George Sand's Jacques as a St. Teresa born out of his time, in *Middlemarch;* or of the animated tableaux from Goethe's *Wahlverwandtschaften* in *Daniel Deronda.* Not parody, not pastiche, not plagiarism—but a good and greedy reading, by a great writer. The phenomenon, then, is not novel. And yet it inevitably looks different in modern novels—because of the pressure of the past, because of the accumulation of literary criticism and because of the weight of anxiety as it shows itself in modern form.

II

Perhaps a paradigmatic case is the development of the career of Angus Wilson. In an illuminating interview with Jonathan Raban, Wilson said, "I nearly always feel when I'm writing a scene that this has been written before." Raban comments, "But life itself tends constantly to the second-hand; our responses are so conditioned, our behaviour so stereotyped, that it is immensely hard for us to extricate ourselves from these literary precedents which plot the course of our own feelings and actions." Wilson's "literariness," Raban adds, is a function of his characters, who read and use literature to interpret their lives, and is not, in this, like "the formal allusiveness of most modernist writing."[6] Indeed, the hero of Angus Wilson's first novel, *Hemlock and After* (1952), is a writer, Bernard Sands. And Angus Wilson requires of his reader that he inhabit Sands's experience, including the writing, but imaginatively, in a "realist" way. The essence of this experience is a vision of aimless evil which undercuts the meliorism of Sands's traditional humanist position, and comes perilously close to undercutting the Religion of Humanity itself. Sands is, like George Eliot, like Angus Wilson, a person who controls an acid wit and a natural cruelty in the interests of justice. His opponent, fat and smiling Mrs. Curry, the procuress, is a two-dimensional Dickensian vision of something irrational, predatory and powerful. Both characters are nineteenth-century, the good one centrally "realist" in morals and presentation, the bad one (whom the reviewers found paradoxically "thin" at the time) suggesting, with hindsight, possibilities of "experimental" fiction techniques, derived from Dickens's grotesque. (Dickens has been behind other "experimental" variants of realism, notably those of Paul Bailey.)

Meg Eliot, in *The Middle Age of Mrs Eliot* (1958), remains, I think, Wilson's most successful attempt at the Jamesian ideal of sustained, inner imagining of a character. She, too, is literary, and has her personal collection of texts, characterised as "the escape she and David had found in the past. *Emma, The Mill on the Floss, The Small House at Allington, The Portrait of a Lady* . . . the basic necessities of the voyage." Reviewers and critics pounce on literary clues in our time. It has been pointed out that all these novels have impulsive, passionate heroines, whose fate is to suffer from forcing their own fantasising vision on reality; that Meg Eliot is in their tradition and is, indeed, their heir. But there are germs of discomfort here. The novels are explicitly "an escape in the past"; Meg's identification with the heroines brings no access of wisdom, but a child-like evasion of present misery. David's literary work, like his boyhood pleasure in "the sad futilities of Emma Bovary's debts," is an evasion of reality. Is this like George Eliot's exposé of Dorothea's desire to dedicate herself to "Milton, when he was old," or is it a doubt about literature itself?

Literary references are also central, obtrusive and pervasive in *No Laughing Matter* (1967), but in a different fashion. The Matthews family's Game deals with unpleasant realities by parody, pastiche, farcical mockery. The Game discovers, exploits, elaborates the sexual, political and aesthetic traits of the characters. It is a primitive, crude and vigorous form of the art of the writer, Margaret, the actor, Rupert, the twee "writings" of the self-deluded Susan, the high camp of Marcus. The characters use the Game, and the Game, directed by Angus Wilson, uses them. He derealises them with overt manipulation, in lengthy parodies of Ibsen, Shaw, Chekhov, Bennett, framing them in a plurality of styles. The result is not realism, but is intimately and uncomfortably related to it. This is because, although Wilson's insistence on the "second-hand" quality of his people and their world renders them papery and insubstantial, they do nevertheless think and feel, and author requires of reader an imaginative response to thought and feeling which belongs with realism.[7] A reverberation is set up between their literary factitiousness and their own sense of this, corresponding to their author's sense of a similar problem in himself and his work, which produces a new, a novel kind of acute disorder and discomfort in the reading experience. This discomfort is intensified in *As If by Magic* (1973), to which I shall return. In that novel, as Raban says, the characters proceed by asking themselves, "How would Birkin, or Myshkin, or Alice, or a Hobbit have felt about this . . .": their answers to these questions produce ludicrously parodic behaviour: the texture of the novel is insistent on its own farcical fictiveness, suggesting that all life is a ghastly fiction "behind" which stands no ratifying or eternal vision of a corresponding reality. When Alexandra declares, "I know I am a fictive device," we are aware that we are out of the world of the realist novel and its norms and in the familiar world of the experimental novel, which proclaims its own artifice and comments on its own procedures. What I want to emphasise at this point is the curiously symbiotic relationship between old realism and new experiment, the way in which Alexandra as "device" grew out of Meg as typical humane reader.

III

An analogous sense of the ambiguous power and restrictiveness of the tradition goes to create the difficulties readers have with the surface of Iris Murdoch's work. She calls herself a realist, and claims that she is in the English tradition: her progress as a whole has been in the opposite direction from Angus Wilson's.[8] *Under the Net* (1954) contains elements of deliberate parody and surreal joke, and is partly a philosophical game with Wittgenstein and Sartre. It corrects, or rereads, *La Nausée* by rewriting scenes of it. Iris Murdoch complained that Sartre "had an impatience, fatal to a novelist proper, with the *stuff* of human life . . ." and lacked "an apprehension of the absurd, irreducible uniqueness of people, and of their relations with each other."[9] Critics have ponderously accused Miss Murdoch of failures in density—"the serious novel calls for intensity of characterization," says F. R. Karl, whereas Iris Murdoch's comedies "frequently decline into triviality."[10] This criticism fails to recognise that *Under the Net* is a fable *about realism,* a conceptual game about the need for the concepts, language and emotional movements of a new realism. It is not intended itself to be a densely realist work.

Her later novels are the result of a sustained attempt, moral and formal, at the realism she and John Bayley admire. When I read *The Bell* in 1959, I felt that something odd was happening; I was able imaginatively to inhabit a fictional universe, to care about the people and their fate, in what I judged to be a "good" book, in a way I thought, then, was confined to my reading of nineteenth-century novels and my stock of non-literary "bad" books or children's books. By *An Unofficial Rose* (1962), my sense of achieved imaginative reality was much more strained. The reason was the obtrusive presence of Henry James, and with him, of John Bayley's reading of *The Golden Bowl;* of Jane Austen, and with her, of Lionel Trilling's reading of *Mansfield Park.* This is difficult, as I suspect the imaginative process involved for Iris Murdoch in writing *An Unofficial Rose* was not essentially different from George Eliot's greedy reworking of Goethe. *An Unofficial Rose* cannot be called parodic, but a trained reader senses its relation to the past in a way that makes its fictional world less accessible, less immediate to the imagination.

Related to this, maybe, is a frequently voiced view that Miss Murdoch is confining her attentions to the "wrong" kind of characters, an "irrelevant" group of the upper bourgeoisie. In terms of her own morality, there is no reason why she should not do so. Free and separate persons can be studied in any social setting. I think part at least of the readers' dissatisfaction is aesthetic, to do with the pressure of the Tradition, which was made by such a society, for such a society, and helped to create and perpetuate it. These are the people of James's and Forster's fiction, and this, perhaps, makes them feel artificial and unreal even where they are not. "Man is a creature who makes pictures of himself and then comes to resemble the picture," Miss Murdoch has said. The world she studies has already "come to resemble" the world of the Victorian and modernist novelists, having seen itself in their mirrors. To be realistic about this world is to encounter pervasive and powerful images of it, in itself, in novels, in readers, which make the imaginative process thinner, more second-hand, more difficult. *An Unofficial Rose* is curiously like *The Middle Age of Mrs Eliot,* even down to its setting and controlling imagery of natural and artificial flowers. They are alike in their attempt at density, and in the literary reverberations which intensify and thin that attempt.

Later still, Miss Murdoch achieved, I think, a striking degree of success as a realist by shifting, partly, her model. The plots of several later novels are parodies, overt, acknowledged by the characters, of Shakespearean plots. *The Nice and the Good* (1968), *A Fairly Honourable Defeat* (1970), *The Black Prince* (1973) play games with *A Midsummer Night's Dream, Much Ado, Hamlet.* These plots could be called experimental devices, obtrusive, making no claims to psychological probability, or development, such as George Eliot or James would have felt essential. They, too, are related to Dickens's comic plotting. Their formality has liberated an imaginative space for reader and character to inhabit; their artifice has created a new-old language for realism. It is this kind of discrimination that makes wholesale advocacy, or rejection, of particular periods and writers, as models, so unhelpful.

In this context one might be able to place the disturbing power and ambiguous effect of David Storey's *Radcliffe* (1963), a novel that derives its terrible energies from a combination of personal obsession, genuinely new realistic observation of things hitherto unobserved and the absorbing literary greed of huge talent. Storey once spoke of the split in himself that developed when he was playing professional rugger in the North to support himself as a student at the Slade in London. *Radcliffe* is about the split, in the artist, between mind and body, mirrored in the split between labourers and a decadent aristocracy, placed against the tradition of English puritanism and the disturbing central figure of Cromwell. Radcliffe and Tolson, intellectual and workman, in their violent attempts either to become incorporate with each other or to destroy each other, mirror, Radcliffe declares in his visionary insanity, "the split in the whole of Western society . . ." and "the division that separates everything in life now, *everything*." The novel makes a heroic attempt at an aesthetic totality like that of the great modernists, offering its protagonists as types of fundamental truths, historical, social, religious, intellectual, biological together, incorporating precise factual records of tent-contracting work with a neo-Brontë, neo-Gothic visionary Yorkshire landscape, a Christian theory of guilt with a Freudian theory of culture, and all with a series of daemonic literary parodies that are almost, not quite, a new form in themselves.

The early chapters of *Radcliffe* I found, on a first reading, paradoxically new and exciting because they had placed, realist, density of observation and imagination. The style was cool, controlled and very energetic: one had a powerful sense of an impending fictional world both thought out and realised. Storey has said that the opening was inspired by the opening of *Madame Bovary*. It reads as a pure example of the greed of novelist-as-reader. The major voices behind the rest of the novel are Lawrence and Dostoevsky. The relation between Tolson and Radcliffe draws on those of Gerald and Birkin, Myshkin and Rogozhin. The style swings wildly between the phantasmagoric grotesque of an American-Gothic comic drama and a Lawrentian intellectual nagging and insistent noise. Radcliffe's fate is Myshkin's, withdrawn, insane, in a silly peace, dead. Lawrentian hollyhocks sprout under Wuthering Heights. It is as though Storey had made as ferocious and doomed and violent an attempt to incorporate literature as Tolson and Radcliffe make on each other. One could compare this to Thomas Mann's incorporation, in *Doctor Faustus,* of Goethe, Nietzsche, Dostoevsky, but the effect is entirely different. Angus Wilson's parodies are joky and papery; Thomas Mann's an act of intellectual appropriation and cultural commentary; Storey's are almost vampiric. That they spring from the same uncomfortable relation to a Tradition as those of Murdoch and Wilson is undeniable, and the reader's sense of muffled power and involuntary thinness is analogous. But it is not the same.

IV

The relation to past novels brings certain firmly "realist" works and certain declared experimental works curiously close together. John Fowles, in *The French Lieutenant's Woman* (1969), writes a Victorian novel within a novel. Within this story the reader is allowed, invited, both to experience imaginatively the sexual urgency and tension it evokes and to place such imagining as a function of that kind of story, that kind of style and, Fowles suggests, that period of history. Obtruded authorial comments offer a "modern" justification of this procedure that has a faintly Murdochian ring. Chapter 12 ends with a Victorian rhetorical question: "Who is Sarah? Out of what shadows does she come?" Chapter 13 opens with a "modern" authorial statement:

> I do not know. The story I am telling is all imagination. These characters I create never existed outside my own mind. If I have pretended until now to know my characters' minds and innermost thought it is because I am writing in (just as I have assumed some of the vocabulary and 'voice' of) a convention universally accepted at the time of my story: that the novelist stands next to God . . . But I live in the age of Alain Robbe-Grillet and Roland Barthes; if this is a novel, it cannot be a novel in the modern sense of the word.
>
> There is only one good definition of God: the freedom that allows other freedoms to exist. . . . The novelist is still a god, since he creates (and not even the most aleatory avant-garde novel has managed to extirpate its author completely); what has changed is that we are no longer the gods of the Victorian image, omniscient and decreeing; but in the new theological image, with freedom as first principle, not authority.

Fowles's understanding of Victorian life and literature is crude and derived from the Bloomsbury rejection of it, which makes his technical nostalgia fascinating as a phenomenon. His theory of "freedom" leads to the experimental alternative endings to the novel, which painfully destroy the narrative "reality" of the central events, which have happily understood authorial shifts in style, interjections and essays on Victorian reality. Fowles claims he did not control his characters, but his projected endings do not suggest a plurality of possible stories. They are a programmatic denial of the reality of any. The future tense, like the future, is a creative lie—necessarily a fiction, as George Steiner has pointed out. But these alternative endings are neither future nor conditional, but fixed, Victorian, narrative past. They therefore cancel each other out, and cancel their participants, rendering Fowles as arbitrary a puppet-maker as he declared his desire not to be. For the writer, whilst the plural endings are possibilities in the head, they intensify the reality of the future world. For the reader, now, they reduce it to paperiness again. (Fowles can manipulate tenses better than this. Chapter 16 opens with some authorial sagacities and apostrophes about Victorian life, and continues in the present tense, with Ernestina's reading of *The Lady of La Garaye*. Two paragraphs later, Fowles is back with his love-story between Sarah and Charles, and in the habitable past tense. *The Lady of La Garaye,* extensively quoted, is thin, high Victorian emotional cliché, possible for Ernestina to be moved by then, blandly farcical now. The present tense, cinematic, distancing, displays her, and it, for judgment. The reader effortlessly and pleasurably switches from watching to imagining with the change of tense. It is a nice game, a typically English experimental game, with layers of literary precedents and nostalgias.)

Such habits of reading can lead to "framing" of passages not presumably intended for it. Here, in another author, is Lord Ryle, pondering his possible love for a woman who

wasn't even really in his taste. Too sharp, too narrow, not free enough. He hadn't been meeting many women, it was a chance and a pity that she had come along. She wouldn't have suited him, nor would he have been much good to her.

In all that he was probably right. There was another reflection which wouldn't have consoled him. The chances with possible partners whom one met produced a sense of fatality: so ought the chances of possible partners whom one didn't meet. The division bell had rung just as Ryle was about to be introduced to Jenny Rastall. As it happened, and it was pure chance, they didn't speak to each other that night, and were not to meet again until it was too late. . . .

It was possible that they were, as Ryle's old mother would have said, made for each other. No one could predict that for certain, there was no one alive who knew them both well, and there was only one test, which they alone could have proved. From their habits, affections, tastes and natures though, it seems more likely than not that they could have fitted one another: certainly more completely than with anyone they actually found. Which, in his mood that evening, Ryle, not a specially sardonic man, would have considered not a specially good joke.

This is a Trollopian authorial interjection, of the chatty kind that James considered a wanton violation of realism, a "suicidal satisfaction in reminding the reader that the story he was telling was only, after all, a make-believe."[11] But, in the context of Fowles's games with authorial interjections, this chapter-ending of C. P. Snow's looks like a game with the conventions of plot, character, probability. It discusses what did not happen, what could not have happened, what the character "would consider" a good joke. Snow is no aesthetician: the qualities he prizes are "a living tradition; reflection; moral awareness; the investigating intelligence."[12] His novels, judged by Jamesian criteria of social realism, or verisimilitude, have been found thin and dry. Yet large areas of Snow's *In Their Wisdom* (1974), if they are read as a self-conscious game with a modern neglect of Victorian themes (death, money) and devices (authorial omniscience), take on the same derivative papery energy as Angus Wilson's puppet-show.

V

All I have so far said could be considered reflection on the use, conscious and unconscious, of the *déjà dit* in current fiction. I would go further and claim that much aggressively "experimental" fiction uses much more distracting devices, in part to legitimise echoes of old styles and straightforward realisms. J. G. Farrell writes omniscient prose, about the past, in the past tense, using a tough narrative voice to prevent his work appearing to be either pastiche or uneasy current Victoriana. But much of John Berger's *G.* (1972) has the same virtues—real, concrete imagining of the past, somehow permitted to be by a politically and linguistically self-conscious framework. The same is true of B. S. Johnson's holes, serifs, columnar and shuffled printed surfaces. Through and athwart them we glimpse a plain, good, unfussy, derivative realist prose that can somehow only come about by declaring that *that* is not what it meant to be, not what it meant at all.

Parody and pastiche are particularly literary ways of pointing to the fictiveness of fiction, gloomily or gleefully. And there is now, amongst some novelists, an almost obsessive concern with the nature of truth and lies, with the problems of veracity, which has also taken oddly "literary" forms. Some of this concern is to do with the history of realist fiction, and later of modernism. George Eliot's scientific "experiments in life" illustrated laws of probability and development which are now seen much more as hypothesis and much less as "truth" than in her time. The aesthetic unities of the high modernists can be experienced as reductive. The apparent flux of *Mrs Dalloway*, even the resistance of Indian reality to Western vision and plotting in *A Passage to India*, are in fact controlled, orchestrated by the writers' metaphors for chaos. And these idiosyncratic visions are only too easy to reject if they seem to claim the status of truth, especially if the reader is looking for "the truth." Virginia Woolf's metaphors require an assent which seems, in certain moods, and particularly for writers, too simple and too exclusive to grant.

There is also our increasing sophistication about the way in which we construct our own world. We study theories of perception and illusion, which show how our biology and its history condition our vision. We study our languages and their limitations, again in terms of biology and history. We deflect our attention from what we perceive to the way in which we perceive it, and this has had its effect on the structure of the novel. Iris Murdoch, discussing Sartre's view of the sickness of language, claimed that "our awareness of language has altered in the fairly recent past. We can no longer take language for granted as a medium of communication. We are like people who for a long time looked out of a window without noticing the glass—and then one day began to notice this too." This self-conscious-ness made the poet feel that "the whole referential character of language had become a sort of irritant or stumbling block. It was as if the poet began to see the world with a dreadful particularity. . . . To lose the discursive 'thingy' nature of one's vision and yet to feel the necessity of utterance is to experience a breakdown of language."[13] This raises problems for the realist novelist even more than for the poet, as Miss Murdoch knows: it is part of Jake's conceptual problem in *Under the Net*.

Gabriel Josipovici, in *The World and the Book* (1971), isolates what he calls "demonic analogy" as a function of modern self-consciousness about lan-guage. For Dante, analogies revealed the mirroring of eternal verities in temporal phenomena. For modern writers

> to discover correspondence in the world around us does not lead to the sensation that we are inhabiting a meaningful universe; on the contrary, it leads to the feeling that what we had taken to be 'the world' is only the projection of our private compulsions: *analogy* becomes a sign of *dementia*. . . . We become aware of it with a shock of recognition, suddenly realizing, what we had dimly sensed all along, that what we had taken to be infinitely open and 'out there' was in reality a bounded world bearing the shape only of our own imagi-nation. . . . The effect of demonic analogy is to rob events of their solidity.[14]

Events are also robbed of their solidity, it has frequently been suggested, by the nature of "modern reality" itself. I am chary about using this phrase, which means all things to all men, from the black heaven untenanted of its God to the television screen flickering with silently screaming children flickering with napalm, or alternatively with the Galloping Gourmet's flambéed soufflé flickering with burning brandy, from social descriptions of "real" homeless families and "unreal" jet sets to psychological deductions from the observed effect on kittens of raising them in a vertically striped or horizontally barred "environment." "Reality" in fiction is ambiguously and uncertainly related to "true facts." Dostoevsky's phantasmagoric and frenetically jerky plots result partly from his fascination with the *improbable* truths of newspaper reports, the murderer who surrounded his corpse with little open bottles of disinfectant to keep off flies. Mary McCarthy in *The Fact in Fiction* argues intelligently that the traditional "facts" of the social novel are now hard to recognise, whilst we are culturally obsessed by facts, Hiroshima, Auschwitz, which are unimaginable because "their special quality is to stagger belief." Such facts render our local world "improbable, unveracious." She concludes: "the novel, with its common sense, is of all forms the least adapted to encompass the modern world, whose leading characteristic is irreality."[15] B. S. Johnson and Giles Gordon, largely without examples, likewise claim that "modern" reality, as opposed to "nineteenth-century" reality, is "chaotic, fluid, random," and our fictional forms must reflect this.[16]

B. S. Johnson is obsessed by truth-telling. So is Iris Murdoch, whose precisely moving rhetoric in "Against Dryness" offers a placing of the word "reality" in a philosophically and historically meaningful context. Johnson's truth-telling entails the abandoning of "stories" as lies, and reduces his subject-matter to a carefully structured autobiography. Iris Murdoch's truth-telling involves an abandoning of solipsism, a recognition that "reality" is other than ourselves, an Eliot-like ideal of the impersonal artist, a return to the "hard idea of truth" as opposed to the facile idea of sincerity. Roquentin in *La Nausée* sees that there are "no stories," because what exists is formless: Miss Murdoch says art is "adventure stories," a necessary technique for discovering truth. Non-realistic autobiography: "impersonal" story-telling—exactly opposite solutions to the problem of the nature of lies and the difficulty of truth.

In *Albert Angelo* (1964), Johnson uses Albert the architect as a paradigm of Johnson, the poet, supporting himself by supply teaching. He plays games—a hole in page 149 reveals a knife-blow which on page 153 is revealed to be the death of Christopher Marlowe, the future glimpsed in the book being in fact the historical past. This is part of the "playfulness" of a novel which is reminding us of its own status as artefact, but Johnson in his outburst at the end claims that his intention in making the hole was "didactic: the novel must be a vehicle for conveying truth, and to this end every device and technique of the printer's art should be at the command of the writer. . . . To dismiss such techniques as gimmicks, or to refuse to take them seriously, is crassly to miss the point." I find this hard to focus or understand. "Truth" in this context is general enough to be meaningless. Clearer is the outburst in which he explodes his illusion:

—fuck all this lying look what im really trying to write about is writing. . . .
   —im trying to say something not tell a story telling stories is telling lies and i want to tell the truth about me about my experience about my truth about my truth to reality about sitting here writing . . .

Aesthetic solipsism, certainly, and a genuine desperation. Later in this section Johnson discusses his fictive substitutions: the girl was called Muriel not Jenny, Balgy was in Scotland not Ireland, the dogs ate Fidomeat not Felixmeat. . . . Lies, lies, lies, rages Johnson, and cannot, *dare* not, be interested in the imaginative process which compels people, writers, to effect such substitutions. Yet this process is an essential part of human thought. He is a case of a born writer, part paralysed, part humiliated, part impelled, part sustained, by an absurd and inadequate theory which is nevertheless a clue to the anxieties of subtler men.

A more complicated response to the problem of veracity and the fictive is Julian Mitchell's *The Undiscovered Country* (1968). This consists of two parts, the first a realist, indeed, factual narrative by the "true" Julian Mitchell, supported by a cast of real people and a plot of real events, about his fictional friend Charles, author of the *New Satyricon,* which is the second part. Within this veracious and conventional first part the two writers discuss the nature of fiction, including their view that they live in a "postliterary" age, and the difficulties of the novel, which is "an impure art-form, inextricably rooted in the real world." Charles criticises the unreal conventionality of "Julian's" (factual) earlier novels, on the ground that they are reticent and untrue. The "sincere" and certainly *déjà dit* ideas and form of this realist section themselves take on a new, riddling energy and opacity when seen as part of the formally unreal, demonically analogic fable, the *New Satyricon,* itself a parody of "possibly the first novel" and containing gratuitous fables, parodies and puns (James Bond, pop music, rubber fetishist news sheets, possibly, Julian teasingly tells us, *actual* news sheets, since impossible to parody). The *New Satyricon* provides versions, visions, analogues of episodes in Part I, which change these. It also provides a "framing" literary critical structure, written by naïve Julian about Charles's "real" meanings—and this includes a parody of literary critical procedure. The novel as a whole, blandly riddling, secretly violent, provides an energetically literary criticism of the relation of the novel, the writer and his world. It plays games with truth, lies and the reader, teasing him with the knowledge that he cannot tell where veracity ends and games begin. It is the game all novelists play anyway, raised to a structural principle.

In this context one could add Muriel Spark's later games with plotting and fictiveness, in which the characters act as surrogate plotters, image-makers, newspaper-informers. One could add Fowles's *The Magus* (1966), a ponderously literary game with the writer as demiurge or puppet-master, and the most recent work of Dan Jacobson, whose *The Rape of Tamar* (1970) and *The Wonder-Worker* (1973) are interested in narration, narrative manipulation, and indeed the reasons for "telling stories" at all. *The Rape of Tamar* is particularly interesting in that its base narrative is an "inspired" biblical text, a canonical episode. Its narrator-manipulator presents it as a political, aesthetic and religious paradigm. Dan Jacobson's early *A Dance in the Sun* (1956) seems to me one of our few clear, good and strong examples of straight realism. He has said he felt a compulsion to describe South African society, which had not been described. In England, he wondered about the value of fiction, and felt that London had been too often described already. This suggests an oblique response to the pressure of the Tradition and the presence of the texts: what his early work proves is that realist narrative, in English, is not in itself either impossible or *déjà dit*. It is a question of subject-matter, as much as of the age of the form.

VI

Finally, three examples of novels which embody, in very different ways, the problems I have been discussing: an awareness of the difficulty of "realism" combined with a strong moral attachment to its values, a formal need to comment on their fictiveness combined with a strong sense of the value of a habitable imagined world, a sense that models, literature and "the tradition" are ambiguous and problematic goods combined with a profound nostalgia for, rather than rejection of, the great works of the past. The novels I have chosen are Iris Murdoch's *The Black Prince* (1973), Angus Wilson's *As If by Magic* (1973) and Doris Lessing's *The Golden Notebook* (1962).

The Black Prince, like *Under the Net,* is best read as a fable about the difficulties of realism, or truth-telling. It contains, like *Under the Net,* two novelists, one prolific and bad, one silent and good—at least in his own opinion, since he is the narrator, condemned (wrongly?) for the murder of the other. Baffin, the bad, distresses people by collecting the "facts" of their lives into his fiction, which Bradley characterises as "inquisitive chatter and cataloguing of things one's spotted," or "a congeries of amusing anecdotes loosely garbled into 'racy stories' with the help of a half-baked unmeditated symbolism. . . . Arnold Baffin wrote too much too fast. Arnold Baffin was just a talented journalist." If Baffin is journalistic, Bradley is crystalline, holding the Murdochian, Eliotian ideal of impersonality and "truth," believing in long suffering and apprenticeship, unable to speak at all. The novel is in fact Bradley's very Baffinesque account of his love for Baffin's daughter and its effect, tragic, comic and literary. A central episode turns on Bradley's disquisition on the paradoxical "truth-telling" in *Hamlet* where Shakespeare, the impersonal genius, wrote a riddling play in which he himself was in fact, for once, the central character, flayed like Marsyas by an Apollo both orderly, loving and cruel. Shakespeare, the true artist, of course combines Baffin and Bradley, reticence with prolific professionalism, endless facts with lucid poetry. *Hamlet* is Shakespeare's purification of the language by a riddling truth-telling. It "transmutes his private obsessions into a rhetoric so public that it can be mumbled by any child. He enacts the purification of speech, and yet also this is something comic, a sort of trick, like a huge pun, like a long almost pointless joke. . . . Being is acting. We are tissues and tissues of different *personae* and yet we are nothing at all. What redeems us is that speech is ultimately divine."

Bradley's tragi-grotesque account of his suffering is enclosed in fictive editorial matter written by Apollo Loxias, and containing various partial and very self-referring postscripts "by" several of the characters. Apollo is the puppet-master, explicitly, of this novel, setting the artists, including Shakespeare, dancing in their excruciatingly funny agonies. Bradley writes Murdoch-like prose on the difficulty of describing "characters," and claims that his "thin layered stuff of ironic sensibility . . . if I were a fictive character, would be that much deeper and denser." Apollo refutes the idea that he himself might be fictive. "I can scarcely be an invention of Bradley's, since I have survived him. Falstaff, it is true, survived Shakespeare, but did not edit his plays. I hear it has even been suggested that Bradley Pearson and myself are both simply fictions, the inventions of a minor novelist. Fear will inspire any hypothesis. No, no, I exist." Apollo, too, assures Julian Baffin that "Art is to do with joy and play and the absurd. . . . All human beings are figures of fun. Art celebrates this. Art is adventure stories."

So *The Black Prince* is a playful adventure story, a comic game, containing fiction within fiction, commentary (and allusion to commentary, Shakespearean, Murdochian) within fiction, ideas about realism endorsed by unreal fictional gods. It does not itself purify the language—Bradley's adventures are Murdochian farce and Murdochian tragi-comedy, his thoughts speak the language of her aesthetic essays which, in our time, are startlingly clear and vernacular. It raises the question of truth and lies, and offers an endless series of receding, unattainable, focused images of truth, but nothing believable, nothing habitable. Like *Under the Net,* it stands beside realism, a papery charade indicating in riddles what it is not doing, but is intensely concerned with.

As If by Magic is also a "literary" artefact, symbiotically involved both in realism and in the modernist aspirations to the completeness of myth. The central theme of "magic" incorporates the economic "miracle" of the new rice, Magic, in underdeveloped economies, the new Oriental, Arthurian, astrological and Tolkienesque cults of the 1960s flower children; and sexual-Lawrentian magic, a rescuing of our culture by "good sex," transfiguring the Dark Gods into beneficent spreaders of sweetness and light. The novel proceeds by indiscriminate literary parody. Hamo, the rice geneticist, with his servant, Erroll, is Frodo with Sam crossing Middle Earth; he is an *Arabian Nights* prince in search of The Most Beautiful Boy; he is a character from a Feydeau farce, or Victorian pornography, falling about, smashing things, disguising himself. Alexandra uses English literature to interpret life and also to plot the novel, rescuing the charlatan (at least nine-tenths) Swami from his incensed followers by recalling in quick succession Toad disguised as a washerwoman, and Panks exposing Casby in *Little Dorrit*. There are parodies of the Angry Young Men (in Alexandra's father) and threadbare identifications—Alexandra comes to see Hamo's clumsiness as Myshkin's divine idiocy.

The novel contains a collapsed myth, in the sense that all the characters are out to redeem the Waste Land with fertility magic: but Hamo's death at the hands of an incensed mob is neither Dionysian nor Orphic, his body is simply a "marionette," and the sex-magic of Ned, Roderigo and Alexandra, designed to redeem the aridity of Birkin's failure to love both Gerald and Ursula, produces a child who is explicitly not allowed to represent harvest or fulfillment. At the end of the novel, Alexandra rejects him as a symbol: unlike Helen's child at the end of *Howards End* he will not reconcile opposites, close circles, inherit the earth or play with the grain. "We've had enough of Forster's harvest predictions. Things may have turned sour for all of us, but we must not heap it all on *him*." Alexandra rejects both literature and stories. After her "plotting" success with Toad and Panks, she stops short of seeing her fatigue in terms of Frodo's. "She said to herself, enough of superstitious imagining. A story is a story is a story, even a good one, like the *Lord of the Rings*." And five lines from the end of the book, having become Shaw's millionairess, she cries, "Damn English Literature!" as though brushing away mental cobwebs. Literature too is a magic spell, an illusion between men and reality.

As If by Magic is nihilistic, but it does not, like Nietzsche and Mann, open windows on blackness with a grim delight in reversals of meaning. It works by reducing everything to the ridiculous, in an intensely, inexorably, exclusively literary way. And it is not the absurd it indicates, it is simply the ridiculous. It is like an onion consisting of allusion, parody, interpretation, misinterpretation, imitative plot and trumped-up analogy, but an onion encasing no green growing point, and putting out no roots. The comparison with Mann is instructive. Mann, writing *Doctor Faustus,* discovered, he said, "my own growing inclination, which I discovered was not mine alone, to look upon all life as a cultural product taking the form of mythic clichés, and to prefer quotation to independent invention." Mann cannibalised the facts of Nietzsche's life, the forms of Dostoevsky's fiction: his book has, as R. J. Hollingdale says, "an airless, a horribly airless quality; it smells of the midnight, and worse of the *midday* lamp." An analogous airlessness permeates *As If by Magic,* but the differences are instructive. Mann was monstrously curious as a writer—he had to *know about* music, tuberculosis, syphilis, in heaped factual detail. Angus Wilson's rice, although clearly researched, was researched, one feels, as a *literary symbol*. Mann's book has an extraordinary vitality, however airless, even if it was, as he said it had to be, the vitality of *fleurs du mal*. Wilson's book is paradoxically less vital because of his residual liberal humanist warmth and duty towards his characters. He feels morally compelled to appreciate and understand Alexandra's true being, from the inside, and his display of this moral effort curiously vitiates the papery energies of his puppetry without really allowing the reader to care for that "fictive device" he has so respectfully put together.

Further, the presence of this moral nostalgia for Forster's procedures curiously blurs Alexandra's rejection of Forster's metaphors. These moral confusions and formal blurrings are also characteristic of our time.

The Golden Notebook began, Doris Lessing has said, as a combination of a novel about artistic narcissism, about art, about the "problems of the artist," and a literary-critical book which would be a series of stylistic exercises combined "in such a way that the shape of the book and the juxtaposition of the styles would provide the criticism." The two books in one would have a shape "so enclosed and claustrophobic—so narcissistic that the subject matter must break through the form." The novel has indeed an airlessness, but it also has a realistic power, almost unique amongst the novels I am discussing, which derives from the fact that in this case form and subject-matter are not a seamless garment, that the subject-matter is not the form, is more and other than it, and does indeed break through.

The novel is about the writing block of the novelist Anna Wulf. During the description of the source, form, symptoms and demolition of this block, Anna, and her author, go into most of the formal problems I have raised in this essay. The nostalgia for Tolstoy, and for Thomas Mann, is raised by Anna's reviewing; the novels she reads, she declares, are typically journalistic, reports on unknown areas of the world, undescribed communities. They reflect psychological and cultural splintering. "Human beings are so divided, are becoming more and more divided, and more subdivided in themselves, reflecting the world, that they reach out desperately, not knowing they do it, for information about other groups. . . . Yet I am incapable of writing the only kind of novel which interests me: a novel powered with an intellectual or moral passion, strong enough to create order, to create a new way of looking at life." The novel itself is subdivided, Black, Blue, Red, Yellow notebooks, separating money from politics, from autobiographical facts, from fictional exercises. Journalism is debased realism: Doris Lessing is also penetrating about Iris Murdoch's "crystalline" alternative, the desire for myth, symbol, dream as a deeper reality. Anna's dialogues with her psychoanalyst show mistrust, and even contempt, for her analyst's facile respect for Art, her assumption that if a dream-vision can be named or placed as myth or folk-tale, Icarus or the Little Mermaid, then that gives it a satisfactory form, allied to the world of the primitive. Anna insists, neurotically and wisely together, that civilisation, truth, consist of a capacity to resist such primitive aesthetic wholeness and delights. Her dreams nevertheless punctuate the novel with a power, colour and certainty that are part of its patchwork toughness and fascination. They work as symbols do work, in dreams, in life. They do not become a sub-mythology nor daemonically reduce intelligent Anna to being their puppet.

Anna Wulf is also obsessed by the relations between truth, veracity and fiction. Large parts of the novel are concerned with her relation to her own first novel, a large commercial success, which she now dislikes, feeling it was the product of a corrupt nostalgia for her life during the war, and such nostalgia breeds "stories" "like cells under a microscope." During the novel Anna tries to reconstruct the "real" events that were transmuted into that fiction. The reader, on the other hand, is offered increasingly simple and corrupt versions of it—American film scenarios, projected television musicals, conventional literary reviews, dogmatic Communist reviews, each reducing it to their own form of banal or farcical cliché. Anna asks herself, "Why a story at all. . . . Why not simply the truth?" But truth is hard, stories do indeed breed like cells, the issue is complex. She makes attempts on the factual, the "true fact" of Dostoevsky and B. S. Johnson, in various ingenious ways. She replaces her diary at one point by a series of newspaper snippings, mostly about freedom and violence, of the kind Mary McCarthy said rendered fictive fact "irreal." She attempts a detailed, unmediated account of one day of her life, not "selecting" what she records, not arranging it. This record turns out to be identifiably "false," like the crystalline dream images. She writes that she had assumed that "If I wrote 'at nine-thirty I went to the lavatory to shit and at two to pee and at four I sweated,' this would be more real than if I simply wrote what I thought." She discovers that thought, concepts, a directing intelligence are as necessary to our sense of truth as Iris Murdoch has said they are.

She broods about the vanishing "character," in relation to the real people behind the rejected first novel. She writes of them that some were "good," some "nice," some not good or nice, and that most people who knew them could recognise and use these simple classifications, although "these are not words you'd use in a novel, I'd be careful not to use them." She remarks that personality can still be recognised by gesture in films, yet has become hard to depict in novels, remembers Maryrose's smile and declares, "All this talk, this anti-humanist bullying, about the evaporation of the personality becomes meaningless for me at that point when I manufacture enough emotional energy inside myself to create in memory some human being I've known." The novel is full of characters: the novelist-character's personality disintegrates almost to collapse under the strain of consciousness.

She contemplates the breakdown of language. Her Communist Writers'

Group discuss Stalin on Linguistics, and Anna broods on their moral incapacity to criticise his bad semantics, brooding also on "novels about the
breakdown of language, like *Finnegans Wake*," and a recurrent experience
of her own, in which words lose their meaning and seem "like a foreign
language. The gap between what they are supposed to mean and what in
fact they say seems unbridgeable." Her parodies in this book are partly
explorations of debased languages of cliché. She reads a fantasy story "by a
comrade," out of a genre of Communist wish-fulfillments, and cannot tell
whether it is to be read as "parody, irony, or seriously." She and a friend
write parodic stories to explore and expose current literary clichés, and find
that editors take them seriously. Such debased group languages create, call
for, parody which they cannot recognise. A plurality of such languages, and
a despairing consciousness that they exist, make it hard for any "realist" to
imagine an audience that can recognise or place a truth, if it is told.

Related to these perceptions are the layered parallel emotions and styles
in the fiction-within-the-fiction, Anna's novel about the end of "Ella's"
love-affair, which parallels her own but distorts it, because the love-affair in
the novel is inevitably analysed in terms of "laws" of breakdown, whereas
the experience did not assume breakdown as the inevitable end. Ella, also
a writer, works, like Anna, with fictions more papery than her own:
women's magazines, containing both lonely-hearts letters and clichéd "stories." Anna remarks that she could retell her first novel in the person of the
sex-obsessed teenager "in" it by changing a few words here and there and
thus the whole style: the Chinese boxes of fiction-within-fiction in *The
Golden Notebook* create the most complex example I know of the study of
such tensions of whole styles, degrees of "realism" or vision. They also, of
course, play games akin to Julian Mitchell's with veracity. "Ella's" son has
"Anna's" lover's name: "Anna" has a daughter, not a son. And Doris
Lessing? A Freudian joke, a writer's joke, a novelist's riddle about truth and
fictiveness. The splendid irony about all this obsessive narcissism and self-
consciousness is that the realistic effect of the whole is amazingly reinforced.
What Anna cannot do, Ms. Lessing does, by an effort of sheer intelligence,
political, psychological, aesthetic. It must be added that Doris Lessing's
advantage, in this novel, is that she is not necessarily or primarily "literary."
Anna remarks earlier that all she has left of the novelist is a huge curiosity.
It is this curiosity that saves the novelist from aestheticism. Communism is
more important in this novel than the Great Tradition, and modern female
sex than fictiveness. If it is a book about books about books, it is haunted
more by the claustrophobia of bad books than by love or fear of good ones,

though these are present. I take it that such untrammelled curiosity is in fact a way out of formal anxiety, and a necessary component of realism.

One of the odd results, for me, of writing this paper, has been an increased respect for Anthony Powell. The thoughts of Nick in the Ritz about the difficulty of writing a novel about English life (in *The Acceptance World*) seem gracefully thrown off, and in fact tell a truth both sober and crucial. Nick thinks about the difficulties of reporting speech in a land where understatement is the normal style of all classes, and how bare facts have "an unreal, almost satirical ring when committed to paper." In *Books Do Furnish a Room,* X. Trapnel's outburst about "naturalism" continues the topic. Its essence is that "naturalism is just a way of writing a novel like any other, just as contrived, just as selective." Powell's own contrivances, his own selection, his own manipulation of memory, above all, his vigorous and detailed and controlled curiosity, seem to me now gifts of a high order. "Naturalism's only 'like life' if the novelist himself is any good," says Trapnel. This essay has been concerned with reading, with the morals of literature, with devices and with anxieties. In fact, to be "good," whatever form you use, takes more primitive gifts of curiosity and greed about things other than literature. That these gifts are harder to discuss in academic essays is maybe part cause of our contemporary unease.

(1979)

9

William Golding:
Darkness Visible

I N THE FIFTIES and into the Sixties we read novels which dealt with the numinous in an almost hectically ordered way. They described a spirituality insecurely and ambivalently attached to any traditional beliefs and symbols, and possibly for that reason tended to be more interested in the apocalyptic vision of disintegration and dark than in the rarer moments of beatitude. I think of Durrell, Patrick White, the savagely Nietzschean Murdoch of *Time of the Angels,* and centrally, of course, of Golding. These writers offer us something different from the huge aesthetic structures and comparatively serene epiphanies of Joyce, Mann and Proust. There is more of a fine frenzy in the way they force visions of light and blackness on the reader, more ambivalence about the value or efficacy of art in the world in which they work. If this kind of novel is no longer so central to our idea of "the contemporary novel," a new novel from Golding, his first full-length one since 1968, may cause us to think again.

Darkness Visible opens with one of the most moving first scenes I have read. The central figure materialises, walking steadily, a naked child, out of a pit of flame in a bomb attack on the Isle of Dogs. "Darkness visible" is Milton's paradoxical description of the "no light" in his Hell. Golding's fireburst, which occurs again in a transmuted form at the end of the novel, is here described both as "burning bush" and as "too much clarity, too much shameful, inhuman light . . . a version of the infernal city." The emotions of the watching firemen are beautifully, humanly done. The brightness of the child's left side is in fact the nakedness of a huge burn which renders him permanently bald and dead-white there. He survives, solitary, largely silent, with a dark side to his face and a blanched one, to become one of those wholly truthful and righteous people who, in life and in fiction, are usually charmless. Besides being physically repellent he has the somewhat alienating sense of vocation of a George Fox or a Bunyan—he believes himself to be at the "centre of things," a battle between good and evil. He performs biblical rituals—heaven-offerings, dust-shakings—and looks for and makes signs, from wearing 666 in his black hatband, written in blood on 6 June 1966, to causing tongues of flame with piles of stones and matchboxes. In Australia he ceases to lust after the "daughters of men" when he is symbolically crucified and truly (if not wholly successfully, it turns out) castrated by a black Aborigine called Willy Bummer. He is a scapegoat: pederastic Mr. Pedigree, his beloved schoolmaster, dismissed after a distraught boy favourite falls to his death from a roof, tells him it is "all his fault," which he takes literally.

He moves from England to Australia to England, where his fate merges with that of the twin Stanhope daughters, Sophia and Antonia, both beautiful, brilliant, charming and ultimately evil. Sophy is a natural killer; as a small child she destroys a swimming dabchick with a stone that fits itself to her hand. She finds orgasm in knifing people, playfully or in earnest. Toni, more shadowy, becomes an international guerrilla. For a time the twins' lives are in no way connected with that of the burning babe, now named Matthew, or Matty, Septimus Windup, Windrove, Windrave, Windgraff, Windgrove—no one seems to get right the name the hospital officer had chosen for him and felt to be peculiarly felicitous. But Sophy forms a plan to kidnap a dark-skinned princeling from a public school where Matty, now conversing with red and blue spirits in "expensive" and "less expensive" hats, is caretaker on a literal and spiritual level. The climax comes when a bomb explosion causes a sea of petrol flames to float on a sea of water from a burst tank.

Golding's English towns, rather like Blake's Jerusalem in England's green and pleasant land, are always violently turbulent microcosms. In Greenfield, a corrupt Eden like Sammy Mountjoy's Rotten Row birthplace, or Beatrice's grey asylum on Paradise Hill, men and women face the darkness Golding finds so compelling. In an essay, "Fable," he wrote that since the Second World War he has believed that man was corrupt and produces "evil as a bee produces honey"—but hides "the sad fact of his cruelty and lust" as he hides his genitalia. Cruelty and lust both go hand in hand with darkness in Golding. He said also, however, that "the two signs of man are a capacity to kill and a belief in God"—and God, in a postscript to *Lord of the Flies,* is called "the thing we turn away from into life, and therefore we hate and fear him and make a darkness there." In *Free Fall* he wrote of man's "unnamable, unfathomable and invisible darkness that sits at the centre of him always awake, always different from what you believe it to be, always thinking and feeling what you can never know it thinks and feels, that hopes hopelessly to understand and to be understood. Our loneliness . . . is the loneliness of that dark thing."

Both Matty and Sophy experience that loneliness, but they make of it completely opposed powers, visions and patterns of life. Sophy's uneasy internal darkness recognises a power with which she wishes to ally herself when she hears a broadcast on entropy, on "the universe running down," and later tells her ex-mercenary lover that "in the mess things are, the heap, the darkness . . . everything's running down . . . towards something that's simpler and simpler—and we can help it. Be a part." Now Golding has said that "the Satan of our cosmology is the Second Law of Thermodynamics which implies that everything is running down and will finally stop like an unwound clock." Sophy wears a shirt with TAKE ME on it; she likes to think of herself as a whore; Matty refers to her as the harlot in his journal. She is the Great Whore of the Apocalypse, who heralds the "second death, even the lake of fire" (Revelation 20:14). She is also Sophia, the Gnostic or Hermetic or Jewish Wisdom, who in some myths of the Creation and Fall was separated from God in the creation of matter, imprisoned in the latter and condemned to be incarnate as a series of women, daughters of men doomed to lust after the sons of God. Also, the imagery suggests, she is the dead cold "bomber's moon," the cruel Artemis who presides over the inferno of the first chapter. Her twin, pale and absent by comparison, is interested in beliefs and ideas, moving from Christianity through Transcendental Philosophy to, presumably, some revolutionary political belief. The people of Greenfield believe they are "everything to each other," but they know better. They are the flesh and intellect, separated, not unified, and thus damned, whore and guerrilla, last heard on the radio after a hijack delivering on behalf of mindless cruelty words that in Golding's microcosm need human identity and minute particulars to have meaning—"the long aria in that silvery voice about freedom and justice . . ."

If the beautiful twins are the fallen Whore, Matty, piebald, mutilated, is the incarnate Second Coming, the figure in the fiery furnace in the Book of Daniel, the alchemical conjunction of opposites in one body and thus the Philosophers' Stone—which was often pictured as a naked child and referred to as the orphan. He is also Horus, Horapollo, one-eyed God of Light, who was imaged as a naked boy with one bald side to his head and one "lock of youth" over his temple. Horus is also falcon-headed, and it is as a great golden bird that Matty finally appears to Mr. Pedigree at the end of the novel, flaming, feathered, golden, loving and terrible. That is why I also believe that the name which came into the hospital superintendent's mind, the name no one speaks, was Windhover—Hopkins's Falcon, the Christ whose blue-bleak embers fall, gall themselves, and gash gold-vermilion. If this sounds far-fetched, consider the superintendent's own metaphor for his surprising idea:

> The name had first jumped into his mind with the curious effect of having come out of empty air and of being temporary, a thing to be noticed because you were lucky to be in the place where it had landed. It was as if you had sat silently in the bushes and . . . there settled in front of you the rarest of butterflies or birds which had stayed long enough to be seen and had then gone off with an air of going forever, sideways, it might be.

If Satan is the Second Law of Thermodynamics, Golding has said that he believes man is "the local contradiction to this rule," that in him "the cosmos is organising energy back to the sunlight level." Matty is the contradictory burning bush that is not consumed.

How does one read a book that is so spattered with clues and signs, clotted with symbols and puns, from the lewd aptness of Willy Bummer's name to the figure with the sword in his mouth straight out of Revelation? After the easy drug-ecstasies and modish spirituality of the late Sixties, we have as novel readers become nervous and austere. "Signs" means semiology and we like books that indicate their own fictiveness, the closed system of language that can only know language. Gabriel Josipovici used Golding's own work as an example of a different problem, named by Mallarmé—"demonic analogy," the modern fear that our metaphors, vehicle *and* tenor, come from our own heads and that nothing "out there" corresponds to them, as Pincher Martin's purgatorial island was only his own decaying tooth.

Neither of these two ways will do for reading *Darkness Visible*. Nor will a realistic reading that hopes to intuit the mystery by attending to the surface of the story. That has its power—Matty's frightful physical presence, the comic limitations of his human intelligence, Sophy's sadism, Mr. Pedigree's fear and love of the "sons of the morning" in the smelly cast-iron urinal have their solidity. But in the end the signs are there and have to be conjured with or left alone. Golding's art has moved from fabulating to conjuring, almost in a Yeatsian sense. Jung, in *Mysterium Coniunctionis,* wrote: "The 'living idea' is always perfect and always numinous. Human formulation adds nothing and takes away nothing for the only question is whether a man is gripped by it or not." Matty, like that other conjurer, Prospero, comes to drown his Book. But Golding's book, although it is about the unspeakable, is there, like a kind of mandala. Unlike Patrick White, who sometimes seems to fake ecstasy as women fake orgasm, Golding conjures vision rather than describing it. And I suspect Jung is right: either one is gripped or not. I tried not to be. And was.

(1979)

10

The *TLS* Poetry Competition

IN THE SUMMER I read 960 poems for the *TLS*/Cheltenham competition. I've judged fiction before, but not poetry; I expected to feel alternate pleasure and amusement and exasperation, and to have great difficulty in reducing the good poems to a shortlist of six. It didn't work out quite like that. I had trouble finding six poems I thought were good enough to print and I felt little, almost no, pleasure. But I was, paradoxically, deeply moved by the bulk of the poems.

The subjects fell into readily distinguishable categories. There were many poems about death, the death of a parent or child, some about the pain of watching beside a hospital bed, some attempting to sum up the meaning of a vanished life. Related to these were a series of pen-portraits of the very old, farm workers, urban pensioners, claiming dignity, asking, "What was it all for?" And related to these again were a series of responses to the sea, the English landscape, trees, seen as threatened or enduring or both, all of which ended lamely and stoically with the acknowledgement that the writer was small and helpless but had dignity, surely?

Then there were the poems of sex, reproach and indignation—the most memorable, a poet's wrath at her mother-in-law for sneering at her secret writing. There was a recognisable subcategory of ageing men inventing warm, responsive girls to share lonely beds. There were poems of divorce, ditties about ducks and bunnies and a great deal of what I came to think of as hortatory citizens' indignation about the Bomb and pollution—"surely we can do better than this?"

Most of the poems were bad because the language was inert. Several began well, with a striking observation, and then petered out in cliché. They were covered by a kind of kettle-fur of imprecision and the untransmuted sounds of ordinary speech. And yet they were moving; they were quite clearly the record of human beings trying to understand themselves and the world. Although much of the language was neo-Georgian rather than neo-Larkin, I rarely felt their badness was a question of stock responses to other poetry—the fleeting bluebells were *seen,* not derivative, but they were not brought to life. The deaths were unique and terrible, but they produced an involuntary conventional mutter of consolation, not placed as poetry but transmitted raw and hopeless to the page.

I came to feel that few of these poets were interested enough in *language.* They had never played with words, they had never read dictionaries, they had never experimented with verse-forms, they had never thought about figures of speech. I found myself privileging little poems that were inert. A poem about a failed marriage stays in my mind because it worked it out in terms of a dry bed—no river of life, no wet sex, no damp children. A poem about making marmalade shines in my memory. But these local felicities emphasise the gulf between their competence and the large muffled cries of the others.

The English believe in instinct and amateurism. Most English, including most writers, will tell you that good writing can't be taught in classes. I'm not sure that is right. Sylvia Plath managed to make her cries of despair arresting and beautiful because of her long apprenticeship to the language, her poetry classes at Harvard, her experiments in syllabics, her interest in form. I'm not ascribing the demotic sameness of the mass of the competition poems to modern education, but I think it is worth looking at how the craft is taught, if it is taught, in schools.

I was a member of the Kingman Committee on the teaching of English language. The writers on that committee were all convinced that learning poetry by heart and experimenting with strict form were essential ways of making children free and at home in the language. The teachers on the committee were more doubtful. One of them suggested to me that learning by heart was "punitive." Many, if not most, of the teachers we met in schools and colleges felt that precise forms were a restriction of freedom and self-expression. We read a most dispiriting anthology of prizewinning poems from a GLC competition on "Freedom." These were all conversational free verse, broken speech with no reason for the line endings, and written out of a uniform hortatory indignation.

If that competition had been for ballads or sonnets about freedom, at least those children would have had to search for words, select, reject, consider, make discoveries. I remember with pleasure from my 960 a rousing ballad of hatred for working conditions in Saudi Arabia. In one excellent primary school we visited, a teacher had her whole class experimenting with forms—the acrostic, the diamant, the limerick. One unusually good pupil had been encouraged to write her own free verses on loneliness and autumn leaves. Her poems were not nearly as interesting or inventive as the rest of the class's exercises. I said I hoped she would be encouraged to play word-games too.

Free verse has come to represent democracy, equal opportunity and self-expression. But in bulk, and unaware of the forms from which it has been "freed"—the iambic pentameters, the alexandrine—it can be extremely depressing. E. J. Thribb at least counts his quantities and has an ear. I ended up shortlisting the poem "Shee," which invokes the Muse in a thoroughly reactionary way, simply because it spoke to my distress. The poet quotes Ben Jonson on Nature: "Men are decay'd and studied. Shee is not." He goes on, possibly petulantly, to accuse "young men" of writing an "impotent vers libre." My fellow judges, all poets as I am not, were indignant at this sweeping judgment and eloquent about the subtleties of good modern verse. But I thought "impotent" was right for the mass of what I had been reading. Here were people with something to say, and powerless to say it, because they didn't care, or think, or know enough about language.

(1988)

11

A Sense of Religion: Enright's God

S TRANGE that a sense of religion should / Somehow survive all this grim buffoonery!" reflects D. J. Enright, recalling his childhood Sundays in *The Terrible Shears*. That "sense" did survive, and indeed is pervasive, in his poetry. In the more recent *Instant Chronicles,* the "short thoughts" include:

> Quite often heard to call on God—
> Though not expecting an answer.
>
> For who else could he call on—
> On some temporal lord and master?
>
> Angry with the one for being there;
> With the other for not, still angrier.
> (CP, 317)[1]

Anger with God for being absent is one form of the Enright religion. Sometimes it appears that God was once there, and good, as in the poem "High-mindedness of an English Poet," which takes on the advocate of Job-like patience in modern politics.

> Job is the case he cites
> Whose readiness to sing

Under the frequent scourge
Was a fine and sacred thing—
But God was living then,

And you and I, my dear,
Seeing the bad go free

The good go by default
Know more than one sole state
Where this sweet bard would be
Appointed laureate.

(CP, 117)

This sense of the past existence of a good God is, however, comparatively rare. (Christ is different; we come to Him later.) Anthropos, feeling his age, also feels the death of God, but more as a loss of a sense of profundity in things. He has fewer things to hide from, we are told. Religions are not supposed to burn him:

. . . Once there were torrents to cross,
Forests to explore, and the nature of God.
The objects that squat on his desk
Afford him no refuge.

(CP, 205-6)

The demonologising of the desk-things is akin to much of the peculiar, not quite malign energy of modern non-mysterious objects in the most recent poems, such as "Psalm for Supersunday."

The nature and origin of Enright's argument with God can be discerned, directly and obliquely, in *The Terrible Shears*. There is a kind of sociological picture of accepted religion, its tedium and its fears and puzzles, that most of us who are old enough will remember, working-class or not. The God of this world is a Sunday God, and the Sundays on which the child goes to Sunday school and the Church are seen, ironically, as, at best, God's time off.

It was a far cry from that brisk person
Who created the heaven and the earth in
Six days and then took Sunday off.

(CP, 133-4)

The tone of the description of the Sunday school is childish mockery and adult pity and indignation mixed:

> In Sunday school a sickly adult
> Taught the teachings of a sickly lamb
> To a gathering of sickly children.

Nevertheless it is at the end of this poem that Enright remarks on the strange persistence of a "sense of religion," and concludes, "Perhaps that brisk old person does exist / And we are living through his Sunday." Connected to this sense of Sunday emptiness, as opposed to fullness, is the child's inability to respond to the masses of flowers in the town's gardens, admission-free on Sundays. They "were emblematic / Of something, I couldn't make out what." They press round him, muttering "too softly for me to hear":

> I never learnt their true names.
> If I looked at them now,
> I would only see the sound of Sunday church bells.
>
> (CP, 127)

The effect here of Sunday is, as so often in these poems, both muffling and deadening, and obscurely enlivening at the same time. The flowers never come to life in terms of the Pathetic Fallacy, but their Sundayness has its vitality.

The accounts of people are both comic and terrible, often both at once, depending on how seriously we take religion at all. The poet's mother is Protestant and has a Protestant mistrust of the religion of his father, a "lapsed Catholic."

> My mother's strongest religious feeling
> Was that Catholics were a sinister lot;
> She would hardly trust even a lapsed one.
> My father was a lapsed Catholic.
>
> (CP, 133)

Here the word "lapsed" carries also the weight of Enright's sense, wholly informing the language and shape of the poems, of man's fallen nature. (Remember the Voice of the Bard, in the *Songs of Experience*, "Calling the lapsed soul.") Various short poems in this sequence enact the Fall, obliquely, ironically. Consider "The Soul of a Schoolboy":

> A woman thrust her way into the house,
> Desirous to save the soul of a schoolboy.
>
> An obliging schoolboy, would do anything
> For peace, excepting kneel in public.
>
> But no, she would not go, she would not go,
> Till crack on their knees they fell together.
> His soul was lost forever.
>
> (CP, 150)

This is an anecdote, but it somehow makes us both smile and see the riddling weight of the words. "Anything for peace" is embarrassed or evangelical. "They fell together" neatly reverses the blundering evangelist's intention, and precisely. They fell *together*. Both sin. And the "crack" is descriptive, and a Mephistophelean firework.

Equally succinct and full of import is the little poem "Two Bad Things in Infant School":

> Learning bad grammar, then getting blamed for it:
> Learning Our Father which art in Heaven.
>
> Bowing our heads to a hurried nurse, and
> Hearing the nits rattle down on the paper.
>
> (CP, 123)

Here God, as throughout Enright's poems, is associated with language and fallen language. Our Father *which* art in Heaven has something grammatically wrong with it. Juxtaposition involves the blame for the grammar in the saying of the prayer. "God is a harsh master, who put his creatures in the way of damning themselves and then went on damning them," said Enright in his introduction to his selection from *Paradise Lost*.[2] And the bowed head from which the nits fall is a secular bowing which echoes the prayer, comic, yes, but spreading into meaning, because the nits rattle down, they fall, like the sinful. Even the idea of paper connects the prayer to the written language, and the nits to bad words.

And the involvement of religion with language and eventually with poetry, for Enright, is seen in the poems "A Sign" and "It Is Poetry." In "A Sign" the young poet retrieves an old broken-backed Bible from the dustbin, describing his scandalised look and restraint from chiding these "blasphemers against God's Word." He makes it quite clear what was sacred to *him*:

> At that tender age I couldn't bear
> To see printed matter ill treated.
> I would have subscribed to the ancient
> Oriental taboo against stepping light-
> Mindedly over paper inscribed with characters.
>
> (CP, 133)

His impressed elders see the episode in terms of religion:

> It was read as a sign. The child
> Is destined to become Vicar of the Parish Church!
> He has rescued Religion from the scrap-heap.

But the poet does not leave us with the contrast between his true respect for print and his supposed respect for religion. Now, he tells us, he could watch unmoved the casting of hundreds of books into dustbins. But would still dive in after Shakespeare and the Bible. And the Bible retains its ambivalent significance.

The poem "It Is Poetry" seems at first to sit oddly in this sequence between a poem which begins "Grandma doddered a bit, / But she was my friend," and one about the gym teacher. It concerns the damned artist of Thomas Mann's *Doctor Faustus,* Leverkühn, and describes his "last address / To the cultivated ladies and gentlemen"; these hearers are at first relieved to diagnose what he is saying as "poetry" and then disturbed to realise they were "hearing about damnation." The poem treats damnation and European literature, two preoccupations of the adult Enright, and is placed where it is *because* it follows the extremely painful, if fiercely understated, description of the dispatch of Grandma to the Workhouse, which she feared. Enright asks:

> Perhaps it had to be done,
> Did it have to be done like that?

And he goes on to tell us:

> It started me writing poems,
> Unpleasant and enigmatic,
> Which quite rightly no one liked,
> But were thought to be 'modern'.
>
> (CP,142)

Here, in the juxtaposition of the local rage against the suffering of the helpless and the innocent, with high modernist art *(Doctor Faustus)* deriving from ancient myth and belief, is a kind of seed or paradigm of Enright's religious poetry.

One steady strand in it is a refusal to understand or accept the pain of the innocent, a refusal local and observed, as in the elegant poem "A Polished Performance" about the large-eyed innocent girl, "Perfect for the part" of a tourist attraction "except for the dropsy / Which comes from polished rice"; but also connected to the theological anger of Ivan Karamazov, when Enright's Faust asks Mephistopheles, "Why is it little children suffer, / Guiltless beyond dispute?" and gets the bureaucratic and hellish answer:

> 'It passes understanding,'
>   came the pious answer.
> 'It may surprise you, but in hell
> We need to keep child-murderers and molesters
> Segregated from the rest. Feelings run high.'
>
> (CP, 220)

Because of his riddling tone of voice, matter-of-fact, funny and terrible, Enright can make us look at children in war, or depicted in the talons of Hokusai's "Laughing Hyena, cavalier of evil," who holds

> a child's head
> Immobile, authentic, torn and bloody—
> The point of repose in the picture, the point of
>   movement in us.
>
> (CP, 13)

Which says much about the relation of art to life, of what it is to be "moved," of evil. In a coolly balanced early poem about the Chinese poets, he begins:

> Only one subject to write about: pity.
> Self-pity: the only subject to avoid.

And ends with a kind of invocation of the absent deity:

> One thing is certain. However studious we are, or tough,
> Thank God we cannot hope to know
> The full horror of this world—or whole happiness.
>
> (CP, 22)

In an essay in *Fields of Vision*, "What happened to the Devil?," Enright is dismissive about modern theology's lack of interest in Evil. He is reviewing Jeffrey Burton Russell's *Lucifer,* and endorses Russell's view that "at a time when evil threatens to engulf us totally, when evil has already claimed more victims this century than in all previous centuries combined," churchmen evince a lack of interest in the concept.

> Russell opines that some modern theologians have been motivated by the thought that the subtraction of Devil / Evil from Christianity would 'remove barriers' and 'be ecumenical.' Yet it is barely credible that theologians could soft-pedal Devil / Evil purely as a tactical, popularizing measure: their personal belief in him / it would surely need to have waned already. (Otherwise, one takes it, they would scarcely leave moral damnation to Chief Constables.) To get rid of God will remove barriers, too, and prove even more ecumenical, for it admits convinced atheists to the Church. Why nibble away at such marginal matters as the Immaculate Conception, the Virgin Birth, the loaves and fishes, the Resurrection? As for the Crucifixion, it was all so very long ago, as they say, that by the grace of God it may not be true.[3]

And again, in this context, he quotes Mann's *Faustus,* where Leverkühn's "polymorphous visitor" tells him that only the Devil now speaks of religion: "Who else, I should like to know, is to speak of it today? Surely not the liberal theologian! After all I am by now its sole custodian! In whom will you recognize theological existence if not in me?" It is as though Enright's interest in, if not need for, religion arises from the certain existence of the principle of evil, which entails the desire, if never the certainty, for the existence of theological good. In his sequences on *Paradise Lost* and *Faust* he takes on the two most persuasive, elegant and verbally inventive literary personifications of evil, Milton's spirited sly snake and Goethe's (and Marlowe's) damned and witty Mephistopheles. Both involve evil in the attractions of language and know about damnation. The God in both sequences, by contrast, is a dubious and detached Creator, a kind of poet who uses poetry to evade humanity and the vigorous human (fallen) users of language. It seems necessary to quote the whole of the following poem, since editing it distorts it.

> *Walking in the Harz Mountains,*
> *Faust senses the presence of God*

God was a brooding presence.
Brooding at present over new metres.
In which his creatures could approach him,
In which they could evade him,

—And he be relieved of their presence,
Through art as Proxy Divine—
Sublimation, as they termed it,
Which could very nearly be sublime—
For which he was truly thankful.

But how active they were, the bad ones!
They brooded rarely.
They talked incessantly,
In poisoned prose from pointed tongues.
How gregarious they were!
They needed friends to wound.

But who had invented tongues?
(One had to be careful when one brooded.)
And even the better ones
(One had to remember)
Were only human . . .
He started to fashion a special measure
For the likes of Gretchen, a still, sad music.

Creation was never finished.

(CP, 241)

This God is weary, reluctant to bother his patrician self (note the use of the reserved "one," isolating the unique divinity from even the "better ones" in plural humanity). He is a travesty of the romantic God as artist—his art is a secularised Christ—a "Proxy Divine"—but its purpose is to distance the creatures. He invents Wordsworth's "still, sad music of humanity" for the likes of Gretchen, the innocent victims, but his concerns are aesthetic. The last line is splendidly ambiguous. It is God's fatigue with creation. It is the human sense that there is something lacking, something indeed not finished about our raw world. The still, sad music plays, but the Devil has all the best tunes. This God as artist is related to an earlier Enright God as poet, working at night, attracting insects to his desk-lamp:

> . . . He gives, He also takes away.
>
> The insects love the light
> And are devoured. They suppose
> I punish them for something,
> My instrument the spring-jawed dragon.
>
> It isn't difficult to be a god.
> You hang your lantern out,
> Sink yourself in your own concerns
> And leave the rest to the faithful.
>
> ("The Faithful," CP, 101)

Both good and evil, and their myths and religious forms, are for En-right bound up in the nature of poetry and the imagination. In the essay on the Devil I've already quoted, he analyses the myth of Frankenstein's Monster (a kind of unfinished Adam, requiring love and dignity from his incompetent creator) and that of Dracula (an embodiment of involuntary evil destructiveness) as persisting relics in our culture of "metaphysical anxieties":

> What this phenomenon, this secret perturbation, has to do with *belief,* to what extent believing is involved, is hard to say. The postulation of a half-way house between belief and disbelief is the best we can manage; that famous 'willing suspension of disbelief for the moment' doesn't fill the bill, nor does the 'hoping' (or fearing) 'it might be so' of Hardy's poem 'The Oxen'. We can agree with William James that what keeps religion going is 'something else than abstract definitions and systems of concentrated adjectives, and something different from faculties of theology and their professors'. And we shall probably find it easier to assent to Octavio Paz's summing-up: 'Although religions belong to history and perish, in all of them a non-religious seed survives: poetic imagination.' Yet the relationship between imagina-tion and belief remains an indecipherable mystery.[4]

It is in this context that the project of reworking, in ironic, cross-referring fragments, the two great myths of Western salvation and damnation, seems so splendidly ambitious. This essay is about God, not about language, even though God originated the tongues in which we damn ourselves so inven-tively. The poem in *Sad Ires* on the "Origin of the Haiku" is a paradigm in little of the procedures, also in little, but not little, of *Paradise Illustrated* and *A Faust Book*. It opens Miltonically:

> The darkness is always visible
> Enough for us to write,

goes on to relate all the "pain" (pains of hell, pains of compassion, strictly incomparable?) of making seventeen syllables, relates how a "desperate faction" proposed to bring in rhyme and how they were defeated:

> We are a conventional lot,
> This is a conventional spot,
> And we take some satisfaction
> In writing verse called *free*.

It goes on to appropriate, miniaturise, and yet to enliven and continue, the language of Milton's great myth:

> In between we make up epigrams.
> 'Not to know me argues yourselves unknown',
> Or 'What is else not to be overcome?'
> The mind is sometimes its own place.

—this last a splendidly ironic statement, since its space is two quotations from God and Satan respectively, and its (original) context is lack of freedom.

> Such petty projects—
> Yes, but even an epic,
> Even *Paradise Lost,*
> Would look puny
> In hell, throughout eternity . . .
>   (CP, 157–8)

Space, time, eternity, poetry, heaven and hell, and a technical exercise, all connected. An equal sense of crafted proportion and huge disproportion. Language, including Milton's, saves. Language does nothing at all about the fact that Enright keeps echoing and half-echoing, "Why, this is Hell, / And we are in it." Or "Y this is L / Nor-my-outfit."

The Paradise myth, Enright claimed, although it had been criticised for not holding any enduring truth, did, on the contrary, engage readers (in diverse Asian countries, for example) who are not Christian either by conviction or, laxly, by environment. For it is the story of our first parents, of the birth of moral consciousness, and pre-eminently of the perversity in human nature whereby man destroys his happiness even when outward circumstance works in its favour and to his benefit. The Christian myth in some of its elements exerts a greater persisting influence on—or is more actively central to—not only our ethics (increasingly international) but also the darker places of the human psyche than is often supposed, even (or especially) by its conscious adherents.[5]

Enright incarnates this myth, in accounts farcical, grim, joky, of our incorrigible sinfulness. I like particularly, in this context, his picture of himself teaching Hopkins in the Orient ("More Memories of Underdevelopment"):

> 'God's most deep decree
> Bitter would have me taste: my taste was me.'

The poet describes himself as a "lapsed Wesleyan" (lapsed again) who is teaching Father Hopkins to "these young though ageless Catholics." He asks:

> A lurching humanist,
> Is it for me to instruct you in the fall complete?

He himself is ironically moved by Hopkins's words:

> Yet these words appal me with recognition,
> They grow continuously in terror.

Yet his innocent charges assume that his response is due to his age:

> Oh yes, they tell themselves, the poor old man,
> His taste is certainly him . . .
> And they turn to their nicer thoughts,
> Of salted mangoes, pickled plums, and bamboo shoots,
> And scarlet chillies, and rice as white as snow.
>
> (CP, 103)

Their image of themselves is an unfallen paradise, yet it contains a hint of Christian iconography in the last line—though their sins are as scarlet, yet they shall be washed whiter than snow—which is ambiguous, if read one way. Either in this land Christian myths are without force, and scarlet and white tastes are nothing to do with original sin. Or the sin lurks in the innocent taste, as it does in the flowery crown of Marvell's Little T. C., for instance. Either way the contrast between the lapsed humanist with his powerful sense of innate evil and the colourfully wholesome young is piquant.

Such ambiguous resonances have been the stuff of religious poetry through the centuries. I want finally to consider a peculiar kind of Christian presence in Enright's presentation of ordinary language and culture in our demythologised world. In *Paradise Illustrated,* language is the naming of things, pre- and post-lapsarian, flowers and creatures before the Fall— "Avalanches, defoliation, earthquakes, eruptions . . . Also perhaps inclemency," as Adam remarks in a fit of "airy" inventiveness (XIII). In the *Faust Book* language is romantic, as we have seen in the Harz Mountains, or may see in Mephistopheles' argument with the simple primrose. In *Paradise Illustrated* (XIX) Raphael tells Adam that a long book will be written about this very matter, and suggests that the real hero is the Son.

In Section XVIII God and the Son have a dialogue:

> 'My sole complacence,
> Radiant image of My Glory!'

> 'What I mean precisely.
> Much further, Father, You must love—
> And love what's hard to love.'

> 'Too much talk of love.
> Die man, or someone else must die.'

> 'Account me man *pro tem*.
> *Pro tem* account me man.'

> Nothing was said about a cross.
> By now the quire was in full swing.
>   (CP, 187)

I think it is not fanciful to see in the accountant's language, *pro tem,* a version of the Incarnation in the vulgar and mundane—and temporal. In the context of the reduced epic, the language has its Herbertian riddling ambiguity. But in our world, as Enright shows, the myths can be strangely inert, can bristle with oddity and a kind of questionable vampiric life.

There is, again, a childish or innocent version of what I mean in *The Terrible Shears,* in which secular things acquire the moral and emotive power of the sacred ones, even challenging them, as when the poet reflects on the worse fate of women ("Religious Phase"):

> He was on secondment. At no time
> Was he ignorant of his state.
>
> His ignorant bewildered mother
> Was another matter.
> In our street the pangs of labour
> Were nearer than those of crucifixion.
> Carpenters were useful, but
> Every family required a mother.
>
> (CP, 149–50)

This draws its strength from its plainness and its relation to what we are told about the poet's mother. More ambivalent in its tone is one of the little poems about Christmas:

> The cracked oilcloth is hidden
> By knife-creased linen.
> On it bottles of Vimto squat,
> A few flakes of browning tinsel
> Settle. It is Christmas—
> Someone will pay for this.
>
> (CP, 123)

"Someone will pay" is the sober truth, and the ironic reference to the atonement that follows the celebration of the birth. Here again the once powerful meanings of the phrases haunt the solid and daily. Something similar is happening in the poem "Remembrance Sunday," from *Sad Ires:*

> The autumn leaves that strew the brooks
> Lie thick as legions.
> 　　　　Only a dog limps past,
> Lifting a wounded leg.

> Was it the rocket hurt it?
> Asks a child.
> And next comes Xmas,
> Reflects the mother in the silence,
> When X was born or hurt or died.
>
> (CP, 173)

This is beautiful and complex, in its contrast of the Miltonic and Dantesque fallen soldiers with the blunt ciphered absence of X, to whom it is all one, whether he was born or hurt or died—he is humanised by the word "hurt," which carries pain and power. Between Milton and X are a dog (a limp and wounded God?—see the *Faust Book* on dogs and poodles) and a child concerned with rockets. But this poem too evokes what has gone from our culture, X.

The "feel" of the presence and absence of Christ is different in a poem like "The Stations of King's Cross," which is bizarrely witty, straining for effect, a kind of modern Gongorism. It finds the Passion in ordinary language with fiendish ingenuity.

> At Hammersmith the nails
> At Green Park the tree
>
> . . . .
>
> He speaks to the maidenforms of Jerusalem
> Blessed are the paps which never gave suck.
>
> . . . .
>
> The first fall, the second fall
> The third fall.
> And more to come.
>
> A sleeve goes, a leg is torn
> A hem is ripped.
> This is the parting of garments.
>
> They mock him, offering him vodka.
> The effect is shattering.
>
> He is taken down from the strap.
> And deposited.
>
> Wilt thou leave him in the loathsome grave?
>
> (CP, 156–7)

What sort of poem is this? Why describe the hazards of modern Tube-travel in terms of the ancient and once-believed-in journey of the god-man to torture and death? It is not, as we have seen, that English takes pleasure in iconoclasm, nor is it any kind of fashionable sick wit. What I think it is is a showing-up of the *vanishing* of what was the centre of our public culture and private myths. Only those of us who know these myths or stories will pick up the system of connections at work. If we do, we will be made uncomfortably aware of the absence from much public life now of any interest in, or ability to make, such connections. Why this is hell, nor are we out of it, might indeed be jocularly said of strap-hanging, but this Hell will not be harrowed, and if there is no Man to speak for the strap-hanger, his small concerns will remain small. The language, however, always for those of us who can read it, has acquired a new and savage vitality, almost demonic.

Some of Enright's very recent poems have made me laugh aloud, almost hysterically, partly because they were verbally funny, but partly because they called up obscure emotions I feel, as a resolute anti-Christian, about the vanishing of the whole culture, the whole spread of heaven, hell and suffering meaning I grew up with. Such poems, or proses, are "Agape," "Psalm for Supersunday" and "Prayer."

"Agape" is about the question of whether God struck York Minster because of the consecration of the Bishop of Durham. It rollicks. It is rather naughty, or wicked, in its suggestion that the old God might after all act in a traditional manner and smite those he was displeased with. But its language is couched in a mad debating form that leaves no opening for such a vision:

> question: Why did God not strike Durham Cathedral? Is it suggested that His aim is uncertain?
>
> answer: In His mysterious way He reveals that He moves in a mysterious way.
>
> question: Though less mysterious, would it not have been more to the point to strike down Arthur Scargill?
>
> rebuke: The Archbishop of Canterbury does not care for talk of divine intervention unless properly vouched for.
>
> (CP, 353)

What is the effect of this? Some people laugh a great deal when I show it to them; some look pained, at bad taste or triviality. I myself believe that the poem *is* a light-hearted but devastating attack on the deadness of modern religion, on the lifelessness acknowledged by Leverkühn's lively visitor. God does not strike any longer. When he appears to, we know it is not him, because we know he is not there (as the Bishop of Durham probably knows also). What religion we have has no poetic or other vitality. To spell this out is to do the poem a disservice. It works in contrast to the God we all learned about in school, in hours of boredom and flashes of sublimity and vision. It proclaims his absence and ineffectiveness. His mysterious ways are merely a tautology.

"Psalm for Supersunday" is naturalised religion with a vengeance—or not, since it is all safe and sanitised? The supermarket is sanitised, but not Enright's demonic language. This psalm addresses the entropic final vision of the Sunday "brisk person" of *The Terrible Shears,* and it presents simultaneously the resolutely unheard cry of this person's Proxy Divine, the incarnate, the ruthlessly demythologised and annihilated Christ:

> There on the right you shall find bread, white and brown, sliced and unsliced; and on the left new wine in new bottles, made to make men glad. Vinegar is displayed everywhere and, in Toiletries, sponges.
>
> This was somebody's flesh and blood, they say, speaking metaphorically. The Supermarket, as likewise the lesser clergy, has set its face against metaphors, save in promotional literature. The beef is immaculately presented, not conceived; the lamb will never rise again.

> (CP, 354)

This is demythologised and desacralised. Bread and wine, vinegar and sponge, are stripped of their associations. The mention of metaphor is particularly interesting, because it is detached from any context of meaning. "They say" this was "somebody's flesh and blood," where "they" is vanishing, gossipy and vague—who say?—and "someone" is more pallid, amorphous and ineffective than the X of the earlier poem, in which he was born or hurt or died. The vanishing of our contexts and meanings is enacted at us, but because we can still pick up these inert references and remember the power that was in them, they are a form of torment for us. I think the absence of metaphor is more unpleasant than the commercial world of the Sunday Supermarket; to my ear the final secular joke about the cash registers—"Hearken to the sound of bells"—is funnier, perhaps because the joke about money as an alternative God is old, whereas the absence of metaphor and myth is not. Though one remembers, as perhaps was appropriate in the earlier context of the Sunday flowers in which the poet would now "see" only "the sound of Sunday church bells," one of George Herbert's lovely, multifarious metaphors for prayer, uniting Heaven and earth, "Church bells beyond the stars heard." Enright's God, whose voice, Christ's voice, Enright's Faust hears in parenthesis, signing his demonic contract:

> (Some other words were heard in Faustus' mind.
> *There is in love a sweetnesse readie penn'd:*
> *Copie out onely that, and save expense—*
> But reason could not tell him what they meant.)

Which brings me to a final poem, appropriately entitled "Prayer." This again looks like a squib, a verbal *tour de force,* a kind of wicked game with the respectably sacred. But it is not finally that, though it depends upon arbitrary puns (sin/sun/cindy/Sunday) for part of its effect. Much of what I have been looking at in this essay is given a new shape here, at once grisly and gentle, bereft of significance and full of pain, immersed in the world of post-Sunday *pro tem* accountancy. It is awfully funny. Like the world, according to Enright.

> O Cindy
> You who are always well-groomed and cheerful
> As we should be
> Who tie your hair back before going to ballet school
> As we should do
> Who take good care of your costly vestments
> As we should take
> Who is put to bed and made to get up
> Who speak in silent parables
> Concerning charm and deportment and a suitable mar-
> riage to a tennis star and yachts and a rich social life
> Who grow old like us
> Yet unlike us remain for ever young
> Whose hair is torn out at times
> Whose arms are broken
> Whose legs are forced apart
> Who take away the sin of the world
> To whom a raggedy doll called Barabbas is preferred
> You who are scourged
> And given vinegar to drink from a jar of pickled onions

Who seem to say, Why have you forsaken me?
Who like us may rise or may not from the dead in a long
   white garment
You after whom the first day of the week is almost named
Into your hands we commend ourselves.

(CP, 355)

(1990)

THE FEMALE
VOICE?

12

Willa Cather

I BEGAN WRITING introductions to the Virago reprints of
Willa Cather's novels in 1979, with *A Lost Lady* and *My
Ántonia*. I was interested in her then—I wouldn't put it more strongly than
that—because I was intrigued by Ellen Moers's account of her work in
Literary Women and because I was teaching American Literature, which
seemed, unlike English Literature, to have few indisputably major women
writers. Cather's place is still not undisputed—Malcolm Bradbury left her
out of his history of American literature altogether. But she seems to me to
be a major writer, who created her own form to suit her own subject-
matter. She also came to matter to me personally, as a writer from whom
I could learn.

What intrigues me about her is the intelligence with which she combines
her formidable learning in European art and literature with her "new"
unformed or formless American subjects, the settlers and pioneers with their
unrecorded lives and their diverse heritages. And beyond that, a kind of
stoic yet fierce interest in the primitive *matter* of human energy over a whole
life—the passionate desire to live, the passive readiness to die. In this she
seemed to me to resemble George Eliot, whom she admired. And beyond
that again, she interested me *technically,* in her sentences, which are so
unexpected, so apparently fluent and artless, so precise and muscular and
exact, in fact. She wove prose like a huge intricate cloth, covered with local
detail yet flowing in large loops and coils and connections.

I wrote prefaces to *A Lost Lady, My Mortal Enemy, My Ántonia, Lucy Gayheart, The Song of the Lark, Shadows on the Rock, O Pioneers!, The Professor's House* and *Death Comes for the Archbishop*. I have reprinted the last three in this collection, largely because they illustrate my three points best—the American–European contrast, the treatment of energy, and the sentences. They also come from the beginning, middle and end of her extraordinary career—her discovery of her own fluid sentence and form in *O Pioneers!,* her own kind of realism and cultural history in *The Professor's House* and her late, legendary, fresco-like style in *Death Comes for the Archbishop*.

O Pioneers!

In 1931 Willa Cather published an essay entitled "My First Novels (There were Two)." They were *Alexander's Bridge* (1912) and *O Pioneers!* (1913). Between them came the decision to leave her job as editor of *McClure's* and become a writer. *Alexander's Bridge* is a psychological, symbolic book which owes much to Cather's thorough literary training, and her admiration for Henry James, Edith Wharton, the well-constructed novel. In *O Pioneers!,* she claims, she found her own voice for the first time. "There is a time in a writer's development," she wrote in a preface to a 1922 edition of *Alexander's Bridge,* "when his life line and the line of his personal endeavor meet. This may come early or late, but after it occurs his work is never quite the same . . ."

"My First Novels" conveys something of the delight she felt when her own life suddenly became accessible to her as an artist, bringing with it an exhilarating ease of formal innovation. *O Pioneers!* was written "entirely for myself; a story about some Scandinavians and Bohemians who had been neighbours of ours in Nebraska when I was eight or nine years old." She dismissed *Alexander's Bridge* as "unnecessary and superficial" (which does not do it justice), whereas in the true first novel "there was no arranging or inventing; everything was spontaneous and took its own place, right or wrong . . . Since I wrote this book for myself I ignored all the situations and accents that were then generally thought to be necessary." On the flyleaf of a copy she sent to a friend, she wrote: "This was the first time I walked off on my own feet—everything before was half real and half an imitation of writers whom I admired."

This account simplifies the history of Cather's discovery of her "own material." It particularly ignores the existence of "The Bohemian Girl," a 16,000-word story published in *McClure's* in 1912, which also treats Scandinavians and Bohemians and takes pleasure in recollected details of speech, customs, values, household objects. But "The Bohemian Girl" is primarily about young people whose energies are directed, as the writer's were, to getting out of the oppressively narrow society, the conventions . . . the land itself. *O Pioneers!,* by contrast, is a celebration, at once of the land and the energy that goes into it and of the writer's capacity to remember, record and contemplate it. Its title and epigraphs are all celebratory. Cather only half approved of Walt Whitman, who used "Pioneers, O Pioneers!" as an ecstatic refrain to one of his rambling catalogues of American life, in *Leaves of Grass*. She added a poem of her own—"Prairie Spring"—which juxtaposes the flaring of young life and the flat and sombre land. And she added a line from Mickiewicz's *Pan Tadeusz,* emphasising both her sense that she, like Mickiewicz and Virgil, was writing national epic, and her sense of the European origin of her cultural roots, of continuities, as well as gaps, between the Old World and the New.

The novel was, like *Middlemarch,* the result of its author's perception that two stories she had embarked on were really parts of one whole. There was a story—"Alexandra"—written before she left *McClure's,* and parts of "The White Mulberry Tree" were also already in existence. Critics have called *O Pioneers!* "episodic and unevenly patterned" (David Daiches) as a result of this. This is in my view a great injustice—the patient length of Alexandra's relationship with the land and the rapid violence ("Prairie Spring") of Emil and Marie's tragedy are stronger and more complex together than either would be alone. To read *O Pioneers!* with a technical attention to the writing is to share the exhilaration which the writer so obviously feels at the way language, like light, like the undifferentiated earth, can hold everything together.

The characters have been said to be idealised, or pastoral. Alexandra, Daiches says, is "a kind of Earth Mother or Corn Goddess . . . whom we are not allowed to know intimately and who is not even convincing as a creation. She moves with calm symbolic motion through the book against a background of golden corn and agricultural routines." This seems to me to oversimplify again. Alexandra is a woman of considerable will and considerable energy who has had since early childhood to be morally and economically responsible for a family and has succeeded. She is *not* a woman of pronounced individual sensibility or powerful personal emotions. She does have a strong, possibly Scandinavian sense of practical justice, somewhat humourless but rock-solid, and a need to organise things, which she recognises and allows to flourish. She is contrasted both with her own dependent and aimlessly locally efficient mother (small flowerbeds, bottled fruit are the extent of her domain) and with Marie Shabata. Marie has as much energy as Alexandra, but in her case the vitality is sexual and leads both to her mistaken early marriage and to her affection for her disappointing husband as well as her tragic love for Emil. Alexandra has patience—consider the way in which she listens to Crazy Ivar, carefully and without ridicule, the way in which she directs her brothers without rousing real opposition. She has patience and judgment, and there is more than some symbolic Corn Goddess, there is genuine human virtue, in her final decision to fight for Frank Shabata's release when he has murdered her brother. "Frank was the only one, Alexandra told herself, for whom anything could be done." The limits of her sympathy and intelligence are economically and brilliantly given to us in a series of moments of vision or decisive comments. Consider the way in which Alexandra decides how to save the pigs. Or the certainty of Willa Cather's summing-up ("The Wild Land") after the vision of Alexandra sitting in her rocking chair with the Swedish Bible. "Her body was in an attitude of perfect repose, such as it was apt to take when she was thinking earnestly. Her mind was slow, truthful, steadfast. She had not the least spark of cleverness."

It is difficult to be precise, critically, about the sureness and authority of the form of this novel. Her friend Elizabeth Sergeant records that

> When I let her know that the only flaw I could find in O Pioneers! was that it had no sharp skeleton she swiftly replied, true enough, I had named a weakness. But the land has no sculptured lines or features. The soil is soft, light, fluent, black, for the grass of the plains creates this type of soil as it decays. This influences the mind and memory of the author and so the composition of the story.

In O Pioneers! first, and later in My Ántonia, Death Comes for the Archbishop and other books, the formal coherence comes from the way Willa Cather relates the time of memory, the time of one human life, the time of the seasons and the land, and the nature of death into a slow, retrospective meditation. Death punctuates and paces O Pioneers!, but the novel refuses the form of a life story or a tragedy that ends with an individual death. One of the finest things in it is the death of John Bergson, who is exhausted by the land. "He was ready to give up, he felt. He did not know how it had come about, but he was quite willing to go deep under his fields and rest, where the plow could not find him. He was tired of making mistakes . . ."

In this passage Alexandra represents young energy:

He heard her quick step, and saw her tall figure appear in the doorway . . . He felt her youth and strength, how easily she moved and stooped and lifted. But he would not have had it again if he could, not he! He knew the end too well to wish to begin again. He knew where it all went to, what it all became.

Willa Cather's *placing* of this passage is in itself amazing. It follows the haunting description of the inhuman formless land. "Of all the bewildering things about a new country, the absence of human landmarks is one of the most depressing and disheartening." The sod houses are grave-like, "only the inescapable ground in another form." "The record of the plow was insignificant, like the feeble scratches on stone left by prehistoric races, so indeterminate that they may, after all, be only the markings of glaciers, and not a record of human strivings."

And yet the end of the same chapter is not Bergson's deathbed—which is never described—but a loving description of Mrs. Bergson's gardening and fruit-preserving habits, her extravagance with sugar, preservation of an old form of life. And the next chapter begins: "One Sunday afternoon in July, six months after John Bergson's death." Death is absorbed in life and energy, trivial and enduring.

The adult Alexandra, by "Neighbouring Fields," before any tragedy, has a sense of a desire for death associated with the land. She tells Carl, "We grow hard and heavy here," and compares herself with Carrie Jensen,

who had never been out of the cornfields, and a few years ago she got despondent and said life was just the same thing over and over, and she didn't see the use of it. After she had tried to kill herself once or twice her folks got worried and sent her over to Iowa to visit some relations. Ever since she's come back she's been perfectly cheerful and she says she's contented to live and work in a world that's so big and interesting.

This may be related to Cather's own ambivalence about the hardness of her land. She told Elizabeth Sergeant when she was writing "The Bohemian

Girl" that on her return to Red Cloud she had felt that a sudden death would overtake her somewhere in the prairie. This feeling, Miss Sergeant says, would come on her obsessively and darken her life for days. She reminisced about originals of Crazy Ivar, farmers, "Norsemen" who went mad and killed themselves during the years of drought which impoverished them during Cather's university years. Distance and memory enable celebration—but the dark aspects persist.

Just as the placing of the death of John Bergson sharpens our vision of the light, the land and Alexandra's energy, so the placing of the murder of Emil and Marie further complicates our sense of death. We see them, as we do not see Bergson, as dying animals, bloody, struggling, losing their last force, from a distance. This would not be so moving if it were not preceded by the sudden death of Emil's friend Amédée and Emil's meditations on it. Emil is full of youth, excitement—

> at that height of excitement from which everything is foreshortened, from which life seems short and simple, death very near, and the soul seems to soar like an eagle. As he rode past the graveyard he looked at the brown hole in the earth where Amédée was to lie, and felt no horror. That too was beautiful, that simple doorway into forgetfulness. The heart, when it is too much alive, aches for that brown earth, and ecstasy has no fear of death.

He goes on through hot ripe wheat into the sunlight—"light was the reality, the trees were merely interferences that reflected and refracted light." It is a dangerous lyricism, a Wagnerian Liebestod, on its own, but in the context of the whole novel, where death becomes part of exhaustion, madness, heaviness, it is a part-truth. It is Emil, not Alexandra, who enters myth, but only briefly and partially in the language. And the bloodiness of his death partly negates and darkens the liveliness of the lovers' blood at the end of this scene.

This brings us to Alexandra's mythical aspect, her recurring dream of the very strong male lover who will carry her away, who is first the earth and then, after Emil's death, "the mightiest of all lovers"—Death, indistinguishable from the land. Emil dies brightly: Alexandra suffers pain, torpor, despair after his death. She comes to her father's state: "She knew at last for whom it was she had waited, and where he would carry her. That, she told herself, was very well."

But Alexandra does not die: she busies herself about Frank, and is reunited to Carl. The last paragraph of the novel is, to modern readers, possibly too easily lyrical and exclamatory. But how exactly it brings together all the threads of Cather's meditation, like a piece of music: the land, death, the failure of energy, the new energy of youth, the classical and biblical echoes in this formless country that was so hard to come to terms with or bring form to. This is pastoral—and part of its embarrassment is that it is a thin echo of other, older pastorals. I don't think that its "yellow wheat" negates or transcends the sod houses or the "light, fluent, black" earth made of decayed grass. They are all part of the same vision.

> They went into the house together, leaving the Divide behind them, under the evening star. Fortunate country, that is one day to receive hearts like Alexandra's into its bosom, to give them out again in the yellow wheat, in the rustling corn, in the shining eyes of youth!

(1983)

The Professor's House

The Professor's House was first published in 1925 when its author, like its hero, was in her early fifties. Lionel Trilling, in 1937, called the novel "lame" but used it as an example of a prevalent American mood after the First War. This was a mood of disgust with money-making machinery, "a régime of sameness," according to Cather herself, and concentration on mass-produced material goods. Cather's earlier novels had been concerned with the rigours and triumphs of settlers and pioneers: it is certainly true that she, like Professor St. Peter, felt exhausted and out of place in the 1920s. Lionel Trilling was eloquent about her message. "She implies that in our civilisation even the best ideals are bound to corruption," he said, and went on to generalise. "Some vestige of the odd striving after new worlds which cannot be gratified seems to spread a poison through the American soul, making it thin and insubstantial, unable to find peace and solidity." Cather, he concluded, advocated (inadequately) "devitalisation" and a nostalgic retreat into "pre-adolescent integration and innocent community with nature."

Here Trilling, unusually for him, seems to be interpreting *The Professor's House* all too easily as a "symbolic" novel, in which St. Peter's human fatigue and readiness to die can be happily equated with cultural tedium and disgust. Cather, whatever her inadequacies as an infrequent, and perhaps for that reason too vehement polemicist, is a better artist than that. She knows about pure biological fatigue as well as about cultural nostalgia. It seems to me to be interesting to try and see how far the two are separated and how far they are integrated in *The Professor's House*.

The novel is certainly, in a very deliberately patterned way, concerned with the history of Western, and American, culture. Consider St. Peter's full name, Napoleon Godfrey St. Peter. The Napoleon is there because there has always been a Napoleon in the family "since a remote grandfather got his discharge from the Grande Armée" and emigrated to Canada rather than witness the disintegration of Emperor and Empire. "Godfrey" derives, I take it, from another triumphant conqueror, Godfrey of Bouillon, who took Jerusalem when other crusaders failed and was the hero of Tasso's *Jerusalem Delivered*. St. Peter is the rock on which the Roman church was built, though Professor St. Peter, ironically, has been cut off from his family's Catholic tradition. Three founding conquerors. And St. Peter's life-work is the eight-volume *Spanish Adventurers in North America*—a subject in which Cather herself had been interested in early youth, using Coronado's description of his expedition in search of "seven golden cities" as a symbol of dream and ambition in an early story, "The Enchanted Bluff" (based on an even earlier adolescent tale), reworking the Western settlers' children's discussions of Coronado in *My Ántonia,* where Jim Burden asks, "Why had Coronado never gone back to Spain, to his riches and his castles and his King? I couldn't tell them. I only knew the school-books said he 'died in the wilderness of a broken heart.' " Compare St. Peter's meditation on Napoleon: "One pays, coming or going. A man has got only just so much in him; when it's gone, he slumps. Even the first Napoleon did." Throughout her life Willa Cather was interested in powerful explorers, men who travelled and discovered and died. She compared the great railroad pioneers in *A Lost Lady* to a generation of heroic chivalric knights. In an early essay (1896) on "The Kingdom of Art" she specifically uses the crusaders as a metaphor for the daring spirit of the artist:

There were other crusades many centuries ago, when all the good men who were otherwise unemployed and their wives and progeny set out for Palestine. But they found that the holy sepulchre was a long way off, and there was no beaten path thereto, and the mountains were high and the sands hot and the waters of the desert were bitter brine. So they decided to leave the journey to the pilgrims who were madmen anyway, without homes; who found the water no bitterer than their own tears and the desert sands no hotter than the burning hearts within them. In the kingdom of art there is no God but one God and his service is so exacting that there are few men born of woman who are strong enough to take the vows. There is no paradise offered for a reward to the faithful, no celestial bowers, no houris, no scented wines; only death and the truth.

The Professor is—I shall come back to that—a pilgrim who has set out, not as a madman without a home but with his wife and progeny. But he is a crusader for the Kingdom of Art, which he equates, quite explicitly, in the only lecture of his that we hear, with religion, contrasting both, rather crudely, with "science," which has as a phase of human development only "given us a lot of ingenious toys; they take our attention away from the real problems of course, and since the real problems are insoluble, I suppose we ought to be grateful for distraction." Whereas the Church makes each life, each human act, mysterious and important. "It makes us happy to surround our creature needs and bodily instincts with as much pomp and circumstance as possible. Art and religion (they are the same thing in the end, of course) have given man the only happiness he has ever had."

This lecture can, and should, be juxtaposed with the lecture given by Father Duchêne to Tom Outland and Blake in the village—the Cliff City—they have discovered on the hidden mesa. The cliff-dwellers are in a sense the opposite of Godfrey, Napoleon, the conquistadores: they have settled and "developed considerably the arts of peace"—beautiful, organically related buildings, cloth, pottery, astronomical observations, "making their mesa more and more worthy to be a home for man, purifying life by religious ceremonies and observances . . . They were perhaps too far advanced for their time and environment."

Willa Cather, a ferociously ambitious woman, had a complex attitude to the "arts of peace." In all her novels she shows understanding of, and profound respect for, the making of gardens in wilderness, traditions of civilised food ceremony. The Professor in this novel has created—in his old house—a French garden, walled-in, tended for twenty years, "the comfort of his life." Willa Cather felt that the French had a continuity that the Americans—brashly importing Norwegian manor houses, and wrought-iron door fittings, like Louie Marsellus—had not, or had lost before it was established. She also had a strong feeling for the Virgilian decorum of the *Georgics,* the classic pastoral. If Godfrey St. Peter, with his face like a Spanish grandee and his swimming mask like a Greek warrior, is a pioneer, Augusta, the German Catholic maid, combines, in her name and occupation, the Christian and classical "arts of peace." In the sewing room that is also the Professor's study, her household stuff is harmoniously stored with his notes. And it is she who tells him, as though art and ceremony flowed naturally from domestic concerns, that "just as soon as the angel had announced to her that she would be the mother of our Lord, the Blessed Virgin sat down and composed the Magnification." St. Peter compares the household work of his womenfolk, while he was writing, to the women who embroidered birds and beasts on the Bayeux tapestry while history unfolded.

Godfrey St. Peter—much more than Thea Kronborg in *The Song of the Lark*—is intensely drawn to civilised family life and to fierce solitary contemplation and endeavour. Cather, I believe, regarded this doubleness as inevitable and fundamental in human relations. In an essay on Katherine Mansfield, she praises the other woman's gift for showing

the many kinds of personal relationships which exist in an everyday "happy family" who are merely going on living their daily lives, with no crises or shocks or bewildering complications to try them. Yet every individual in that household (even the children) is clinging passionately to his individual soul, is in terror of losing it in the general family flavour . . . One realises that even in harmonious families there is this double life; the group life, which is the one we can observe, in our neighbours' household, and underneath, another—secret and passionate and intense—which is the real life that stamps the faces and gives character to the voices of our friends . . . One realises that human relationships are the tragic necessity of human life; that they can never be wholly satisfactory, that every ego is half the time greedily seeking them, and half the time pulling away from them. In those simple relationships of loving husband and wife, affectionate sisters, children and grandmother there are innumerable shades of sweetness and anguish which make up the pattern of our lives day by day, though they are not down in the list of subjects from which the conventional novelist works.

One of Willa Cather's most triumphant depictions of these tensions is her cool and yet precisely sympathetic portrayal of the egos and co-existing family warmth and indifference in the generations of women in "Old Mrs. Harris." In *The Professor's House* Godfrey St. Peter moves, as the story progresses, further away from the "general family flavour" towards a resurgence of his old childish solitary self. At the end of the novel, awaiting his family's return from France, he broods that "In great misfortunes people want to be alone. They have a right to be. And the misfortunes that occur within one are the greatest. Surely the saddest thing in the world is falling out of love—if once one has fallen in." It might seem significant at this point that the ship on which his wife, his daughter and his son-in-law Louie Marsellus are returning is called the *Berengaria*. Berengaria was, of course, the wife abandoned by Richard Coeur de Lion for his crusades—I associate this with the contrast in the passage in "The Kingdom of Art" in which the good unemployed men "with their wives and progeny" are contrasted with the true solitaries who simply seek "death and the truth."

Louie Marsellus's name is interesting. He is not the heir or son-in-law St. Peter would have chosen: he has replaced the pilgrim Tom Outland, who quotes the *Aeneid* effortlessly and has "fine long hands with backspringing thumbs which had never handled things which were not symbols of ideas." Louis Napoleon could not carry on the Napoleonic ideal. Aeneas in the underworld meets two Marcelluses: one a soldier who has carried off the *spolia optima,* the spoils of war, and the other Augustus's much-mourned adopted son who married his daughter and died young. Marsellus in the book is Jewish, sensuous, vulgar, generous, and is cast in a pageant by St. Peter as Saladin, confronting his other son-in-law, the not-too-bright Scott McGregor, a non-artistic versifier, as Coeur de Lion. (It is of Louie that St. Peter's wife remarks sagely that "The Oriental peoples didn't have an Age of Chivalry. They didn't need one.") Louie Marsellus is said to be partly a portrait of Jan Hambourg, a Jewish musician who married Willa Cather's close friend and companion Isabelle McClung, in whose house Cather had had her first writing room, "a sewing-room at the top of the house fitted up for her as a study," according to a later friend, Edith Lewis, who said that the young journalist in 1899 "enjoyed a tranquillity and physical comfort" which she had not known earlier in the McClung household, "with its solidity and comfort, its well-trained servants and ordered routine." *The Professor's House* is dedicated to Jan Hambourg, and prefaced with a quotation from Louie Marsellus about Outland's Indian jewel—"a turquoise set in silver." But the novel embodies complex—and unresolved—feelings about families, solitude, generosity and possessions.

If there is a resolution, it is in the art, in the careful relating of the parts of the whole, which can perhaps best be considered by considering the idea of the "house" itself, and the house in relation to the open spaces near it. At the beginning of the novel the Professor is still working in his "ugly," "dismantled house," in his sewing-room study surrounded by Augusta's ambivalent female "forms"—dressmakers' models, one made of "a dead, opaque, lumpy solidity, like chunks of putty or tightly packed sawdust," one in wire, with no legs, no viscera and a bosom like a bird-cage. These are not works of art, but they are the familiar "forms" amongst whom—unreal women—he *works*. He will not move to his smart new house, purchased with the prize money gained for his *Spanish Adventurers*. Contrasted with both houses are the ostentatious vulgarity of the Marselluses' Norwegian residence on the shores of Lake Michigan, and Scott and Kathleen's bungalow with its colonial glass knobs. Contrasted with all of them are the pre-Christian houses clustered in the clear air on Tom Outland's mesa, which have the qualities of high eternal art and perfect domestic proportion together.

> Far up above me, a thousand feet or so, set in a great cavern in the face of the cliff, I saw a little city of stone, asleep. It was as still as sculpture—and something like that. It all hung together, seemed to have a kind of composition: pale little houses of stone nestling close to one another, perched on top of each other, with flat roofs, narrow windows, straight walls, and in the middle of the group, a round tower . . .
>
> A fringe of cedars grew along the edge of the cavern, like a garden. They were the only living things. Such silence and such stillness and repose—immortal repose. That village sat looking down into the canyon with the calmness of eternity . . . I knew at once that I had come upon the city of some extinct civilisation, hidden away in this inaccessible mesa for centuries, preserved in the dry air and almost perpetual sunlight like a fly in amber . . .

Yet in that little town, so aptly compared by Edward Brown, Miss Cather's biographer, to the "little town" in the "Ode on a Grecian Urn," is the body of a woman probably stabbed for adultery . . .

Cather has written of the effect she wished to achieve by inserting, so boldly, the *Nouvelle* ("Tom Outland's Story") into the *Roman*—imitating the early French and Spanish novelists. The technique seems to me extraordinarily successful in this case—the contrast, as she says, of "Professor St. Peter's house, rather overcrowded and stuffy with new things; American properties, clothes, furs, petty ambitions, quivering jealousies" and "the fresh air that blew off the Blue Mesa." But the effect is more complex than one of simple contrast. In the letter I have just quoted she uses the "domestic interiors of old and modern Dutch paintings" as an example of what she had tried to achieve. "In many of them the scene presented was a living-room warmly furnished, or a kitchen full of food and coppers. But in most of the interiors, whether drawing-room or kitchen, there was a square window, open, through which one saw the masts of ships, or a stretch of grey sea. The feeling of the sea that one got through those square windows was remarkable, and gave me a sense of the fleets of Dutch ships that ply quietly in all the waters of the globe . . ."

In the final part, after stuffiness and air, St. Peter nearly allows himself to die passively of gassing in his attic, which overlooks the inland waters of Lake Michigan. (It was the discovery of a gas by Outland whose patent, bequeathed to Rosamond, made Louie rich.) He is rescued by Augusta, moral in her respect for life and decency. But not before he has contemplated—as Cather and her thoughtful people always do—man's final house. This is not "devitalisation" as Trilling claimed. It is strong knowledge that all energy ends in death, which is as powerful a truth as any uttered by Grecian Urn or mesa village. Cather misquoted it. It is Longfellow's translation of an Anglo-Saxon poem. As she has it, it runs:

> For thee a house was built
> Ere thou wast born;
> For thee a mould was made
> Ere thou of woman camest.

The Professor on his old couch is reminded by the sagging springs of "the sham upholstery that is put in coffins."

"Just the equivocal American way of dealing with serious facts, he reflected. Why pretend that it is possible to soften that last hard bed?" And he thinks that he would rather lie alone than with his wife. "He thought of eternal solitude with gratefulness, as a release from every obligation, from every form of effort. It was the Truth."

Death and the Truth, as Cather had written so long ago. But the truths seen by her dying are not the truths seen by her living heroes: all weigh. She was a true novelist and her book contains without finally "evaluating" bright air, human muddle, stuffy rooms and the truth of the last hard bed, looked at straight. She was wiser than she was clever, which is admirable: but by the time of writing *The Professor's House* she was an unobtrusively great economical artist, too.

(1980)

Death Comes for the Archbishop

Death Comes for the Archbishop was first published in 1927. Willa Cather had been working on, reading about and visiting the deserts and Indian villages of the Southwest for fifteen years before she wrote it, and had come, she says in a letter published in *Commonweal*, to the conclusion that "the story of the Catholic Church in that country was the most interesting of all its stories." In earlier novels she had dealt with the experiences of pioneers and settlers in the raw, featureless land of Nebraska: from very early days she had been interested in texts like Castaneda's account of the Coronado expedition, and in the great American historian and explorer Francis Parkman's accounts of his own journeys amongst Indians and frontiersmen, as well as in his series of historical accounts of French settlers and missionaries in the New World. During a visit to Santa Cruz in New Mexico, Cather formed a friendship with a Belgian priest, Father Haltermann, from whom she learned much about "Indians and their traditions" and also about the nineteenth-century French missionaries, who are the heroes of *Death Comes for the Archbishop*. She tells us (in the letter published in *Commonweal*) that Archbishop Lamy, the first bishop of New Mexico, "had become a sort of invisible personal friend" long before she conceived the idea of writing about the missionaries. A bronze statue of him in Santa Fe interested her in "a pioneer churchman who looked so well-bred and distinguished. In his pictures one felt the same thing, something fearless and fine and very, very well-bred—something that spoke of race. What I felt curious about was the daily life of such a man in a crude frontier society."

Father Lamy must be one of the most immediate and deliberately identifiable originals of any fictive character. However, his companion and friend, Father Machebeuf, who was to become Willa Cather's Father Vaillant, is even more directly identifiable, since Willa Cather read, in 1925, Father W. J. Howlett's *Life of the Right Reverend Joseph P. Machebeuf, Pioneer Priest of Ohio, Pioneer Priest of New Mexico, Pioneer Priest of Colorado, Vicar Apostolic of Colorado and Utah, and First Bishop of Denver* (Pueblo, Colorado, 1908). She drew extensively and in detail on Father Howlett's account, which included Father Machebeuf's letters to his sister in Auvergne. Indeed, as Edward and Lillian Bloom have demonstrated in a well-illustrated article, she reproduced large passages of the book almost verbatim—notably Father Vaillant's season of special devotion to Mary, in May, "when he was a young curate in Cendre." It was Father Howlett's "gentle reminder" that she had not acknowledged her indebtedness, according to the Blooms, which prompted the open letter to *Commonweal* from which we derive considerable insight into what Miss Cather thought she was doing in the novel.

As she herself points out in the *Commonweal* letter, "novel" is a misleading term in some ways. Reviewers, she says, found the book hard to classify—to which she characteristically responds, "Why bother?" and goes on: "Many more reviewers assert vehemently that it is not a novel. Myself, I prefer to call it a narrative." In that, it bears some resemblance to other American writing of the time—such as William Carlos Williams's brilliant and very influential *In the American Grain,* first published in 1925, a work of art which recounts the making, discovery, racial mix of America, from Red Eric through Cortez, Raleigh, the *Mayflower,* Daniel Boone, to Aaron Burr and Lincoln. D. H. Lawrence said of this book: "All America is now going hundred per cent American. But the only hundred per cent American is the Red Indian, and he can only be canonized when he is finally dead . . . the unravished *local* America still waits, vast and virgin as ever, though in the process of being murdered." And Williams himself said of the aesthetically exciting patchwork quality of *In the American Grain:* "In letters, in journals, reports of happenings I have recognised new contours suggested by old words so that new names were constituted. Thus, where I have found noteworthy stuff, bits of writing have been copied into the book for the taste of it. Everywhere I have tried to separate out from the original records some flavour of an actual peculiarity, the character denoting shape which the unique force has given."

Williams's America went to the making of Hart Crane's *The Bridge:* I do not know if it affected Cather, but I do feel that Williams's concern with the specific, the local, the *name* is akin to many of Miss Cather's own concerns, and that her sense of "American" history is illuminated by a comparison with his. Willa Cather had been confirmed in the Episcopal Church in 1922, but her preoccupation with religion, with church buildings, with missions is profoundly a preoccupation with culture and its transmission, and was there long before she felt any personal desire or need to join a particular church. Her discrimination of something "very, very well-bred—something that spoke of race" in Bishop Lamy's face, with its complete approval of this racial stamp, is indicative of her attitude. She believed that the French were sanely and humanly civilised, and that they had developed the arts of peace to a high degree—it is as important to her that the missionaries bring excellent soup, well-roast lamb, wine for the table and methods of gardening to the culture of New Mexico as that they bring true doctrine or even a cathedral. Her admiration of the French caused her to change the emphasis in passages she based, particularly in *Shadows on the Rock* (1931), on Parkman's histories. Parkman saw history in terms of a struggle between progress and reaction, represented by England and France, and placed his personal faith in some middle way, a "conservative republic." Cather wholeheartedly admired the French aristocratic way, the way of Bishop Latour, as well as of Count Frontenac (whom Parkman admired) and Bishop Laval (whom he disapproved of severely) in the seventeenth-century Quebec of *Shadows on the Rock*. It is significant that when she died she was writing a book about Provence, whose unchanging indigenous culture she admired.

As she frequently did, when talking about the art of writing, Willa Cather invoked the art of painting to explain her aesthetic aims. What she got from Father Machebeuf's letters, she wrote, "was the mood, the spirit, in which they accepted the accidents and hardships of a desert country, the joyful energy that kept them going. To attempt to convey this hardihood of spirit one must use language a little stiff, a little formal, one must not be afraid of the old trite phraseology of the frontier. Some of those time-worn phrases I used as the note from the piano by which the violinist tunes his instrument." The aristocracy of spirit, the old common speech of the frontier, gave her the stuff of "legend," which was what she wanted to do. As she points out, her book was "a conjunction of the general and the particular, like most works of the imagination." She goes on:

> I had all my life wanted to do something in the style of legend, which is absolutely the reverse of dramatic treatment. Since I first saw the Puvis de Chavannes frescoes of the life of St. Geneviève in my student days, I have wished that I could try something like that in prose; something without accent, with none of the artificial elements of composition. In the Golden Legend the martyrdoms of the saints are no more dwelt on than are the trivial incidents of their lives; it is as though all human experiences, measured against one supreme spiritual experience, were of about the same importance. The essence of such writing is not to hold the note—not to use an incident for all there is in it—but to touch and pass on. I felt that such writing would be a kind of discipline in these days when the 'situation' is made to count for so much in writing, when the general tendency is to force things up.

In much of her earlier work she had already been attempting to write "without accent," and also to treat all incidents as "of about the same importance." In *O Pioneers!* and *My Ántonia,* violent death, moments of vision, the careful preparation of food are treated at the same leisurely narrative pace, described but not angled from any "point of view," so that ultimately all do indeed seem to be part of the same experience, the whole of which is both simpler than, and greater than, the sum of its component parts. That is why, I think, there has been some legitimate critical confusion over the title *Death Comes for the Archbishop.* It arouses expectations in the reader which are not fulfilled—that death and the Archbishop are of equal importance in the narrative, whereas in fact the Archbishop's death is only one further incident in the series of frozen gestures, moments of insight, small comedies and agonies which make up the fresco. In the novel, as he did not in life, the Archbishop outlives his life-companion, Father Vaillant, and this in some sense, by making the Archbishop's own death a gentle part of his solitary and peaceful retrospective contemplation of his life in that land, does remove from it any dramatic quality it might have had. Other deaths are briefly dramatic—the legendary, comic-terrible execution of Friar Baltazar at Acóma, the boy executed for a momentary flash of anger at a cockfight, Padre Lucero's oracular and bizarre last words—but the death that comes for the Archbishop is simply the close of the narrative. Willa Cather says she chose the title from Holbein's *Dance of Death*—another visual series of figures arrested in mid-gesture—and in that sense, though not obviously, it is related to her ambition to write as Puvis painted. My own response to the analogy with Puvis de Chavannes was originally to think that the soft, other-worldly mournful quality of the gestures of his figures represented something much less tough and wild and complex than the world of *Death Comes for the Archbishop,* however eternally still its landscape, whatever peaceful human eternity of repetition is found in the actions of celebrating Mass or cooking a gigot. It is interesting to note, however, that the works of Puvis excited Van Gogh for much the same reasons that they excited Willa Cather—he described his paintings as representing "a strange and providential meeting of *very* far-off antiquities and *crude* modernity." They were, he said, "prophetic" like those of Delacroix: "Before them one feels an emotion as if one were present at the continuation of all kinds of things, a benevolent renaissance ordained by fate."

In her essay "The Novel Démeublé" Cather compares her desired art to the operations of modern painters, not primarily concerned with verisimilitude. "The higher processes of art are all processes of simplification. The novelist must learn to write and then he must unlearn it; just as the modern painter learns to draw and then learns when utterly to disregard his accomplishment . . ." She admired Thomas Mann as a novelist who was modern, who "belongs immensely to the forward-goers . . . But he also goes back a long way, and his backwardness is more gratifying to the backward." In her collection of essays, *Not Under Forty,* she classed herself firmly as a "backward" writer for "backward" readers. Her expressed admiration for Mann's depiction of the beginnings of our culture, in *Joseph and His Brethren,* tells us much about what she herself hoped to achieve in her depiction of Indian culture and early Christian churches alike. Mann described his ancient Hebrews as "much like ourselves, aside from a measure of dreamy indefiniteness in their habits of thought." Cather commends this "indefiniteness" as one of "the most effective elements of verity in this great work" and claims it "belongs to a people without any of the relentless mechanical gear which directs every moment of modern life towards accuracy":

> We are among a shepherd people; the story has almost the movement of grazing sheep. The characters live at that pace. Perhaps no one who has not lived among sheep can recognize the rightness of the rhythm. A shepherd people is not driving towards anything. With them truly, as Michelet said of quite another form of journeying, the end is nothing, the road is all. In fact the road and the end are literally one.
> There is nothing in *Joseph and His Brethren* more admirable than the tempo, the deliberate sustained pace.

Nothing in *Death Comes for the Archbishop* is more admirable than the pace, either, though, as I have already suggested, it is not exactly or simply the pace of a shepherd people. Cather is dealing with various elements of New Mexican culture, of American culture, which, although they exist side by side in the same landscape and fresco, are part of the same world, are not *blended,* but clearly differentiated. The American frontiersman, represented by Kit Carson, a real friend of the real Bishop Lamy, stands beside the quite different Hispanic world of the Olivares and the aristocratic Don Manuel Chavez, Indian-hater, which again are different from the excesses of the native Mexican priests, and from the mysterious, partly apprehended world of the Indians. In her letter to *Commonweal,* Cather describes the sense she had of the *difference* of the churches, with their "countless, fanciful figures of the saints, not two of them alike." "In lonely, sombre villages in the mountains the church decorations were sombre, the martyrdoms bloodier, the grief of the Virgin more agonised, the figure of Death more terrifying. In warm, gentle valleys everything about the churches was milder." These differences she has conveyed. Underlying them, as she tells us of *Joseph and His Brethren,* is

> the Book of Genesis, like a faded tapestry deep in the consciousness of almost every individual who is more than forty years of age . . . We are familiar with Mann's characters and their history, not only through Moses and the Prophets, but through Milton and Dante and Racine, Bach and Haydn and Handel, through painters and architects and stone-cutters innumerable. We begin with the great imaginings and the great imaginators already in our minds—we are dyed through and through with them.

Something of this inevitable quality too, whatever her, or our, religious beliefs, she has given to the life of the Church in its new land.

Her two major characters are also distinct. Like Christian and Faithful, they are named for what they represent. Vaillant, valiant-for-truth, goes out on journeys: associated with him are his mules, waggons, litter, cooking, social encounters. Latour, the Tower, is conscious culture, well-read, reserved, just, whose crowning achievement is his cathedral, built like the Palais des Papes in Avignon, Midi Romanesque, "the first Romanesque church in the New World," but built in, and of, the local golden rock, as part of the landscape. It is a central part of Cather's skill as a novelist that she can convey both Latour's aesthetic passion and Father Vaillant's curious reluctance to share it, or care about buildings, without feeling it necessary to judge between them. In the same way, describing the relations of the Indians to the rocks on which they live, she can comment: "It was the Indian manner to vanish into the landscape, not to stand out against it." They decorate pots and cloth, but they have not "the European's desire to 'master' nature, to arrange and re-create." Her descriptions of the Indian mesa towns on the rock are as beautiful, as unjudging, as lucid, as her description of the Bishop's cathedral. It is an art of "making," of clear depiction—of separate objects, whose whole effect works slowly and mysteriously in the reader and cannot be summed up.

Rebecca West, reviewing *Death Comes for the Archbishop* in 1927, recognised it as a masterpiece, and recognised its mastery in Cather's command of the sensuous. "She builds her imagined world almost as solidly as our five senses build the universe around us." She observes, interestingly, that "The Roman Catholic Church has never doubted that sense is a synthesis of the senses; and it has never doubted that man must take the universe sensibly." That is witty, profound and true. It leads to "an art" not remote from William Carlos Williams's desideratum, "No ideas but in things," though the two writers began very differently. Rebecca West also observes that "some of the recent work of D. H. Lawrence" is concerned with the consciousness of Indians, and its inaccessibility to modern man: she discusses the "Stone Lips" chapter where Latour decides he cannot know about Jacinto's beliefs and customs and does not ask. "He didn't think it polite, and he believed it to be useless." His European mind cannot know Jacinto's tradition, and he is content to rest with the mystery. Lawrence, as Rebecca West sagely remarks, would not have been so content: he would have attempted "irritably and with partial failure, but also with greater success than any previous aspirant," to imagine, to become, the invisible snake and hidden river. Is his art therefore, West asks, greater than Willa Cather's classic discretion? She does not answer herself. Nor need we. But Willa Cather's composed acceptance of mystery is a major, and rare, artistic achievement.

(1981)

13

Elizabeth Bowen:
The House in Paris

M Y RELATIONSHIP with *The House in Paris* has been odd, continuous and shifting for many years. It has had a disproportionate influence, both good and bad, on my ideas about the writing of novels and, indeed, about the nature of fiction. It seems proper to begin by explaining this, since I do now believe it to be both the best of Elizabeth Bowen's novels and a very good novel by any critical standards. But the reading process behind these judgments has been complicated.

I was given *The House in Paris* by my father when I was quite a small child, maybe ten or eleven, roughly the age of Henrietta in the novel itself. My father was under the impression that the book was a historical novel, having mistaken Elizabeth Bowen for the historical writer Marjorie Bowen. I began the book, a compulsive reader, having already worked my way through most of Scott and much of Dickens, expecting to find a powerful plot, another world to inhabit, love, danger. I found instead my first experience of a wrought, formalised "modern" novel, a novel which played tricks with time and point of view. A novel, also (and this I remember clearly as being supremely important), which clarified, or would have clarified if I had been clever enough to focus it, the obscure, complex and alarming relationships between children, sex and love. There were powerful phrases which lodged in my mind and have stayed there. "Years before sex had power to touch his feeling it had forced itself into view as an awkward tangle of motives." Or, "The mystery about sex comes from confusion and terror: to a mind on which these have not yet settled there is nothing you cannot tell." Or, "There is no end to the violations committed by children on children, quietly talking alone." I finished the book, deeply uncertain about what was happening, deeply troubled about how to judge the relative weight of any of the events or people. I read it, in fact, with a social, sexual and narrative innocence which was the equivalent of Henrietta's own. I learned, from that reading, two things. First, that "the modern novel" was difficult: it stopped and analysed little things, when you wanted to get on with the big things—it made it clear to you that you did not understand events, or other people. And, more important, more durable, I learned that Elizabeth Bowen had *got Henrietta right*. Adult readers are too given to saying, of children like Henrietta, that "real" children are not so sophisticated, so articulate, so thoughtful. What I remember with absolute clarity from this reading was a feeling that the private analyses I made to myself of things were vindicated, the confusions I was aware of were real, and presumably important and interesting, since here they were described. There is a sense in which Henrietta, and indeed Leopold, are more subtle images of the innocent or immature perception of adult behaviour than James's Maisie, in *What Maisie Knew*. Maisie is a *tour de force,* a brilliant creation, a vehicle both for James's technical mastery and for his moral commentary. But Leopold, and still more Henrietta, are children equipped with the language of the secret thoughts of intelligent children, with no more and no less than that. They make Maisie seem very much a creature of adult artifice.

After this innocent reading I put the book away for some years. In my late teens I read it again, several times; focused now much more on Karen and the central section of the novel, on love, passion, the breaking of convention, the moment of truth, the definition of identity. At that stage I think I saw the novel very strongly as a model of good writing, an example of how to be precise about thought, emotion, passion and character. To me then the restaurant scene in Boulogne, the bedroom scene in Hythe, seemed to be the central scenes, remarkable for concentrating so much passion in so few words, for the violence of life one looked for in books and feared to miss in reality.

Later still I came to think less well of the novel, dismissing it as too much a work of "fine-drawn sensibility." It seemed too much the novel-as-object, inexorably shaped and limited by its own internal laws. I had by then read James, Forster, Woolf, Ford: "modernism" no longer shocked or confused me. I became a discriminating reader and saw merits in the heavy, broad, open-ended Victorian novels, admired by Dr. Leavis and Iris Murdoch, which made Elizabeth Bowen's precise distinctions, her craftsmanship, appear minor virtues, and her world, so economically, so selectively presented, appear shadowy. And then, recently, I read the novel again and saw that it is one of those books that grow in the mind, in time. As it is impossible at Henrietta's age to realise the nature of sex, however aware one is of its presence, so at the age when one is necessarily interested in imperative passion, the identity of the character stripped for action decisive or disastrous, it is impossible to *realise* that sex has a history, that children are the result of sex, that children are people produced by other people's sexual behaviour, and that with children, as with lovers and husbands, relationships of some complexity exist. One may think as a child reader, as a young reader, that one is aware of the relationship of Leopold to the plot of the book. But to recognise the full emotional force of his existence one has simply and necessarily to have lived through a certain amount of time. As with Henrietta, I came to realise that Elizabeth Bowen had got Leopold right. His claims on the reader's attention, on the other characters' attention, are justified morally and artistically.

I have described this reading and rereading at such length because it is at the least an indication of some imaginative force in Elizabeth Bowen, but also because it was, with this novel, a peculiarly valuable way into its themes and subject-matter. *The House in Paris* is a novel about sex, time and the discovery of identity. That my readings of it in some way reflected the process it was dealing with was, in the end, my good luck.

"Plot might seem to be a matter of choice. It is not. The particular plot is something the novelist is driven to: it is what is left after the whittling-away of alternatives." Elizabeth Bowen opened her "Notes on Writing a Novel" (1945, reprinted in *Collected Impressions,* 1950) with this statement. I think, finally, it is in the simple brilliance of the plot that the power of *The House in Paris* lies. It is a plot of considerable primitive force—child in search of unknown parents, parents in search of unknown child, love and death as identical moments of extremity. It works by playing these powerful emotions and events off against the confusions, the limitations, the continuities created by a particular civilisation, a particular time and culture. Thus in the first part, "The Present," Leopold and Henrietta are both attempting to define, or assert, their own identities, which are thrown into relief by the alien quality of the enclosing Anglo-French house in Paris inhabited by adult passions, and equally by adult social conventions, with which they are not used to dealing. Leopold is in a state of disaster and crisis; Henrietta is a normal little girl, trying to deal with tragedy through a set of responses formed only for controlled social situations.

"Today was to do much to disintegrate Henrietta's character, which, built up by herself, for herself, out of admonitions and axioms (under the growing stress of: If I am Henrietta, then what is *Henrietta?*) was a mosaic of all possible kinds of prejudice. She was anxious to be someone, and, no one having ever voiced a prejudice in her hearing without impressing her, had come to associate prejudice with identity. You could not be someone without disliking things . . . Now she sat biting precisely into her half of roll, wondering how one could bear to eat soppy bread." Henrietta "longed already to occupy people's fancies, speculations, and thoughts." Whereas Leopold, brought up by his adopted parents, was "over understood . . . He knew too well these people found him remarkable . . . Where he came from, kindness thickened the air and sentiment fattened on the mystery of his birth. Years before sex had power to touch his feeling it had forced itself into view as an awkward tangle of motives. There was no one he could ask frankly: 'Just how odd *is* all this?' The disengaged Henrietta had been his first looking-glass." Leopold's situation of extremity and indefiniteness is emphasised by the letter he reads from the adopted parents, with its complete ignorance of his nature and needs, its grotesque emphasis on his dangerous heredity and possible digestive upsets.

> We do not consider him ripe for direct sex-instruction yet, though my husband is working towards this through botany and mythology. When the revelation regarding himself must come, what better prototypes could he find than the Greek and other heroes, we feel. His religious sense seems still to be dormant. We are educating him on broad undenominational lines such as God is Love.
>
> We have of course no idea *what* revelations Leopold's mother may see fit to make, but we do trust you will beg her to be discreet and have regard for his temperament and the fact that he has not yet received direct sex-instruction. Almost any fact she might mention seems to us still unsuitable.

Leopold's reading of this letter, at a point when the reader is as unaware as he is of the possible nature of his mother's "revelations" and indeed of his mother, is a brilliant piece of plotting. So is the transition from Leopold's quest for self in Part I to Karen's quest for self in Part II, "The Past." The transition from Leopold's mother's non-appearance to the account she did not give him of how he had come to be is masterly. It is not simply authorial sleight-of-hand that gives Elizabeth Bowen the authority to open her fictional account of Leopold's origins with a claim that an *imaginary* mother, like a work of art, can tell the truth because she is not encumbered by either time or conventions. "The mother who did not come to meet Leopold that afternoon remained his creature, able to speak the truth . . . He did not have to hear out with grave discriminating intelligence that grown-up falsified view of what had been once that she, coming in actually, might have given him. She, in the flesh, could have offered him only that in reply to the questions he had kept waiting for so long for her: 'Why am I? What made me be?'" And Elizabeth Bowen adds that "the meeting he had projected could take place only in Heaven—call it Heaven; on the plane of potential not merely likely behaviour. Or call it art, with truth and imagination informing every word."

Elizabeth Bowen's definition of the object of a novel is directly relevant here. It is also as good a statement of the complex relations of truth and fiction as I know. "Plot must further the novel towards its object. What object? The non-poetic statement of a poetic truth . . . Have not all poetic truths already been stated? The essence of a poetic truth is that no statement of it can be final." Earlier in the same essay she said that plot, as well as being story, "is also 'a story' in the nursery sense = lie. The novel lies in saying something happened, that did not. It must, therefore, contain uncontradictable truth to warrant the original lie." Thus Leopold's projected talk with Karen is a lie, as Elizabeth Bowen's novel is a lie, but both are charged with "poetic truth" and related to each other. And there is a sense, one of the real achievements of the book, in which the following flashback to Karen's love for Max carries the plot forward. The "poetic truth" of this novel, as I see it, is about the discovery of identity, and in this sense the woman, Karen, and the man, Max, are continuations of the children Leopold and Henrietta, although they are also means to the redefinition, the restatement, of the child Leopold, in the light of our knowledge of them. That is, the reader moves forward from childhood to young adult love, although the narrative time shifts backwards.

Karen, like the children, defines herself by plotting extremity, disaster, against convention. Her family is happily, successfully conventional in a way nothing in the house in Paris is. They have an "unconscious sereneness behind their living and letting live" which "Karen's hungry or angry friends could not tolerate." "Nowadays such people rarely appear in books; their way of life, though pleasant to share, makes tame reading . . . Karen saw this inherited world enough from the outside to see that it might not last, but for that reason, obstinately stood by it." Ray, whom she is to marry, is of it. Max, like his son, powerful and over-sensitive, has no available conventions, so has to define himself. "Intellect, feeling, force were written all over him; he did in fact cut ice." Mrs. Michealis, Karen's mother, sees that Karen is shaken by him, and makes one of those generalisations, true and inadequate, that together make the tone of this book: careful definition, redefinition, judgment, further judgment.

"She thought, young girls like the excess of any quality. Without knowing, they want to suffer, to suffer they must exaggerate; they like to have loud chords struck on them. Loving art better than life they need men to be actors; only an actor moves them, with his telling smile, undomestic, out of touch with the everyday that they dread. They love to enjoy love as a system of doubts and shocks. They are right: not seeking husbands yet, they have no need to see love socially." Karen's dying Aunt Violet, held even when dying by the everyday, the continuous, the social, sees Karen wistfully as a woman of "character" who could and should have "an interesting life." Karen, in bed with Max, contemplating the possibility of Leopold, thinks that Leopold would be disaster and realises that Aunt Violet "saw Ray was my mother: did she want this for me? I saw her wondering what disaster could be like. The child would be disaster."

Karen's reflections on the impossible disaster represented by the possible Leopold are the next stage in the movement of the plot around the themes of death, sex, identity, time, violence and convention. Imagined Leopold is the imagined, improbable future. "If a child were going to be born, there would still be something that had to be . . . I should not see the hour in the child, I should not have rushed on to nothing." Karen is afraid that her act has been unreal, will come to seem unreal because it has no past or future. In fact, disaster, Leopold's birth, Max's death, are reality, the real future; they are what is, and not what is imagined.

In Part II, Karen and Max, who have no shared past and do not know that they share a future, talk about history. We are told: "side by side in the emptying restaurant, they surrounded themselves with wars, treaties, persecutions, strategic marriages, campaigns, reforms, successions and violent deaths. History is unpainful, memory does not cloud it; you join the emphatic lives of the long dead. May we give the future something to talk about." In Part III it is Ray Forrestier and Leopold together who engineer a continuity, a movement from past through present to future which is on Leopold's part dramatic and on Ray's the product of a profound sense of the saving value of convention, of love as seen by Karen's dead mother (who "died of Leopold"), as protective, practical, normal. Leopold is told by Madame Fisher that he is in a story whose plot has the necessity of fairy-tale. "No doubt you do not care for fairy-tales, Leopold? An enchanted wood full of dumb people would offend you; you are not the young man with the sword who goes jumping his way through. Fairy-tales always made me impatient also. But unfortunately there is no doubt that in life such things exist . . ." Ray, described as looking like "any of these tall Englishmen who stand back in train corridors unobtrusively to let foreigners pass to meals or the lavatory . . . was the Englishman's age: about thirty-six . . . He had exchanged the career he once projected for business, which makes for a more private private life." Ray, that is, appears to be anonymous. But Karen's dramatic act has changed him too; he is in a fairy-tale, and his wife sees him as a fanatic. He is aware that he and Karen are not alone, are not two—they are haunted, as Max and Karen, momentarily, were not—by the absent third, Leopold. Ray, mystically according to Karen, practically according to himself, sets out to rectify the situation. And when Ray meets Leopold, the identities of both are defined, in action. Elizabeth Bowen's description of this action is a marvellous continuation of the fairy-story metaphor and the practical detail of the "non-poetic" novel working together. Leopold is both the prince and the cross, bewildered, egotistical little boy, clearly seen and taken in hand. The story has moved, in our minds, from innocence through violence to insight, from the child's eye, through the obsessive eye of love and the momentary act to the extraordinary and I think unpredictable ending, where expectations are more than fulfilled and the disparate elements of plot and vision are brought together.

There is much more that could be said. This is both a very elegant and a very melodramatic novel. Again in the "Notes on Writing a Novel" Elizabeth Bowen discusses the concept of "relevance," which she declares is "imperative." Everything, she concludes, Character, Scene, Dialogue, must be strictly relevant to the Plot. The elegance of this novel bears witness to her triumphant skill in this field. Not a dialogue in the book does not turn in some way on the central problems and forces it deals with. No situation is described which does not illuminate others. (Consider Madame Fisher's marriage, as it is presented by Madame Fisher to Henrietta, and its relation both to Leopold's idea of love and marriage and to Henrietta's own.) Images recur: mirrors, and eyes as mirrors of identity, Leopold as a growing tree. There are times when such formal elegance, such energetic pursuit of total relevance, can seem narrowing or claustrophobic or detracting from our sense of reality and importance. Elizabeth Bowen learned much from James, and much from Virginia Woolf. One of the things she learned was James's respect for developed form in fiction, his sense that one could achieve subtleties unavailable to the creators of the "loose, baggy monsters" of the nineteenth century. In her weaker works this preoccupation can create a sense of strain, contrivance, even fuss, which diminish the force of the poetic truth. In this novel her priorities seem to me vindicated by the power of the plot. She writes, for all her elegance, with a harshness that is unusual and pleasing. There are moments of vision and metaphor, akin both to James and to Virginia Woolf, but recognisably Elizabeth Bowen's own. As when Naomi's "sudden tragic importance made her look doubtful, as though a great dark plumed hat had been clapped aslant on her head." Or Henrietta, who, "feeling like a kaleidoscope often and quickly shaken, badly wanted some place in which not to think." But the characteristic tone is the author's cool judgment of the power of events, the true nature of events, of the Plot, as she sees it. As a child, I thought I was learning sensibility and fine discrimination from this novel. Now, more important, I feel that Elizabeth Bowen's description of Ivy Compton-Burnett's quality applied also to her own work. She wrote of her in 1941: "Elizabethan implacability, tonic plainness of speaking, are not so strange to us as they were. This is a time for *hard* writers—and here is one."

(1976)

14

Sylvia Plath:
Letters Home

The *Disquieting Muses* offers a clue to the relationship between the fine and terrible poet of *Ariel* and the Sylvia Plath whose *Letters Home* are now edited by her mother. The poem is addressed to a story-telling mother whose witches "always, always/Got baked into gingerbread." It enquires whether she saw, or said spells against, the three ladies like darning eggs who watched the child nightly, "mouthless, eyeless, with stitched bald head." The mother praised the child's music: the child, watched by the bald muses, knew her touch to be "oddly wooden." The mother "cried and cried" when the child, immobilised at a school concert, stood heavy in her twinkle-dress. In a hurricane the mother cheered the children by chanting rhymes. "Thor is angry: we don't care." Those ladies burst the windows. The mother floats off on a green balloon amongst flowers and unreal bluebirds. The child remains with the now stony ladies. "But," she promises, "no frown of mine/Will betray the company I keep." Here is the ambivalent power of the archetypes of magic tale: control of terror, creation of terror. Here is one relationship between bright art and appalling reality. Here is a child frightened permanently by a real and imagined horror she believes her mother cannot or will not acknowledge.

Aurelia Schober Plath, in her introduction, describes the death of her husband. Otto Plath, mostly German, a little Polish, much older than his wife, was a scholar, an expert on bees, a domestic authoritarian. He became ill, and for some years refused to see a doctor, having diagnosed his complaint as lung cancer. It was in fact diabetes. In 1940 he had a gangrenous leg amputated and died. Sylvia Plath was then eight. In the autobiographical *Bell Jar* the heroine's suicide bid follows a visit to her father's grave, where she weeps and realizes she did not do so earlier. She remarks with chilly ambivalence:

> I had a great yearning lately to pay my father back for all the years of neglect and start tending his grave. I had always been my father's favourite and it seemed fitting I should take on a mourning my mother had never bothered with.

Aurelia Plath is distressed by her daughter's attitude to this issue of mourning. She says she wept alone. "What I intended as an exercise in courage for the sake of my children was interpreted years later by my daughter as indifference." She herself had felt her world shaken by seeing her own mother in tears. It is clear that she set herself to shield her children, to secure for them all the moral, material and intellectual advantages they might have had, to make them happy. It is also clear that her self-denial, ideals and expectations were a strain on Sylvia Plath, who probably carried a further strain from her mother's unfulfilled ambitions. Destined to be a "businesswoman," Mrs. Plath lectured in Medical Secretarial Procedures. What she cared for was literature and culture. I fear Mrs. Plath's gallantry will meet with less sympathy than it should. It is easy and customary to blame "the Mother" for many inner horrors. It can be forgotten that mothers, in other lights, are also daughters and women, that the death of a husband creates strains to be endured just as much as the death of a father, that death cannot be undone, either by mourning or by courage.

It is entirely natural that Mrs. Plath should appear unduly concerned that Sylvia not think of "depressing" things: once tragedy has struck a family all the members seem perpetually vulnerable. There is nevertheless something distressing about Sylvia's persistent tone of gay and solicitous reassurance, even accompanying a potentially "depressing" poem with an admonition to "understand that it's done tongue in cheek." Mrs. Plath is disturbed by Sylvia's discovery that sad stories sold better to teenage magazines than "her exuberant, joyous outbursts." In the turmoil of the collapse of Sylvia's marriage, Sylvia writes irritably, for once, rejecting advice to write about "decent courageous people." She published *The Bell Jar* under a pseudonym and felt great guilt over writing it.

The letters were selectively edited and have been cut. This may, or may not, be responsible for the fact that even those Mrs. Plath apologetically calls "desperate," written in 1963, seem strenuously cheery, at worst irritable or briefly glum. The prevailing tone throughout is Pollyanna's "being glad"—a mixture of euphoria, lists of social, publishing and academic successes and a women's magazine self-examination for signs of "maturity." I knew Sylvia Plath very slightly at Cambridge and found her hard to talk to: she was very gracious, very deliberately outgoing, almost aggressively an image of the healthy American girl, blonded hair, red mouth, full of bouncy wonder. I can imagine that girl writing these letters: not those poems. The letters show her creating herself deliberately as a success, in both conventional social terms and competitive academic ones. There was tension between these—at high school, after her early lyrics had pleased a teacher, she wrote in her diary: "I am doubtful about poetry's effect on the little strategy of 'popularity' I have been building up." She made her A grades into an incredulous joke for dancing partners, hid her publishing successes from potentially jealous contemporaries. She worked with obsessive perfectionism, writing fifteen hundred words a day as "scales and exercises," even, after her breakdown, producing the best occupationally therapeutic weaving in her mental hospital—"though Sylvia claimed it was awful."

Her intelligence worked at another level on this process of mask-making and character-building. At seventeen, in her diary she analyses a conscious and complex narcissism. She is afraid of marriage. She would prefer to be a disembodied God. But "I have a terrible egotism. I love my flesh, my limbs with overwhelming devotion . . . I pose and prink before the mirror . . . I have erected in my mind an image of myself,—idealistic and beautiful. Is not that image, free from blemish, the true perfection?" At twenty-two, after the suicide bid, the resurrected intellect was working on Dostoevsky's "doubles." She writes of the delights of Freud, Frazer and Jung—

> all fascinating stuff about the ego as symbolised in reflections (mirrors and water), shadows, twins—dividing off and becoming an enemy, or omen of death . . . or a means by which one denies the power of death (e.g. by creating the idea of the soul as the deathless double of the immortal body).

When she met Ted Hughes at Cambridge she was an accomplished craftsman, a fiercely competitive intellectual, a woman afraid of being too powerful, seeing herself as a "queen" among men, or "the princess on the glass hill." Ted Hughes was "the only man in the world who is my match." Marriage to him produces a vatic note in her letters:

> I am a woman and glad of it and my songs will be of the fertility of the earth and the people in it, through waste, sorrow and death. I shall be a woman singer and Ted and I shall make a fine life together.

The marriage broke the forms and ambitions which had so far sustained and strained her. She decided, Hughes says, "with great difficulty and against great tactical opposition from individuals she regarded as benefactors, to leave teaching and throw herself on writing." Ted, she writes, "doesn't demand Immediate Success and Publication and is teaching me not to." She rejects the "academic writer" who doesn't *feel* reality, but thinks and needs "symbols irony archetypal images and all that. Well, we will try to get along without such conscious and contrived machinery. We write and wake up with symbols on our pages but do not begin with them." The fastidious aesthete slowly making verbal mosaics with a Thesaurus is suddenly able to improvise rapidly on themes suggested by a ouija board. The poets devised "exercises of meditation and invocation" to "break down the tyranny, the fixed focus and public persona" of poems. Sylvia Plath found that meditation, magic, folklore and the figures—vampires, witches and serpents—of her private nightmare world cohered. "With the birth of her first child," Hughes says, "she received herself and was able to turn to her advantage all the forces of a highly-disciplined, highly intellectual style of education which had, up to this point, worked mainly against her . . ."

The rest is by now history and mythology. The marriage failed. Hughes's successful presence clearly threatened her attempts to reassert her social and intellectual selves in his milieu. She wrote *The Bell Jar,* thus, presumably, calling up the emotions and images of that earlier terror and failure. She also wrote, before her suicide, the triumphantly powerful *Ariel* poems in which witch and woman, waxen image and perfected death-mask, angry wife and mother and daughter cohere; in which the savagely personal achieves the impersonality of high art. The cool American wit and intellectual control of the well-trained poet handle explosive material literally conjured up by the release of a concrete imagination. Magic tales, mythic monsters are ways an imagination may come to terms with the dark. But they also give it shape and substance. The father died, the hurricane really smashed the windows. Ted Hughes taught the poet to turn round, confront and conjure up the bald ladies and the black daddy who in nursery rhyme rhythms "bit my pretty red heart in two." The last poems are a deliberate exploration of the nature of death and the poet's enduring relationship with it. They made it real.

(1976)

15

Toni Morrison: *Beloved*

Beloved begins "124 was spiteful." 124 is a house in Cincinnati in 1873, inhabited by Sethe, once a runaway slave from the horribly named "Sweet Home" Kentucky farm, and her daughter, Denver. The house is spiteful because it is haunted by the terrible fury of a baby whose throat was cut to make her safe from repossession after the infamous Fugitive Slave Act. This sad ghost, possessed by infant rage and an infant's absolute and peremptory need for love, manages to materialise herself just as Sethe is cautiously attempting to come to terms with the affection offered by Paul D., the only survivor of the six "Sweet Home Men" who worked with her and loved her. Beloved—as she names herself after the one word on her pink tombstone—exacts love and payment in a wholly credible and comically disastrous way from her mother, her sister and the generous and dignified Paul D. In the early days Sethe suggested to Baby Suggs, her mother-in-law, that they move. "What'd be the point?" asked Baby. "Not a house in the country ain't packed to its rafters with some dead Negro's grief."

If Beloved represents the terrible pain and suffering of a people whose very mother-love is warped by torture into murder, she is no thin allegory or shrill tract. This is a huge, generous, humane and gripping novel. In the foreground is the life of the black people whose courage and dignity and affection are felt to be *almost* indomitable. Their names are the no-names of non-people and are as alive as jazz with their quiddity and idiosyncrasy.

Baby Sugg's owner has always believed her to be called Jenny but never asked Baby herself. The Sweet Home Men are Paul D. Garner, Paul F. Garner, Paul A. Garner, Halle Suggs and Sixo the wild man. (Garner was their owner's name: all the acknowledged individuality of Paul D.—one of the most convincing gentle adult men I have met in a book for years—resides in his D.) They do not love, or almost do not, the land whose beauty they respond to, which is not theirs, where they are not at home, though they try to make families and keep their pride. This is an adult book, but all the characters have the essential *virtue* of fairy-tale heroes and exact our primitive affection unquestioningly. Toni Morrison's love for her people is Tolstoyan in its detail and greedy curiosity; the reader is *inside* their doings and sufferings.

The world of the whites, by contrast, is almost wholly distanced—rising to the surface of consciousness only as and when the blacks can briefly bear to contemplate what it has done to them. The Civil War slips by almost without mention. Those whites who might think of themselves as good or kind are judged by Sethe's dismissive and patient acceptance of their obtuseness and ignorance about the essentials of her life. Those who whipped and tortured and hanged are judged implacably by the brief accounts of reminiscences the blacks cannot suppress, however they try to numb themselves.

The emotional condition of all the people of this story is a deliberate limitation of memory. Dying, Baby Suggs thinks "Her past had been like her present—intolerable—and since she knew death was anything but forgetfulness, she used the little energy left her for pondering colour." The women do not remember the children they have borne to be sold away like fatstock, because it would hurt too much. Paul D. and Sethe, meeting after terrible years, do each other the essential courtesy of sparing themselves from their worst things, which they pass over vaguely. They do not speak of the bits and collars they have been forced to wear. But the past rises up and cries for blood like Beloved. Paul D., witched into making love to this beautiful dead thing, finds his heart, which he thinks of as a tobacco tin rusted shut, is red and alive. This living redness connects him to Baby Suggs's sermon to the black people, in which she exhorts them to love their own living bodies—neck and mouth and skin and liver and heart—since *"they"* will not.

The book is full of the colours whose absence distresses the defeated Baby Suggs so that she hungers for yellow, or lavender, or a pink tongue even. It is also—and connectedly, through the name "coloured people"—full of marvellous descriptions of the brightness and softness of black bodies—

pewter skins of women skating in the cold, Sixo's indigo behind as he walks home naked after meeting his girl. Whiteness is evil and nothingness—Melville in his chapter on Whiteness in *Moby-Dick* called it "the colourless no-colour from which people shrink." Beloved perceives whites as skinless. Sethe, full of rage and distress, turns on Paul D. "a look like snow."

Another profound and patterning metaphor is related to Sethe's horror when the two brutal and inhuman nephews of her schoolmaster owner write—with ink she has made for them—"a list of Sethe's animal characteristics." When Paul D. discovers what she did and attempted to do to her children in her desperation, he reproaches her, "You got two feet, not four." This image works subtly all ways. During her escape Sethe *crawls* towards the river, pregnant, desperate to reach her other unweaned baby (already in Ohio), ripped open by whipping, reduced to animal level by white man's beastliness. The child she is trying to get to—Beloved—is always described as "crawling—already?" moving on all fours and aspiring to walk straight. The slaves whose stories lie behind Toni Morrison's novel were thought by whites at this time to be in some way animal. The case for slavery was argued on these grounds. What Toni Morrison does is present an image of a people so wholly human they are almost superhuman. It is a magnificent achievement.

Toni Morrison has always been an ambitious artist, sometimes almost clotted or tangled in her own brilliant and complex vision. *Beloved* has a new strength and simplicity. This novel gave me nightmares, and yet I sat up late, paradoxically smiling to myself with intense pleasure at the exact beauty of the singing prose. It is an American masterpiece, and one which, moreover, in a curious way reassesses all the major novels of the time in which it is set. Melville, Hawthorne, Poe wrote riddling allegories about the nature of evil, the haunting of unappeased spirits, the inverted opposition of blackness and whiteness. Toni Morrison has with plainness and grace and terror—and judgment—solved the riddle, and showed us the world which haunted theirs.

(1987)

16

An Honourable
Escape:
Georgette Heyer

THE ONLY responsible position I ever held at my respectable boarding-school was a place on the Library Committee. I was relieved of it after one term. I assumed that this was because of general incompetence, but discovered later that it was because I had vetoed the purchase of Georgette Heyer's books, which the staff had taken as conclusive proof of intellectual arrogance, narrow-mindedness, the moralism of the Cambridge English school creeping up on me already. The truth was exactly opposite. The sharpness of my veto was a desperate attempt to conform to what I took to be *their* moralism. I had read every word of Georgette Heyer. I was a secret, illegal member of two circulating libraries to get more of her books. I had purloined exercise books to write two Regency romances and half a novel about the amours of Charles II. These were shockingly bad, and their badness led me to realise how difficult good escape literature is to write. Georgette Heyer still seems to me a superlatively good writer of honourable escape. This article is an attempt to exorcise my own past cowardice and hypocrisy by trying to say why.

Escape literature can exist to satisfy people's fantasies—sexual and social—at the expense of probability and "truth." But there is another kind, which exists less to satisfy hidden desires than to provide simple release from strain—the story with simple streamlined rules of conduct and a guaranteed happy ending. Both kinds like to create other worlds—imaginary lands of legend and fairy-tale, the past, the future, outer space, Tahiti, the aristocracy, the desert of the sheikhs and the American frontier.

There are various uses of costume drama. Much of it depends on the universal childhood desire to *be* someone else, somewhere else, usually someone more powerful and important. An incredible number of people claim to be reincarnations of Cleopatra, and even more read novels about her. Purely sexual costume drama probably derives from a time when there was more licence to describe sexual activity in other periods than in our own—which produced a spate of watered-down versions of *Fanny Hill* and *Moll Flanders*. A bastard version of these is the pruriently suggestive novel for nice girls, which has it both ways—describes the life of some great whore, courtesan, society lady, with suggestive details but has a moral scheme which ensures that the sex is narrowly avoided (except perhaps once), the tart has a heart of gold and *really* loves her dull, neglected husband all the time. There is straight cloak and dagger, as in Baroness Orczy; there is real curiosity about shifting cultures and beliefs, as in the best of Scott. There is "serious" work "explaining" some glamorous figure of the past in terms of modern psychiatry and sociology. The film *The Lion in Winter,* with its simplified Freudian explanations of Richard I's homosexuality and the power structure of mediaeval Europe, is one of these. It is bastard Albee—the "family romance," infantile needs controlling the language and behaviour of big business, the "deals" dictated by terror of incest and sibling rivalry. It diminishes both big business and the Plantagenets in the process.

Which brings me back to the "serious" literary-critical dismissal of escape literature. The Penguin literary history's *Modern Age* imperceptively lumps Georgette Heyer together with several other historical best-sellers as a "formula" writer who simply dresses up "modern bodies and feelings" in period disguise. It claims that the values and drift of her dialogue are essentially modern, despite the Regency phraseology. This, although true of the ponderously significant *The Lion in Winter,* does not seem to me to apply to Miss Heyer's lighter fantasies. They satisfy, too, much simpler emotions: the perennial need for a happy ending and, increasingly, a curiosity about historical *facts* of daily life and thought.

It is necessary to distinguish between her books. The earliest seem to be written out of a simple desire to create more of Baroness Orczy's world of bright colour and danger—rather as my unsuccessful Regency pieces were written out of frustration because I could get no more Heyer. She began by adapting Baroness Orczy's solid, large English hero, whose lazy good looks and "inanity" hid a keen intelligence and a grip of iron. (Other descendants of this aristocratic hero are Lord Peter Wimsey and Albert Campion in their version of the streamlined escape world.) The heroes of *The Black Moth* (gentleman turned highwayman) and *The Masqueraders* are of this kind. In *The Masqueraders* the lazy, large gentleman casually unmasks the girl, who is disguised, for no very good reason, as a man.

In Miss Heyer's early novels great use is made of the fantasy-fulfilling cliché of sex-changing disguise; later she gets too subtle to need it. Romantic heroines in real life were clearly possessed by the same need to get into the comparative freedom of the man's world: both Mary Queen of Scots and Lady Caroline Lamb were fond of disguising themselves as beautiful page boys.

Another costume-novel cliché which appears in Miss Heyer's early work is the villain with the fascinating sneer, cold thin mouth, complete *sang-froid* and complete ruthlessness—except to his lady. The rather mechanically wicked villain of *The Black Moth* was resuscitated with a new name as Justin Alastair, Lord Avon, or Satanas, in *These Old Shades* and *Devil's Cub*. I imagine that the charm of Justin Alastair and his reckless son, Dominic, accounts for the names of small sons of many of my contemporaries.

In these two books Miss Heyer comes her nearest to playing with her readers' sexual fantasies. She is so successful because she avoids coming very near. In the first, the young heroine-disguised-as-a-boy, with conventionally flaming hair and huge violet eyes, is rescued, unmasked and finally married to a coldly "wicked" father-figure. This provides the faint *frisson* of danger which appeals to female masochism, and the appeal of achieving the impossible which (psychoanalysts would say) satisfies the Oedipal desires. In *Devil's Cub* Miss Heyer uses one of the stocks-in-trade of the romantic novel: the characters are in close proximity and without a chaperon almost from the beginning. This provides a sense of danger and drama and heightened expectation—the declarations of love, and the bedding, are of course delayed by points of honour and twists of the plot until the end.

Both these novels are successful escape literature—particularly the second—for two reasons. There is the minimum of sexual titillation—only, indeed, the proximity and the romantic appearance of the hero—and there is an increasing clever balance between genuine romance and a saving comic mockery of romance within romance.

The Convenient Marriage (1934) and *Friday's Child* (1944) both play with a variant of the delayed bedding trick: this one has been used by romantic novelists from Ethel M. Dell and Marie Corelli onwards. Hero and heroine are married for purely practical reasons at the beginning of the novel, but declarations of love are postponed to the end. No clue is given as to whether these marriages were consummated, although the reader must clearly be wondering and imagining. In *The Convenient Marriage* I *think* we are meant to assume that the hero—a gentleman and a Marquis—is waiting with superhuman patience until his schoolgirl wife really trusts him: this trust is delayed by the dastardly plotting of his ex-mistress and one of her beaux.

In *Friday's Child,* a much more successful novel, Georgette Heyer blandly and blatantly ignores the sexual issue until she makes a light joke about it on the very last page. In this novel the hero's ex-mistress is only mentioned when his wife asks at the Opera if *that* is his opera-dancer. Her sexual jealousy is sketched in very lightly indeed—but his rage at her public *faux pas* is crushing. Miss Heyer is beginning to employ the technique of her most successful work—the shifting of attention from the sexual imagination to the details of conventional behaviour and daily life. She employs increasingly less of the props of high passion—highwaymen, Jacobites, duels and disguise. She is playing romantic games with the novel of manners.

Miss Heyer is most successful with the artificial conventions of fashionable Regency society—a world of elegance, good taste, meaningful trifles and the high significance of *manners*. It has been said that in no other period were the ruling classes so secure in wealth, privilege and power. Some were politically active, many were without responsibilities except their estates, which they often left to others to manage. They developed eccentricities and mannerisms to use up their time and wealth. Lord Petersham collected snuff boxes, Lord Alvanley won a bet that he could produce the most expensive dish at a meal (a pie made from three hundred small back pieces of thirteen different birds and costing £108 5s). The Green Man of Brighton dyed his clothes, furniture, carriages, livery and hair bright green. "Romeo" Coates took the Theatre Royal in Bath to play Romeo himself and drove an all-white curricle shaped like a shell. Max Beerbohm described an ordinary day in the life of a rich man:

> To spend the early morning with his valet, to saunter round to Whites for ale and tittle-tattle and the making of wagers, to attend 'a drunken *déjeuner*' in honour of 'la belle Rosalie,' to drive far out into the country in his pretty curricle followed by two well-dressed and well-mounted grooms . . . and stop at every tavern on the road . . . to reach St James's in time for a random toilet and so off to dinner . . . dinner done, to scamper off to Ranelagh to dance and sup.

Into this leisured world Beau Brummell introduced the ideal of artfully achieved simplicity. He had clean, starched neckcloths, perfectly cut plain clothes, perfectly shining boots, and, unusually, he *washed*. "No perfume, but clean linen, plenty of it, and country washing." A biographer explains his success as "the perfect art which conceals art, that satisfying spontaneity which can be achieved only by taking intense thought."

The description would, curiously, fit the novels of Brummell's contemporary Jane Austen, who also held up the perfect manners of the perfect gentleman as an aesthetic and moral ideal.

In Jane Austen's world, as in Brummell's, keeping off boredom is a major emotional force—Emma's silliness, Anne Elliot's solitary pensiveness, Darcy's distant pride are functions of boredom. Nobody *need* work; neither men nor women were exhausted by hours of office labour like Dickens's heroes, let alone those career men and women with whose devotion of the major part of their lives to the strife of job and ambition the modern novel, serious or romantic, is singularly incompetent to deal. And in such a world marriage, the rituals of courtship and the subsequent family life were much more real, much more essentially important than they are now.

Georgette Heyer's awareness of this atmosphere—both of the minute details of the social pursuits of the leisured classes and of the emotional structure behind the fiction it produced—is her greatest asset. Her most attractive heroes are lazy, bored men—dandies, Corinthians, entirely in control of their clothes and amusements, enjoying them—but in need of something more. Her heroines are lively, resourceful girls, usually not rich, with natural moral taste combined with a certain unworldly innocence that arouses the masculine protectiveness of the heroes.

In these novels, besides the leisurely, decorous good-temper of the plots, it is the details of life which are satisfying. It has been said that Miss Heyer's slang—boxing cant, thieves' slang, the fashionable adjectives of the *ton*—is right to the year in which her book is set. Her clothes are certainly right—anyone leafing through the contemporary periodicals *La Belle Assemblée, The Lady's Magazine,* the *Beau Monde* after reading her novels will discover, as I did, a world of details of tissues, trimmings and cosmetic hints, already familiar turns of phrase, twists of the language I had always known through her novels. She can do shops and entertainments—fashionable milliners, the Pantheon Bazaar, Astley's theatre. The mechanical genius's interests in *Frederica* are fully documented. He wants to see a pneumatic lift in Soho and Trevithick's steam-locomotive—*not* the Puffing Devil, which burnt itself out on the road, but the one that was exhibited on its own track near Fitzroy Square.

W. H. Auden said that Jane Austen was good at describing "the amatory effects of brass." Miss Heyer is good at money and the lack of it, too. In *Black Sheep* there is an excellent portrait of a gentleman Nabob from India, who has made his fortune and is prepared to throw over certain conventions. In *Frederica* and *Arabella* there is a wealth of fascinating detail about how to contrive ball dresses on a tiny budget. And she is aware of, and knowledgeable about, the ways in which men of birth used up their energy when not devoted to leisure or politics, the army and agriculture. She knows all about sheep-breeding, the "new" crops of turnips, swedes and mangel-wurzels, about Coke of Norfolk, Tull's Drill, manures and rotation of crops. Her two most realistic novels deal with the army and with finance. These are the early *An Infamous Army* and the fairly recent *A Civil Contract*.

An Infamous Army is a skilful reconstruction of the battle of Waterloo—included in the bibliography of Lady Longford's new biography of Wellington. It is meticulously researched and documented: the Iron Duke, Miss Heyer tells us, says nothing in the novel that he did not, in fact, say at some point of his life.

A Civil Contract comes nearest of Miss Heyer's novels to abandoning the streamlined escape world for real emotion and real causation. It deliberately reverses the romantic bed-trick of *The Convenient Marriage*. Adam inherits his father's title, estates and very heavy debts. He marries Jenny, the daughter of a rich Cit, despite his love for the beautiful Juliana, to save his estates. Jenny's father wants the title for Jenny; Jenny, who loves Adam, can only aspire rather bleakly to "make him comfortable" and give him an heir—both of which she does. She never becomes beautiful; although slightly improved by contact with Adam's family she remains essentially tasteless about clothes and flashy horses, although the crimp in her hair, the number of her jewels and her plumes are reduced. Adam copes with her generous, blundering, vulgar father with his own innate moral taste: he suffers because he is taking everything and really giving nothing—and since he does not come to love Jenny, only to settle with her, this problem has no easy solution. Sex enters this book more than any other, but on the same practical, flat, anti-romantic note. The couple are seen, apprehensive and nervously polite, heading towards a purposeful but unromantic honeymoon. There is no kiss, no sudden tension as in the novel of delayed romantic recognition—but Jenny's pregnancy, a sickly one, is documented in detail with appropriate medical regimens and errors, and Adam's protectiveness comes out. In this novel the denouement is provided not by love but by economics. Adam, a military man, is warned by his father-in-law to sell government stock in the panic before Waterloo; instead, gambling on his own professional skill and knowledge of Wellington, he *buys,* and repairs his fortune. I know of no other romantic novel in which the high tension is supplied by the Stock Exchange. And throughout the book attention is concentrated on daily life, family life, financial repairs, domesticity and agriculture.

Romantic love of Jane Austen's kind, if not of Caroline Lamb's, is an ideal image of a society which often had to make do with marriages of this kind. Miss Heyer knows about the relationship between the ideal and the actual; Jenny knows what she has got, and does not deny the reality of what she has not got.

Marghanita Laski has said that Georgette Heyer is a genius and defies description. I am painfully conscious that my description of her world leaves out the sparkle and comfort of the flesh and blood for the sake of largely irrelevant literary-critical bones. Why *is* she so good? Partly because she has good taste—her stories are deliberately innocent, not because she does not know about the seamier side of Regency life, but because she chooses to hint mockingly at it or ignore it.

Partly because she is neither prurient nor working out fantasies—her own or the reader's—and by deflecting attention from the passions to the daily life of her romantic characters, she manages to create an escape world of super-sanity in her fantasy. I think the clue to her success is somewhere here—in the *precise* balance she achieves between romance and reality, fantastic plot and real detail. Her good taste, her knowledge and the literary and social conventions of the time she is writing about all contribute to a romanticised anti-romanticism: an impossibly desirable world of prettiness, silliness and ultimate good sense where men and women really *talk* to each other, know what is going on between them and plan to spend the rest of their lives together developing the relationship. In her romantic novels, as in Jane Austen's, it is love the people are looking for, and love they give each other, guaranteed by the cushions, bonnets, and dances at Almack's and by the absence of sex-in-the-head. It is a myth and an idealisation, but it is one we were brought up to believe whether or not we really had Jane Austen in our schoolroom. And because of Georgette Heyer's innocence and lack of prurience we can still retreat into this Paradise of ideal solutions, knowing it for what it is, comforted by its temporary actuality, nostalgically refreshed for coping with the quite different tangle of preconceptions, conventions and social emphases we have to live with. Which is what good escape literature is about.

(1969)

17

Barbara Pym

BARBARA PYM'S novel *An Academic Question* was begun in 1970, in a mistaken attempt to write something "sharp" and "swinging" about a provincial university. She wrote and abandoned two drafts, one in the first and one in the third person, which have been amalgamated and "smoothed" by her diligent editor Hazel Holt, who also provided the title.

The result is thin and unappealing. Its heroine, Caro, is a graduate wife, married to a characterless anthropologist—she chose her diminutive in deference to Lady Caroline Lamb but, like all Pym's women, is a distinct failure in Byronic terms. There is an exiguous anthropological plot, concerning some papers improperly filched from a dying missionary, and an even more exiguous adulterous plot. There is also a usual Pym eccentric spinster, this one preoccupied with a tragi-comic vision of hedge-hog-turds and the eternal jumble-sale jumpers. This character, Dolly, produces an innocent vision of the transience of human life that is Pym at her best:

Kitty and I living here as young girls, going to dances and wearing flesh-coloured artificial silk stockings. Kitty used to have hers ironed to make them shiny. *Such* detail and now people wear nylon tights and we shall all soon be gone anyway.

It is a moment comic and appalling like the one where Belinda in *Some Tame Gazelle,* sitting in bed with a slight chill and some old copies of *The Gentlewoman,* murmurs, *"Timor mortis conturbat me."*

Caro, on the other hand, is simply horrid. It is hard to know if her creator, who treats all her creations with a muted blanket irony, knew how very horrid she was. She combines the usual malice of Pym's self-centered observers with a wholly unsuccessful attempt on the sharp "satirical" note of the 1960s. The angry graduate wives of that decade, who wrote to *The Guardian* complaining of kitchen and confinement, claimed they wanted to use their minds. Caro has none. She judges people on their clothes and little stylistic failings. (She has a child, also judged in terms of style. Her possible rival has "a boy and a girl named Luke and Alice. I felt a little scornful when I heard the names, though my own Kate was not much better.") An academic wife at a party remarks the flamboyant dress of a male acquaintance. "I suppose that's quite the latest," says Heather, implausibly, and Caro tells the reader, "Evidently a life spent with card indexes did not make for generosity of spirit, I thought."

This remark could be self-directed—Miss Pym was a card-indexer—but its tone is typical of Pym's more unworthy undercurrents, tiny snap judgments vaguely addressed to the mockery of nuances of social style, petty about pettiness. Early reviewers of Pym's work praised her "sparkling feminine malice." A harsh view of her work would add that its central characteristics are indeed malice and a kind of narcissistic self-pity, since the reader's generous sympathy for the unperceived virtue or agony is usually required for the excellent woman, the sharp observer whose need for love goes unrequited and unremarked.

Why, therefore, in the last few years has there been such a sudden blossoming of attention to Pym's *œuvre?* It is easy enough to understand why she has a devoted following of *readers*—she has the ability to create a comfortable little world in which they can relax, locate themselves with ease, confirm their prejudices and enjoy their own superiority. But why the Ph.D. dissertations, the academic conferences, *La Narrativa di Barbara Pym,* "Text and Subtext in the novels of Barbara Pym," etc.? In England, a curious combination of unlikely allies brought her to our attention. First came Lord David Cecil (who praised Pym in the *Times Literary Supplement*), followed by fogies of various ages, all of whom feel a nostalgia for memorable manners and habits of small folk in the days of England's greatness, or anyway England's certainty of its own cultural identity. With this kind of pleasure in comic self-deprecation goes the English terror of anything that could possibly be called pretentious, phoney or pseud. Malice is all right, as long as it's unpretentious and not too loud.

A quite different part of our cultural life produced the flowering of Virago and the rehabilitation of the library novel and good read (which has been marvellous). But the feminist-academic seriousness with which this "good read" has been taken is arguably less healthy, even perhaps pretentious or phoney. The resuscitation of women's novels has run into taught courses in popular literature or women's literature, where a moral and academic imperative is that we must not disparage (or criticise?) what the people (or women) do in fact read and like, and we must by no means talk about what these patronisingly located bodies of readers find it difficult, even initially, to read or like. We must also, of course, not mock women, blacks, gays or any other disadvantaged group: Barbara Pym is eminently safe in that her targets are safely in the past, in a bourgeois world which may then have been cramped and painful but now has the discreet charm of a peepshow. The new philistinism and the old thus unite to produce an academic field in which Pym can be seen as meriting the same kind of attention as Murdoch or Lessing or Spark.

It is harder to see why this interest should have extended to Europe or the United States. Robert Emmett Long, the author of *Barbara Pym* (1986), is an American who has written us a full-length critical study. It is old-fashioned, as befits its subject, the bulk of it consisting of a retelling of the plots of the novels, occasionally pointing out the moments of "high comedy." Long's tone suggests he is faintly dubious about his own enterprise. He is possibly not sure how good Pym is—he sounds half-bemused, as did her anthropologist friend recently in the *Sunday Telegraph,* who wrote, "Barbara Pym was not perceived by any of us as any kind of *major* novelist," and went on to give good reasons why she should not be.

Long makes one substantial critical point. Pym's people, he claims, and not only her people, but her whole world and the Anglican Church in her world, and the English society at large, are "marginal." He writes oddly and memorably in his peroration of Pym's "radiant identification with marginal people," though he doesn't quite see this as a placed artistic strategy. "It is one of the brilliant strokes of Pym's fiction that she should have projected her own disabilities and uncertainty of role upon her novels." It is possible to connect this perception of Pym's world as "marginal" with the post-modernist American obsession with entropy, running-down, lack of centrality. There is truth in this, but it is more a sociological truth than a literary-critical one; it explains Pym's vogue but doesn't endorse claims for her as a major artist.

Pym's most persuasive advocate was, of course, Philip Larkin. In the preface to his own novel *Jill* he remarked with approval of his own wartime generation that events had cut them ruthlessly down to size. Pym was also of that generation who were cut down to size; a good joke is socially acceptable, but a romantic gesture, unless heavily disguised with irony and deprecation, is not. Everyone in Pym's books is cut down to size, no less ruthlessly because she is so deceptively mild. It is one way of looking at the world, stoical and ironic. It is part of our contemporary English aimlessness and gloom.

In 1937 Q. D. Leavis, in the pages of *Scrutiny,* fulminated against Dorothy Sayers for pretentions to literary merit when she was only writing vulgar best-sellers. Mrs. Leavis's rage is unattractive (and can be immediately classed as pretentious). She could not understand Miss Sayers's vogue amongst intelligent readers in Common Rooms. Dorothy Sayers has since been cut down to size quite efficiently—university teachers are much more likely to sneer at Lord Peter Wimsey's sexual prowess, *noblesse oblige* and cricket than to confess to a *tendresse* for his milieu. Barbara Pym wanted, we are told, to write novels like Angela Thirkell, a good comic library novelist who disrupted her own comfortable world with shrill hostility to the 1945 Labour Government and (maybe for that reason, or because of the under-standable hostility of her son Colin MacInnes) has proved unrevivable.

In the end, I think, Miss Pym does belong with Thirkell and Sayers. She lacks Muriel Spark's metaphysical wit and icy eye for moral and spiritual inadequacies. She lacks the mad logical rigour and the tolerant detachment of Fay Weldon's moral satire. If we want an analysis of the world in which the mass of men lead lives of quiet desperation, we might turn to Stanley Middleton, who is less charming but in the end more poetic and wiser. Her prose lacks the flexibility of all of these; too much of it is good school-magazine jokiness. She appears gentler than Spark or Weldon but is also infinitely less generous, humane and imaginative. Good relaxing reading is a matter of personal choice, *pace* Queenie Leavis. I'd rather have cloth-of-gold wedding dresses, quotations from *Urne Buriall* and tigerish passion in crime writers acquitted of murder than brown frocks, knitted socks in clerical grey and cauliflower cheese.

(1986)

18

Monique Wittig:
The Lesbian Body

T HE THEME OF Monique Wittig's third book is Lesbianism, which she claimed had until now been largely
unmentioned and unmentionable. *The Lesbian Body* (1974) is explicitly an
act of cultural warfare on various fronts. "Only the women's movement,"
says Mlle. Wittig, "has proved capable of producing lesbian texts in a
context of total rupture with masculine culture, texts written by women for
women, careless of male approval." This total rupture entails a rupture of
the patterns of written language, a more pressing problem for the French,
with French's ubiquitous indications of gender, than for the English. The
Lesbian subject must show her separation from "tout ce que est humain,"
since what is human is masculine, "il" or "ils" grammatically. Monique
Wittig is not "*un* ecrivain."

The female writer must break into, or do violence to, the language of the
text. This is done by writing "je" as "j/e" and "mon" and "ma" as "m/on"
and "m/a." The strokes indicate both the sex of the speaker and the "lived,
rending experience," the "cutting in half" imposed by the male-dominated
culture. David Le Vay, the anatomist and surgeon, who has translated *Le
Corps lesbien* with precision and some elegance, has had some trouble with
the split "j/e." He has chosen to italicise the capital "I," which has had the
odd effect of making the writing seem even more obsessively narcissistic
than it is, and emphasising its aggressiveness at the expense of its awareness

of wounds and disruption to the self. But this has virtues as well as disadvantages in the case of this text.

(I was, parenthetically, amused by Mrs. Thatcher's precisely opposite solution to this problem of gender in an interview with Robin Day. "A leader, if he wants to be Prime Minister . . ." she said. "Or she?" said Day archly. "He embraces she," replied Mrs. Thatcher, speaking "as one lawyer to another." In Monique Wittig's world Mrs. Thatcher's legal phrase would be foolishly innocent or craven, and would be an expression of an intolerable male dominance, erotically and culturally. In Mrs. Thatcher's world, I suppose, and in English, "as one lawyer to another" achieves a kind of gracious unconcessionary neutrality?)

Despite Monique Wittig's revolutionary claims, Lesbianism is now a fashionable subject, a shock for which we are culturally fairly well prepared by *La Bâtarde,* Gay Liberation, Kate Millett and others. Equally fashionable is her concern with the nature of texts, the fictiveness of reality and the reality of fiction. Like Barthes, she sees the reader's relation to the text as an erotic one. Barthes writes, in *Le Plaisir du texte,* that the text is a fetishist object and that *"the text desires me"* (his italics). He elaborates this erotic relationship in various ingenious ways, claiming, for instance, that there is a perverse erotic pleasure to be derived from de Sade's and other writers' rupturing the codes of cultural expectation by, for instance, offering pornographic messages in the purest classical prose. "Neither culture nor its destruction is erotic. But the opened cleft between the two becomes so."

Something analogous is being deliberately invoked in *The Lesbian Body.* Monique Wittig claims that the new Amazonian female culture does not need to distinguish between "fictional, symbolic and actual functions" since they are all anyway "fictifs" (Le Vay translates, too softly, "illusory") for the male-dominated culture. It must bring itself into being, the Lesbian culture, and this can be done by the writing of fiction, since "everything that is written exists." And thus, logically, she *writes* the Lesbian body, enumerating all its parts, functions, acts, fantasies. Here the erotic, fictive and revolutionary functions become one: "to recite one's own body, to recite the body of the other, is to recite the words of which the book is made up. The fascination for writing the never previously written, and the fascination for the unattained body proceed from the same desire." If these propositions are dubious, and if, as I believe, they are permeated by a horrible intellectual inconsequentiality, the train of thought is at least clear. And it is in terms of this train of thought that we must consider *The Lesbian Body* as a work of art.

It consists of two kinds of writing. One, recurring at intervals of several pages, is an unpunctuated capitalised naming of parts, thus: THE OESOPHAGUS THE BRAIN THE CIRCULATION THE RESPIRATION THE NUTRITION THE ELIMINA- TION THE DEFAECATION THE REPRODUCTION $(XX + XX = XX)$ and so on, from follicles to womb writhings. The other writing is a series of brief encounters, a page or a page and a half long, between *I* and the beloved. The first opens, "in this dark adored gehenna," and adjures the beloved to say farewell "to what they, the women, call affection tenderness or gracious abandon," since none "will be able to bear seeing you with eyes turned up lids cut off your yellow smoking intestines spread in the hollow of your hand your tongue spat from your mouth long green strings of your bile flowing over your breasts . . ." The second invokes Sappho to "give me the lips the tongue the saliva which draw one into the slow sweet poisoned country from which one cannot return."

The slow sweet poisoned country is a kind of Lesbian island and shark-infested sea in which a community of women perform rather trite and on the whole palely neo-classical or palely neo-Sadist rites (casting garlands on the sea, human sacrifice, the "ceremony of the vulvas lost and found," in which the vulvas are represented by "blue yellow green black violet red butterflies"). In this land, Achillea (of the tendon) tenderly loved Patroclea, Archimedea made discoveries displacing scented bathwater, and Christa suffered horribly in the garden of Gethsemane. In this land love-making is a constant, careful, savage reconstitution of it. Or a subjection of it to one intense absolute experience after another: burial in sand, in mud, in water, petrification, permeation by air, burning alive. Or metamorphosis into wolf, giraffe, bird, monstrous insect. Some examples:

I begin with the tips of your fingers, *I* chew the phalanges *I* crunch the metacarpals the carpals *I* slaver at your wrists, *I* disarticulate the ulna with great delicacy . . . *I* tear away the biceps from the hu- merus, *I* devour it, *I* eat my fill of you m/y so delectable one, m/y jaws snap, *I* swallow you *I* gulp you down . . .

It is at that moment that *I* spit a part of m/y right lung a soft bland mass to the back of m/y throat and palate . . . *I* hold it pale pink still living before your eyes, *I* shake it, *I* squeeze it, *I* crush it on your skin against the pearl-shaped weals ranged one beside the other. . . . There is no smile on your face but the puckering that precedes tears. *I* forbid you to weep. Untiringly *I* anoint you with m/y living cement.

David Le Vay is quoted as saying that these descriptions add up to a minute celebration of all that goes to make up life. There is a sense in which the appalling resilience of these much and ingeniously mutilated bodies does add up to a celebration of life, as there is a sense in which the persistent recovery of de Sade's heroines can be said to do so. It might be worth trying to analyse what kind of celebration and what kind of life.

One could argue that the erotic experiences in this book are a carrying out in full of sexual fantasies most of us know the dim first stirrings of. "I could eat you," "I could *squeeze* you to death" are common enough, as is the frantic wish to be the beloved, for the body of the lover to become completely assimilated to, involved in, the body of the beloved. This wish presumably feels different if the two bodies are identical in sex, and different in women where the sexual organs are mostly internal. Monique Wittig is most ingenious with these wishes, as she is with more conventional flagellations, scrapings and scratchings with iron claws and spikes and so on. Her speaker penetrates the beloved through the ear, the stomach, the anus, curls a long tongue round an eyeball or grows fingers long enough to reach up through all the lower orifices, thread the central organs and clutch the brain. Indeed, most precisely, to quote a queen much possessed by forbidden if heterosexual passion:

> Ce n'est plus une ardeur dans mes veines cachée:
> C'est Vénus toute entière à sa proie attachée.

It is a world of polymorphous perversity run wild. The Lesbian body can be penetrated anywhere, since penetration has no constricted meaning, and huge wounds opened for hands, tongues and feet to dabble in. Swallowing and vomiting become acts of penetration and orgasm in themselves. It is a world of perpetual orgasm in which the sense of proportion and space occupied by the body expands and contracts, alarmingly, delightfully. One can be a fly on the beloved's uvula: one can cover the sky.

This repeated de-creation and re-creation of the Lesbian body is of course also connected to the aesthetic theme, the bringing to life of the text, the reality. One of the things I dislike about this book is the limpness with which it adheres to traditional myths, simply changing the gender of a few names. This might be seen as guerrilla warfare, taking over the past while the male enemy is not looking, but it feels more like the classical nostalgia for the lovely Greek homosexual world, felt in Lowes Dickinson's Cambridge and Forster's *Maurice.* And if one is looking for that emotion, one is, I think, better satisfied by Mary Renault's hot romantic realism than by this etiolated aesthetic joking.

Monique Wittig's central myth is perhaps that of Isis and Osiris, although Orpheus and Eurydice appear, and Demeter and Persephone. There is an explicit section in which the narrator is identified with Isis, reconstructing the shredded and dead god, or goddess, in this case:

> I search hastily for your fragments in the mud, m/y nails scrabble at the small stones and pebbles, *I* find your nose a part of your vulva your labia your clitoris, I find your ears your tibia . . . *I* reconstruct you. . . . *I* hurriedly produce tears vaginal juice saliva in the requisite amount, *I* smear them all your lacerations. . . . *I* decree that you live as in the past Osiris, *I* say that as in the past we shall succeed together in making the little girls who will come after us . . .

Sexual intercourse and reproduction are means of creation and have always been used as images, analogues of artistic creation. How then do Isis and Osiris make the little girls? The answer seems to be in the form of the book, in the kind of static perpetuity of the present-tense fragments that compose and decompose it. All programmatically erotic literature exists in a perpetual present, both because it desires to be as it is eternally and because it does not choose to envisage other modes of experience. Thus the explanation of reproduction I quoted earlier—XX + XX = XX—is not only a witty reference to the homogeneity of the coupling but to its undifferentiated, invariable circularity. Lesbian lovers make each other by imagining each other. *This* is reproduction and creation. *The Lesbian Body* is a series of episodes in which XX penetrates XX and becomes XX. It seems to me also to be a bit like a tapeworm, proliferating endless similar disjunct segments.

There is an apotheosis in which the heroine becomes a kind of female infernal trinity and declares that her new triune nature transcends "the sense of morning and evening and the stupid duality with all that flows therefrom." That is, it transcends dualities of time and space, and male and female and life and death. The narrator is now the Whore of Babylon and triple Hecate, "she who bellows with her three horns, the triple one," and able to cause the beloved, "blessed art thou among women," "to conceive yourself as I at last see you over the greatest possible space." And conceiving itself over the greatest possible space is exactly what this Lesbian text has set out to do. The Lesbian body is the new trinity, first and last and without end, its second person produced by a virgin birth.

If I write that this text is both unforgettable and boring I shall almost inevitably be accused of *mauvaise foi*. Barthes himself points out that boredom is not simple, which is true, and goes on to claim that there is no *sincere* boredom. "If personally, I am bored by a babbled text, that is because, in reality, I don't like that sort of demand." I am not, in fact, in sympathy with most of Mlle. Wittig's assumptions—I would rather take Mrs. Thatcher's way than hers to deal with a male-dominated culture. I like change, not revolution. I like subtle distinctions with a continuing language, not doctrinaire violations. (And why should she stop her textual violations at names and subjects? Why should the second-person pronouns and adjectives not be rent in two? Why not change the gender of all the parts of the Lesbian body?) I do not, indeed, like the sort of demand this book makes, because the vision it imposes is so thin and chill and simple and dogmatically, narrowly erotic. The way in which it imposes this vision is intense enough, and has enough virtuosity to make it unforgettable. So my boredom is perhaps prejudiced, perhaps insincere, but I still can't find a better word. Wallace Stevens required of the supreme fiction that it must be abstract, it must give pleasure and it must change. *The Lesbian Body* fulfils only the first of these requirements for me, and that, *pace* Barthes, makes it boring. I am truly glad that, having written this review, I am liberated to read something else.

(1974)

VISION AND REALITY

19

Coleridge:
An Archangel
a Little Damaged

Coleridge," said Wordsworth, "is a subject which no Biographer ought to touch beyond what he himself was eye witness of." A reading of his works—prose, poetry, letters, notebooks, marginalia—gives an impression of a personality, contradictory perhaps, but immediately impressive and to be engaged. He was plaintive and self-castigating, but nevertheless immensely alive and observant. He had a greater, more patient power to analyse the movements of thought than almost anyone else, but was always afraid he was "exercising the strength and subtlety of the understanding without awakening the feelings of the heart." He had an almost religious respect for the domestic virtues and was largely incapable of living peacefully with others. He was an enormous talker, in public and private, and a man who compelled others to talk about him; and somewhere amongst all the talk he remains a difficult and elusive figure.

Both amongst his contemporaries and amongst Coleridge students, he calls up a vigorous and contradictory mixture of judgments and reactions. After his death, Wordsworth said he was the only *wonderful* man he had ever known. There is Lamb's famous description of him reciting "Kubla Khan" in middle age: "His face hath its ancient glory; an archangel a little damaged." De Quincey's relationship with him began as passionate worship of an unknown idol—he ended by writing histrionic and vituperative attacks on Coleridge's opium-eating and his plagiarisms.

Hazlitt too began with hero-worship—to Coleridge, he said, he owed it that "my understanding did not remain dumb and brutish and at length found a language to express itself." But he wrote a series of damaging reviews of Coleridge's work, and claimed that

> Coleridge only assents to any opinion when he knows that all the reasons are against it . . . Truth is to him a ceaseless round of contradictions: he lives in the belief of a perpetual lie, and in affecting to think what he pretends to say . . . He would have done better if he had known less. His imagination thus becomes metaphysical, his metaphysics fantastical, his wit heavy, his arguments light, his poetry prose, his prose poetry, his politics turned—but not to account.

The mazy motion of Coleridge's walk, constantly shifting from side to side of the path, struck Hazlitt as "an odd movement; but I did not at that time connect it with any instability of purpose or involuntary change of principle as I have done since." He criticised even the poet's nose. "The rudder of the face, the index of the will, was small, feeble, nothing—like what he has done."

Modern writers repeatedly call him the greatest English critic. Coleridge scholarship goes on in an atmosphere of primary emotional and intellectual identification from sympathetic readers—not so much idolatry as passionate justification from very differing minds. But he retains his capacity to disappoint and enrage. Dr. Leavis claimed that it was scandalous that his work should be considered worthy of serious study in a university. Professor Norman Fruman's study *Coleridge the Damaged Archangel* claims with great cogency that Coleridge's deviousness, poetic and intellectual thefts and downright lying cannot be simply dismissed by anyone seeking to assess the final importance of Coleridge's work. Professor Fruman says he writes with "profound respect and a sense of deep personal affection for Coleridge," but his book is angry, and is angry rather as Hazlitt and De Quincey were angry. Respect and personal affection have been misled and betrayed.

Coleridge, of course, habitually provoked in others, and himself indulged in, these extremes of reaction to his personality. From the beginning he mocked and disparaged himself—his looks, his vacillations, even his Christian name. As a child, he wrote, he was "fretful and inordinately passionate; and as I could not play at anything and was slothful, I was despized and hated by the boys . . . before I was eight years old I was a *character*." He wrote a poem in which he mentioned his "fat vacuity of face." He was capable of using self-disparagement childishly to ingratiate himself with angry or disappointed friends. But the Journals, especially those written in Malta, during the worst days of his realisation of his enslavement to opium, express a real sharp and profound self-hatred.

On the other hand, he was aware of his own brilliance, and when he felt secure could make a public display of it in an amazing and enthralling manner. Crabb Robinson recorded his first meeting with him.

> He kept me on the stretch of attention and admiration from half-past three till 12 o'clock. On politics, metaphysics and poetry, more especially on the Regency, Kant and Shakespeare, he was astonishingly eloquent.

But Robinson found Coleridge easy to destroy in argument.

> I used afterwards to compare him as a disputant with a serpent—easy to kill if you assume the offensive, but if you let him attack, his bite is mortal. Some years after this, when I saw Mme de Stael in London, I asked her what she thought of him. That, she replied, he is very great in monologue, but he has no idea of dialogue.

There is a deeper truth in this witty judgment than is immediately apparent. Coleridge could indeed always impress with a brilliant monologue, but he was easily daunted and he was always afraid that a monologue was all it was.

He was the youngest of eight brothers and was sent away to school at the age of nine when his father died; he developed early a habit of attracting attention by impressing people, in order to mask an inner terror and loneliness. He spent his life trying to establish contacts and relationships, seeking in turn an ideal friend, an ideal community, an ideal woman, driven to expect too much and to provoke the rejection his whole history led him to recognise and anticipate. He attached himself to Robert Southey and the experimental ideal political settlement in America, the Pantisocracy; he married Southey's sister-in-law, Sara Fricker, whom he did not love, at Southey's insistence. When Southey abandoned Pantisocracy Coleridge attached himself to another friend, the wise and steady Thomas Poole at Nether Stowey, and tried to live well in rural retirement. It was at this point that he met William Wordsworth, and began what has always been seen as one of the most powerful dialogues and friendships in literary history. There followed Coleridge's wonderful year, 1797–98, in which most of his great poetry was written, and the *Lyrical Ballads* put together.

In *Biographia Literaria* Coleridge described the ideal poet as combining, among other things, "a more than usual state of emotion with much more than usual order." Much has been written about how, during this year, he was able to fuse years of disparate readings, speculations, observations, into powerfully original forms. It seems certain that without Wordsworth he might never have found this combined force of emotion and order. But the source of power was in itself a danger.

Walter Jackson Bate pointed out percipiently that Coleridge's real sense of the nature and difficulty of true poetic achievement, combined with his great critical gifts, must have inhibited him as a poet. His ideals as well as his understanding were high. The ideal great poem should combine all human powers at their highest. In 1797 he wrote:

> I should not think of devoting less than 20 years to an Epic Poem. Ten to collect materials and warm my mind with universal science. I would be a tolerable Mathematician, I would thoroughly know Mechanics and Hydrostatics, Optics and Astronomy, Botany, Metallurgy, Fossilism, Chemistry, Geology, Anatomy, Medicine—then the *mind of man,* then the *minds of men*—in all Travels, Voyages and Histories. So I would spend ten years—the next five to the composition of the poem—and the five last to the correction of it.

The programme is inspiring and daunting; an example of Coleridge's powerful sense of the interrelated unity of all human knowledge and of an impossibly high valuation of poetic genius. Coleridge was, perhaps, historically, the last poet who could even aspire to know and work with what was known and thought about. The effect on him of his recognition of Wordsworth's genius and, later, of the very different nature of that genius from his own, is perhaps impossible finally to assess or describe. The personal relationship between the two men was for Coleridge the most intense version of his inevitable pattern of responses. Initially he identified his interests with Wordsworth's own, went to Germany, then to the Lakes with Wordsworth, devoted his time to Wordsworth's proofs and fell in love with Wordsworth's sister-in-law, Sarah Hutchinson. Later, inevitably, followed quarrels and rejection. In the early days Poole warned Coleridge of possible dangers. He retorted:

You charge me with prostration in regard to Wordsworth. Have I affirmed anything miraculous of W? Is it impossible that a greater poet than any since Milton should appear in our days? Have any *great* poets appeared since him? . . . Future greatness! Is it not an awful thing, my dearest Poole? What if you had known Milton at the age of 30 and believed all you now know of him?

Coleridge was right about Wordsworth's greatness. But the greatness was not of the kind for which Coleridge had been preparing himself: Wordsworth did not need either the universal knowledge or the philosophical complexities or his sense of the history of literature and ideas from which Coleridge, despite his perpetual fear of losing the "natural man" in "abstruse research," drew so much energy and insight. Keats distinguished Wordsworth's poetical temperament as "the egotistical sublime": Wordsworth himself saw the great artist as "a man preferring the cultivation and exertion of his own powers in the highest possible degree to any other object of regard." Coleridge's curiosity was boundless and at his best he lost his sense of himself in his identification with some object or set of ideas or another man's work. Both "The Ancient Mariner" and "The Leech Gatherer"—to stretch a point—are about solitary men facing extremes of human privation. Coleridge's poem is a vision: Wordsworth's, although invested with visionary dreariness, is set firmly on the earth, and is entitled "Resolution and Independence." These were precisely the qualities both men felt Coleridge lacked. During the terrible time of Coleridge's illness in the Wordsworth household, culminating in Sarah Hutchinson's departure at Wordsworth's instigation, Wordsworth repeatedly reproached Coleridge for failures in resolution and independence.

He also published, in the 1800 edition of the *Lyrical Ballads,* an ungracious note apologising for the shortcomings of "The Ancient Mariner" partly on the grounds that "the principal person has no distinct character and does not act but is continually acted upon." He complained too that "the imagery is somewhat too laboriously accumulated." Coleridge later complained of "the Wordsworths' cold praise and effective discouragement of every attempt of mine to roll onward in a distinct current of my own." But he was aware that Wordsworth's "*practical* Faith that we can do but one thing well and that therefore we must make a choice" was part of his genius, and something that he himself lacked. Wordsworth could tolerate solitude of the spirit. He could not. Yet Wordsworth was surrounded by loving and devoted women, and Coleridge himself "must not be beloved *near* him except as a satellite." At the crucial time he accepted Wordsworth's valuation of his poems with eager self-abasement, agreed to the exclusion of "Christabel" from the *Lyrical Ballads* and claimed: "I would rather have written 'Ruth' and 'Nature's Lady' than a million such poems."

To Godwin in 1801 he wrote, as though it were settled:

> The Poet is dead in me—my imagination (or rather the Somewhat that had been imaginative) lies, like a Cold Snuff on the circular Rim of a brass candlestick, without even a stink of Tallow to remind you that it was once cloath'd and mitred with Flame. . . . If I die and the Booksellers will give you anything for my Life be sure and say— Wordsworth descended on him like the γνῶθι σε αυτόν from Heaven; by shewing to him what fine Poetry was, he made him know, that he himself was no Poet.

Wordsworth, initially at least, found strength in isolation, although Coleridge was arguably right when he wrote: "dear Wordsworth appears to me to have hurtfully segregated and isolated his being." In the same letter he claimed his own "many weaknesses are an advantage to me; they united me more with the great mass of my fellow-beings."

This brings us back to the crucial paradox of Coleridge's nature. He was capable himself of unique achievement in solitude, and that solitude terrified him. He was a man temperamentally condemned to create through monologue and solitary vision, who was haunted by a phantom hope of warm community, love, direct communication. His poem "Fears in Solitude" is a rather hysterical picture of the solitary contemplative who has a political vision of the close communion of Britain and the British. His "Mother Isle must be at once a son, a brother and a friend/A husband and a father." It is arguable that most of his second-rate poems and deeply felt letters strike the same extravagant note—agitated, pleasing, displaying his own insufficiencies to someone or something which *must* provide a total, harmonious response and forgiveness. His great work, on the other hand, either treats of solitary vision, or, in the case of the marvellous, intricate prose of the notebooks, has the hardness, clarity and wit of a mind contemplating in solitude, drawing strength from its own solitary activity. In the moments of strength his reality was his own inner life.

> In looking at objects of Nature while I am thinking, as at yonder moon dim-glimmering through the dewy window-pane, I seem

rather to be seeking, as it were *asking,* a symbolical language for something within me that already and forever exists, than observing anything new.

It has often been said that his most persistent preoccupation was the search for unity underlying diversity. He describes the rapid associative process of his own mind with amusing brilliance but is always afraid that this mind is simply self-inclosed and self-referring. Describing in a notebook one of his own characteristic monologues, he explains that his proliferating illustrations swallow his thesis and continues:

> Psychologically my brain-fibres, or the spiritual Light which abides in the brain marrow as the visible Light appears to do in sundry rotten mackerel and other *smashy* matters, is of too general an affinity with all things, and though it perceives the *difference* of things, yet is eternally pursuing the likenesses, or rather that which is common. Bring me two things that seem the very same, and then I am quick enough to show the difference, even to hairsplitting—but to go on from circle to circle till I break against the shore of my hearer's patience, or have my concentricals dashed to nothing by a snore—this is my ordinary mishap.

He was afraid, too, that this incessant mental activity muffled the directness of his vision.

> O said I as I looked on the blue, yellow, green and purple green sea, with all its hollows and swells and cut-glass surfaces—O what an ocean of lovely forms! and I was Teazed, that the sentence sounded like a play of words. But it was not, the mind within me was struggling to express the marvellous distinctness and unconfounded personality of each of the million millions of forms, and yet the individual unity in which they subsisted.

Coleridge's "Dejection" ode is one of the most moving pictures of the power and failure of the mind in solitude that we have. Wordsworth believed that contemplation of the powers of nature healed the human mind: Coleridge observed the forms of the outer world, remarked, "I see, not feel, how beautiful they are," and concluded, "I may not hope from outward forms to win/The passion and the life, whose fountains are within." The published poem is a condensed, impersonal version of a long verse-letter to Sarah Hutchinson. The verse-letter is discursive, plaintive, self-accusing, pleading, psychologically acute and very moving. But the final Ode has gained a new power from its compression. The contrast between the sharply observed, almost hallucinating outer world of the poem and the passive suffering of the solitary mind is harsher and stronger without the throbbing appeals to Sarah.

In "The Ancient Mariner," "Christabel" and "Kubla Khan" the observed worlds have a unique glittering clarity of extreme states of being, sunny pleasure dome, caves of ice, burning sun, slimy sea. The central characters are passive and suffering, unbearably isolated, waiting, at best, to revive within themselves "that symphony and song," the vanished passion and life whose sources are within. At his best, Coleridge was aware that the sources of his power and his intolerable solitude were very close together. He was like his own mariner, condemned to pluck the sleeve of the wedding guest who was returning to the human feast and community, and hold him spellbound with an almost incomprehensible monologue about the torture of the solitary spirit and its transient vision of the nature of things.

(1979)

20

Charles Rycroft:
The Innocence of Dreams

CHARLES RYCROFT is a psychoanalyst who has shown an interest in the conscious activity of the healthy mind, as well as a remarkably wise and tactful capacity for vivid description of the thought processes of the deranged. His purpose in *The Innocence of Dreams* is to examine dreams as part of a process of imagination which is "a natural, normal activity of an agent or self." Later he discloses another latent theme, "an exploration of the source or origin of creative activity." He hopes to relate Freud on dreams to Coleridge on the Imagination, and so discusses, besides Freud and Jung, a number of dreams really dreamed, and the relationship between dreams, the human body, culture and poetry.

Freud, Dr. Rycroft says, believed his major discovery was the existence of two kinds of mental functioning—the primary and secondary processes. The primary works with symbols, hallucinations and visual images, following no rules of logic, space or time. The secondary process is conscious thought governed by reason, respect for grammar and logic, part of the formation of a healthy, well-adapted personality. Freud, for whom dreams were crucial evidence of the existence of the primary process, described this process as archaic, primitive, and maladaptive: dreams he initially classified as neurotic symptoms, wish-fulfilling hallucinations or distorted symbolic images of repressed fantasy. "The range of things given symbolic representation in dreams is not wide," he said, and instanced "the human body as a whole, parents, children, brothers and sisters, birth, death, nakedness—

and something else besides." The "something else" is sex and its processes. Dr. Rycroft concludes that a major theme of our dreaming is indeed the nature of our bodily fate and identity—ancestry, birth, sex, posterity, death. But he finds Freud's descriptions of the processes of symbol-forming unsatisfactory.

The aspect of Jung's theory Dr. Rycroft is most concerned with is the putative Collective Unconscious which, as well as the personal unconscious, sends us messages and manifestations in dreams. It is the active agent: we are passive. "One does not dream: one is dreamed." Dr. Rycroft is sympathetic to the attempt to account for the sense that the creator of events, or images, of our dreams is, like Groddeck's It, not ourselves, but feels that there are good enough biological reasons for the recurrence of certain images in different times and cultures without invoking a Collective Unconscious. One reason why many writers, including myself, seem to prefer Freud's fleshly pessimism to the apparently more aesthetically and culturally enriching Jungian archetypes is given by Lionel Trilling in his excellent essay "Freud, Within and Beyond Culture," where Trilling argues that Freud's respect for "a hard, irreducible stubborn core of biological urgency and biological necessity, and biological *reason,* that culture cannot reach . . ." is actually a liberating force in the face of cultural and political determinisms.

Dr. Rycroft too admires Freud's biological courage, but doubts whether the relationship between primary and secondary processes is as sharply divided, or as simple, as Freud described it. He points out that Freud seems not to have thought with visual images when awake, and that he confessed that his own dreams were "less rich in sensory images than I am led to suppose is the case of other people." Dr. Rycroft adduces Galton's 1883 findings in support of the idea that an absence of mental imagery accompanying thought is common among scientists and intellectuals. John Beer, in *Coleridge the Visionary* (1959), on the contrary, cites the famous case of Kékulé's vision of atoms forming the shape of a serpent devouring its tail, as an example, among others, of a scientist thinking with images rather than words or logical signs, and relates it to Coleridge's interest in dream, reverie, ocular spectra and other such phenomena as modes of thought.

Freud, as Dr. Rycroft points out, inherited a scientific language and attitude which predated the discoveries of Einstein, linguistic philosophy, and modernist art, which, partly indebted to him, exploited the modes of illogic, dream, symbol and non-representation. Freud made an anatomical "model" of the psyche—Id, Ego and Superego—itself a metaphor and verbal symbol. This led to various difficulties: the tendency to classify symbols and dreams as abnormal and neurotic symptoms, products of the inaccessible and irrational and amoral Id, led to the classification, at one stage, of art as a product also of maladjustment and neurosis. Dr. Rycroft patiently qualifies and redefines the description of the relationship between images, language, thought, consciousness and unconsciousness. Not all dreams or all meanings are, as he points out, inaccessible to the dreamer. He discusses "punning" dreams which "like waking puns . . . reveal the existence of phonetic connections between ideas and images which cut across their logical connections."

He discusses dreams in which metaphors, dead or live, are made actual by the visionary embodiment of vehicle and tenor: a woman "puts her shirt" on a lover, and finds "more fish in the sea." In an earlier book, *Imagination and Reality,* he discussed the symbolic nature of the whole activity of psychoanalysis, including particularly the language both analyst and patient use. In this book he tries to replace the ideas of primary and secondary processes by those of discursive and non-discursive symbolism and comes much nearer to describing, by this means, the relations between the languages of sleep and waking than the early analysts did. From here he connects the *intended* dreams of patients in analysis to those of peoples whose cultures expect them to have certain dreams at certain rites of passage, and to art. One can "dream towards" a work of art, or even a work of analytic thought, as I know.

It is our loss that Dr. Rycroft, whilst (somewhat dubiously) attaching Coleridge's difficult concepts of the Primary and Secondary Imaginations to his own distinctions, does not examine Coleridge's psychological work, in the Notebooks and elsewhere, on the nature of dreaming. Coleridge was fascinated by the "*streamy* nature of association" in dreams, uncontrolled by the will, and saw this powerlessness as a possible point of entry for evil in man. He had inherited a strong evangelical conscience and a weak will. Dr. Rycroft considers Freud's Id, "a chaos, a cauldron, filled with energy . . . with no organisation, no collective will . . . contrary impulses exist side by side . . . no judgment of value, no good and evil, no morality . . ." This, he says, defining by negatives and analogy an entity whose only positive attribute is energy, is like the God of apophatic or negative theology. From here, by a verbal sleight-of-hand which is pleasing rather than irritating, he proceeds to claim that "there is something about the imagination . . . that can only be stated in negative terms."

And this brings him, inevitably, to Keats's Negative Capability, "of being in uncertainties, mysteries, doubts, without any irritable reaching after fact or reason." This is a state of mind, he points out, which is "the exact opposite to that of the healthy, well-adapted ego sanctified by Freudian theory." Coleridge, too, although it is he who is being criticised by Keats for irritable reaching, wrote of the imaginative apprehension of *Paradise Lost* as "that *illusion,* contradistinguished from *delusion,* that *negative* faith, which simply permits the images present to work by their own force, without either denial or affirmation of their existence by the judgment."

Psychoanalytical descriptions of "creativity" are, I have found, usually unsatisfactory and somehow beside the point. Dr. Rycroft's comes at the end of an elegantly written book in which his clear, gnomic prose, his rigorous sense of order, his grip on the various languages of dream imagery, science, theology, logic and art, give his own work some of the quality of a poem, dissolving, diffusing and dissipating in order to recreate. He describes the creative person as one who "lacks that sense of opposition between their Ego and both the outside world and their own unconscious . . . ," someone who, neither identifying masculinity with action, nor femininity with passion, "can oscillate between active and passive states of being, between objectivity and subjectivity, without feeling that their identity is threatened." With an ego so relaxed and unarmoured, such people can mediate between their private symbols and those of their culture. This conclusion could look misleadingly glib in a review: in this book it is achieved and worked for. Dr. Rycroft has his own symbol for the imaginative life—Hopkins's Windhover, riding the air, active and passive in its element.

(1979)

21

Van Gogh,
Death and Summer

T<small>HIS ESSAY</small> began as a review of a heap of books about Van Gogh, published in his centenary year. It was meant to be a thousand words long. I asked for more, and was given three thousand. In the event, I found I had written more like fifteen thousand, linking all sorts of things I had been thinking about, both as a writer and as a reader, for the last twenty years. The only book under review which has survived in the present version is Tsukasa Kodera's excellent study of Van Gogh's thematics, to which I am indebted. This essay discusses, among other things, De Quincey's idea of the "involute"—a "perplexed combination of concrete objects" or "compound experience incapable of being disentangled." The ideas and writings brought together here are for me such an inextricable involute, which I hope makes sense also as a kind of cultural and aesthetic history.

I

Van Gogh, like Blake and the Brontë quartet, has become part of the iconography of the religion of art. His life is a hagiography, of one kind or another—the uncomprehended sufferer, or the flaming and bloody visionary. He is a figure pathetic and gesturing, wheedling his patient brother for money for bread and paint, haunted by the image of his still-born brother

(Vincent Van Gogh, exactly a year older than himself), disastrously incapable of forming real or understanding relations with women, incapacitated by absinthe and venereal disease. Even the great, wise, intelligent letters are alarming in their obsessive humourlessness. And yet he both represented and understood the knotted religious and artistic tensions of his time. He made the icons and was an icon, partly by choice, partly by absurd accident.

Van Gogh as a young man framed his life as a Christian pilgrimage. In London as a schoolteacher he was already deeply involved in a kind of vocation as a preacher, which he later carried to extremes in the south Belgian mining country, the Borinage. In the late autumn of 1876 he preached a sermon at the Wesleyan Methodist Church in Richmond, taking as his text Psalm 119:19, "I am a stranger on the earth, hide not Thy commandments from me."[1] The sermon is like his letters of that time, rhapsodic and driven, thickly informed with biblical quotations and swaying between the knowledge that "our nature is sorrowful" and the conventional hope for salvation and heaven in Christ. He uses the image of the pilgrim on the road, calling it a pilgrim's progress, and quoting Christina Rossetti, "Does the road wind up-hill all the way?" Towards the end of the sermon he describes a landscape from a picture, with hills and "the splendour of the sunset, the grey clouds with their linings of silver and gold and purple." The pilgrim is walking towards a heavenly city, and meets "a woman, or figure in black, that makes one think of St. Paul's word: As being sorrowful yet always rejoicing." The dark woman is, he says, an Angel of Charity. I do not think it is fanciful hindsight to find something threatening in these images of hope.

Accounts of his ministry in the Borinage show how much he was trying to become an imitation of Christ. He gave ferocious and determined assistance during the frequent explosions at the mines, and the *Complete Letters* includes a translation of the memories of a baker who knew him in those days:

> Immediately putting himself on a level with the working class, our friend sank into the greatest humiliations, and it was not long before he had disposed of all his clothes.
>
> Having arrived at the stage where he had no shirt and no socks on his feet, we have seen him making shirts out of sacking. I myself was too young then.
>
> My kind-hearted mother said to him: Monsieur Vincent, why do you deprive yourself of all your clothes like this—you who are de-

scended from such a noble family of Dutch pastors? He answered: I am a friend of the poor like Jesus was. She answered: You're no longer in a normal condition.[2]

He was indeed no longer in a normal condition, self-starved, self-abased, smelly and obsessive. He changed vocation from pastor to painter during the dark years in the Borinage, drawing the labouring peasants and the blackness of the light in the earthy secular supper of the potato eaters, as black as the earth they dug.

A book which comes to grips with something essential in Van Gogh is the brief but cogent one by Tsukasa Kodera, a doctoral thesis written and published in Holland by a Japanese, which studies Van Gogh's "thematics," and is subtitled "Christianity versus Nature."[3] Kodera looks at Van Gogh's dormant ideas from a useful cultural distance—he has a good chapter on Japan and primitivist Utopia—and picks his way intelligently and rigorously through the Christian symbolism, and the natural supernaturalism, of the works. He has traced certain of Van Gogh's recurrent motifs—the sower, the reaper, the digger, light in darkness—from his early theological reading to his interest in the secular thinkers of France, Michelet and Renan, and in the novels of Zola. The line through from Christ's parable of the sower to Millet's realistic sowers and Van Gogh's later visionary ones is clear enough: Kodera concentrates on the diggers and points out that the figure of the digger is absent from the paintings during the time in Arles, recurring during the painter's illness in hospital, along with Christian themes copied from Rembrandt and Delacroix. Kodera points out that Van Gogh characteristically thought of the diggers in terms of the biblical expulsion from Paradise. He quotes particularly two letters written to his brother Theo from The Hague in 1883, referring to Zola's novel *La Faute de l'Abbé Mouret,* where a priest is tempted and falls in a garden called Le Paradou:

> I am glad you are having a good time now—Le Paradou must have been glorious indeed. Yes, I should not mind trying my hand at such a thing: and I do not doubt you two would be very good models. However I prefer to see diggers digging, and have found glory outside Paradise, where one thinks rather of the severe 'Thou shalt eat thy bread in the sweat of thy brow.' My Peat Cutters is quite different from 'Le Paradou', but I assure you I feel also for 'Le Paradou.' Who knows, someday I may attack such a Paradou subject.[4]

The diggers represent the Adamic curse, and also the nineteenth-century socialist concern with the workers, the men of *Germinal*. *La Faute de l'Abbé Mouret,* to which Kodera devotes a whole cautious chapter, is a different kind of novel. Zola's project for this novel summed it up as a study of *"the great conflict of nature and religion."* It is a strange work, simply and rigidly symbolic, minimally realistic. The priest, Serge Mouret, is *curé* of the village of the Artauds in the Midi. The Artauds are one family who form the whole village and seem to propagate by incest, outside the normal human laws or conventions. The village bakes in the inexorable heat of the southern sun. The *abbé* has a devotion to the Virgin, and becomes ill, in a kind of epileptic seizure, in an ecstatic and sexualised vision of her. He is carried away to Le Paradou, where a child of nature, called Albine, fifteen years old, cures him, and introduces him to the swooning abundance of a pleasure-garden run wild, where they eat harmless fruit and finally make love under a sinister Tree. Their nakedness is discovered by the misogynist Frère Archangias, who chastises Serge and removes him to his church again, where he becomes devoted to the suffering figure on the Cross. Albine comes to seek him; he repulses her, loses his contact with Christ, goes back to the garden and finds himself impotent and feeble. Albine, pregnant, kills herself with the poisonous breath of armfuls of flowers. An odd circumstance, of which Kodera does not make too much, is that her Voltairean uncle slices off the ear of Frère Archangias over her grave. Another oddity is the silent presence of a red-haired acolyte called Vincent. The whole takes place in a world alternately baked dry with the sun and swarming with animal and vegetable energies. Serge has a sister, Désirée, who lives at ease among randy cocks, warm-smelling goats, breeding rabbits and a fat pig whose snout she strokes as his throat is cut, telling him that this is all natural and good. Her joyful description of the bull mounting the cow is a *tour de force* of one kind of natural piety. Serge has a hallucinated vision of the natural world invading the white interior of his church, the sun, the trees, the plants, breaking up the stones and shooting phallic stems through the roof. The ferocity of this vegetation, the energy of this heat, has much in common with Van Gogh's depiction of the South when he arrived there. Kodera does not suggest too much direct influence, though he points out that Van Gogh read and admired the book and referred to Le Paradou several times. What he does suggest, convincingly, is a connection between the natural religion of works such as Michelet's natural histories—*La Montagne, La Mer, L'Oiseau, L'Insecte*—which both Van Gogh and Zola read, and the world of Van Gogh's

Arles paintings, lit by the physical sun, which nevertheless appears in physically impossible places, standing, as it were, symbolically for itself.

A transitional painting between the blackly Christian and the sunlit Provençal Van Gogh, in every sense, is the 1885 *Still Life with Open Bible*. In this painting Van Gogh's father's huge dark Bible, open at Isaiah 53, looms over a yellow novel, Zola's *La Joie de Vivre*. The Bible, painted shortly after the death of Van Gogh's father, resembles the huge still lifes of ancient books painted in seventeenth-century Holland as mementoes mori, but the words shimmer with muted colours. Isaiah 53 is the chapter describing the one who was "despised and rejected of men, a man of sorrows and acquainted with grief," an Old Testament prophecy taken to refer to the Christian Passion and central to Van Gogh's Christian vision. Kodera has traced Van Gogh's use of the phrase "la joie de vivre" through his letters, claiming that it was for him a symbolic sense, obscured in translation by variants like "zest for life." La joie de vivre, Kodera says, is characteristically associated by Van Gogh with the happy communal artistic life he projected for himself in his yellow house at Arles and, more ambivalently, with sexual love and happiness. The yellow novel is life; the Bible is the crucifixion. Serge Mouret tells Albine what is indeed clear from his name, that he is dedicated to death, that the true life is through the death of Christ. Zola's book makes both natural random fecundity and sunlight, and the negations of Christianity, at once true and threatening.

The Van Gogh of the Arles years was driven by a desire to make an art that would contain and express the spiritual meanings he had once seen in his religion, in real and natural objects. His diggers were real and symbolic, and so are the olives and sunflowers of Arles and St.-Rémy, but there is a difference. He saw his secular art as the successor to Christian art, and suggested that certain of his paintings should be arranged as triptyches—his painting of Mme. Roulin rocking a cradle, a secular Mother, was to be hung between two of his sunflowers, for instance.

Shortly before he left the asylum at St.-Rémy, he wrote about a triptych—"olive grove, book shop, wheat field"—

> I think that I still have it in my heart to paint a book shop with the front yellow and pink, in the evening, and the black passers-by—it is such an essentially modern subject. Because it seems to the imagination such a rich source of light, say, there would be a subject that would go well between an olive grove and a wheat field, the sowing

season of books and prints. I have a great longing to do it like a light in the midst of darkness.[5]

The idea of "light in the midst of darkness" is as essentially biblical as it is modern, even if the yellow novels have replaced the Black Book. Kodera shows how Van Gogh's idea of the symbolic sun derives as much from the nineteenth-century religious emblem books and prints as it does from the substitution of natural energy for divine. The process of demythologising, yet clinging to, religion in the nineteenth century is complex, and Kodera's analysis of popular religious works in the "dominocratie" of Pastor Van Gogh is a valuable contribution. He also illuminates the iconography of Van Gogh's rejection of the Church, his images of churches shrunk in the light of the starry night or battered in the darkness. Interestingly, he tells us, Van Gogh only ever painted the inside of a church once, as far as is known—and that is only a picture of rows of grim or crossly patient congregational faces on a white ground. He expressed, in his letters, a distaste for "cold, hard whitewashed church walls."

> I still felt chilled, through and through, to the depth of my soul, by the above-mentioned real or imaginary church wall. And I did not want to be stunned by that feeling. Then I thought, I should like to be with a woman—I cannot live without love. . . . the damned wall is too cold for me.[6]

The Abbé Mouret, before his sin, loves his bare white church, into which the sun intrudes. After his fall, he paints the church walls, to the disapproval of Frère Archangias. Van Gogh saw his yellow house as a natural or artistic place of worship—his sunflowers were to be bursts of colour for Gauguin, like church windows; his painting of Mme. Roulin, a fecund woman rocking her cradle, was to stand between the sunflowers like an altarpiece.

Yet there was something altogether tougher and more uncompromising about his rejection of religion than these secular visions of ecclesiastical meanings. His letters to Emile Bernard, rejecting the painting of imaginary Christs in imaginary Gethsemanes, are rooted in the visible and the solid in a different way. In a crucial letter to Bernard, written from St.-Rémy in December 1899, he takes Bernard to task for painting biblical subjects.

> Now, look here, I am too charmed by the landscape in the 'Adoration of the Magi' to venture to criticize, but it is nevertheless too much of

an impossibility to imagine a confinement like that, right on the road, the mother starting to pray instead of giving suck; then and there those fat ecclesiastical frogs kneeling down as though in a fit of epilepsy, God knows how and why!

No, I can't think such a thing sound, but personally, *if* I am capable of spiritual ecstasy, I adore Truth, the possible, and therefore I bow down before that study—powerful enough to make a Millet tremble—of peasants carrying home to the farm a calf which has been born in the fields. Now this my friend all people have felt from France to America . . .

So I am working at present among the olive trees, seeking after the various effects of a grey sky against a yellow soil, with a green-black note in the foliage; another time the soil and the foliage all of a violet hue against a yellow sky; then again in a red-ochre soil and a pinkish green sky. Yes, certainly this interests me far more than the above-mentioned abstractions.[7]

He goes on to offer Bernard descriptions of two of his own asylum canvases, one of the park, with the trunk shrunk by lightning and sawn off:

This sombre giant,—like a defeated proud man—contrasts, when considered in the nature of a living creature, with the pale smile of a last rose on the fading bush in front of him. Underneath the trees, empty stone benches, sullen box trees; the sky is mirrored—yellow—in a puddle left by the rain. A sunbeam, the last ray of daylight, raises the somber ocher almost to orange. Here and there small black figures wander among the tree trunks.

You will realize that this combination of red-ochre, of green gloomed over by gray, the black streaks surrounding the contours, produces something of the sensation of anguish, called 'noir-rouge' from which certain of my companions in misfortune frequently suffer. Moreover the motif of the great tree struck by lightening, the sickly green-pink smile of the last flower of autumn serve to confirm this impression.

Another canvas shows the sun rising over a field of young wheat; lines fleeting away, furrows rising up high into the picture toward a wall and a row of lilac hills. The field is violet and yellow-green. The white sun is surrounded by a great yellow halo. Here, in contrast to the other canvas, I have tried to express calmness, a great peace.

I am telling you about these two canvases, especially about the first one, to remind you that one can try to give an impression of anguish without aiming straight at the historic Garden of Gethsemane; that it is not necessary to portray the characters of the Sermon on the Mount in order to produce a consoling and gentle motif.[8]

And later still, in the same letter, he asks if Bernard has seen "a study of mine with a little reaper, a yellow wheat field and a yellow sun? It isn't *it* yet, however, I have attacked that devilish problem of the yellows in it again. I am speaking of the one with the heavy impasto, done on the spot, and not of the replica with hatchings, in which the effect is weaker."[9] This reaper, in the sun, is Van Gogh's natural image of death, to set beside his image of the sower, sowing the yellow seeds of light into the purple clods of earth, beneath a golden sky. I shall come back to these figures, both painted in the complementary colours of the day, like Van Gogh's own empty chair, yellow and wholesome, which is contrasted with Gauguin's "effet de nuit" painted in the red and green which Van Gogh elsewhere referred to as the "terrible colours of human passion." This chair contains a yellow novel and a lighted candle, whereas Van Gogh's own contains an extinct pipe, though behind it onions sprout with vegetable life.

II

Van Gogh's ideas of sexuality are wound into his thought about Christianity, nature and la joie de vivre, and painting. We have seen how his distaste for the cold church wall was followed immediately by the desire to be with a woman. His Christian mission culminated in his doomed attempt to make a family life with the suicidal prostitute Sien, whom he depicted as "Sorrow" and "The Great Lady," with awkwardly chunky drooping breasts. If his Christian vision was preoccupied with the woman taken in adultery and the repentant sinner, his natural and aesthetic vision was preoccupied with the connection between painting and virility. He lectures Bernard at one and the same time on Dutch realist painting and the necessity of not fucking too much in order that his painting may be more spermatic. He instances Degas:

Why do you say Degas is impotently flabby? Degas lives like a small lawyer and does not like women, for he knows that if he loved them and fucked them often, he, intellectually diseased, would become insipid as a painter.

Degas's painting is virile and impersonal for the very reason that he has resigned himself to be nothing personally but a small lawyer with a horror of going on a spree. He looks on while the human animals, stronger than himself, get excited and fuck, and he paints them well, exactly because he doesn't have the pretension to get excited himself.[10]

This comment is succeeded by praise of Balzac, "that great and powerful artist" who praised "relative chastity," and the Dutchmen who were *"married men and begot children,* a fine, a very fine craftsmanship, and deeply rooted in nature." And in the previous paragraph, he has praised the Dutch artists for exact representation of things as they are, a gift he opposes to the worked up Christs in Gethsemane.

Now we see the Dutch paint things just as they are, apparently without reasoning, just as Courbet paints his beautiful nude women. They painted portraits, landscapes, still lifes. Well, one can be stupider than that, and commit greater follies.

If we don't know what to do, my dear comrade Bernard, then let's do as they did, if only not to let our rare intellectual power evaporate in sterile metaphysical meditations which cannot possibly put the chaos into a goblet, as chaos is chaotic for the very reason that it contains no glass of our calibre.

We can, and this is done by those Dutchmen who are so desperately naughty in the eyes of people with a system,—we can paint an atom of the chaos, a horse, a portrait, your grandmother, apples, a landscape.[11]

When Van Gogh is feeling for his certainty about the importance of representation without a system, without reasoning, he becomes eloquent about colour, as though there was the clue to the truth he grasps. He describes Rembrandt's angels—which are, for Van Gogh, the self-portraits, old, wrinkled, toothless, wearing a cotton cap, a picture from nature, in a mirror. He describes Delacroix's Christ in these words:

Delacroix paints a Christ by means of the unexpected effect of a bright citron-yellow note, a colourful, luminous note, which possesses the same unspeakable strangeness and charm in the picture as a star does in a corner of the firmament. Rembrandt works with tonal values in the same way Delacroix works with colours.

Now there is a great distance between Delacroix's and Rembrandt's method and that of all the rest of religious painting.[12]

Van Gogh's ideas about colour were derived from the discoveries of Chevreul about complementary colours in the 1820s, which had influenced Delacroix, and from his encounter in Paris with the divisionism of Signac and Seurat. Kodera shows, most interestingly, that not only the synthetist theorists of art had theories about colours as the natural language of light and the earth, with correspondences with music and mathematics, but even certain of the dominies had discussed the language of colour as the immanent language of God, with reference also to Goethe's colour theory.

In the autumn of 1888 Van Gogh wrote to Theo that he wished to "say something comforting as music is comforting. I want to paint men and women with that something of the eternal which the halo used to symbolise, and which we seek to confer by the actual radiance and vibration of our colouring."[13] Later in the same letter he writes of his own attempts to combine complementary colours as the depiction of the union of two lovers. "So I am always between two currents of thought, first the material difficulties, . . . and second the study of colour. I am always in hope of making a discovery there, to express the love of two lovers by a marriage of two complementary colours, their mingling and their opposition, the mysterious vibrations of kindred tones."[14] It is surely significant that Kodera finds that the motif of the two lovers, like the depiction of the sun as the source of light, is confined to the visionary years in Arles and St.-Rémy. Orange and blue, red and green, are like the married Dutchmen, begetting children, "a fine, a very fine craftsmanship, and rooted in nature."

For Van Gogh himself, who wrote, "I have always had the coarse lusts of a beast,"[15] there were the prostitutes, for whom, he told Bernard, he felt more sympathy than compassion. "Being a creature exiled, outcast from society, like you and me who are artists, she is certainly a friend and sister."[16]

And it was to the whore Rachel, after the quarrels with Gauguin about the merits of Rembrandt, that Van Gogh delivered his sliced-off ear. In the hospital, after this episode, he said, he was tormented by religious hallucinations and visions—it would be interesting to know the form these took, but as far as I know, he did not say. He did paint religious subjects, notably a version of Rembrandt's *Raising of Lazarus*. In this painting the dead man resembles the painter, and Rembrandt's Christ has been replaced by an angry circle of ruddy gold on a thick gold ground, not shining like the immortal wheat, but somehow indifferently and thickly yellow, with two female figures squatting at the entrance to the tomb.

What did he mean by his self-mutilating gesture? There have been many explanations. Kodera cites critics of Zola, who have seen the mutilation of the fiery Father Archangias in the churchyard as connected to St. Peter's rash slicing off of the ear of the soldier in the Gethsemane garden. Christ restored that ear, as he restored Lazarus, but priest and painter remained damaged. There are other interpretations of the gesture, or sacrifice, to which we may now turn.

III

"Le soleil ni la mort ne se peuvent regarder fixement" (Neither the sun nor death can be looked at steadily), wrote La Rochefoucauld. There is a whole tradition of modernist criticism that sees Van Gogh's sacrifice as a penalty for looking too fixedly at the sun. Bataille, in various essays,[17] compares him to madmen who have heard voices emanating from the sun, ordering them to mutilate themselves, to Prometheus and to the priests of Mithras.

In "Van Gogh Prométhée" Georges Bataille argues that Van Gogh's ear was for him "un SOLEIL," a solar sacrifice of a solar deity in some sort. Van Gogh–Prometheus attempted to steal the fire of heaven and was mutilated by the divine hand.

It must be said that after that December night in 1888 when his ear met in the house where it ended up a fate which no one yet knows (one can only vaguely imagine the laughter and the anxiety which preceded some mysterious decision), Van Gogh began to give the sun a meaning that it had not hitherto possessed. He included it in his paintings, not as part of the background but as the sorcerer whose dancing slowly excites the crowd and then sweeps them along with him. It is at this moment that all of his painting fully became *radiance, explosion, flame,* and he himself became lost in ecstatic wonder before a *radiant, exploding, flaming* light-source. When this solar dance began, nature itself was suddenly shaken into movement, the plants blazed up and the earth rippled like a fast-running sea or exploded: nothing remained of the stability which is the foundation of all things. Death appeared as a form of transparency, just as the sun shines through the blood in a living hand, between the bones which sketch shadows. The blazing and faded flowers and the face whose haggard radiance depresses, the 'sunflower' Van Gogh—anxiety? domination?—put an end to the power of immutable laws, of foundations, of everything that gives to many faces their repugnant look of walled closure.[18]

This vision of the ecstatic shamanic or destabilising dance of the painter before a solar flux is very different from anything Van Gogh himself claimed he was doing, and yet the images of explosion and flowing and bursting earth are recognisably to do with him. Bataille sees the piston movement of sexual penetration and ejaculation, and the rotary movement of the wheel, as the fundamental forces of the universe (see "L'Anus solaire"). His solar religion is sexualised in a way Van Gogh's decorous spermatic painting heroes (despite his own beastly passions) were not. Modernism and surrealism made of Van Gogh a post-Christian sacrificial victim. Bataille has an illuminating article, "Soleil pourri," in which he distinguishes between the sun, not looked at, as the source of mathematical serenity and (at the midday zenith) of *elevation*. Looked at, it produces madness, the experience of combustion and consequent waste. "In practical terms, the sun at which one stares is identified with a mental ejaculation, a frothing mouth, an epileptic fit. . . . In mythological terms, the sun at which one looks is identified with a man who slits the throat of a bull (Mithras), with a vulture which eats a man's liver (Prometheus) . . ."[19] He goes on to describe the Mithraic rite where the priest in the pit receives the warm flood of the bull's blood and hears the bull's roaring. The clear yellow sunlight has become hot and red in another aspect. (Coleridge records a tradition that the damned felt the sun's heat without "its" light.) Bataille, with one of his strokes of genius, points out that it is only in the paintings of Picasso that this double sun, the "rupture of the elevated," is adequately depicted. Picasso is the master of bull worship.

Critics of Van Gogh have speculated about the possible taurine, as opposed to Petrine, signification of the sacrifice of the ear. Van Gogh had seen bullfights and knew that the matador gave the ear of the bull to the lady of his choice. The quarrel with Gauguin that precipitated the mutilation seems to have been fuelled partly by Van Gogh's anger at Gauguin's superior virility, confused with Gauguin's inadequate appreciation of Dutch depiction of reality—he himself was the brute beast sacrificed to the whore. Bataille at the end of his essay "Van Gogh Prométhée" tells us grandly that Van Gogh belongs, not to the history of art, but to the bloody myth of our existence as humans. Bataille approves of this achievement of the terrible "point d'ébullition" (boiling point) which destroys the stable world of all of us, as well as that of the sufferer. Such violence is a source of power, and it is in power that he is interested.

Bataille's ideas about Van Gogh are related to those of Antonin Artaud, who in "Van Gogh, the Man Suicided by Society" (1947) sees the painter as a scapegoat, a victim of power-hungry apelike psychiatrists—he wrote his essay while in an asylum in Rodez. He too sees the painter as the archetype of the explosive.

> No, Van Gogh was not mad, but his paintings were like bursts of Greek fire, atomic bombs, whose angles of vision, unlike all other paintings popular at the time, would have been capable of seriously upsetting the spectral conformity of the Second Empire bourgeoisie and of the myrmidons of Thiers, Gambetta, and Félix Faure, as well as those of Napoleon III.[20]

Artaud's effusion on Van Gogh is a curious, wild, indeed mad structure, which proceeds in an unexpected direction. At first it wallows in magical and surrealist imagery:

> One can speak of the good mental health of Van Gogh who, in his whole life, cooked only one of his hands and did nothing else except once to cut off his left ear, in a world in which every day one eats vagina cooked in a green sauce or penis of newborn child whipped and beaten to a pulp. . . .[21]

But as he proceeds through the berating of collective magical conspiracies against such as "Baudelaire, Poe, Gérard de Nerval, Nietzsche, Kierkegaard, Hölderlin, Coleridge—"[22] and Van Gogh, and through the berating of the psychiatrists who want to straighten out his poems, he seems to fall under the spell of Van Gogh's sense of the real.

Somewhere between the Christian myth of the origins of nature and our life on the earth and the frenetic modernist-primitivist myth of Van Gogh the sacrificial victim of conspiracy and madness, lies Van Gogh's sense of the real. It has to do with his craft of representation, as a way of relating to things as they are, as Artaud also sees. He has different ways, more and less frantic, of apprehending Van Gogh's sense of the real. For instance:

> I see, as I write these lines, the blood-red face of the painter coming toward me, in a wall of eviscerated sunflowers,

in a formidable conflagration of cinders of opaque hyacinth and of fields of lapis lazuli.

All this amid a seemingly meteoric bombardment of atoms which would appear a particle at a time, proof that Van Gogh conceived his canvases like a painter, of course, and only like a painter, but one who would be *for that very reason*
a formidable musician.[23]

This passage is about equally haunted by Artaud's own frantic metaphors ("eviscerated") and by a real apprehension of what is going on in the paintings themselves.

Or we could take his description of the cornfield with crows, which like many others he believed to be Van Gogh's last painting.

It is not usual to see a man, with the shot that killed him already in his belly, crowding black crows onto a canvas, and under them the kind of meadow—perhaps livid, at any rate empty—in which the wine colour of the earth is juxtaposed wildly with the dirty yellow of the wheat.

But no other painter besides Van Gogh would have known how to find, as he did, in order to paint his crows, that truffle black, that 'rich banquet' black which is at the same time, as it were, excremental, of the wings of the crows surprised in the fading gleam of the evening.[24]

Here too is a romanticising of the sinister, the explosive and the violent, though the colouring is good. But at the centre of the piece of writing Artaud suddenly quotes three passages from the letters, all of them descriptions of Van Gogh's way of working, of his choice of colours, with the remark that he was "as great a writer as he was a painter." I give the quotations in full because without them it is impossible to convey the effect they have on Artaud's ejaculatory rhapsody.

What is drawing? How does one do it? It is the act of working one's way through an invisible wall of iron which seems to lie between what one *feels* and what one can do. How is one to get through this wall, for it does no good to use force? In my opinion, one must undermine the wall and file one's way through, slowly and with patience.

8 September 1888
In my painting *The Night Café* I have tried to express that the café is a place where one can ruin oneself, go mad, commit crimes. I have

tried by contrasting pale pink with blood red and maroon, by contrasting soft Louis XV and Veronese greens with yellow greens and hard pure greens, all this in an atmosphere of an infernal furnace, of pale sulphur, to express, as it were, the evil power of a dive.

And yet in the guise of Japanese gaiety and the good fellowship of *Tartarin*.

23 July 1890
Perhaps you will see the sketch of the garden of Daubigny—it is one of my most studied paintings—I am enclosing with it a sketch of old stubble and the sketches for two twelve-inch canvases representing vast stretches of wheat after a rain.

Daubigny's garden, foreground of green and pink grass. To the left a garden and lavender bush and the stump of a plant with whitish foliage. In the middle a bed of roses, a wattle, a wall, and above the wall a hazel tree with violet leaves. Then a hedge of lilacs, a row of rounded yellow linden trees, the house itself in the background, pink, with a roof of bluish tile. A bench and three chairs, a dark figure with a yellow hat, and in the foreground a black cat. Pale green sky.

Artaud comments, "How easy it seems to write like this," and goes on:

Well, try it then, and tell me whether, not being the creator of a Van Gogh canvas, you could describe it as simply, succinctly, objectively, permanently, validly, solidly, opaquely, massively, authentically, and miraculously as in this little letter of his. (For the distinguishing criterion is not a question of amplitude or crampedness but one of sheer personal strength.)

So I shall not describe a painting of Van Gogh after Van Gogh, but I shall say that Van Gogh is a painter because he recollected nature, because he reperspired it and made it sweat, because he squeezed onto his canvas in clusters in monumental sheaves of colour, the grinding of elements that occurs once in a hundred years, the awful elementary pressure of apostrophes, scratches, commas, and dashes, which, after him, one can no longer believe that natural appearances are not made of.

There is something very important here. Artaud has understood the truth that what is extraordinary about the letters, in the end, is the descriptions of the paintings, their authority, the way in which they combine things seen and the representation of them. It is *not* easy to write like that. And the writings, like the painting, do indeed give rise to Artaud's most important aperçu:

> I believe that Gauguin thought the artist must look for symbol, for myth, must enlarge the things of life to the magnitude of myth,
>   whereas Van Gogh thought that one must know how to deduce myth from the most ordinary things of life.
>   In which I think he was bloody well right.
>   For reality is frighteningly superior to all fiction, all fable, all divinity, all surreality.
>   All you need is the genius to know how to interpret it.[25]

In cutting off this quotation where I do, it is only honourable to record that it continues without a break to state Artaud's belief that mythic reality itself is in the process of becoming flesh in "this month of February 1947." It is not possible to avoid the myth of incarnation for long. We slip into metaphor and fiction. But Artaud has located and described the sense we have that Van Gogh, choosing his colours and subjects, was somehow strong enough to reveal something essential about the nature of the real, human and inhuman in their places.

IV

Rilke, during his period of intense contemplation of the representation of the world in colour, came to place Cézanne above Van Gogh, partly because of the humanity and individuality of Van Gogh's letters. His praise of Cézanne resembles, *mutatis mutandis,* the feeling Artaud had before the plainness of Van Gogh's descriptions. Rilke wrote to Clara on 21 October 1907:[26]

> There's something else I wanted to say about Cézanne: that no one before him ever demonstrated so clearly the extent to which painting is something that takes place among the colours, and how one has to leave them alone completely, so that they can settle the matter among themselves. Their intercourse: this is the whole of painting. Whoever meddles, arranges, injects his human deliberation, his wit, his advocacy, his intellectual agility in any way, is already clouding and disturbing their activity.[27]

He goes on to make the point

That Van Gogh's letters are so readable, that they are so rich, basically argues against him, just as it argues against a painter (holding up Cézanne for comparison) that he wanted or knew or experienced this and that; that blue called for orange and green for red: that secretly listening in his eye's interior, he had heard such things spoken, the inquisitive one.[28]

It is interesting that it is not Van Gogh's sentimental or moralising outbursts that Rilke objects to, but precisely his *theorising* in relation to colour, which Rilke saw as in the way of the completely impersonal, selfless work of looking and representing that for him was both art and the only possible spiritual life. This desire for selflessness is another form of romanticism, very potent at the beginning of this century in conjunction with the difficult apprehension that human beings are animals on a smallish planet turning round the physical sun, but animals which for some reason have developed the capacity 'to reflect on their state and to make representations of it.

Rilke's most famous statement about Cézanne and colour is worth quoting at length.

Without looking at a particular [painting] standing in the middle between the two rooms, one feels their presence drawing together into a colossal reality. As if these colours could heal one of indecision once and for all. The good conscience of these reds, these blues, their simple truthfulness, it educates you; and if you stand beneath them as acceptingly as possible, it's as if they were doing something for you. You also notice, a little more clearly each time, how necessary it was to go beyond love, too; it's natural, after all, to love each of these things as one makes it: instead of *saying* it. One ceases to be impartial; and the very best—love—stays outside the work, does not enter it, is left aside, untranslated: that's how the painting of sentiments came about (which is in no way better than the paintings of things). They'd paint: I love this here; instead of painting: here it is.[29]

Earlier (on 12 October 1907), Rilke records Mathilde Vollmeier's remarks about Cézanne's impersonal precision.

But imagine my surprise when Miss V., with her painterly training and eye, said: 'He just sat there in front of it like a dog, just looking, without any nervousness, without any ulterior motive.' And she said some very good things about his manner of working (which one can decipher in an unfinished picture). 'Here,' she said, pointing to one spot, 'this is something he knew, and now he's saying it (a part of an apple); right next to it there's an empty space, because that was something he didn't know yet. He only made what he knew, nothing else.' 'What a good conscience he must have had,' I said.[30]

There is a sense of the truth of things which is hard to put into words, if not to point to, which comes out in Rilke's apprehension of the relations between Cézanne's work and his vision (in both the literal and the figurative sense of this word) of reality. A similar sense comes through Rilke's own lines about *saying* things in the ninth of the *Duino Elegies*[31]—a quotation I first met as a student, in John Beer's descriptions of Coleridge's sun-worship in *Coleridge the Visionary,* where Beer is quoting at second hand from Erich Heller's *The Disinherited Mind,* a paradigm in itself of a series of thoughts about the withdrawal of religious certainty, even philosophical certainty, from a bare, but possibly beautiful, world.

Bringt doch der Wanderer auch vom Hange des Bergrands
nicht eine Hand voll Erde ins Tal, die Allen unsägliche, sondern
ein erworbenes Wort, reines, den gelben und blaun
Enzian. Sind wir vielleicht hier, um zu sagen: Haus,
Brücke, Brunnen, Tor, Krug, Obstbaum, Fenster,—
höchstens: Säule, Turm . . . aber zu sagen, verstehs
oh, zu sagen so, wie selber die Dinge niemals
innig meinten zu sein.

(Yet the wanderer too doesn't bring from mountain to valley
a handful of earth, of for all untellable earth, but only
a word he has won, pure, the yellow and blue
gentian. Are we perhaps, *here,* just for saying: House,
Bridge, Fountain, Gate, Jug, Fruit tree, Window,—
possibly: Pillar, Tower? . . . but for *saying,* remember,
oh, for such saying as never the things themselves
hoped so intensely to be.)

Rilke goes on to speak of the earth urging a pair of lovers to draw everything into their feeling.

Ist nicht die heimliche List
dieser verschwiegenen Erde, wenn sie die Lebenden drängt,
dass sich in ihrem Gefühl jedes und jedes entzückt?

This passage seems to me to be connected with Van Gogh's priorities in the letter to Bernard, in his list of what could be rescued from chaos. "We can paint an atom of the chaos, a horse, a portrait, your grandmother, apples, a landscape." The ingredients of Rilke's listed reality, like Van Gogh's, include yellow and blue, the abstract pair of lovers and, earlier, the sense of death as earthly, final and natural.

> Ein mal
> jedes, nur ein mal. Ein mal und nichtmehr. Und wir auch
> ein mal. Nie wieder. Aber dieses
> ein mal gewesen zu sein, wenn auch nur ein mal:
> irdisch gewesen zu sein, scheint nicht widerrufbar.
>
> (Just once,
> everything only for once. Once and no more. And we, too,
> once. And never again. But this
> having been once, though only once
> having been once on earth—can it ever be cancelled?)

Where is all this leading? It is easy to say, simply, that Western art of the nineteenth century, novels and poems as well as paintings, is all involved in the slow stripping away of the Christian certainties and frameworks. (I have discussed this process in earlier essays in this collection, on Browning and George Eliot.) Eighteenth-century German biblical critics were already interpreting the Bible in terms of older myths of fertility and sun-worship—Coleridge and Hölderlin, to take examples brilliantly analysed by Elinor Shaffer,[32] were influenced by these thoughts. The resolutely agnostic George Eliot wrote about a particular incarnate carpenter's son, Adam Bede, in a demythologised world, who drinks wine and breaks bread at moments of tragic crisis, not as symbols but for themselves, or, as Feuerbach said, in sacramental celebration of their earthly truth, the bread symbolising bread, the wine symbolising wine, the baptismal water, water, without which we cannot live. Vincent Van Gogh read and pondered *Adam Bede* as he read and pondered *La Faute de l'Abbé Mouret,* a work wholly informed by, and incomprehensible without the power of, the biblical myth. Some later writers took the way out suggested by Bataille's mythologising of Van Gogh, or T. S. Eliot's acceptance, through *The Golden Bough,* that if dying and resurrected human gods were a kind of cultural universal, there might also be a kind of universal truth there. We all make meanings by using the myths and fictions of our ancestors as a way of making sense, or excitement, out of our experience on the earth. We believe and half believe and reject, we respond to certain powerful symbols and feel repelled by others whose death we sense.

We play, in a sense, with so few essentials, since the myths became defined as fictions. The earth, bare and chaotic, or brilliant with thoughtless life; the sun, which makes life, and thought, possible, and is a huge physical object, flaming and burning, not a choir of the heavenly host, nor any God. Our own short lives, birth, copulation and death. Perhaps what is interesting about Van Gogh is exactly the way in which he stands between the old myth of sacrifice, death and resurrection and the new world, in which all we can do seems to be to look clearly, as Rilke's Cézanne looked.

V

Van Gogh painted the light of the sun, and the earth under the sun. He painted what men had made of it, and he painted it naked, as far as any man can. This nakedness, and ways of representing it, are part of a modern apprehension of reality I find deeply moving because of what has been stripped from it.

Take, for instance, a myth of Freud's which seems to tell an undisplaced truth about our place on the earth. *Beyond the Pleasure Principle* was written in response to Freud's interest in the repetitive dreams of the shell-shocked, which seemed to contradict his then theory that dreams procured pleasure, fulfilled wishes. He discovered a natural desire for death, which he places in a denuded mythic universe of solid earth and warming sun. He has spent some time establishing that the activity of instinctual behavior is to restore a former state of things, which he relates to his own discovery of the repetition compulsion in human behaviour.

> This view of instincts [he writes] strikes us as strange because we have become used to see in them a factor impelling towards change and development, whereas we are now asked to recognise in them the precise contrary—an expression of the *conservative* nature of living substance.[33]

He continues a little later:

> In the last resort, what has left its mark on the development of organisms must be the history of the earth we live in and of its relation

to the sun. Every modification which is thus imposed upon the course of the organism's life is accepted by the conservative organic instincts and stored up for further repetition. These instincts are therefore bound to give a deceptive appearance of being forces tending towards change and progress, whilst in fact they are merely seeking to reach an ancient goal by paths alike old and new. Moreover it is possible to specify this goal of all organic striving. It would be in contradiction to the conservative nature of the instincts if the goal of life were a state of things which had never been attained. On the contrary, it must be an *old* state of things, an initial state from which the living entity has at one time or another departed and to which it is striving to return by the circuitous paths along which its development leads. If we are to take it as a truth that knows no exception that everything living dies for *internal* reasons—becomes inorganic once again—then we shall be compelled to say that 'the aim of all life is death,' and, looking backwards, that 'inanimate things existed before living ones.'³⁴

In the context of these observations Freud makes the remark that the "germ-cell"—or what we might now call the genes—is potentially immortal, whilst the individual body, or *soma*, is striving for death. It is thus the sexual instincts that are in some kind concerned with immortality. He goes on to offer his version of an old myth, Aristophanes' account in Plato's *Symposium* of the origin of love in hermaphrodite creatures who were torn apart and ceaselessly seek completeness. Freud likes this story, "because it traces the origin of an instinct *to need to restore an earlier state of things.*" From this myth Freud builds his own scientific myth, or hypothesis, of a primary living substance that "at the time of coming to life was torn apart into small particles which have ever since endeavoured to reunite through the sexual instincts."³⁵

VI

I have quoted all this because it can be seen as a resolutely atheist vision of the same myth of sun, earth, death and lovers that appeared so differently in *La Faute de l'Abbé Mouret,* Van Gogh's paintings and Rilke. I should also perhaps say plainly that I am working partly by instinct—that the passages and paintings I quote, connecting these things, and craftsmanship and looking steadily in this way have over many years come to represent some truth for me about the possibility and nature of, and need for, art in the world we live in. Such coloured interest in the play of the light and the mind on sun and earth also informs the work of Wallace Stevens, who seems to me to have absorbed and understood the nineteenth- and turn-of-the-century responses to mythology, art and bareness in a singularly complete way.

We could take "Sunday Morning."[36] The poem opens with

> Complacencies of the peignoir, and late
> Coffee and oranges in a sunny chair,
> And the green freedom of a cockatoo

—colours and light almost like a Matisse painting, which are set against

> The holy hush of ancient sacrifice,

and the figure in the poem dreams of passing across wide water without sound,

> Over the seas, to silent Palestine,
> Dominion of the blood and sepulchre.

The poem is a meditation on the nature of divinity. The second verse argues that

> Divinity must live within herself:
> Passions of rain, or moods in falling snow

and creates a landscape out of human emotion in a way the Rilke of "Here it is" would not quite have approved. The third verse describes the "inhuman birth" of the mythic divinity, Jove in the clouds, and describes the possible incarnation as a result of

> . . . our blood, commingling, virginal,
> With heaven, brought such requital to desire
> The very hinds discerned it, in a star.

This is ambiguous. Our blood is the blood of Paradise and it is asked:

> And shall the earth
> Seem all of Paradise that we shall know?

The next verse states that there is no haunt of prophecy, no old chimera of the grave, golden underground nor isle melodious,

> Nor visionary south, nor cloudy palm
> Remote on heaven's hill, that has endured
> As April's green endures.

"She" states that she still feels the need for some imperishable bliss, and we are told:

> Death is the mother of beauty, hence from her,
> Alone, shall come fulfilment to our dreams
> And our desires.

The next verse is a vision of a static and unchanging Paradise, with heavy fruit always perfect, and insipid lutes. The next invokes the shamanic fire dancing, delicately and ironically, like Matisse's unreal and strangely moving creations of *La Danse* and *La Musique,* rather than Bataille's frantic conjuring.

> Supple and turbulent, a ring of men
> Shall chant in orgy on a summer morn
> Their boisterous devotion to the sun,
> Not as a god, but as a god might be,
> Naked among them, like a savage source.

But the last verse changes this demythologised religion again. The connection of "our blood" and the "chant of Paradise" returning to its source in stanza VII is replaced in stanza VIII by the setting up of a divorce between the religion of the death of Jesus and free, inhuman, wild creatures. Christ's death is simply death.

> She hears, upon that water without sound,
> A voice that cries, 'The tomb in Palestine
> Is not the porch of spirits lingering.
> It is the grave of Jesus, where he lay.'

And Stevens continues with one of the most striking and memorable of what I think of as the "naked" or "bare" images of our place among things:

We live in an old chaos of the sun
Or old dependency of day and night,
Or island solitude, unsponsored, free,
Of that wide water, inescapable.
Deer walk upon our mountains, and the quail
Whistle about us their spontaneous cries;
Sweet berries ripen in the wilderness;
And, in the isolation of the sky,
At evening, casual flocks of pigeons make
Ambiguous undulations as they sink,
Downward to darkness, on extended wings.

The words that dispose of the old Adamic vision of the world as made for Man, or the Christian vision of the source of light and life, the Word incarnate in our blood, are so delicately chosen, so excellent. Our solitude is both free and *unsponsored*. The mountains are described as "ours," but this possessive is quickly shown to be no more than a statement of where "we" are. Quails whistle about "us" their *spontaneous* cries, nothing to do with us. The fruit is in the wilderness, the sky is isolated, and the pigeons, which in Christian mythology were the Holy Ghost demonstrating election, are *casual*, ambiguous and go downwards to darkness, naturally.

One of the many glories of this poem is its Janus nature. It is a high modernist poem, and yet in the perfection of its blank verse, its elegant echoes of the vocabulary of Keats and Browning (I once found the line about the pigeons in Browning's "Paracelsus," but could never find it again), it is acquainted with the history of Romanticism and its ambivalent relations with religion.

There is a passage in De Quincey's *Suspiria de Profundis* which seemed to me, when I read it accidentally because I was reading De Quincey, to be a prime source of the terms of the "Sunday Morning" meditation. It seems to me remarkable enough, in terms of Stevens, and in terms of this essay, to quote at length.

It happened that among our nursery collection of books was the Bible, illustrated with many pictures. And in long dark evenings, as my three sisters with myself sat by the firelight round the *guard* of our nursery, no book was so much in request amongst us. It ruled us and swayed us as mysteriously as music. One young nurse whom we all loved, before any candle was lighted, would often strain her eye to read it for us and sometimes, according to her simple powers, attempt to explain what we found obscure. We, the children, were all constitutionally touched with pensiveness; the fitful gloom and sudden lambencies of the room by firelight suited our evening state of feelings; and they suited also, the divine revelations of power and mysterious beauty which awed us. Above all, the story of a just man—man and yet *not* man, real above all things, and yet shadowy above all things, who had suffered the passion of death in Palestine—slept upon our minds like early dawn upon the waters. The nurse knew and explained to us the chief differences in Oriental climates; and all these differences (as it happens) express themselves in the great varieties of summer. The cloudless sunlights of Syria—those seemed to argue everlasting summer, the disciples plucking the ears of corn—that *must* be summer, but above all the very name of Palm Sunday (a festival in the English church) troubled me like an anthem. 'Sunday!' What was *that?* That was the day of peace which masked another peace deeper than the heart of man can comprehend. 'Palms!' What are they? *That* was an equivocal word; palms, in the sense of trophies, expressed the pomps of life; palms as a product of nature, expressed the pomps of summer. Yet still even this explanation does not suffice; it was not merely by the peace and by the summer, by the deep sound of the rest below all rest, and of ascending glory, that I had been haunted. It was also because Jerusalem stood near to those deep images both in time and in place. The great event of Jerusalem was at hand when Palm Sunday came, and the scene of that Sunday was near in place to Jerusalem. Yet what then was Jerusalem? Did I fancy it to be the *omphalos* (navel) of the earth? That pretension had once been made for Jerusalem, and once for Delphi; and both pretensions had become ridiculous, as the figure of the planet became known. Yes, but if not of the earth, for earth's tenant, Jerusalem was the *omphalos* of mortality. Yet how? There, on the contrary, it was, as we infants understood, that mortality had been trampled underfoot. True, but for that very reason, there it was that mortality had opened its very gloomiest crater. There it was, indeed, that the human had risen on wings from the grave; but for that reason, there also it was that the divine had been swallowed up by the abyss; the lesser star could not rise before the greater would submit to eclipse. Summer, therefore, had connected itself with death, not merely as a mode of antagonism, but also through intricate relations to scriptural scenery and events.[37]

De Quincey uses this description as an example of the way in which the human mind thinks and feels in "perplexed combinations of *concrete* objects" or "compound objects, incapable of being disentangled" to which he gives a name he has himself coined, *"involutes."* These involutes, he says, contain our deepest thoughts and feelings, which we do not apprehend "*directly* and in their own abstract shapes."

The long passage I have quoted is part of his explanation of how he came to associate the ideas, or experiences, of summer and death. The whole account is indispensable to the "involute"—the narrative of the writer's childhood, the experience of the Bible, as Book and history, of the death of Jesus, the ideas of Sunday, palms and the sun, mortality and the incarnation. I think the whole of the involute is at work in "Sunday Morning," which makes a new, more abstract involute, containing the same combinations of words, with new additions, birds, colours and fruits.

De Quincey writes of how the story of "a just man—man and yet *not* man, real above all things, and yet shadowy above all things, who had suffered the passion of death in Palestine—slept upon our minds like early dawn upon the waters." Stevens's "she" "dreams a little" of "some procession of the dead / Winding across wide water without sound / . . . Stilled for the passing of her dreaming feet / Over the seas to silent Palestine / Dominion of the blood and sepulchre." And he asks:

> What is divinity if it can come
> Only in silent shadows and in dreams?

Both De Quincey and Stevens meditate on the meaning of Sunday, both speak of the "visionary south, [and] cloudy palm / Remote on heaven's hill," both meditate on death and summer, the experience of seasons and mortality, the ripeness of harvest. Even Stevens's extended pigeon-wings, sinking downwards to darkness, are an intricate part of De Quincey's rhetoric about the Jerusalem where "the human had risen on wings from the grave."

De Quincey's Romantic involute, and Stevens's abstract and sensuous meditation on the relations between sun, earth, mortality, myth and metaphor, have become, with Van Gogh's letters and paintings, part of a new involute for me. De Quincey's fireside Bible reading, with its contemplation of death and summer, is like Van Gogh's early reflections on Christian truths and incarnation, on the human pilgrimage and the meeting with sorrow. Van Gogh loved emblematic prints of just such scenes as the nurse reading to the living children with the dead child in the next room. Stevens's poem, which grew out of, and steadfastly rejects, De Quincey's meditation on incarnation, or anyway the Incarnation, is like Van Gogh's paintings of natural objects, including the sun, the savage source of light, as images of themselves, meaning themselves. Stevens's poem and Van Gogh's secular triptychs acknowledge their cultural source, the Sunday of the palms and sepulchre, the Mother of God between the symbolic flowers of light, but the cockatoo is "green freedom" and the sunflowers are merely flowers, living and dying.

Stevens's poem is intricately related to the other writings considered in this essay. He sets the freedom and colour of the world of things as they are, as painted by Matisse or Bonnard, in the green freedom of the cockatoo, the coffee and oranges and sunny chair, against the "dark encroachment of that old catastrophe." The catastrophe is old, a word which recurs in the "old chaos of the sun / Or old dependency of day and night," this is the world of things natural, and older than that real and mythological death. This world bears some relation to that of *Beyond the Pleasure Principle* in its underpinning of old myths with an image of even older relations between earth, sun and organic life, including death. Stevens's desiring, aspiring blood is Freud's immortality-seeking germs, again natural, in the end, not supernatural, part of the whole.

And Stevens, like Rilke, finds in the painted object, in attention to light and colour, the Angel of Reality, who gathered up the words the poet of the elegies spoke in his lists. *Angel Surrounded by Paysans,* was, Stevens said, a description of a still-life painting of a bowl amongst fruits,* something that could not be guessed from reading this dialogue between the angel who makes no annunciation to the countrymen who sense

A welcome at the door to which no one comes.

*In a letter to Paul Vidal in October 1949 (*Letters*, p. 649) Stevens described how he had given this name to a still life by Tal Coat. "Tal Coat is supposed to be a man of violence but one soon becomes accustomed to the present picture. I have even given it a title of my own: *Angel Surrounded by Peasants*. The angel is the Venetian glass bowl on the left, with the little spray of leaves in it. The peasants are the terrines, bottles and glasses that surround it. This title alone tames it as a lump of sugar might tame a lion." The wit of this taming of violent still life by naming it out of a vanished religious order of art bears a riddling and real relation to Van Gogh's procedures that could make another essay.

The angel:

> I am the angel of reality,
> Seen for a moment standing in the door.
>
> I have neither ashen wings nor wear of ore,
> And live without a tepid aureole . . .
>
> Yet I am the necessary angel of earth
> Since in my sight, you see the earth again
>
> Cleared of its stiff and stubborn, man-locked set . . .

"Notes towards a Supreme Fiction" deals with the pleasure principle, the earth, the shifting weather and colours, the invention and absence of gods, the nature of the real and our relation to it, with endless wit and variations. It is a post-religious and also a post-metaphysical poem that understands the importance—I baulk at the words "religious," "spiritual," even "contemplative," so what is left?—of looking clearly like Rilke's Cézanne, like Van Gogh's realist Dutchmen. The green, the fluent mundo of "Notes" celebrates several pairs of lovers who make up different marriages, like the craftsmanship again of Van Gogh's Dutch lovers, Nanzia Nunzio and Ozymandias, the great captain and the maiden Bawda, the cold copulars who engender the particulars of rapture.

> Two things of opposite nature seem to depend
> On one another, as a man depends
> On a woman, day on night, the imagined
>
> On the real. This is the origin of change.
> Winter and spring, cold copulars, embrace
> And forth the particulars of rapture come.
>
> Music falls on the silence like a sense,
> A passion that we feel, not understand.
> Morning and afternoon are clasped together
>
> And North and South are an intrinsic couple,
> And sun and rain a plural, like two lovers
> That walk away as one in the greenest body.

Reality in "Notes" is intrinsically to do with the demythologised sun, the study of the ephebe, who must learn

> The sun
> Must bear no name, gold flourisher, but be
> In the difficulty of what it is to be.

On the sun depends weather, and it is in terms of weather that Stevens gives us the *discovery* of order and reality.

> But to impose is not
> To discover. To discover an order as of
> A season, to discover summer and know it,
>
> To discover winter and know it well, to find,
> Not to impose, not to have reasoned at all,
> Out of nothing to have come on major weather.
>
> It is possible, possible, possible. It must
> Be possible.

Stevens's poem celebrates the priority of the earth and the sun.

> But the first idea was not to shape the clouds
> In imitation. The clouds preceded us.
>
> There was a muddy centre before we breathed.
> There was a myth before the myth began.
> Venerable and articulate and complete.
>
> From this the poem springs: that we live in a place
> That is not our own and, much more not ourselves,
> And hard it is in spite of blazoned days.

What I have been talking about is a kind of bareness that succeeded natural supernaturalism, and a kind of contemplation that raised the sensuous and the pleasurable—which includes even Van Gogh's description of his infernal intentions in *The Night Café*, which he wanted to be in the guise of Japanese gaiety and the good fellowship of Tartarin, to a kind of truth beyond hedonism. Years ago I was struck by Marshall McLuhan's discussion[38] of A. H. Hallam's essay on Tennyson's *Poems 1830* in which Hallam praises Tennyson for grounding his vision of reality in Keats's "O for a life of sensations rather than thoughts!" McLuhan claimed that Hallam and Tennyson failed to make the further step into symbolism, the world of Mallarmé and the mental landscape. I thought then, and I think now, that there is something to be said for the artists who keep in touch with the hard world outside them. If religion, Mithraic, shamanistic or Christian, is anthropomorphic, symbolist and abstract art can easily become solipsist and thus again anthropomorphic. Stevens—and Van Gogh and Cézanne and Rilke and that great analyst of men's self-deception, self-projection and self-love, Sigmund Freud—knew that the world was not ourselves and not our own, and that it was hard in spite of blazoned days. (I failed to persuade Frank Kermode that "hard" in that context might be taken to mean solid, in the sense of *terra firma,* and not merely hostile and rejecting.)

VII

Jacques Derrida, in "La Mythologie blanche," has much to say about the sun, that gold flourisher, about our persistent anthropomorphism and about Van Gogh's sunflowers, or alternatively about heliotropes.

He takes his title from Anatole France, *Le Jardin d'Epicure,* where, in a philosophical dialogue, one of the characters claims that all abstract ideas can only be allegories.

> I think I have sufficiently made you realise, Aristos, that any expression of an abstract idea can only be an allegory. By an odd turn of fate, the very metaphysicians who think to escape the world of appearances are constrained to live perpetually in allegory. Sad poets, they bleach the fables of antiquity, and are themselves but gatherers of fables. They produce white mythology.[39]

Derrida's white mythology touches, at one point, on the fact that philosophical discourse, like Freud's life of the instincts, is inexorably part, in its dead, or extinct, metaphors, of the relations between the earth and the sun. ("Extinct" in French is *éteinte,* which is to say extinguished, the light put out.) He discusses the "archaic" tropes which seem to give "fundamental" concepts. The values of words such as "concepts," "foundation," "theory," he says, are metaphoric, and at the same time resist all attempts to form a metaphoric description. "What is fundamental corresponds to the desire for a solid and ultimate ground, a construction site, the earth as the support of an artificial structure."[40]

He illustrates this with a description of Kant's use of "Grund," "fondement," "foundation" in his thinking about intuitions, and later with a discussion of Locke's "light of reason" or Descartes's "clear and distinct ideas" with their metaphoric dependence on the sun. "The appeal to the criteria of lightness and darkness suffices to confirm what I stated above: this entire philosophical delimitation of metaphor already lends itself to being constructed and worked by 'metaphors.' "[41]

The discussion of the metaphors of the sun in "La Mythologie blanche" moves from this "extinct" metaphor of light for thought to the discussion, in Aristotle and Plato, of the idea of the sun as father, source of all good, sower of seed. Aristotle discusses metaphor as analogy, Derrida reminds us, and adds that sometimes one of the terms of the analogy is lacking, and has to be invented.

> Aristotle illustrates this with an example: an example that is the most illustrious, that is illustrative *par excellence,* the most natural lustre there is. It is when considering the generative power of this example that the question of the missing name comes to be posed and that one of the members of the analogical square has to be supplied or replaced.[42]

After all this metaphorical play with light, illustration and the illustrious, we come to *The Republic.*

> In *The Republic* (VI–VII), before and after the Line which presents ontology according to the analogies of proportionality, the sun appears. In order to disappear. It is there, but as the invisible source of light, in a kind of insistent eclipse, more than essential, producing the essence—Being and Appearance—of what is. One can look directly at it only under the pain of blinding and death. Keeping itself beyond all that is, it figures the Good of which the physical sun is the son: source of life and visibility, of seed and light.
>
> Here is the case of the Sun in the *Poetics* (1457b): 'It may be that some of the terms thus related have no special name of their own, but for all that they will be metaphorically described in just the same way. Thus to cast forth seed corn is called "sowing" (*speirein*), but to cast forth its light, as said of the sun, has no special name (*to de tēn phloga apo tou hēliou anōnymon*).[43]

How, asks Derrida, shall we supplement this anonymity (namelessness, nounlessness) if the action of the sun is the same as that of sowing? And he asks where has it ever been seen that there is the same relation between the sun and its rays as between seeding and seeds (*"l'ensemencement et la se-*

mence''). This last correspondence leads to the remark that there is a running analogy available to French speakers that is not available to the English, since Van Gogh's seed is also the source of the art of semantics, of meanings, here. But, Derrida goes on to claim, Aristotle does not here see the terms— the sun, the rays, the act of sowing, the seeds—as tropes.

> Here metaphor consists in a substitution of proper names having a fixed meaning and referent, especially when we are dealing with the sun, whose referent has the originality of always being original, unique and irreplaceable, at least in the representation we give of it. *There is only one sun in this system* [my italics]. The proper name, here, is the nonmetaphorical prime mover of metaphor, the father of all figures. Everything turns around it, everything turns toward it.[44]

If the sun can sow *(semer)* it is because his name is inscribed in a system of relationships which constitute him. Derrida cites Aristotle's definition of man as a maker of representations; mimesis is essentially human. And metaphor, like mimesis, he says, returns continually to *physis,* to its truth and its presence. In Aristotle's world, nature finds natural resemblances, analogies, and the power of metaphor-making is a natural gift, though more natural to men than to beasts, more natural to philosophers than to mere men. Some men are more natural than others, have more genius, generosity, seed *(semence)*.

Human beings cannot know the sun. Our metaphors are tournesols (sunflowers) or heliotropes, but these metaphors are always imperfect, because of our incapacity. "Heliotropic metaphors are always imperfect metaphors. They provide us with too little knowledge because one of the terms directly implied in the substitution (the physical sun) cannot be known in its physicality."[45]

Derrida uses the figure of the heliotrope (double in its ambiguity, our turning towards the sun, the turning of the sun itself) to image the death of metaphor, the death of philosophical thought inextricably involved in our natures as mimetic creatures. "Metaphor thus always carries its death within itself. And this death is undoubtedly also the death of philosophy."[46] It is both the death of philosophy, thinking itself through, recognising itself and accomplishing its end, and the death of a philosophy which doesn't see itself die and no longer rediscovers itself. Derrida has an elegant peroration on the heliotrope of the two deaths.

Such a flower carries within itself its double, whether it be seed or type, the chance structure of its programme or the necessity of its diagram. The heliotrope can always be derived from itself and raised to a higher level. And it can always become a dried flower in a book. There is always, absent from every garden, a dried flower in a book . . .[47]

The two sun metaphors I have isolated from Derrida's discourse could be seen as more and less anthropomorphic. In Kant's metaphor of ground and solid foundation, allied to the Cartesian light of reason illuminating clear and distinct ideas, the metaphor is an acknowledgement of something beyond metaphor. Without sun and solid earth there would be no thought. The other, that of the sun scattering his seed, is pure anthropomorphism, elevating man (if woman is seen as the passive and fecundated earth) to the power of the blazing star.

It is clear [Bataille tells us in *L'Anus solaire*] that the world is purely parodic, that is to say, every thing that we see is a parody of some other thing, or even the same thing in some deceptive guise.

Ever since sentences have been *circulating* in the brains of those committed to thinking, there has been a movement towards absolute identification, since, with the help of a *copula,* each sentence links one thing to another; and everything would be visibly linked if we were suddenly to discover in its entirety the diagram traced by an Ariadne's thread, leading thought within its own labyrinth.

But the *copula* of linguistic terms is no less irritating than that of bodies. And when I cry out: I AM THE SUN, the result is a full erection, for language is the vehicle of erotic fantasy.[48]

One may think of Stevens's cold copulars, but Bataille's reconstruction of the old neoplatonic myths of the Logos as the fecundator of Hyle, or the birth of Aphrodite as the result of the fall of Saturn's seed on the waves of the sea, is involved in his personal idea of violation and violence, which he extends by sleight of language, and, as he says, parody, to earth and sun.

All animal life came from the movement of the seas and, within all bodies, life continues to emerge from salt water.

The sea thus played the role of the female organ which liquefies as the penis excites it.

The sea never ceases to masturbate.

The solid elements contained and stirred up by the water animated by an erotic movement spring forth as flying fish.

Erections and the sun scandalise just like corpses and the darkness of cellars.

Plants turn uniformly towards the sun, while, on the other hand, human beings, although they are phalloid, like trees and unlike other animals, necessarily turn their gaze away from it.

Human eyes can bear to see neither the sun nor copulation nor corpses nor darkness, though always with different reactions.[49]

So love cries out in my own throat: I am the *Jesuvus,* a disgusting parody of the torrid, blinding sun.

I long to have my throat cut as I am raping the girl to whom I could have said: you are night.

The Sun loves Night alone and directs at the earth its luminous violence, its vile penis . . .[50]

This, though extreme, and truly shocking, is not eccentric, in that it represents a way of thought that is old and human, and pervasive in many cultures.

VIII

Sanity, perhaps, is to find a way to escape from such parodies, such bloody and semantic self-projections.

Like Van Gogh, whose realism seems to be an essential part of this sanity, which at any given point we feel to be luminous, precarious, and hard-won.

It is not a slavish realism, a desire to copy. Coleridge distinguishes between true imitations, or representations, and simple copies, between the live painting and the cold dead feel of the marble peach—a fruit rather like the heavy ones that hang in the arrested and unreal Paradise dismissed in "Sunday Morning." Van Gogh could not paint from the imagination—he disliked the invented and mythological paintings of Bernard and Gauguin because he could not work without the close looking at what he was representing. But his work was about colour itself, as much as about cypresses, sun, corn, his own face on a malachite ground, sunflowers, olives.

He wrote to Theo from Nuenen in 1885, before Provence:

'Les vrais peintres sont ceux qui ne font pas de la couleur locale'—that was what Blanc and Delacroix discussed once.

May I not boldly take it to mean that a painter does better to start from the colours on his palette than from the colours in nature? I mean, when one wants to paint, for instance, a head, and sharply observes the reality one has before one, then one may think: that head is a harmony of red-brown, violet, yellow, all of them broken—I will put a violet and a yellow and red-brown on my palette and these will break each other.

I retain from nature a certain sequence and a certain correctness in placing the tones, I study nature, so as not to do foolish things, to remain reasonable—however I don't mind so much whether my colour corresponds exactly as long as it looks beautiful on my canvas, as beautiful as it looks in nature. . . .

Always and intelligently to make use of the beautiful tones which the colours form of their own accord, when one breaks them on the palette, I repeat—to start from one's palette, I repeat—to start from one's palette, from one's knowledge of colour-harmony, is quite different from following nature mechanically and obsequiously.

Here is another example: suppose I have to paint an autumn landscape, trees with yellow leaves. All right—when I conceive it as a symphony in yellow, what does it matter whether the fundamental colour of yellow is the same as that of the leaves or not? It matters *very* little. Much, everything depends on my perception of the infinite variety of tones of *one and the same family*.

Do you call this a dangerous inclination towards romanticism, an infidelity to "realism," a "peindre de chic," a caring more for the palette of the colourist than for nature? Well, que soit. Delacroix, Millet, Corot, Dupré, Daubigny, Breton, thirty names more, are they not the heart and soul of the art of painting of this century, and are they not all rooted in romanticism, though they *surpassed* romanticism?

Romance and romanticism are of our time, and painters must have imagination and sentiment. Luckily realism and naturalism are not free from it. Zola creates but does not hold up a mirror to things, he creates *wonderfully*, but creates, poetises, that is why it is so beautiful. So much for naturalism and realism, which nevertheless stand in connection to romanticism.[51]

Our perception of colour, like our language, like our power to make representations, is something that is purely human. We know now that other creatures see different wave-lengths, that the bee and the octopus, the bull and the dog, see different shades and tones, that flowers are painted with ultra-violet patterns of which we are quite unaware. Our gold flour-isher, our violet and malachite, are ours and only ours, varying from one pair of eyes and brain to the next. We know that we live in a flow of light and lights, as we live in a flow of airs and sounds, of which we apprehend a part, and make sense of it as best we can. The pigments on Van Gogh's palette, with their chemistry and their changing tones, are as much part of this perceived flow as the trees and the variable sky. We relate them to each other, and to ourselves, from where we are. It seems to me that at the height of his passion of work Van Gogh was able to hold all these things in a kind of creative or poetic balance, painting the tiny decorous lovers in a corner of his Poets' Garden, which was also the everyday public garden of Arles, to welcome Gauguin to the community of artists in the yellow house, under its cobalt sky. I do see this as human sanity, which is always threat-ened by forces from inside and outside itself.

The pictures to which I always return again and again when thinking about this balance, of human and inhuman, vision and artifice, are the purple and yellow sower, painted in June 1888, and the reaper of St.-Rémy.

Van Gogh wrote of the Sower to Theo, contrasting Millet's *The Sower* with Delacroix's *Christ in the Boat*. The Delacroix he says, "speaks a sym-bolic language" through the colour alone—"blue and green with touches of violet, red and a little citron-yellow for the nimbus, the halo."

> Millet's 'Sower' is a colourless *gray,* like Israels's pictures.
>
> Now, could you paint the Sower in colour, with a simultaneous contrast of, for instance, yellow and violet (like the Apollo ceiling of Delacroix's which *is just that,* yellow and violet,) yes or no? Why, *yes.* Well do it then. That is what old Martin said, 'The masterpiece is up to you.' But try it and you tumble into a regular metaphysical philoso-phy of colour à la Monticelli, a mess that is damnably difficult to get out of with honour.
>
> And it makes you as absent-minded as a sleepwalker. And yet if only one could do something good.[52]

He describes to Bernard what he did.

> As for myself I feel much better here than I did in the North. I work even in the middle of the day, in the full sunshine, without any shadow at all, in the wheat fields, and I enjoy it like a cicada. My God,

if I had only known this country at the age of twenty-five, instead of coming here when I was thirty-five . . . In that period I had become enthusiastic about gray, or rather colourlessness, I was always dreaming of Millet . . .

Here is a sketch of a sower: large plowed field with clods of earth, for the most part frankly violet.

A field of ripe wheat, yellow ochre in tone with a little carmine.

The sky, chrome yellow, almost as bright as the sun itself which is chrome yellow no. 1, with a little white, whereas the rest of the sky is chrome yellow nos 1 and 2 mixed. So very yellow.

The Sower's shirt is blue and his trousers white.

Size 25 canvas, square.

There are many hints of yellow in the soil, neutral tones resulting from mixing violet with yellow; but I have played hell somewhat with the truthfulness of the colours. . . .[53]

The Sower bridges earth and sky, and seems to catch seeds of light out of the sky to mix with the violets of earth. The brush strokes shine like turned clods, like commas and dashes as Artaud said, a language that represents itself, in some way. The Sower is larger than life, in a haze of hot sunlight and intense unreal colour of early day—he is somehow balanced, a man on the earth, the right size, in relation to soil and sun.

I always think of the brighter Reaper as a companion picture, the beginning and the end of life, in the real and symbolic wheatfields, under the real sun. Van Gogh went on thinking of life in terms of his early image of the pilgrimage, and, thinking of the faces of his dead father and uncle, wrote wistfully that it was hard not to think of the idea that there was life after death. But the Reaper, painted in St.-Rémy in fear of more attacks, in what he described to Theo as a "dumb fury of work"—"very slowly—but from morning to night without slackening—and the secret is probably this— work long and slowly"—the Reaper comes as near as any human being has done to looking steadily at Death and the Sun. When it was finished Van Gogh told Theo it was "an image of death as the great book of nature speaks of it—but what I have sought is the 'almost smiling.' It is all yellow, except a line of hills, a pale, fair yellow. I find it queer that I saw it like this from between the iron bars of a cell."[54] In the book of nature the metaphorical Reaper is real and pale yellow.

Work is going pretty well—I am struggling with a canvas begun some days before my indisposition, a 'Reaper'; the study is all yellow, terribly thickly painted, but the subject was fine and simple. For I see in this reaper—a vague figure fighting like a devil in the midst of the heat to get to the end of his task—I see in him the image of death, in the sense that humanity might be the wheat he is reaping. So it is—if you like—the opposite of that sower I tried to do before. But there's nothing sad in this death, it goes its way in broad daylight with a sun flooding everything with a light of pure gold.[55]

(1990)

Notes

1. Still Life/Nature morte

First published in *Cross References: Modern French Theory and the Practice of Criticism,* ed. David Kelley and Isabelle Llasera, Society for French Studies (London, 1986). Quotations from French authors have been translated for this edition; the notes below refer to original sources.

1. John Milton, *Paradise Lost,* v, 479–85.
2. Gabriel Josipovici, *The World and the Book* (London, 1971), p. 299.
3. Ezra Pound, *Polite Essays,* pp. 50 and 53, quoted in Hugh Kenner, *The Poetry of Ezra Pound* (London, 1951), p. 264.
4. Kenner, op. cit., p. 256.
5. Marcel Proust, "A propos du 'style' de Flaubert," in *Correspondence,* II, (Paris, 1971), p. 586.
6. Gérard Genette, "Métonymie chez Proust," in *Figures III* (Paris, 1972), p. 60, quoting Proust, op. cit., p. 586.
7. Vernon Lee, *The Handling of Words and Other Studies in Literary Psychology* (London, 1923), pp. 241–51.
8. Paul Ricœur, *La Métaphore vive* (Paris, 1975), p. 252.
9. Ibid., p. 266.
10. Ibid., p. 253.
11. Leo Bersani, *The Death of Stéphane Mallarmé* (Cambridge, 1982), p. 30.
12. Michel Foucault, *Les Mots et les choses* (Paris, 1966), pp. 49–50.
13. Ibid., p. 51.
14. Ibid., p. 132.

15. Ibid., p. 118.
16. M. Proust, *Du Côté de chez Swann* (Bibliothèque de la Pléiade, 1978), I, p. 387.
17. Ludwig Wittgenstein, *Remarks on Colour* (Oxford, 1977), p. 17e.4.
18. Ibid., p. 17e.8.
19. H. R. Rookmaaker, *Synthetist Art Theories* (Amsterdam, 1959). See in this book, p. 204: "By the word Iconic we want to express something that might be indicated by the Dutch word 'beeld-spraak' (speaking in images). If this term were not a little confusing as it means metaphor . . . iconically we can express something by means of lines, colours and three-dimensional forms in a way similar to what happens in language by means of sounds."
20. Jean-Paul Sartre, *La Nausée* (Gallimard, Collection "Holio," 1982), pp. 178ff.

2. "Sugar"/"Le Sucre"

Written as an introduction to the French translation of "Sugar," Editions des Cendres (Paris, 1989).

3. Robert Browning: Fact, Fiction, Lies, Incarnation and Art

A shorter version of this essay appears as the Introduction to the Holio Society edition of *Robert Browning: Dramatic Monologues* (London, 1991).

1. Letter to Elizabeth Barrett Browning, 13 January 1845. *The Letters of Robert Browning and Elizabeth Barrett Browning, 1845–1846,* ed. Elvan Klintner (Cambridge, Mass, 1989) p. 7.
2. For a fascinating and authoritative account of all this speculation see Elinor Shaffer, *Kubla Khan and the Fall of Jerusalem* (Cambridge, 1975), which includes an excellent account of "A Death in the Desert."
3. Charles Darwin, *Autobiography,* ed. T. H. Huxley (Oxford, 1983 edn), p. 50.
4. David Friedrich Strauss, *Life of Jesus,* trans. Marian Evans (George Eliot) (London, 1846), III, pp. 441–44.
5. Ibid.
6. Browning to Mrs. Orr, in Mrs. S. Orr, *A Handbook to the Works of Browning* (London, 1885), p. 879, quoted by K. Badger in *Robert Browning: A Collection of Critical Essays,* ed. K. A. P. Drew (London, 1966).
7. Ernest Renan, Preface to the Thirteenth Edition of the *Vie de Jésus,* ed. Jean Gaulmier (Paris, 1974), pp. x and xi.
8. Ibid., p. liv.
9. Strauss, *Life of Jesus,* II, p. 378n.
10. Letter to Isabella Blagden, 19 November 1863, in *Dearest Isa: Robert Browning's Letters to Isa Blagden,* ed. Edward McAleer (Austin, 1951), p. 80.
11. J. A. Froude, *The Nemesis of Faith* (1849: 1988 edn, with an introduction by Rosemary Ashton [London, 1988]), pp. x and xi.

12. Jules Michelet, *Le Peuple* (Paris, 1974 edn), pp. 72–93.
13. Ibid., p. 67.
14. Jules Michelet, *Journal*, ed. P. Viallaneix, 4 vols (Paris, 1959–62), 23 July, Vol II (1849–60) 1850.
15. Ibid., 11 August 1850.
16. Ibid., 5 September 1850.
17. Ibid.
18. *The George Eliot Letters*, ed. Gordon S. Haight, 7 vols (New Haven, 1954–55) Oxford, Vol III, p. 99.
19. Ludwig Feuerbach, *The Essence of Christianity*, trans. Marian Evans (George Eliot) (1854; Harper Torchbook edition, New York, 1957), p. 81.
20. Ibid., p. 74.
21. Ibid., pp. 130 and 132.
22. Strauss, op. cit., Conclusion, p. 432.
23. Letter to Ruskin, 10 December 1855.
24. My thoughts about "Mr. Sludge, 'the Medium' " owe a great deal to Isobel Armstrong's excellent essay on the poem, in *Victorian Poetry* II, 1964, 1–9.

4. George Eliot: A Celebration

First published as a special pamphlet for the Penguin boxed set of George Eliot's novels (Harmondsworth, 1980).

5. George Eliot's Essays

This is a slightly edited version of the Introduction to *George Eliot: Selected Essays, Poems and Other Writings* (Harmondsworth, 1990). References are made throughout to particular passages in that selection.

1. *Athenæum*, 28 November 1885.
2. See Gordon S. Haight, *George Eliot and John Chapman* (London and New Haven, 1940), p. 22.
3. *The George Eliot Letters*, VIII, p. 23.
4. Haight, *George Eliot and John Chapman*, pp. 41–42.
5. Gordon S. Haight, *George Eliot: A Biography* (Oxford and New York, 1988), p. 97.
6. Herbert Spencer, *Principles of Psychology* (London, 1855), p. 162.
7. Herbert Spencer, *Autobiography*, I (London, 1904), pp. 394–95.
8. *Letters*, v, p. 58.
9. Ibid., I, p. 284.
10. Ibid., v, p. 106.
11. Thomas Pinney, *Essays of George Eliot* (London, 1963), p. 157.
12. *Letters*, II, p. 15.

13. Ibid., v, pp. 160–61.
14. *Daniel Deronda*, ch. 51.
15. *Journal*, 12 September 1856 (Pinney, p. 301).
16. *Letters*, II, p. 258.
17. "The Ilfracombe Journal," *Essays*, pp. 214–30.
18. "Evangelical Teaching: Dr Cummings," and "Worldliness and Other Worldliness: The Poet Young," *Essays*, pp. 38–67; pp. 164–213.
19. *Letters*, VI, p. 210: "Lord Brougham's Literature," *Essays*, pp. 302–7.
20. *Letters*, II, pp. 205–7.
21. Ibid., p. 362.
22. J. S. Mill, *Auguste Comte and Positivism* (London, 1865), pp. 9ff: "R. W. Mackay's Progress of the Intellect," *Essays*, pp. 268–85.
23. *Life*, p. 464, citing *Century Magazine*, vol. 23 (November 1881), pp. 62–63.
24. "The Natural History of German Life," *Essays*, pp. 107–39.
25. *Modern Painters*, IV, Part 5, ch. 1, section 5.
26. Friedrich Nietzsche, *Twilight of the Idols* (London, 1889), Penguin edition, p. 69.
27. *Letters*, II, pp. 48–49.
28. For Strauss, see *Essays*, pp. 447–58; and Feuerbach, pp. 459–72. The extracts in the Penguin selection were especially chosen to illustrate Eliot's thinking on incarnation and narrative.
29. *Letters*, II, p. 153.
30. Ludwig Feuerbach, *The Essence of Christianity*, trans. Marian Evans (George Eliot), end of Chapter 3. The phrase translated as "the justice of sensuous life" is "Das Rechtsgefühl der Sinnlichkeit."
31. U. C. Knoepflmacher, *Religious Humanism and the Victorian Novel* (New Haven, 1965), pp. 55ff.
32. Shakespeare, *A Midsummer Night's Dream*, Act V, scene 1, lines 12–17.
33. "The George Eliot–Frederic Harrison Correspondence," *Essays*, pp. 241–57.
34. Harrison was greatly puzzled as to the characters of Zarca and Fedalma, and how they could be judged in normal ethical terms: "I am not sure that either are real types of human nature. I am not sure if the conduct of both of them, or of one of them is not treason to human life." *Essays*, p. 254.
35. Quoted in Richard Stang, *The Theory of the Novel in England 1850–70* (London, 1959), p. 154.
36. Ibid.
37. See James F. Scott, "George Eliot, Positivism and the Social Vision of *Middlemarch*," in *Victorian Studies*, vol. 16 (September 1972), pp. 59–76, and Martha Vogeler, "George Eliot and the Positivists," in *Nineteenth-Century Fiction*, vol. 36 (1980), pp. 406–31.
38. *Middlemarch*, ch. 21, Penguin edition, p. 243.

6. Accurate Letters: Ford Madox Ford

This essay draws on two separately published pieces: a review of the Bodley Head reissue of Ford's novels, *Times Literary Supplement*, January 1981, and a Preface to the World's Classics edition of *The Fifth Queen* (Oxford, 1981).

7. "The Omnipotence of Thought"

First published in *Sir James Frazer and the Literary Imagination*, ed. Robert Fraser (London, 1980).

1. Lionel Trilling, "On the Teaching of Modern Literature," in *Beyond Culture* (London, 1961), p. 14.
2. "*Ulysses*, Order and Myth," *The Dial*, November 1923; repr. in *Selected Prose of T. S. Eliot*, ed. Frank Kermode (London, 1975), pp. 175–78. See especially pp. 177–78.
3. Trilling, *Beyond Culture*, p. 17.
4. Page references to these novels are given parenthetically in the text. The editions cited are as follows:
   Iris Murdoch, *A Severed Head* (1961), *The Unicorn* (1963), *The Good Apprentice* (1985), all London.
   Anthony Powell, *The Kindly Ones* (London, 1962), cited from Fontana reprint (London, 1977); *Temporary Kings* (London, 1973); *Hearing Secret Harmonies* (London, 1975).
   Saul Bellow, *Henderson the Rain King* (New York and London, 1959), cited from Penguin reprint (Harmondsworth, 1987).
   Muriel Spark, *The Takeover* (London, 1976), cited from Panther reprint (London, 1985).
   Norman Mailer, *The Armies of the Night: The Novel as History, History as the Novel* (New York and London, 1968), cited from Penguin reprint (Harmondsworth, 1970).
5. Sigmund Freud, *Totem and Taboo* in *The Pelican Freud Library*, XIII: *The Origins of Religion* (Harmondsworth, 1985), pp. 183–84, citing Frazer, *Totemism and Exogamy* (London, 1910), IV, pp. 97ff.
6. *The Pelican Freud Library*, XIII, p. 106.
7. Ibid., p. 140, quoting *Golden Bough*, 3rd edn, London 1906–15, vol I, p. 420.
8. *The Pelican Freud Library*, XIII, p. 142.
9. Ibid., pp. 143–44.
10. Ibid., pp. 148–49.
11. Ibid., p. 130.
12. Iris Murdoch, "On 'God' and 'Good,'" in *The Sovereignty of Good* (London, 1970), p. 51.
13. Iris Murdoch, *Sartre: Romantic Rationalist* (London, 1953), p. 62.
14. *The Pelican Freud Library*, XIII, p. 92, quoting *Golden Bough*, vol. I, p. 295.

15. *The Pelican Freud Library*, XIII, p. 73, quoting *The Encyclopaedia Britannica*, 9th edn, XXIII (Edinburgh, 1887), pp. 15–18. Frazer's article is reprinted in *Garnered Sheaves* (London, 1931), pp. 80–92.

16. Murdoch, *The Sovereignty of Good*, p. 68.

17. *The Pelican Freud Library*, XIII, pp. 98–99, quoting *Golden Bough*, vol III, pp. 7ff.

18. *The Pelican Freud Library*, XIII, p. 99.

19. *Golden Bough*, vol. III, p. 258.

20. Ibid., vol. IV, p. 265.

21. *The Pelican Freud Library*, XIII, p. 104.

22. Ibid.

23. Ibid., p. 133.

24. Ibid., pp. 121–2.

25. The news of Sarajevo occurs on p. 72.

26. *Golden Bough*, vol. I, p. 297.

27. Herman Melville, *Moby-Dick*, ch. 59; p. 382 in the Penguin edition (Harmondsworth, 1972).

8. People in Paper Houses

First published in *The Contemporary English Novel,* ed. Malcolm Bradbury and David Palmer (London, 1979).

1. See Rubin Rabinowitz, *The Reaction Against Experiment in the English Novel 1950–1960* (New York and London, 1967), p. 98.

2. Ibid., p. 40.

3. B. S. Johnson, *Aren't You Rather Young to be Writing Your Memoirs?* (London, 1973), pp. 12ff.

4. Nathalie Sarraute, "Rebels in a World of Platitudes," in *The Writer's Dilemma: Essays from the TLS* (London, 1961), pp. 35–41.

5. See Harold Bloom, *The Anxiety of Influence: A Theory of Poetry* (New York, 1973).

6. Jonathan Raban, "Angus Wilson: A Profile," *The New Review,* I, I (April 1974), pp. 16–24.

7. There is a very helpful discussion of this aspect of *No Laughing Matter* in Malcolm Bradbury's *Possibilities* (London, 1973), to which I am indebted.

8. I have discussed this in chapter 2 of my book *Degrees of Freedom* (London, 1965).

9. Iris Murdoch, *Sartre, Romantic Rationalist* (London, 1953), p. 75.

10. F. R. Karl, *A Reader's Guide to the Contemporary English Novel* (London, 1963), section on Iris Murdoch.

11. Henry James, "Anthony Trollope" (1883), repr. in *The House of Fiction,* ed. Leon Edel (London, 1957).

12. See Rubin Rabinowitz, op. cit., p. 98.

13. Iris Murdoch, *Sartre*, pp. 26–27.

14. Gabriel Josipovici, *The World and the Book* (London, 1971), p. 299.
15. Mary McCarthy, *The Fact in Fiction*.
16. B. S. Johnson, op. cit.; Giles Gordon, New Fiction Society publicity material for the collection *Beyond the Words,* ed. Giles Gordon (London, 1975).

9. William Golding: *Darkness Visible*

First published in *The Literary Review,* May 1979.

10. The *TLS* Poetry Competition

First published in the *Times Literary Supplement,* December 1988.

11. A Sense of Religion: Enright's God

First published in *Life by Other Means: Essays on D. J. Enright,* ed. Jacqueline Simms (Oxford, paperback edition, 1990).

1. CP stands for *Collected Poems 1987* (Oxford paperback edn, 1987).
2. *A Choice of Milton's Verse,* ed. D. J. Enright (London, 1975), p. 12.
3. D. J. Enright, *Fields of Vision: Essays on Literature, Language and Television.* (Oxford, 1988), p. 99.
4. Ibid., p. 110.
5. *A Choice of Milton's Verse,* p. 11.

12. Willa Cather

This essay incorporates an Afterword and two Introductions to Virago Modern Classics editions of *O Pioneers!* (London 1983), *The Professor's House* (London, 1980) and *Death Comes for the Archbishop* (London, 1981).

13. Elizabeth Bowen: *The House in Paris*

This formed the Introduction to the Penguin Modern Classics edition of *The House in Paris* (Harmondsworth, 1976).

14. Sylvia Plath: *Letters Home*

Review of *Letters Home*, ed. Aurelia Schober Plath, in *New Statesman*, April 1976.

15. Toni Morrison: *Beloved*

Reviewed in *The Guardian*, October 1987.

16. An Honourable Escape: Georgette Heyer

First published in *Nova*, June 1969.

17. Barbara Pym

A review of Barbara Pym, *An Academic Question*, and Robert Emmett Long, *Barbara Pym*, in *Times Literary Supplement*, August 1986.

18. Monique Wittig: *The Lesbian Body*

Review of *The Lesbian Body*, trans. David Le Vay, in *The New Review*, July 1974.

19. Coleridge: An Archangel a Little Damaged

Review of Norman Fruman, *Coleridge, the Damaged Archangel*, in *New Statesman*, May 1979.

20. Charles Rycroft: *The Innocence of Dreams*

Review of *The Innocence of Dreams* in *New Statesman*, May 1979.

21. Van Gogh, Death and Summer

This essay grew from a relatively short review in the *Times Literary Supplement*, July 1990.

1. *The Complete Letters of Vincent Van Gogh* (London, 1958, repr. 1978), I, pp. 87–91. All quotations from Van Gogh's letters are taken from this edition, hereafter referred to as *Letters*.

2. *Letters*, I, p. 225.

3. Tsukasa Kodera, *Vincent Van Gogh: Christianity versus Nature* (Amsterdam and Philadelphia, 1989).

4. *Letters*, II, letters 286 and 287, pp. 36 and 41.

5. *Letters*, III, letter 615, p. 235. Kodera, op. cit., p. 47.

6. *Letters*, I, letter 164, p. 285.

7. *Letters*, III, letter B21, pp. 521ff.

8. Ibid.

9. Ibid.

10. *Letters*, III, letter B14, p. 509.

11. Ibid., pp. 508–9.

12. *Letters*, III, letter B12, p. 504.

13. *Letters*, III, letter 532, p. 25.

14. Ibid., p. 26.

15. Letter to Gauguin, *Letters*, III, letter 544a, p. 64.

16. *Letters*, III, B14 [9], p. 510.

17. All references to Bataille are from Tome I of his *Œuvres Complètes*, 6 vols (Paris, 1970–73).

18. Ibid., pp. 498–48.

19. Ibid., p. 231.

20. Antonin Artaud, "Van Gogh, the Man Suicided by Society" (Paris, 1947), in *Selected Writings of Antonin Artaud*, ed. Susan Sontag (New York, 1976), p. 483.

21. Ibid.

22. Ibid., p. 486.

23. Ibid., p. 502.

24. Ibid., p. 489.

25. Ibid., p. 491.

26. All quotations from Rilke's letters are from Rainer Maria Rilke, *Letters on Cézanne*, trans. Joel Agee (London, 1988).

27. Ibid., p. 75.

28. Ibid., p. 50.

29. Ibid., p. 46.

30. Ibid., p. 50.

31. All quotations and translations of the Ninth Elegy are taken from *The Duino Elegies*, ed. and trans. J. B. Leishman and Stephen Spender (4th rev. edn, London, 1963).

32. See Elinor Shaffer, *Kubla Khan and the Fall of Jerusalem* (Cambridge, 1975).

33. Sigmund Freud, *Beyond the Pleasure Principle*, in *The Pelican Freud Library*, XI, p. 309: *On Metapsychology*, ed. Angela Richards (Harmondsworth, 1984).

34. Ibid., pp. 310–11.

35. Ibid., p. 332.

36. Wallace Stevens "Sunday Morning," *Collected Poems* (London, 1955).

37. Thomas De Quincey, *Suspiria de Profundis* (London, 1845). From Part I, "The Affliction of Childhood" (Signet Classic edition, New York, 1966), pp. 130–31.

38. Reprinted in John Killham, *Critical Essays on the Poetry of Tennyson* (London, 1960).

39. Derrida's essay "La Mythologie blanche" is collected in *Marges de la philosophie* (Editions de Minuit, Paris, 1972), p. 253. All quotations are from that edition.

40. Ibid., p. 267.

41. Ibid., p. 301.

42. Ibid., p. 289.

43. Ibid.

44. Ibid., p. 290.

45. Ibid., p. 299.

46. Ibid., p. 323.

47. Ibid., p. 324.

48. Bataille, op. cit., p. 79.

49. Ibid., pp. 84–85.

50. Ibid., p. 50.

51. *Letters*, ɪɪ,, letter 429, p. 427.

52. *Letters*, ɪɪ, letter 503, p. 597.

53. *Letters*, ɪɪɪ, letter B7, pp. 491–92.

54. *Letters*, ɪɪɪ, Letter 604, p. 205.

55. *Letters*, ɪɪɪ, p. 202.

Index